T0319796

A Research Agenda for Tourism and Development

Elgar Research Agendas outline the future of research in a given area. Leading scholars are given the space to explore their subject in provocative ways, and map out the potential directions of travel. They are relevant but also visionary.

Forward-looking and innovative, Elgar Research Agendas are an essential resource for PhD students, scholars and anybody who wants to be at the forefront of research.

Titles in the series include:

A Research Agenda for Entrepreneurship
Education
Edited by Alain Fayolle

A Research Agenda for Service Innovation
*Edited by Faïz Gallouj and Faridah
Djellal*

A Research Agenda for Global
Environmental Politics
*Edited by Peter Dauvergne and Justin
Alger*

A Research Agenda for New Institutional
Economics
*Edited by Claude Ménard and Mary M.
Shirley*

A Research Agenda for Regeneration
Economies
Reading City-Regions
*Edited by John R. Bryson, Lauren Andres
and Rachel Mulhall*

A Research Agenda for Cultural Economics
Edited by Samuel Cameron

A Research Agenda for Environmental
Management
*Edited by Kathleen E. Halvorsen, Chelsea
Schelly, Robert M. Handler, Erin C. Pischke
and Jessie L. Knowlton*

A Research Agenda for Creative
Tourism
*Edited by Nancy Duxbury and Greg
Richards*

A Research Agenda for Public
Administration
Edited by Andrew Massey

A Research Agenda for Tourism
Geographies
Edited by Dieter K. Müller

A Research Agenda for Economic
Psychology
*Edited by Katharina Gangl and Erich
Kirchler*

A Research Agenda for Entrepreneurship
and Innovation
*Edited by David B. Audretsch, Erik E.
Lehmann and Albert N. Link*

A Research Agenda for Financial Inclusion
and Microfinance
*Edited by Marek Hudon, Marc Labie and
Ariane Szafarz*

A Research Agenda for Global Crime
Edited by Tim Hall and Vincenzo Scalia

A Research Agenda for Transport Policy
*Edited by John Stanley and David A.
Hensher*

A Research Agenda for Tourism and
Development
*Edited by Richard Sharpley and David
Harrison*

A Research Agenda for Housing
Edited by Markus Moos

A Research Agenda for Tourism and Development

Edited by

RICHARD SHARPLEY

Lancashire School of Business and Enterprise, University of Central Lancashire, UK

DAVID HARRISON

The Business School, Middlesex University, UK

Elgar Research Agendas

Edward Elgar
PUBLISHING

Cheltenham, UK • Northampton, MA, USA

Published by
Edward Elgar Publishing Limited
The Lypiatts
15 Lansdown Road
Cheltenham
Glos GL50 2JA
UK

Edward Elgar Publishing, Inc.
William Pratt House
9 Dewey Court
Northampton
Massachusetts 01060
USA

A catalogue record for this book
is available from the British Library

Library of Congress Control Number: 2019938735

This book is available electronically in the **Elgar**online
Social and Political Science subject collection
DOI 10.4337/9781788112413

ISBN 978 1 78811 240 6 (cased)
ISBN 978 1 78811 241 3 (eBook)

Typeset by Servis Filmsetting Ltd, Stockport, Cheshire

Printed and bound by CPI Group (UK) Ltd, Croydon, CR0 4YY

Contents

Figures

Tables

Contributors

Emmanuel Akwasi Adu-Ampong is Lecturer in Cultural Geography in the Cultural Geography Chair Group, Wageningen University and Research, the Netherlands, and a research associate at the School of Tourism and Hospitality Management, University of Johannesburg, South Africa. He obtained his PhD from the Department of Urban Studies and Planning at the University of Sheffield, UK. His interdisciplinary research interests are in the allied fields of tourism policy and planning, urban studies and international development planning in the context of Sub-Saharan Africa generally and Ghana in particular. His work is published in leading international journals in the field of tourism and international development such as *Annals of Tourism Research, Current Issues in Tourism, Tourism Planning and Development, International Development Planning Review* and *Development Policy Review.*

Julio Aramberri is Sitting Professor at Dongbei University of Finance and Economics, Dalian, China. He has previously held academic positions at Hoa Sen University, Saigon, Vietnam (2009–13), Drexel University, Philadelphia, USA (1999–2009) and Universidad Complutense de Madrid (1964–84). Prior to that, he undertook post-doctoral studies at the London School of Economics (1971–74). He worked for the Spanish Tourist Administration (1985–99) where he became its director general (1987–90). Aramberri has authored or co-authored eight books on sociological subjects and over 50 refereed articles. His *Modern Mass Tourism* (2010) was translated into Spanish (2012) and Chinese (2014). He is Charter Fellow of the International Academy for the Study of Tourism.

Helene Balslev Clausen is an anthropologist and holds a PhD in migration studies, Copenhagen Business School, Denmark. She is Associate Professor and Coordinator at the Department of Culture and Global Studies, Aalborg University. Her mission is to create new knowledge on ways in which tourism, activism and development can play a significant role in creating social change, stimulating local economies, conserving the environment and generating human wellbeing. She has conducted extensive fieldwork mainly in Latin America and Morocco. She has published extensively on tourism and sustainable development in high-ranking journals and edited various books. Recent publications include 'The Tourism Model in Post-Castro Cuba: Tensions between Ideology and Economic Realities' in the *Journal of Tourism Planning and Development* (2018) and 'Los norteamericanos que re-inventaron a los pueblos de México' in *Latin American Research Review* (2019). Currently she is coordinating a major research project in Mexico about sustainable tourism development and informal economies and regulation.

Ingrid Barradas-Bribiesca holds a BA and master's degree from the Institute of Education, University of London, UK. She was born in Germany but has been working at the University of Guanajuato for the last 32 years at the Division of Human Sciences and the Economic Administrative Sciences (DCEA). She has taught BA courses in Teaching English as a Foreign Language and in Education. At present she is teaching courses related to cultural heritage, cultural tourism and intercultural communication. During her time at the University of Guanajuato she has also worked as Coordinator of the Language Department and the Department of Internationalization of DCEA. She has published articles and book chapters in the field of education, popularization of science and tourism.

Tom Baum is Professor and Head of the Department of Work, Employment and Organisation in the University of Strathclyde, Glasgow, UK. Tom's research focuses on the social, cultural and economic context of work in frontline services, primarily hospitality and tourism from a comparative, international perspective. He has contributed to debate in this area for over 30 years, challenging the relative neglect of employment issues in wider discourse relating to tourism development and sustainable tourism. Tom has worked extensively with international agencies and supervised over 35 successful PhD candidates in this area.

Christine Budke is Professor of Epidemiology in the Department of Veterinary Integrative Biosciences at A&M University, College Station, USA. Budke's research focuses on epidemiology, burden of disease indicators, zoonotic diseases, international veterinary medicine and public health. She is a strong proponent of the One Health approach and has acted as a resource adviser for the World Health Organization's Foodborne Disease Burden Epidemiology Reference Group and has contributed to the Global Burden of Disease Study.

Dianne Dredge is Visiting Professor in the Department of Service Management and Service Studies, Lund University, Sweden. She has 20 years' practical experience as a tourism and environmental planner and policy analyst in Australia. She has completed consulting assignments in Canada, Mexico and China and undertaken work for international agencies such as the European Commission and the Organisation for Economic Co-operation and Development. Her research focuses on tourism as an agent of change from macro to micro contexts wherein she employs story-telling, policy ethnographies, policy network analysis and social learning approaches. Dianne is currently Chair of the Tourism Education Futures Initiative and a member of the International Academy for the Study of Tourism.

David Harrison is Professor of Tourism at Middlesex University, London, UK. Before that, he was Professor and Head of the School of Tourism and Hospitality Management at the University of the South Pacific, Fiji. He has carried out research on the impact of tourism in the Caribbean, Eastern Europe, Southern Africa, Southeast Asia and the South Pacific and is author of numerous peer-reviewed papers in tourism journals. In addition, he wrote *The Sociology of Modernization and Development* (1988) and has since edited and co-edited more than a dozen books, including *Tourism and the Less Developed Countries* (1992) and *Tourism and the Less Developed World: Issues and Case Studies* (2001). In 2003 he edited

Pacific Island Tourism and later, with Stephen Pratt, he co-edited *Tourism in Pacific Islands*. More recently, with Richard Sharpley he co-edited *Mass Tourism in a Small World* (2017) and with Victor T. King and Jerry Eades he co-edited four volumes, *Tourism in East and Southeast Asia* (2018).

Tazim Jamal is Professor in the Department of Recreation, Park and Tourism Sciences at A&M University, College Station, USA. Her primary research areas are sustainable tourism, collaborative tourism planning and cultural heritage management. She also teaches on theoretical, applied and methodological issues in tourism research, with particular interest in critical and interpretive research as well as issues related to justice and ethics. She is the co-editor of *The SAGE Handbook of Tourism Studies* (2009) and is the author of *Justice and Ethics in Tourism* (forthcoming). She is on the editorial board of nine peer-reviewed journals.

Shelagh Mooney is Senior Lecturer in Organizational Behaviour and Human Resources Management, as well as hospitality postgraduate program leader in the School of Hospitality and Tourism, at Auckland University of Technology, New Zealand. Shelagh's career research explores the effects of gender and other dimensions of diversity in employment, focusing on organizational processes within specific societal and industry contexts. The studies have been widely published in employment journals as well as in tourism and hospitality-specific publications. Shelagh's current research projects focus on sustainable human resources management, talent management, gendered organizations and how universities may best 'future-proof' students in a shifting and dynamic employment landscape.

Marina Novelli is an internationally renowned tourism and international development expert and an established academic based at the University of Brighton, UK, where she is Professor of Tourism and International Development and Academic Lead for the Responsible Futures Research and Enterprise Agenda across the university. With a background in economics and a keen interest in international development issues, she has written extensively in the field of international tourism policy, planning, development and management. She has advised on numerous projects funded by the World Bank, the European Union, the United Nations (UN) Educational, Scientific and Cultural Organization, the UN Industrial Development Organization, the UN World Tourism Organization, the Commonwealth Secretariat, national ministries and tourism boards, regional development agencies and non-governmental organizations in Sub-Saharan Africa, Europe and Asia. Her volume *Tourism and Development in Sub-Saharan Africa: Current Issues and Local Realities* (2016) conveys her extensive empirically grounded research and consultancy engagements and collaborations in some 15 Sub-Saharan Africa destinations.

Stephen Pratt is Head of the School of Tourism and Hospitality Management at the University of the South Pacific, Fiji. Previously, he worked in the School of Hotel and Tourism Management at the Hong Kong Polytechnic University. Steve holds bachelor and master's degrees in economics from the University of Sydney, Australia and a PhD from the University of Nottingham, UK. His research interests include sustainable tourism development (economic, socio-cultural and environmental impacts of tourism), tourism in small island states and film tourism. Steve is co-creator of the popular YouTube channel *The Travel Professors*. This channel provides a brief overview of current trends and issues in tourism and relates them to academic research. The channel provides additional educational resources for students and lecturers and for anyone curious about travel and tourism.

Amy Scarth is a specialist in tourism, community development and protected areas, particularly in East Africa. Formerly a research analyst for the commercial travel industry in London, followed by a range of consultancy projects in the tourism and development fields, Amy founded and spent six years directing a tourism and philanthropy-related social enterprise in remote parts of Uganda, Malawi and Ethiopia. She is the recipient of an Economic and Social Research Council doctoral scholarship and is currently researching for her PhD at the University of Brighton, UK focusing on the complexity of charity, gift giving and philanthropy through tourism in Sub-Saharan Africa. With her research she intends to enrich the understanding of this topic from an academic and practitioner's perspective. Amy is passionate about the role of tourism in African development and conservation and contributing to a deeper understanding of this field.

Richard Sharpley is Professor of Tourism and Development at the University of Central Lancashire, Preston, UK. He has previously held positions at a number of other institutions, including the University of Northumbria and the University of Lincoln, where he was Professor of Tourism and Head of Department, Tourism and Recreation Management. He is co-editor of the journal *Tourism Planning and Development*, a resource editor for *Annals of Tourism Research* and a member of the editorial boards of a number of other tourism journals. His principal research interests are within the fields of tourism and development, island tourism, rural tourism and the sociology of tourism. His books include *Tourism and Development: Concepts and Issues* (2002, 2015, with David Telfer); *Tourism and Development in the Developing World* (2008, 2016, with David Telfer); *Tourism, Tourists and Society* (5th Edition, 2018); *The Darker Side of Travel: The Theory and Practice of Dark Tourism* (2009, with Philip Stone); *Tourism, Development and Environment: Beyond Sustainability* (2009); and, co-edited with David Harrison, *Mass Tourism in a Small World* (2017).

David J. Telfer is Associate Professor in the Department of Geography and Tourism Studies at Brock University, Canada. His research interests are in the areas of the relationship between tourism and development theories, tourism planning, heritage tourism and rural tourism in Japan. He is co-author of *Tourism and Development in the Developing World* (2nd edition, 2016) and co-editor of *Tourism and Development: Concepts and Issues* (2nd edition, 2015), both with Richard Sharpley.

1 Introduction: tourism and development – towards a research agenda

Richard Sharpley and David Harrison

Introduction

The *raison d'être* of tourism is development. In other words, since the 1950s – not coincidentally, from the time when 'development' first became established as a global project in an emerging post-colonial world (Rist 2014) – tourism at both the national (domestic) and international scale has primarily been considered an effective catalyst of economic and social development. Indeed, almost four decades ago this role of tourism was officially endorsed by the World Tourism Organization (now United Nations World Tourism Organization, or UNWTO) in its Manila Declaration: 'world tourism can contribute to the establishment of a new international economic order that will help eliminate the widening economic gap between developed and developing countries and ensure the steady acceleration of economic and social development and progress, in particular in developing countries' (WTO 1980, p.1). Since then, not only has the UNWTO supported the development of tourism through knowledge generation and dissemination, policy guidance and more direct intervention (UNWTO 2017a) but also tourism itself has come to occupy a prominent position in the development policies and processes of an increasing number of countries and regions (Telfer & Sharpley 2016). In some cases, particularly where few if any other viable alternatives exist, especially small island states, it may be an option of 'last resort' (Brown 1998; Harrison 2001; Harrison & Prasad 2013; Lea 1988); in other cases, it has been employed as a means of diversifying economies dependent on a single sector, such as oil (Morakabati et al. 2014; Sharpley 2002), of stimulating the regeneration of peripheral rural areas (Gannon 1994; Roberts & Hall 2001) and post-industrial cities (Law 1992; Murphy & Boyle 2006), or more generally contributing to economic and social development (Sharpley & Telfer 2015). Irrespective of the context, however, tourism has, over the last half century or so, become a ubiquitous agent of development in almost every corner of the globe.

It is perhaps not surprising, therefore, that academic attention has long been paid to the relationship between tourism and development. Initially, such attention adopted a typically critical stance. That is, in contrast to the enthusiasm with which tourism was embraced by destinations eager to exploit the burgeoning demand for tourism, particularly from the late 1960s and with the emergence of international tourism on a relatively mass scale, early studies began to question its alleged developmental benefits. For example, Diamond (1977), drawing on research in Turkey, concluded that tourism did not necessarily represent a panacea to the economic problems facing many developing countries in particular, whilst a number of now seminal texts challenged tourism's developmental contribution more generally (de Kadt 1979; Turner & Ash 1975; Young 1973). Moreover, such criticism continued into the early 1980s, albeit more specifically from a political-economic perspective, with some arguing that tourism's developmental contribution was restricted by the inherent power relations within the international tourism sector that served to perpetuate a condition of dependency in destinations (Britton 1982; Høivik & Heiberg 1980; Husbands 1981).

However, the pendulum soon began to swing in the opposite direction as academic attention became focused more positively on means of enhancing the benefits of tourism to destinations. For example, reflecting the emergence of the alternative development paradigm (Pieterse 1998), alternative tourism, a blanket term applied to forms of tourism that allegedly offer an alternative to the perceived problems associated with mass tourism, gained widespread support during the latter half of the 1980s (Butler 1990; Smith & Eadington 1992), whilst the roots of the now popular concept of community-based tourism (CBT), drawing on the 'bottom-up' or grassroots philosophy of alternative development, also date back to this time (Murphy 1983, 1985). Thus, over a period of some 30 years, theory and understanding of the relationship between tourism and development progressed, according to Jafari (1989), through three stages: an initial advocacy stage, extolling the benefits of tourism, superseded by a cautionary stage that highlighted the negative consequences of tourism and then an adaptancy stage manifested in the alternative tourism movement.

Significantly, since the early 1990s we have witnessed the advent and subsequent maturation of a fourth, knowledge stage (Jafari 1989) during which understanding of tourism's developmental processes has expanded and deepened. Specifically, the locating of tourism within the conceptual framework of sustainable development provided – and continues to provide – a fruitful though controversial context for research into tourism and development (Mowforth & Munt 2016; Sharpley 2009), as well as the basis for much tourism planning and policy (though not necessarily implementation) in practice. At the same time, following the lead of a number of notable studies that established an initial link between the fields of tourism and development studies (for example, Brohman 1996; Harrison 1992; Opperman & Chon 1997), a more nuanced, theoretically informed understanding of tourism and development benefiting from contributions from a variety of disciplines has evolved. Indeed, knowledge and understanding of tourism as a social and economic phenomenon in general, as well as of its potential to contribute to development in particular, has advanced rapidly over the last two decades.

Nevertheless, tourism is dynamic, as both the demand for and supply of tourism are constantly transformed in response to economic, socio-cultural and technological change, and the external world within which the so-called tourism 'system' (Leiper 1990) is located and with which it interacts is also in a constant state of flux. A variety of influences and processes, from shifts in the global political-economic landscape to such challenges as climate change, have direct consequences for tourism, whilst tourism may also contribute to these processes. And more specifically in the context of this book, understandings of development, how it may be measured, the policies for and goals of development and the mechanisms for its achievement are equally dynamic. For example, once considered to be synonymous with economic growth (Mabogunje 1980), the concept of development has evolved into a broader concern for human well-being (Knutsson 2009) with specific global development objectives defined in the UN's 17 Sustainable Development Goals (UN 2017). Similarly, theories of development, or development paradigms, have also evolved, reflecting not only greater knowledge and understanding of developmental opportunities and challenges but also transformations in the global political economy (de Janvry & Sadoulet 2016; Todaro & Smith 2014).

The concept of development (as the explicit purpose of promoting tourism) is considered in more detail later in this chapter. The important point here, however, is that although ever increasing academic attention has been paid to the relationship between tourism and development, that relationship continues to change as both tourism and the challenges of development also undergo change. As a consequence, new questions arise and new gaps in knowledge emerge. For example, are typically growth-focused tourism policies becoming increasingly detrimental to destination development? Can mass forms of tourism in fact generate more benefit to the destination than alternative forms of tourism? Does the role of the state in supporting tourism-induced development require reconsideration? How effective is tourism-related philanthropy in contributing to development? Is CBT a realistic development policy? And, to what extent can tourism contribute to what is still the most pressing development challenge, namely poverty reduction? In short, despite the more recent advances in knowledge and understanding of the relationship between tourism and development, there exists the need for further research or, more precisely, for an agenda for research that addresses these and other questions and issues.

The purpose of this book is to establish such an agenda. That is, it sets out to identify and justify gaps in extant knowledge and understanding of tourism and development and, in so doing, to propose a number of themes and issues that would benefit from further research. As such, it is not the intention to suggest specific research projects; rather, the aim of the book is to identify potential avenues of research that might be followed from a variety of disciplinary or contextual perspectives, thereby ultimately contributing to the overall tourism and development body of knowledge. Hence, the remainder of this introductory chapter is concerned with establishing the background to this research agenda, first summarizing the factors that justify the widespread adoption of tourism as an agent of development before going on to review briefly the evolution of the concept of development and development theory. It then highlights key themes and perspectives within the extent research in tourism and development as a basis for introducing the chapters that comprise this book.

Development: why tourism?

As noted above, tourism has not only enjoyed long recognition and endorsement as a potentially valuable catalyst of development, but also this role is widely manifested in practice. By the early 1990s, it was observed that tourism had been adopted as 'an important and integral element of . . . development strategies' (Jenkins 1991a, p. 61) in many countries around the world. Unsurprisingly, however, it is primarily in the context of developing countries that: 'the development of tourism has long been seen as both a vehicle and a symbol of . . . progress and modernization' (Roche 1992, p. 566). Consequently, attention was, and continues to be, focused largely on tourism and development in the developing world. This is not to say, of course, that tourism has not been embedded in the development and regeneration policies of modern, industrialized nations; in Europe, for example, tourism's role in economic development enjoys a long history (Williams & Shaw 1991) whilst nowadays there is much evidence of national and supranational policy responses across the continent to the developmental opportunities afforded by tourism (Costa et al. 2013; EU n.d.). Nevertheless, in academic circles at least, it is developing countries that have benefited most from research, immediately pointing to a potential gap in extant knowledge (see Chapter 11).

Irrespective of the context, however, the principal reason for tourism to be adopted as a development strategy has always been its perceived economic contribution (Mihalič 2015; Sinclair 1998). Indeed, there can be no doubting the economic value of tourism on a global scale. In 2016, for example, worldwide international tourism receipts (payments for all goods and services in the destination and for international transport) amounted to US$1,220 million (UNWTO 2017b). If domestic tourism is also taken into account then, according to the World Travel and Tourism Council (WTTC 2016), the total direct economic contribution of tourism amounts to around US$2.3 trillion, or 3 per cent of global gross domestic product (GDP), rising to over US$7 trillion (9.8 per cent of GDP) if tourism's indirect contribution is also taken into account.

Such remarkable figures deserve to be treated, perhaps, with a degree of caution. Nevertheless, as one of the world's largest export sectors, international tourism represents a significant source of income and foreign exchange earnings, particularly for developing countries and, most especially, for many small island states that lack a range of natural resources and for which tourism can represent an overwhelming percentage of their GDP. Indeed, even though the absolute number of international tourists visiting such destinations is but a tiny percentage of international trips, small island states have long constituted the vast majority of world destinations most economically dependent on international tourism (Harrison 2001, p. 10; Harrison & Prasad 2013). Equally, it may also make a vital contribution to any country's balance of payments, not least to the travel account of major tourism-generating countries. In 2016, for example, international tourists in the UK spent £22.5 billion, around half of the £43.8 billion spent by UK residents on overseas visits (ONS 2017). At the same time, tourism is widely considered to be a labour-intensive sector and may be a significant source of employment in destination areas, whether direct or indirect. Again, according to the WTTC (2016), tourism supports around 284 million jobs worldwide, or almost 10 per cent of employment although, as discussed later in this chapter, issues surrounding tourism-related employment remain surprisingly underrepresented in the literature (see Chapter 10).

It should be noted, of course, that tourism may also incur significant economic costs (Wall & Mathieson 2006), hence the 'tourism development dilemma' (Telfer & Sharpley 2016) that many destinations face. Nevertheless, except in those instances where tourism represents the only viable choice, it may be assumed that, generally, destination administrations make a positive decision to integrate tourism into their development strategies in the expectation that the economic benefits will outweigh the costs. And indeed, there are innumerable examples around the world of cities, rural regions, islands, coastal resorts and entire nations where that expectation has proved to be correct, although the challenge of so-called 'overtourism', long prophesied in the literature, suggests that excessive emphasis tends to be placed on economic gain above other developmental needs. There are, however, a number of other factors, discussed at some length in the literature, that serve to enhance the attraction of tourism as a development option (Sharpley 2015), as follows.

Tourism is a growth sector

Tourism, particularly international tourism, is characterized by a history of remarkable growth. In 1950, the year that international statistics were first collated and published, just over 25 million international arrivals were recorded. Over the following six decades, international tourism grew, in terms of arrivals, at an average annual rate of 6.2 per cent, whilst receipts achieved an average annual growth rate of more than 10 per cent. As can be seen from Table 1.1, rapid growth in arrivals and receipts was achieved throughout the latter half of the twentieth century; at the turn of the new millennium, almost 690 million arrivals were recorded and, just over a decade later, in 2012, the 1 billion mark was surpassed for the first time. Since then, the growth in arrivals has continued although it should be noted that, on a decade-by-decade basis, the growth rate in both arrivals and receipts has not only steadily declined but also continues to do so (see Table 1.2). For example, the average annual growth rate in arrivals between 2010 and 2015 was 3.9 per cent (UNWTO 2016). Although recent figures suggest that an annual growth rate of around 4 per cent may be maintained into the future, it is unlikely that the UNWTO's long-standing prediction of 1.6 billion arrivals and receipts of over US$2 trillion by 2020 will be achieved (WTO 1998).

Three other points should also be noted. First, international tourism is susceptible to a variety of external factors and, at times, has experienced low or even negative growth worldwide. Following the events of 9/11, for example, an overall decline in global tourist arrivals was recorded in 2001 whilst, similarly, a decline also occurred in 2009 as a result of the global financial crisis. However, such falls are rare with more frequent declines typically experienced at the regional or destinational level,

Table 1.1   International tourist arrivals and receipts, 1950–2016

Year	Arrivals (million)	Receipts (US$bn)	Year	Arrivals (million)	Receipts (US$bn)
1950	25.3	2.1	2000	687.0	481.6
1960	69.3	6.9	2001	686.7	469.9
1965	112.9	11.6	2002	707.0	488.2
1970	165.8	17.9	2003	694.6	534.6
1975	222.3	40.7	2004	765.1	634.7
1980	278.1	104.4	2005	806.1	682.7
1985	320.1	119.1	2006	847.0	742.0
1990	439.5	270.2	2007	903.0	856.0
1991	442.5	283.4	2008	917.0	939.0
1992	479.8	326.6	2009	882.0	851.0
1993	495.7	332.6	2010	940.0	927.0
1994	519.8	362.1	2011	995.0	1,042.0
1995	540.6	410.7	2012	1,035.0	1,075.0
1996	575.0	446.0	2013	1,087.0	1,159.0
1997	598.6	450.4	2014	1,130.0	1,252.0
1998	616.7	451.4	2015	1,184.0	1,196.0
1999	639.6	465.5	2016	1,235.0	1,220.0

Source: Adapted from UNWTO data.

Table 1.2   International tourism arrivals and receipts growth rates, 1950–2000

Decade	Arrivals (average annual increase %)	Receipts (average annual increase %)
1950–60	10.6	12.6
1960–70	9.1	10.1
1970–80	5.6	19.4
1980–90	4.8	9.8
1990–2000	4.2	6.5

Source: Adapted from UNWTO 2005.

sadly often as a result of terrorist activity. For example, following two separate terrorist attacks against tourists in Tunisia in 2015, the country's tourism sector suffered a serious decline for two years with international arrivals only beginning to increase again in late 2017.

Second, international tourism has traditionally been polarized and regionalized (Shaw & Williams 1994). That is, the major flows of international tourists have tended to be between particular places (for example, between Northern and Southern Europe and between North America and the Caribbean) and within particular regions; until very recently, Europe accounted for more than half of all international tourist arrivals. This dominance is gradually changing with the Asia and Pacific region in particular claiming a larger share of global arrivals and the emergence of China as the world's largest international tourism generator (Harrison 2016), yet the overall figures mask a continuing inequity in the share of international tourism. In other words, the growth of international tourism has not been universal, with implications for many countries most in need of development.

And third, tourism data collated and presented on a worldwide basis exist only for international tourism. Although many individual countries, particularly in the developed world, collect domestic tourism data, few if any attempts have been made to undertake international comparisons, one notable exception being Bigano et al.'s (2007) study. Even this is limited in scope and provides no indication of the overall scale and growth of domestic tourism on a global basis yet, in addition to clear evidence that, generally, it is of significantly greater economic value than international tourism (and hence an equally if not more powerful economic growth catalyst), it would be safe to assume that domestic tourism has also grown consistently. Overall, then, despite a slowing growth rate and inequities in the share of that growth, tourism (both international and domestic) remains a safe development option.

Tourism redistributes wealth

It has long been recognized that one of the principal challenges to development is inequality both within and between nations (Seers 1969). Indeed, although significant progress has been achieved in recent years in reducing poverty around the world, particularly during the Millennium Development Goals programme (UN 2015), there is evidence that such inequality is actually on the increase (UN 2017). However, as a potentially effective means of transferring wealth from richer countries or regions to poorer, less developed or peripheral areas, tourism may contribute to the alleviation of inequality, whether through direct tourist expenditure on goods and services in the destination (with spending in the local informal economy in particular transferring wealth to the poor) or through foreign direct investment in the local tourism sector. Moreover, at the national scale, domestic tourism may play a significant role in the redistribution of wealth in both developed and developing countries. On the one hand, however, this redistributive effect may be limited by the nature and scale of tourism in the destination; for example, all-inclusive resort-based tourism is considered to restrict the spread of wealth locally (Freitag 1994). On the other hand, additional, philanthropic expenditures and activities beyond the tourism sector may help relieve inequalities (Chapter 5).

Backward linkages

While in the destination, tourists inevitably require a variety of goods and services, including accommodation, food and beverages, local transport, entertainment, souvenirs and so on. Hence, in principle, tourism offers significant opportunities for individuals and businesses within the local economy to respond to these needs, such as through the provision of food to hotels and restaurants (Telfer & Wall 2000; Torres 2003) or the production of arts and crafts for sale to tourists. Again, however, the extent to which these backward linkages can be successfully developed and exploited is dependent on a variety of factors, including the diversity and maturity of the local economy, the availability of finance and the volume and quality of locally produced goods. In some cases, the failure or inability to establish backward linkages may result in a high level of 'leakage', whereby earnings from tourism are spent on imports to service tourists' needs (see, for example, Anderson 2013). As a consequence, the potential contribution of tourism to poverty reduction must be questioned (Chapter 6).

No trade barriers

Tourism is often considered an attractive development option because, unlike many other industries or sectors, it faces no trade barriers. In other words, it is not uncommon for individual countries or trading blocs, such as the European Union, to impose restrictions on imports such as tariffs or quotas in order to protect and support their internal markets. By contrast, international tourism suffers no such restrictions. In general, tourism-generating countries place no limits on how many of their citizens may travel overseas, where they go, how often and how much they may spend although there are exceptions, such as the long-standing ban on Americans flying directly from the USA to Cuba. This ban was lifted during the Obama era, only to be partly reinstated in 2017 by the Trump administration. Hence, by and large, destinations have free and equal access to international tourism markets and are able to exploit 'an export opportunity free of the usual trade limitations' (Jenkins 1991b, p. 84). They must still, however, operate in an increasingly competitive international market, and transport links and the extent of local tourism infrastructure may also serve to limit the growth of tourism at the destination.

'Free' resources

Compared to many other industries, tourism is considered to have relatively low start-up costs inasmuch as many of the resources that attract tourists, whether natural, such as mountains and beaches, or built heritage, already exist and thus are, in a simplistic sense, 'free'. Of course, they are not free as, inevitably, costs are incurred in their upkeep and protection and many argue that an economic value should be placed on their use and included as part of the price that tourists pay (Mihalič 2015). At the same time, substantial investment might be required in infrastructure and facilities to enable tourists to travel to and enjoy these resources. Nevertheless, tourism is often favoured as a development option given the pre-existence of these basic resources.

Social and environmental benefits

In addition to the above factors, the development of tourism offers a number of 'spin-off' benefits to the destination and the local community. For example, infra-structural, facility and amenity developments for tourism, from power supplies and transport infrastructure to restaurants, entertainment facilities and other services such as policing and health care are also of benefit to and utilized by the local community. At the same time, the destination may be improved for the local community by general environmental protection and enhancement schemes whilst specific policies, such as national park designation, provide additional environ-mental and recreational resources for local people. Moreover, tourism may also serve to strengthen or revitalize local cultural identity through stimulating cultural performances, the production of traditional arts and crafts or the organization of culturally based festivals.

There are, then, compelling reasons for the adoption of tourism as opposed to other industries or economic sectors as a catalyst of development. These are, for the most part, related specifically to the economic benefits that accrue from tourism; that is, as a global economic sector of significant scale and value – simply stated, as big business – tourism acts primarily as an engine of economic growth. However, as observed above, although once considered synonymous with economic growth, development has evolved into a much broader concept. Hence, in order to consider the relation-ship between tourism and development and, as is the intent of this book, to propose a research agenda to enhance understanding of that relationship, it is now necessary to review briefly what development 'is' and transformations in development theory.

Development: definitions and processes

The academic study of development first emerged in the 1950s as a branch of devel-opment economics and, subsequently, development studies as a discrete, albeit interdisciplinary, field of academic endeavour became established in the 1960s. Since then, it has evolved and transformed, addressing development from a vari-ety of disciplinary and practical perspectives (Desai & Potter 2013). According to Harriss (2005), however, the future direction of development studies remains uncertain, not least reflecting wider concerns and debates surrounding the validity of development itself as a global 'project' (Sidaway 2007). That is, since the 1990s, proponents of the so-called 'post-development' school have suggested that the notion of global development is flawed, unjust, has failed in its objectives and, hence, should be abandoned or replaced with an alternative approach (Rahnema 1997). Similarly, Payne and Phillips (2010, p. 3) suggest that 'contemporary development studies, although still a sizeable academic enterprise in many Western countries, is at the same time an uncertain and under-confident discipline'. However, their solution to this impasse is to 'relocate the study of development squarely within the intellectual project of political economy and the diverse theoretical traditions associated with it' (Payne & Phillips 2010, p. 181).

It is not possible to consider these debates in detail here, although they are of undoubted relevance; that is, given the widespread support for and dependence upon tourism as a development strategy, it is logical to question that role from a critical perspective on development itself. Nevertheless, for the purposes of this chapter, two issues demand brief consideration: first, how development may be defined or thought of and, second, the evolution of development paradigms (for more detail, see Telfer 2015).

Defining development

An immediate challenge in considering development is that it is a concept that 'seems to defy definition' (Cowen & Shenton 1996, p. 3). On the one hand, it is typically used to refer to a process of social change and, implicitly, 'betterment'; on the other hand, it may be seen as a philosophical concept alluding to a desirable future state or condition. Either way, however, a universal definition would appear to be optimistic and, hence, development should perhaps be considered in relation to the needs or aims of particular societies and the ways in which those societies seek to address their specific societal challenges (Hettne 2009). Nevertheless, it can broadly be thought of as the process and outcome of a specific kind of social change; as Goulet (1968, p. 388) puts it, development 'refers both to the destination of a journey and to the journey itself'.

That 'destination' has changed over time. The initial alignment of development with economic growth in the 1950s and early 1960s referred to earlier in this chapter was soon challenged when it came to be recognized that in many countries, economic growth was not only failing to solve social and political problems but was also causing or exacerbating them. In particular, it was argued that, beyond overall economic growth, fundamental to development is solving the three problems of poverty, unemployment and inequality (problems that to varying extents still remain unresolved in both developed and developing countries). According to Seers (1969), even if just one of these has become more acute then, even if per capita income has grown significantly, development cannot be considered to have occurred.

To these three challenges Seers (1977) later added a fourth, namely, self-reliance. That is, in an era of increasing dependence emphasized by the 1970s oil crisis, the notion of self-determination also became fundamental to development. Putting it another way, the concept of freedom, later to be considered synonymous with development (Sen 1999), entered the equation; the path to development required freedom of choice for individual members of societies and freedom from servitude to ignorance, nature, other societies, beliefs and institutions (Sharpley 2015). Thus, development came to be seen as a broad concept embracing at least five dimensions (see Goulet 1992):

- an economic component – wealth creation and equitable access to resources
- a social component – improvements in health, housing, education and employment

Table 1.3 Sustainable Development Goals

1	No poverty	10	Reduced inequalities
2	Zero hunger	11	Sustainable cities and communities
3	Good health and well-being	12	Responsible production and consumption
4	Quality education	13	Climate action
5	Gender equality	14	Life below water
6	Clean water and sanitation	15	Life on land
7	Affordable and clean energy	16	Peace, justice and strong institutions
8	Decent work and economic growth	17	Partnerships for the goals
9	Industry, innovation and infrastructure		

Source: Adapted from UN 2017.

- a political dimension – assertion of human rights, appropriate political systems
- a cultural dimension – protection or affirmation of cultural identity and self-esteem
- the full-life paradigm – preservation and strengthening of a society's symbols, beliefs and meaning systems.

To these, perhaps, should be added an ecological component, reflecting not only the emergence of environmental sustainability as a fundamental parameter of contemporary approaches to development but also its centrality to the concept of sustainable tourism development which, as considered later in this chapter, has been a dominant theme in the tourism and development literature since the early 1990s. It is also notable that these components of development are broadly reflected in the current Sustainable Development Goals (see Table 1.3), whilst the most widely accepted measure of development is the annual UN Development Programme (UNDP) Human Development Index which ranks countries according to a variety of economic and social indicators.

To summarize, then, development may be considered to be essentially a social phenomenon focusing on the betterment of the human condition, or what a recently devised development index refers to as social progress: 'Social progress is the capacity of a society to meet the basic human needs of its citizens, establish the building blocks that allow citizens and communities to enhance and sustain the quality of their lives, and create the conditions for all individuals to reach their full potential' (Porter et al. 2013, p. 7). Putting it another way, development may be defined as the continuous and positive change in the economic, social, political and cultural dimensions of the human condition, guided by the principle of freedom of choice and limited by the capacity of the environment to sustain such change (Sharpley 2015, p. 22). This is reflected in the UNDP's most recent definition of human development (UNDP 2010, p. 22) as: 'the expansion of people's freedoms to live long, healthy and creative lives; to advance other goals they have reason to value; and to engage actively in shaping development equitably and sustainably on a shared planet'.

Development paradigms

Just as definitions and understandings of development have evolved over the last half century, so too have development paradigms or theories of development (that is, a combination of the ideological ends of development and the strategic means of achieving them). These are addressed at length in the literature (for example, Peet & Hartwick 2015) although, as with the preceding discussion of definitions, an overview of key points will suffice for the purpose of this chapter. That is, it is important to consider the means by which tourism may contribute to development and, in particular, whether contemporary paradigms are applicable to the specific context of tourism (Telfer 2015).

Broadly speaking, development paradigms have evolved along a trajectory from top-down economic growth-based approaches to a broader focus on enhancing human well-being with an emphasis on endogenous, bottom-up development. For some, this evolution is evident in a journey from traditional modernization theory through to sustainable development, the latter still occupying a dominant position in development policies in general and tourism development policies in particular; for others, that journey has continued into human development and beyond into global development. Table 1.4 summarizes a chronology of development paradigms, although it should be noted that emerging paradigms have not replaced but rather supplement preceding ones which remain of relevance to particular contexts. For example, in some instances, tourism and its potential developmental contribution may be best explained by modernization theory; in others, such as pro-poor tourism interventionist policies, human development is more in evidence whilst, as noted earlier, CBT is most closely aligned to alternative development. Each paradigm is now explained briefly.

Modernization

Modernization theory combines the notion that all societies follow an inevitable evolutionary path from traditional to economic, political and social modernity with the belief that, once a particular point along that path has been reached – the so-called 'take-off' stage (Rostow 1967) – then development based upon economic growth can occur. Significantly, that development may be stimulated by the introduction of a 'growth pole' (that is, an industry or economic sector) from which 'growth impulses' diffuse throughout the region. There is, then, a direct corollary with tourism. A tourist resort may act as a growth pole, the growth impulses being the backward linkages referred to earlier in this chapter. Cyprus (Sharpley 2003) and Mexico (Clancy 2001) are examples of the application of tourism-related modernization theory.

Dependency

Dependency theory, which emerged in the 1960s as a critique of the modernization paradigm, is essentially a neo-Marxist explanation of why development does

Table 1.4   The evolution of development theory

Period	Development paradigm	Theoretical perspectives
1950s–1960s	*Modernization*	Stages of growth Diffusion: growth impulses/trickle-down effect
1950s–1970s	*Dependency*	Neo-colonialism: underdevelopment caused by exploitation by developed countries Dualism: poverty functional to global economic growth Structuralism: domestic markets, state involvement
mid-1970s–1980s	*Economic neo-liberalism*	Free market: free competitive markets/privatization Structural adjustment: competitive exports/market forces One world: new world financial systems
1970s–early 1980s	*Alternative development*	Basic needs: focus on food, housing, education, health Grassroots: people-centred development Gender: gender relations/empowerment Sustainable development: environmental management
Late 1980s–early 1990s	*The impasse and post-development*	Post-modern critique of metanarratives of development discourse; pluralistic approaches that value local knowledge and solutions
1990s–2000s	*Human development*	Human development: freedom, democratic and human rights, poverty reduction State-led development Focus on civil society and social capital Transnational social movements: environment, peace, etc. Culture: different world views are accommodated Human security; challenging the 'failed state'
2000s and 2010s	*Global development*	Focus on enhancing global international relations and governance through yet to be built supranational political institutions

Source: Adapted from Telfer 2015, pp. 36–7; also Telfer & Sharpley 2016, p. 16.

not occur. Its fundamental premise is that a country's underdevelopment reflects the external and internal political, economic and institutional structures that keep it in a dependent position relative to developed countries. More precisely, dependency theory argues that global political and economic relations are such that wealthier, more powerful Western nations are able to exploit weaker, peripheral nations (often mirroring earlier colonial ties), thereby limiting developmental opportunities within developing countries. Various theoretical perspectives on dependency theory exist although tourism has long been considered a manifestation of the paradigm (Bastin 1984; Britton 1982; Nash 1989).

Economic neo-liberalism

The 1980s Reagan-Thatcher era was characterized by a return to the politics of economic liberalism. In the context of international development, this was manifested in policies that sought to counter existing excessive state intervention, promoting instead development lending contingent on market liberalization, the privatization of state enterprises and the overall reduction in the role of the state. So-called Structural Adjustment Lending Programmes became popular yet soon became widely discredited for enhancing rather than solving development challenges (Harrigan & Mosley 1991). Consequently, these were superseded by Poverty Reduction Strategy Papers, which encouraged local participation in development strategy, though these have also proved to be unsuccessful (Lazarus 2008).

Alternative development

The alternative development paradigm offers, literally, an alternative to the preceding top-down interventionist approaches to development. Instead, it adopts a resource-based, bottom-up approach that focuses primarily on human and environmental concerns, based on the fundamental tenet that development should be endogenous. In other words, the development process should start within and be guided by the needs of each society rather than being externally imposed. Hence, alternative development also emphasizes the importance of satisfying basic needs and of encouraging self-reliance (Galtung 1986). Significantly, it underpinned the subsequent emergence of sustainable development, a concept that continues to dominate global development policy, whilst as discussed earlier in this chapter, the 1980s concept of 'alternative tourism' not coincidentally adapted the principles of alternative development to the specific context of tourism.

The impasse and post-development

The 1980s were considered by some to be a lost decade of development. Not only had the developmental gap between rich and poor nations failed to diminish but also the collapse of socialism as a political system, the inherently oxymoronic nature of sustainable development, the diminishing role of the nation-state in an increasingly globalized world, as well as the perceived failure of preceding development policies (including sustainable development) led to claims that the concept of development as a global project had not worked. Consequently, it was also suggested by some that development thought had reached an impasse, hence the emergence of the 'post-development' school, an eclectic collection of approaches to development that, broadly, favoured traditional, non-modern/Western philosophies and cultures and emphasized local engagement, community involvement and autonomy from the state in development processes. Within the context of tourism, however, development policies continued to be framed by the sustainable development paradigm.

Human development

As discussed in the preceding section, the concept or definition of development has evolved over time, most recently being considered the process and objective of improving human well-being. This is reflected in the human development paradigm which, rather than promoting a specific 'blueprint' of development, embraces a variety of approaches and practices unified by a focus on improving the human condition. In addition to the adoption of measures such as the UNDP's annual Human Development Index with a focus on indicators such as life expectancy, education and income, issues including human rights, democracy and good governance, debt cancellation and poverty reduction are also embraced by human development. The UN's Sustainable Development Goals (see Table 1.3) are evidence of the centrality of human well-being in development, each goal arguably requiring different policies and processes for its achievement. Within the tourism context, more recent approaches to and forms of tourism, such as pro-poor tourism (Harrison 2008; Scheyvens 2015) and volunteer tourism (Wearing & McGehee 2013) are examples of a focus on human development although, in the context of tourism development globally, these arguably remain on the margins.

Global development

According to Held (2010, p. 220):

> Today, there is a newfound recognition that global problems cannot be solved by any one nation-state acting alone, nor by states just fighting their corner in regional blocs. What is required is collective and collaborative action – something the states of the world have not been good at, and which they need to reconsider and advance if the most pressing issues are to be adequately tackled.

In short, despite recognition of the right of nations to individually address their development challenges, in an increasingly interconnected globalized world that faces global problems, the establishment of new supranational political organizations is clearly necessary. To some extent, such as in the context of climate change, this is already occurring; within tourism in particular, however, despite the existence of the UNWTO and other bodies committed to enhancing international co-operation in tourism, it has long been recognized that, as a fragmented and multi-sectoral industry, global consensus on policies and processes is unlikely to be achieved (McKercher 1993).

Overall, then, it is evident that over time, both the processes and objectives of development have evolved from relatively simplistic economic growth models through the more complex notion of sustainable development to a more specific focus on human development. It is also evident that, in some respects, tourism policies and processes in particular have reflected this evolution. Nevertheless, given that tourism, as observed at the outset of this chapter, has long been considered a vehicle of development, the next task is to explore the various approaches proposed within the literature for realizing this potential; that is, for establishing an effective link between tourism and development. This will provide the basis for then outlining future research needs within the field of tourism and development.

Tourism and development: conceptual approaches

As observed earlier, the academic study of and research into tourism and development has advanced through a number of stages, the last two decades in particular being characterized by more theoretically informed, multi-disciplinary perspectives on the relationship between tourism and development. As a consequence, a variety of conceptual approaches have been proposed in the literature – and to an extent adopted in practice – that seek to enhance both the benefits accruing from tourism to the local community and an understanding of how such benefits might be transferred. Most of these approaches have attracted significant attention and have become discrete themes in tourism studies in their own right, some becoming the focus of a substantial literature. In particular, the concept of sustainable tourism development has not only spawned innumerable books, chapters and articles and special issues but, for more than 20 years, also enjoyed its own dedicated journal (*Journal of Sustainable Tourism*), as has also the concept of ecotourism.

The purpose here is to present a brief overview of each theme, in so doing providing an overall 'flavour' of extant research in tourism and development and highlighting key questions or areas of contention that arguably would justify further research.

Tourism and development: economic perspectives

Tourism is primarily an economic phenomenon. That is, although it is manifested in the movement of significant volumes of people within and across national borders, it is the spending by those people on the goods and services that collectively comprise the tourist product or experience that endows tourism with significance as a catalyst of development in destination areas. In other words, it is primarily in the economic benefits of tourism, as reviewed earlier in this chapter, that the attraction of tourism lies, whether as a stimulus of economic growth in general or as a means of achieving specific objectives, such as enhancing foreign exchange earnings or poverty reduction, in particular. It then follows that, as the primary developmental outcomes of tourism are economic, subsequent social development may follow, though not inevitably. That is, at the destinational level, a variety of factors such as the nature of tourism development and other political and socioeconomic variables may determine the extent to which tourism contributes to wider development.

Importantly, however, even positive economic benefits cannot be assumed as an inevitable outcome of tourism development; indeed, as Mihalič (2015, p. 80) observes, destinations may often exaggerate or take for granted the potential contribution of tourism to economic growth whilst overlooking the economic costs that may limit the benefits that accrue. Such economic costs (and benefits) have long been considered in the literature, both in general texts exploring the economics of tourism (for example, Bull 1995; Dwyer & Forsyth 2006; Tribe 2005; Wall & Mathieson 2006) and more specific studies of, for example, backward economic linkages (Telfer & Wall 2000), tourism multipliers (Archer 1982), supply chains (Ashley & Haysom 2008; Zhang et al. 2009) and employment generation (Farver 1984; Leiper 1999). Equally, not only has knowledge and understanding of tourism's economic contribution become more detailed and nuanced through, for example, the development of satellite accounting (Smeral 2006) and, in practice, models for the more realistic measurement of tourism spending, but also research into tourism's economic potential, taking into account factors such as the structure and maturity of the local destination economy, has become more sophisticated. Indeed, in the context of this book, it could be argued that, from an economics disciplinary perspective, the economic dimension of tourism and development is well understood, in particular at the level of individual destinations. Where research remains necessary, however, is in the ways in which the translation of the economic contribution of tourism into non-economic developmental benefits (for example, greater equity within and between societies) can be optimized or, indeed, if there are alternative, non-economic parameters by which the success (or failure) of tourism as an agent of development might be better measured.

Alternative tourism and its derivatives

Alternative tourism emerged, as observed by Cohen (1987, p. 13) in an early critique of the concept, as 'a fashionable idea among those . . . dissatisfied with the nature of mass tourism'. By definition, it was proposed by its early proponents (for example, Holden 1984) in response to the perceived negative impacts of mass tourism development; that is, as an alternative to mass tourism. Its foundations, therefore, were to be found in the growing concern over the consequences of the rapid and seemingly uncontrolled growth and development of tourism from the 1960s onwards, perhaps best epitomized not only in the rapid spread of large-scale homogenous resorts along the Spanish 'costas' but also in the annual mass migration of tourists to the sun on cheap package holidays. Indeed, as Cohen (1987) noted, alternative tourism is as much about alternative tourists seeking more individualistic, non-commoditized experiences as it is about planning and managing tourism development.

Alternative tourism, then, is essentially an umbrella term that refers to an approach to tourism supply and demand that is distinctive from (or the opposite to) mass tourism. Hence, an enormous variety of types of tourism, such as green tourism, nature tourism, adventure tourism, responsible tourism and, of course, ecotourism, can be thought of as derivatives of the concept of alternative tourism, yet all share a number of characteristics, as summarized in Table 1.5.

Table 1.5   Characteristics of mass versus alternative tourism

Conventional mass tourism	Alternative forms of tourism
General features	
Rapid development	Slow development
Maximizes	Optimizes
Socially/environmentally inconsiderate	Socially/environmentally considerate
Uncontrolled	Controlled
Short term	Long term
Sectoral	Holistic
Remote control	Local control
Development strategies	
Development without planning	First plan, then develop
Project-led schemes	Concept-led schemes
Tourism development everywhere	Development in suitable places
Concentration on 'honeypots'	Pressures and benefits diffused
New building	Re-use of existing building
Development by outsiders	Local developers
Employees imported	Local employment utilized
Urban architecture	Vernacular architecture
Tourist behaviour	
Large groups	Singles, families, friends
Fixed programme	Spontaneous decisions
Little time	Much time
'Sights'	'Experiences'
Imported lifestyle	Local lifestyle
Comfortable/passive	Demanding/active
Loud	Quiet
Shopping	Bring presents

Source: Telfer & Sharpley 2016, p. 57, adapted from Lane 1990 and Butler 1990.

Undoubtedly, many examples can be found of such alternative tourism developments (and tourists) in practice which may bring fewer negative consequences and greater benefit to local communities. However, this may not always be the case; many of the criticisms raised by Cohen in 1987 and subsequently by others remain current. In a practical sense, negative impacts may still be keenly felt whilst the implicit idealism of the concept and its condemnation of mass tourism not only overlooks the potential for alternative developments to become mainstream but also the fact that, as they are by definition small and local, so too are the benefits that accrue from alternative tourism. In other words, in many instances conventional mass tourism may bring greater net benefits to a destination whilst, as recently suggested (Harrison & Sharpley 2017), alternative tourism might be more realistically considered a sub-category of the contemporary global phenomenon that is mass tourism.

Community-based tourism

As a specific manifestation of alternative tourism development, a community-based approach to tourism was first proposed by Murphy (1983, 1985). Since then, it has attracted support and criticism in equal measure (Blackstock 2005; Joppe 1996; Scheyvens 2002; Tosun 2000), yet remains not only a popular focus of academic attention but also a highly contested concept (Jamal & Dredge 2016).

In a sense, all forms of tourism development are concerned with bringing benefits to destination communities; as stated at the outset of this chapter, in principle this is the fundamental purpose of tourism although, in reality, such benefits may often be coincidental to the more pragmatic pursuit of tourism as a business. CBT, however, is a specific approach that seeks to enhance the developmental benefits of tourism through maintaining, to varying degrees, the local community's involvement in tourism. In practice, CBT may take many forms and communities may benefit from numerous kinds of association with external agencies (Simpson 2007) but, for many commentators, the local community should not only be involved in the planning of tourism but also have ownership of it, managing it on a day-to-day basis and sharing its benefits (Telfer & Sharpley 2016, pp.192–8). Hence, CBT is, essentially, a means of empowering communities (Campbell & Vainio-Mattila 2003; Scheyvens 2002), supporting local social development through tourism that meets local needs, respects local culture and traditions and supports environmental conservation. As such, it can be considered the counterpoint to large-scale resort developments controlled and owned by 'outside' organizations on which the local community become dependent for income and employment.

Inevitably, perhaps, much of the research explores or proposes ways in which CBT might be implemented, typically within conceptual frameworks of differing levels and types of community involvement and participation, such as Arnstein's (1969) and Pretty's (1995) widely cited models. Equally, issues surrounding collaboration and partnership are of relevance, particularly when a broader definition of community is applied (Bramwell & Lane 2000). Overall, however, studies demonstrate that, in practice, not only is the concept of CBT widely interpreted but also that, often, it may be less successful than envisaged in bringing benefits to local communities (Goodwin & Santilli 2009). Hence, there appears to be a mismatch between the continuing support for and promotion of the concept of CBT and its viability as a means of enhancing the developmental benefits to destination communities. This, in turn, points to the need for objective empirical research that considers the circumstances under which CBT may represent a realistic approach and how it may be achieved.

Sustainable tourism development

Sustainable tourism development has dominated research into tourism and development since the early 1990s, both as a concept in its own right and as a context for justifying and exploring more specific forms of tourism development. At the same time, it has remained the objective of tourism planning and management in practice; the UNWTO is committed to the concept, suggesting that 'sustainable tourism development guidelines and management practices are applicable to all forms of tourism in all types of destinations, including mass tourism and the various niche tourism segments' (UNWTO 2018), whilst destinations, industry sectors and other organizations actively seek to encourage the sustainable development of tourism. Moreover, 2017 was designated as the UN's International Year of Sustainable Tourism for Development.

Despite the widespread support for sustainable tourism development, however, debate continues to surround its viability in practice, reflecting, perhaps, long-expressed criticisms of its parental paradigm, sustainable development (for example, Redclift 1987). Indeed, given the more recent emphasis on human development within development circles (see Table 1.4), sustainable tourism development might arguably be considered to be anachronistic. While the arguments are many and sometimes complex, for present purposes a number of observations can be made (Sharpley 2009). First, a definitional distinction exists between sustainable tourism – a parochial emphasis on the sustainability of tourism itself (Hunter 1995) – and sustainable tourism development, the focus of which is on the achievement of sustainable development through tourism (Cronin 1990). The former (sustainability) is a prerequisite for any economic activity or business and is, unsurprisingly, the concern of much of the research, whereas the latter remains, perhaps, an idealistic (and contested) objective. Second and related, sustainable tourism development was considered from the outset as an alternative to mass tourism (Pigram 1990), a dichotomy that persists, not least in many sets of guidelines for sustainable tourism development. Hence, attention has primarily been focused on the nature of tourism itself rather than on its developmental outcomes (although specific approaches, such as pro-poor tourism as discussed below, go some way to addressing this limitation). Third, it has been demonstrated that, as a social and economic phenomenon, tourism cannot be mapped on to the principles and objectives of sustainable development (Sharpley 2000); specifically, the fundamental principles of futurity, equity and an holistic perspective cannot be met by tourism. And fourth, an often overlooked fact is that, as an activity involving primarily fossil fuel-dependent travel, tourism is inherently environmentally unsustainable (Høyer 2000). Hence, although there is clearly a need to explore ways of enhancing the sustainability of tourism itself, the time has perhaps come to draw a line under the concept of sustainable tourism development.

Pro-poor tourism

Whilst tourism has long been considered a catalyst of development in general, it is only relatively recently that tourism's potential to contribute to the alleviation of poverty in particular has attracted increasing interest. Indeed, it was only around the start of the new millennium that policies and projects targeting poverty reduction through tourism were first proposed, most notably through the work of the now defunct Pro-Poor Tourism Partnership funded initially by the UK's

Department for International Development. The World Tourism Organization launched its Sustainable Tourism – Eliminating Poverty Programme (ST-EP) at the World Summit on Sustainable Development in Johannesburg in 2002 (see http://step.unwto.org/content/st-ep-initiative-1) and only subsequently did academic attention turn to what is generally referred to as pro-poor tourism. Hence, it was in developmental circles that the notion of poverty reduction through tourism first emerged, the mantle subsequently being taken over by academics (Scheyvens 2015) and, since then, a burgeoning literature on the subject has evolved (for example, Ashley & Mitchell 2010; Blake et al. 2008; Holden 2013).

As discussed later in this book (Chapter 6) as well as elsewhere (Harrison 2008), pro-poor tourism is not a specific type of tourism; any form of tourism, including mass tourism, might be pro-poor. Rather, it is an approach to tourism that seeks to provide the poor or those excluded from the tourism sector access to tourist markets, in so doing offering them the opportunity to earn income through tourism. The UNWTO's ST-EP programme, referred to above, proposes seven different strategies for engaging the poor in tourism, from employment in tourism enterprises to targeted/philanthropic schemes (see below), whilst there are examples of successful pro-poor tourism projects in practice. However, as essentially interventionist schemes (it is market forces that typically exclude the poor) dependent on funding and, usually, non-governmental organization (NGO) support, their longer-term viability is often questioned, as is the overall concept of pro-poor tourism (Harrison 2008).

Tourism planning and governance

If tourism is to contribute effectively to the wider socio-economic development of destinations or, indeed, if simply the economic benefits of tourism are to be optimized, appropriate planning and management is, inevitably, required. Put differently, if tourism is to meet its developmental objectives, then effective planning is a prerequisite; it should, in principle, establish what those objectives are and, within the context of available resources and opportunities, not only set out a path for the achievement of those objectives but also propose mechanisms for measuring the extent to which they have been achieved.

It is not surprising, therefore, that much of the literature is concerned, either directly or indirectly, with tourism planning and governance. Numerous texts explore the topic in detail, either from a 'pure' planning perspective (for example, Gunn & Var 2002; Hall 2008; Inskeep 1991), from a strategic management perspective (Evans 2015) or from a public policy/governance perspective (Bramwell & Lane 2012; Hall & Jenkins 1995). Equally, the planning and management of specific forms of tourism, such as island tourism (Carlsen & Butler 2011), urban tourism (Page & Hall 2003) or tourism in protected areas (Eagles & McCool 2002) have attracted significant attention, whilst a variety of approaches, such as community or participatory planning, as well as alternative perspectives (Burns 2004) are also considered.

Importantly, however, the effective planning of tourism is not always (or perhaps even rarely) in evidence in practice (Ruhanen 2013). In other words, much of what is proposed in the extensive academic literature on tourism planning and governance is not reflected in the way in which tourism is often developed in reality. For example, although sustainable tourism development has remained the dominant tourism development paradigm in both academic and policy circles for more than two decades, a growth-focused 'industrial' model of tourism development persists (Pollock 2012). Equally, the so-called phenomenon of 'overtourism' is increasingly in evidence around the world, again pointing to the failure of planning or, perhaps, policies (Kerr 2003) in tourism development, as well as a disconnect between the academic study and the practice of tourism. There is, then, a pressing need for research into the planning and governance of tourism to identify not only the factors that have brought about planning failure (or success) but also to explore alternative means of establishing and implementing tourism policy and planning.

Philanthropy: volunteer tourism

Although the notion of 'responsible tourism' initially referred to an alternative approach to tourism planning in general (Haywood 1988; Wheeller 1991), it has re-emerged as a more actor-centred approach demanding responsibility on the part of all stakeholders in the tourism system (see below). One specific form of tourism that arguably reflects such responsibility, at least on the part of tourists themselves, is so-called volunteer tourism (Wearing 2001) in which individuals pay to travel and engage in development-related voluntary activities, typically in developing countries, for all or part of their trip. Often, such activities involve conservation work although many volunteer tourists also seek to work on socio-economic projects including education, medical assistance or social care.

Of course, the concept of travelling overseas (and domestically) to work voluntarily is not new; as observed elsewhere (Sharpley 2018), organized international volunteering has existed since the mid-twentieth century, though usually involving individuals with identified skills for longer periods of time. In recent years, however, volunteer tourism has become a recognized and increasingly popular sector of the overall tourism market as, in particular, growing numbers of younger people, often as part of their 'gap year' either before or after attending university, join volunteering projects organized and sold by an also growing number of specialist organizations. At the same time, as Wearing and McGehee (2013) note, much of the academic research into the phenomenon, perhaps unsurprisingly, also emerged during this period. Initially, volunteer tourism was advocated as an effective means of contributing directly to local sustainable development, although soon a number of negative consequences came to be identified, such as the reinforcement of cultural stereotyping (Raymond & Hall 2008; Simpson 2004) or highlighting inequality (Lyons et al. 2012; Sin 2010). The popularization of volunteer tourism as a commercial tourism product has also stimulated debates surrounding the altruistic or self-interest motives of those participating in it, with many suggesting that it is no more than an ego-centric tourism experience (Daldeniz & Hampton 2010) involving a self-therapeutic retreat from public policies and a diminution of political and moral agency (Butcher & Smith 2015).

Interestingly, however, less attention has been paid to the benefits of volunteer tourism accruing to host communities (Lupoli et al. 2014); that is, it remains unclear to what extent volunteer tourism brings positive developmental benefits to destinations and host communities. Moreover, the relative benefits of volunteer tourism compared with other, often 'hidden' tourism-related philanthropy, such as the private establishment of charitable projects by tourists visiting developing countries, have yet to be explored.

Responsible tourism: a 'moral' approach?

As noted in the preceding section, the concept of responsible tourism first emerged in the late 1980s and early 1990s as a more environmentally and socially appropriate alternative to mass tourism development (Cooper & Ozdil 1992; Harrison & Husbands 1996). It referred to a more responsible approach (to destination environments and communities) in planning and managing tourism. In more recent years, however, it has re-emerged and, indeed, garnered significant support within some sectors of the tourism industry as an approach to tourism that emphasizes the requirement for all stakeholders, including tourism businesses and tourists themselves, to take responsibility for their roles and actions in tourism (Goodwin 2011). In practice, this has been evidenced in the promotion and adoption of principles for responsible tourism by (some) businesses and industry bodies alike, reflecting its alleged benefits as defined in the Cape Town Declaration on Responsible Tourism (ICRT 2010):

- minimizes negative economic, environmental, and social impacts;
- generates greater economic benefits for local people and enhances the well-being of host communities, improves working conditions and access to the industry; involves local people in decisions that affect their lives and life chances;
- makes positive contributions to the conservation of natural and cultural heritage, to the maintenance of the world's diversity;
- provides more enjoyable experiences for tourists through more meaningful connections with local people, and a greater understanding of local cultural, social and environmental issues;
- provides access for physically challenged people; and
- is culturally sensitive, engenders respect between tourists and hosts, and builds local pride and confidence.

As such, and as discussed by Harrison and Pratt in this book in their chapter on tourism and poverty, it may be considered a form of tourism-specific corporate social responsibility (CSR).

Interestingly, it has also been promoted as a tourism product – responsible travel – with the focus very much on tourist experiences that are the antithesis to the organized, mass form of travel (see www.responsibletravel.org). In other words, although its proponents suggest that responsible tourism should be the objective of all tourism businesses, all tourists and all destinations, its roots in alternative tourism remain.

Whilst it is difficult to argue against the principle of responsible tourism (as it is similarly difficult to argue against the principle of sustainable tourism development with which it might be considered synonymous), its viability in practice has long been criticized (Sharpley 2012). In particular, it is suggested that, despite surveys that suggest otherwise, tourists themselves are generally unlikely to adopt so-called responsible behaviour, whilst it also remains uncertain to what extent businesses across the tourism sector have adapted their practices to meet responsibility guidelines. That is, although a number of larger, higher-profile organizations support the concept of responsible tourism, significant doubts surround its more general adoption. Hence, further research is required to address the question: is responsible tourism a realistic objective, or is it simply an example of what has been described as the moralization (Butcher 2002) of tourism?

Towards a research agenda: contributions to this book

Recent academic critiques of tourism often bear more than a passing similarity to many of those first voiced in the 1970s. It can also be argued that the research agenda for tourism academics has not kept pace with the truly remarkable changes in forms of tourism and their perceived relationship to development over the last four decades. It is here that our contributors become especially relevant for, more or less explicitly, they address the research issues relating to modern tourism we have identified in the previous pages.

For Dianne Dredge, in Chapter 2, standard approaches to tourism policy making are driven by the private sector and are too narrowly based on neo-liberal notions of trickle-down economics and market self-regulation. Such tourism policies do not lead to poverty reduction and/or development, and benefit only the higher echelons of society (a claim further discussed in other chapters of this book). Instead, defining policy as a socially constructed, emergent process aimed at the redistribution of resources, involving the agency, *inter alia*, of both academics and policy makers, she advocates a tourism research agenda which recognizes an underlying structure of capitalist power relations. In such 'deep' research, nine themes are considered especially relevant: ideologies, public versus private interests, the redistribution of resources, diverse values, representation in policy making, issue identification, policy consequences, knowledge needs and a future orientation. They are the basis of her tourism research agenda, and help determine the appropriate policy questions and 'practical policy knowledge', a kind of 'to do' list as to how to go about researching the key issues.

How far Dredge's radical agenda will reduce the scepticism of policy makers towards academics, which she correctly identifies, is open to question. However, her insistence on the crucial role of the state in tourism development is echoed by Adu-Ampong in Chapter 3. His focus is specifically on governance, and he directs us to the state and other institutional actors and interest groups with key roles in the policy-making process as it pertains to tourism and development. As he notes, research into the political arena where tourism occurs has tended to emphasize the need to manage tourism firms and destinations, but this omits the wider context of tourism development. What is needed, instead, is (again) a wider political economy approach, where governance is conceptualized as the bringing together of a variety of actors to achieve some collective goal, and where the historical and current role of the state and its changing interaction with other major players on the tourism development stage is crucial.

In Chapter 4, Clausen examines the influence of another major tourism stakeholder, the NGO. Her contribution is worrying. She notes the power held by NGOs and international NGOs in sustainable tourism development, especially as fundraisers and implementing agencies. They increasingly participate in such apparently 'niche' areas as ecotourism, volunteer tourism, pro-poor, fair trade and celebrity tourism, all of which she describes, but the tourism projects in which they are involved, and the aims and objectives they espouse, are neither regularly monitored nor evaluated. Similarly, little attention is accorded to the ethical and political framework within which they operate. According to Clausen, research is urgently needed into such NGO activities, not only of Northern-based NGOs working across the North-South divide, but also of those (of increasing importance) operating across countries within the South. She also recommends research into how NGOs intersect with the state and the market – in short, the manner they articulate with two other sets of major stakeholders in sustainable tourism development.

In Chapter 5, Scarth and Novelli highlight the most obvious tourism stakeholder of all – the tourist – and the extent travel(ler) philanthropy can contribute to development, especially in Sub-Saharan Africa. They note the growing importance of donations, in cash or kind, received directly from individuals or by or through tour operators, who may also operate their own programmes of CSR. Such highly 'moral' contributions, found across a wide range of holiday providers, can be an add-on feature of a vacation or even a central feature of the holiday experience, promoting a 'feel-good' factor for the tourist. However, as Scarth and Novelli argue, individual 'feel good' does not necessarily translate to 'do good' at the community level. Rather, such donations can lead to communal dependency on handouts, or corruption and, more generally, there is little empirical evidence of the development role of tour operators. Put simply, the circumstances of much tourist giving are unaccountable and lack transparency, and the consequences of travel(ler) philanthropy are unresearched and unknown.

Numerous claims have been made – and contested – concerning tourism's role in poverty alleviation. Harrison and Pratt, in Chapter 6, point to clear macro-economic evidence that international tourism does contribute to economic growth and poverty reduction (though they recognize it can also contribute to social inequality). It does so through the conventional capitalist activities of tourism enterprises, including mass tourism, or through smaller tourism enterprises that 'piggy back' on larger private-sector organizations. As also discussed in Chapters 4 and 5, poverty reduction can occur through tourism activities of NGOs that are targeted at the poor, and through private-sector CSR programmes. Finally, some small, non-profit (and sometimes indigenous) enterprises engage in tourism simply to meet basic needs. Harrison and Pratt argue that research should identify those kinds of tourism most effective in reducing poverty and, also, that comparative research is required on how other stakeholders can influence the distribution of tourism's benefits, including such community benefits as roads and electricity. We know tourism *can* reduce poverty; as yet, it is difficult to say precisely how, where and when.

Case studies sometimes clarify wider issues of tourism and development. That by Jamal, Budke and Barradas-Bribiesca in Chapter 7, of development in La Cuadrilla, an Otomi community in Mexico, is informed by a 'hard' model of CBT, and situated within a 'One Health' understanding of sustainable development, where human, animal and environmental sub-systems are in balance. This perspective, clearly at odds with neo-liberal perceptions of 'development', is (implicitly) tested in their analysis of women's cooperatives, spearheading the move from a low-paid agricultural base to a more diversified, commoditized economy, based on the sale of traditional embroidery. While some traditional practices were in decline, considerable success was also reported: community engagement and civic learning increased, and women became individually and collectively more empowered, socially, economically and culturally. Inevitably, the short research period, small focus groups, unelaborated role of tourism and significant NGO involvement means results can only be indicative. However, such case studies can inform further research on how sustainable development can be more widely achieved.

In Chapter 8, Sharpley emphasizes the relationship of tourism consumption and development. Tourists attach changing cultural significance to the tourism 'product', which may influence their self-esteem, and he suggests three especially significant themes in research on the consumption of tourism. First, tourist *motivation* has been a major focus of tourism studies, though, he notes, they have been more conceptual than empirical. Second, there has been extensive research on the *demand* for tourist experience – the pushes, pulls and conditioning factors – and, finally, there are *tourist roles and experiences*, which can be theorized at length (for example, the ubiquitous topic of authenticity) or considered major areas of empirical study. All such aspects of tourism require further research. If tourism is to be planned and managed, present and future international trends must be understood, including their underlying demographic causes. Also, despite much rhetoric on 'responsible' tourism, we urgently need research on values espoused by tourists, including the extent to which they can be active and 'responsible' contributors to 'development'.

Moving to the macro level, in Chapter 9, Aramberri traces the historical realignment or 'unbundling' of global relations of production, consumption and communication, in two great movements: first, since the 1800s, from pre-industrial to industrial, capitalist production and the emergence of powerful G7 industrial nations and, second, the 1990s outsourcing of information and communication technologies to an additional Industrial Six nations, notably, China, India, Korea, Indonesia, Thailand and Poland. Into this mix comes post-1950s mass tourism, operating an extensive global value chain for travel and hospitality services. The process is illustrated by reference to mass tourism in Majorca (dominated by powerful West European tour operators in a low-wage Spanish economy), low-cost carriers, first in the West and later in South and Southeast Asia and, finally, the growth of nautical tourism, notably in Croatia, initially among an elite but increasingly – with the development of yacht charters – for the aspiring international middle class. Such patterns of tourism clearly relate to 'development', in that they radically increase the GDP of international tourist destinations, but point to challenges facing the nature of employment in tourism, an issue also highlighted in Chapter 10 as well as raising important questions about not only the potential of non-economic contributions to development through tourism but also the ability of destinations to manage the nature and direction of tourism development at the destinational level.

Mooney and Baum direct attention to another, much neglected category of stakeholders, the underpaid, undervalued, and underresearched workforce in tourism and (especially) hospitality. In Chapter 10, they describe at length the current state of research in a wide range of areas, notably critical hospitality studies, human resource management, strategic human resource approaches, peripheral tourism workforce studies, labour geographies and diversity management in tourism and indigenous tourism. Included in their discussion are, *inter alia*, links between hospitality and sex work, the management orientation of hospitality research, the poor application of human resource principles, short termism and resistance to change in the hospitality and tourism sector, and the multi-disciplinarity of much hospitality research which, nevertheless, has failed to engage with diversity – including indigenous employees – in the workforce. Concluding, Mooney and Baum advocate a macro-level research agenda level that prioritizes ethical policies for a less exploited and more empowered workforce and, at the management level, one that focuses on the possible organizational and community benefits from a similarly orientated Sustainable Human Resource Management model.

Finally and fittingly, in Chapter 11, Telfer focuses on tourism's importance in developed countries. After noting how research questions emerge from prevailing development paradigms, he argues that, since the 1970s, developed countries have been characterized by increased inequality. Nevertheless, tourism, especially domestic and regional tourism, has promoted economic growth, though more research is needed on why and when successes have been achieved. In addition to theory-led research questions, Telfer isolates several major topics requiring urgent research:

- gentrification, overtourism and the emerging sharing economy (for example, Airbnb and Uber), which bring undoubted benefits to individuals but also create

problems in the community (for example, inflated accommodation costs);
- the connection of tourism growth, increased carbon emissions and low-cost carriers, together forming another example of overtourism;
- as also indicated by Mooney and Baum, the underresearched, undervalued and underregulated employment structure of hospitality and tourism, especially when threatened by technological innovation; and
- the potential for tourism to reduce poverty and promote inclusive growth, and the role played by government policies in redistributing the financial benefits brought by tourism.

From their very different perspectives, contributors to the following chapters offer a rich vein of potential research into tourism and its relationship to development. Some point to (what they consider to be) the 'big picture' of tourism in a global economy dominated by neo-liberalism and elsewhere we, too, have recognized the systemic global interconnections that link tourism in developing and developed societies (Harrison & Sharpley 2017). Others focus on social and economic institutions and stakeholders in tourism, including NGOs, the state, women, workers in hospitality and tourism and the tourists themselves. Most also ask how far tourism does (or can) reduce poverty and bring about inclusive growth. This is perhaps the biggest question of all, which can be asked of any kind of tourism – mass or 'alternative' – in any kind of society – developing or developed – and while at present there is much rhetoric on the topic, there is still very little evidence. We can indeed examine growth rates and gross national product, but we must also ask what is happening *within* economies, societies and regions. Put differently, the size of the cake is important, but so, too, is how it is divided, according to what criteria and by whom.

References

Anderson, W. (2013), 'Leakages in the tourism systems: Case of Zanzibar', *Tourism Review*, **68**(1), 62–76.

Archer, B. (1982), 'The value of multipliers and their policy implications', *Tourism Management*, **3**(4), 236–41.

Arnstein, S. (1969), 'A ladder of citizen participation', *Journal of the American Institute of Planners*, **35**(4), 216–24.

Ashley, C. and Haysom, G. (2008), 'The development impacts of tourism supply chains: Increasing impact on poverty and decreasing our ignorance', in A. Spenceley (ed.) *Responsible Tourism: Critical Issues for Conservation and Development*, Abingdon: Earthscan, pp. 129–56.

Ashley, C. and Mitchell, J. (2010), *Tourism and Poverty Reduction: Pathways to Prosperity*, London: Earthscan.

Bastin, R. (1984), 'Small island tourism: Development or dependency?', *Development Policy Review*, **2**(1), 79–90.

Bigano, A., Hamilton, J.M., Lau, M., Tol, R.S. and Zhou, Y. (2007), 'A global database of domestic and international tourist numbers at national and subnational level', *International Journal of Tourism Research*, **9**(3), 147–74.

Blackstock, K. (2005), 'A critical look at community-based tourism', *Community Development Journal*, **40**(1), 39–49.

Blake, A., Arbache, J., Sinclair, M.T. and Teles, V. (2008), 'Tourism and poverty relief', *Annals of Tourism Research*, **35**(1), 107–26.

Bramwell, B. and Lane, B. (eds) (2000), *Tourism Collaboration and Partnerships: Politics, Practice and Sustainability*, Clevedon: Channel View Publications.

Bramwell, B. and Lane, B. (eds) (2012), *Tourism Governance: Critical Perspectives on Governance and Sustainability*, Abingdon: Routledge.

Britton, S. (1982), 'The political economy of tourism in the Third World', *Annals of Tourism Research*, **9**(3), 331–58.

Brohman, J. (1996), 'New directions in tourism for the Third World', *Annals of Tourism Research*, **23**(1), 48–70.

Brown, F. (1998), *Tourism Reassessed: Blight or Blessing?* Oxford: Butterworth Heinemann.

Bull, A. (1995), *The Economics of Travel and Tourism*, 2nd edn, Melbourne: Longman.

Burns, P. (2004), 'Tourism planning: A third way?', *Annals of Tourism Research*, **31**(1), 24–43.

Butcher, J. (2002), *The Moralisation of Tourism: Sun, Sand . . . and Saving the World?* London: Routledge.

Butcher, J. and Smith, P. (2015), *Volunteer Tourism: The Lifestyle Politics of International Development*, Abingdon: Routledge.

Butler, R. (1990), 'Alternative tourism: Pious hope or trojan horse?', *Journal of Travel Research*, **28**(3), 40–5.

Campbell, L. and Vainio-Mattila, A. (2003), 'Participatory development and community-based conservation: Opportunities missed for lessons learned?', *Human Ecology*, **31**(3), 417–37.

Carlsen, J. and Butler, R. (eds) (2011), *Island Tourism: Sustainable Perspectives*, Wallingford: CABI.

Clancy, M. (2001), *Exporting Paradise: Tourism and Development in Mexico*, Bingley: Emerald Group.

Cohen, E. (1987), 'Alternative tourism: A critique', *Tourism Recreation Research*, **12**(2), 13–18.

Cooper, C. and Ozdil, I. (1992), 'From mass to responsible tourism: The Turkish experience', *Tourism Management*, **13**(4), 377–86.

Costa, C., Panyik, E. and Buhalis, D. (eds) (2013), *Trends in European Tourism Planning and Organisation*, Bristol: Channel View Publications.

Cowen, M. and Shenton, R. (1996), *Doctrines of Development*, London: Routledge.

Cronin, L. (1990), 'A strategy for tourism and sustainable developments', *World Leisure and Recreation*, **32**(3), 12–18.

Daldeniz, B. and Hampton, M. (2010), *Charity-Based Voluntourism versus Lifestyle Voluntourism: Evidence from Nicaragua and Malaysia* (working paper 211), Canterbury: Kent Business School.

de Janvry, A. and Sadoulet, E. (2016), *Development Economics: Theory and Practice*, Abingdon: Routledge.

de Kadt, E. (1979), *Tourism: Passport to Development?* New York: Oxford University Press.

Desai, V. and Potter, R. (2013), *The Companion to Development Studies*, 2nd edn, Abingdon: Routledge.

Diamond, J. (1977), 'Tourism's role in economic development: The case reexamined', *Economic Development and Cultural Change*, **25**(3), 539–53.

Dwyer, L. and Forsyth, P. (2006), *International Handbook on the Economics of Tourism*, Cheltenham, UK and Northampton, MA, USA: Edward Elgar Publishing.

Eagles, P. and McCool, S. (2002), *Tourism in National Parks and Protected Areas: Planning and Management*, Wallingford: CABI.

EU (n.d.), *Overview of EU Tourism Policy*, European Commission. Accessed 2 January 2018 at http://ec.europa.eu/growth/sectors/tourism/policy-overview_en

Evans, N. (2015), *Strategic Management for Tourism, Hospitality and Events*, 2nd edn, Abingdon: Routledge.

Farver, J. (1984), 'Tourism and employment in the Gambia', *Annals of Tourism Research*, **11**(2), 249–65.

Freitag, T. (1994), 'Enclave tourism development: For whom the benefits roll?', *Annals of Tourism Research*, **21**(3), 538–54.

Galtung, J. (1986), 'Towards a new economics: On the theory and practice of self-reliance', in P. Ekins (ed.) *The Living Economy: A New Economy in the Making*, London: Routledge, pp. 97–109.

Gannon, A. (1994), 'Rural tourism as a factor in rural community economic development for economies in transition', *Journal of Sustainable Tourism*, **2**(1–2), 51–60.

Goodwin, H. (2011), *Taking Responsibility for Tourism*, Oxford: Goodfellow Publishers.

Goodwin, H. and Santilli, R. (2009), *Community Tourism: A Success?* ICRT Occasional Paper No. 11. Accessed 28 January 2018 at www.haroldgoodwin.info/uploads/CBTaSuccessPubpdf.pdf

Goulet, D. (1968), 'On the goals of development', *Cross Currents*, **18**, 387–405.

Goulet, D. (1992), 'Participation in development: New avenues', *World Development*, **17**(2), 165–78.

Gunn, C. and Var, T. (2002), *Tourism Planning: Basics, Concepts, Cases*, London: Routledge.

Hall, C.M. (2008), *Tourism Planning: Policies, Processes and Relationships*, Harlow: Pearson Education.

Hall, C.M. and Jenkins, J. (1995), *Tourism and Public Policy*, London: Thomson.

Harrigan, J. and Mosley, P. (1991), 'Evaluating the impact of World Bank structural adjustment lending', *Journal of Development Studies*, **27**(3), 63–94.

Harrison, D. (ed.) (1992), *Tourism and the Less Developed Countries*, London: Belhaven Press.

Harrison, D. (2001), 'Islands, image and tourism', *Tourism Recreation* Research, **26**(3), 9–14.

Harrison, D. (2008), 'Pro-poor tourism: A critique', *Third World Quarterly*, **29**(5), 851–68.

Harrison, D. (2016), 'Looking East but learning from the West? Mass tourism and emerging nations', *Asian Journal of Tourism Research*, **1**(2), 1–26.

Harrison, D. and Prasad, B. (2013), 'The contribution of tourism to the development of Fiji and other Pacific island countries', in C.A. Tisdall (ed.) *Handbook of Tourism Economics: Analysis, New Applications and Case Studies*, Singapore: World Scientific Publishing, pp. 741–60.

Harrison, D. and Sharpley, R. (2017), 'Introduction: Mass tourism in a small world', in D. Harrison and R. Sharpley (eds) *Mass Tourism in a Small World*, Wallingford: CABI, pp. 1–14.

Harrison, L. and Husbands, W. (1996), *Practising Responsible Tourism: International Case Studies in Tourism Planning, Policy and Development*, Chichester: John Wiley & Sons.

Harriss, J. (2005), 'Great promise, hubris and recovery: A participant's history of development studies', in U. Kothari (ed.) *A Radical History of Development Studies: Individuals, Institutions and Ideologies*, London: Zed Books, pp. 17–46.

Haywood, K. (1988), 'Responsible and responsive tourism planning in the community', *Tourism Management*, **9**(2), 105–18.

Held, D. (2010), *Cosmopolitanism Ideals and Realities*, Malden: Polity Press.

Hettne, B. (2009), *Thinking about Development*, London: Zed Books.

Høivik, T. and Heiberg, T. (1980), 'Centre-periphery tourism and self-reliance', *International Social Science Journal*, **32**(1), 69–98.

Holden, A. (2013), *Tourism, Poverty and Development*, Abingdon: Routledge.

Holden, P. (1984), *Alternative Tourism with a Focus on Asia*, Bangkok: Ecumenical Coalition on Third World Tourism.

Høyer, K. (2000), 'Sustainable tourism or sustainable mobility? The Norwegian case', *Journal of Sustainable Tourism*, **8**(2), 147–60.

Hunter, C. (1995), 'On the need to reconceptualise sustainable tourism development', *Journal of Sustainable Tourism*, **3**(3), 155–65.

Husbands, W. (1981), 'Centres, peripheries, tourism and socio-spatial development', *Ontario Geography*, **17**, 37–60.

ICRT (2010), *Cape Town Declaration*, International Centre for Responsible Tourism. Accessed 5 February 2018 at http://responsibletourismpartnership.org/cape-town-declaration-on-responsible-tourism/

Inskeep, E. (1991), *Tourism Planning: An Integrated and Sustainable Development Approach*, New York: Van Nostrand Reinhold.

Jafari, J. (1989), 'Sociocultural dimensions of tourism: An English language literature review', in J. Bystrzanowski (ed.) *Tourism as a Factor of Change: A Sociocultural Study*, Vienna: Vienna Centre, pp. 17–60.

Jamal, T. and Dredge, D. (2016), 'Tourism and community development issues', in R. Sharpley and D. Telfer (eds) *Tourism and Development: Concepts and Issues*, 2nd edn, Bristol: Channel View Publications, pp. 178–204.

Jenkins, C. (1991a), 'Tourism development strategies', in L. Lickorish (ed.) *Developing Tourism Destinations*, Harlow: Longman, pp. 61–77.

Jenkins, C. (1991b) 'Tourism and development', in L. Lickorish (ed.) *Developing Tourism Destinations*, Harlow: Longman, pp. 79–89.

Joppe, M. (1996), 'Sustainable community tourism development revisited', *Tourism Management*, **17**(7), 475–9.

Kerr, W. (2003), *Tourism Public Policy, and the Strategic Management of Failure*, Oxford: Elsevier.

Knutsson, B. (2009), 'The intellectual history of development: Towards a potential widening repertoire', *Perspectives* No. 13, Gothenburg: School of Global Studies. Accessed 29 December 2017 at www.gu.se/digitalAssets/1272/1272997_Perspectives_13.pdf

Lane, B. (1990), 'Sustaining host areas, holiday makers and operators alike', *Conference Proceedings, Sustainable Tourism Development Conference*, Queen Margaret College, Edinburgh, November.

Law, C.M. (1992), 'Urban tourism and its contribution to economic regeneration', *Urban Studies*, **29**(3–4), 599–618.

Lazarus, J. (2008), 'Participation in poverty reduction strategy papers: Reviewing the past, assessing the present and predicting the future', *Third World Quarterly*, **29**(6), 1205–21.

Lea, J. (1988), *Tourism and Development in the Third World*, London: Routledge.

Leiper, N. (1990), *Tourism Systems: An Interdisciplinary Perspective*, Palmerston North, New Zealand: Massey University Printery.

Leiper, N. (1999), 'A conceptual analysis of tourism-supported employment which reduces the incidence of exaggerated, misleading statistics about jobs', *Tourism Management*, **20**(5), 605–13.

Lupoli, C., Morse, W., Bailey, C. and Schelhas, J. (2014), 'Assessing the impacts of international volunteer tourism in host communities: A new approach to organizing and prioritizing indicators', *Journal of Sustainable Tourism*, **22**(6), 898–921.

Lyons, K., Hanley, J., Wearing, S. and Neil, J. (2012), 'Gap year volunteer tourism: Myths of global citizenship?', *Annals of Tourism Research*, **39**(1), 361–78.

Mabogunje, A. (1980), *The Development Process: A Spatial Perspective*, London: Hutchinson.

McKercher, B. (1993), 'Some fundamental truths about tourism: Understanding tourism's social and environmental impacts', *Journal of Sustainable Tourism*, **1**(1), 6–16.

Mihalič, T. (2015), 'Tourism and economic development issues', in R. Sharpley and D. Telfer (eds) *Tourism and Development: Concepts and Issues*, 2nd edn, Bristol: Channel View Publications, pp. 77–117.

Morakabati, Y., Beavis, J. and Fletcher, J. (2014), 'Planning for a Qatar without oil: Tourism and economic diversification, a battle of perceptions', *Tourism Planning and Development*, **11**(4), 415–34.

Mowforth, M. and Munt, I. (2016), *Tourism and Sustainability: Development, Globalisation and New Tourism in the Third World*, 4th edn, Abingdon: Routledge.

Murphy, C. and Boyle, E. (2006), 'Testing a conceptual model of cultural tourism development in the post-industrial city: A case study of Glasgow', *Tourism and Hospitality Research*, **6**(2), 111–28.

Murphy, P. (1983), 'Tourism as a community industry: An ecological model of tourism development', *Tourism Management*, **14**(3), 180–93.

Murphy, P. (1985), *Tourism: A Community Approach*, London: Routledge.

Nash, D. (1989), 'Tourism as a form of imperialism', in V. Smith (ed.) *Hosts and Guests: The Anthropology of Tourism*, 2nd edn, Philadelphia, PA: University of Pennsylvania Press, pp. 37–52.

ONS (2017), *Travel Trends 2016*, Office for National Statistics. Accessed 2 January 2018 at www.ons.gov.uk/peoplepopulationandcommunity/leisureandtourism/articles/traveltrends/2016

Opperman, M. and Chon, K. (1997), *Tourism in Developing Countries*, London: International Thomson Business Press.

Page, S. and Hall, C.M. (2003), *Managing Urban Tourism*, Harlow: Prentice Hall.

Payne, A. and Phillips, N. (2010), *Development*, Cambridge: Polity Press.

Peet, R. and Hartwick, E. (2015), *Theories of Development: Contentions, Arguments, Alternatives*, New York: Guilford Press.

Pieterse, J. (1998), 'My paradigm or yours? Alternative development, post-development, reflexive development', *Development and Change*, **29**(2), 343–73.

Pigram, J. (1990), 'Sustainable tourism: Policy considerations', *Journal of Tourism Studies*, **1**(2), 2–9.

Pollock, A. (2012), 'Conscious travel: Signposts towards a new model for tourism', in *2nd UNWTO Ethics and Tourism Congress: Conscious Tourism for a New Era. September 12th, Quito*. Accessed 6 February 2018 at http://3rxg9qea18zhtl6s2u8jammft.wpengine.netdna-cdn.com/wp-content/uploads/2012/09/presentacion-anna-meira-pollock.pdf

Porter, M., Stern, S. and Artavia Loría, R. (2013), *Social Progress Index 2013*, Washington, DC: Social Progress Imperative.

Pretty, J. (1995), 'The many interpretations of participation', *Focus*, **16**(4), 4–5.

Rahnema, M. (1997), 'Towards post-development: Searching for signposts, a new language and new paradigms', in M. Rahnema and V. Bawtree (eds), *The Post-Development Reader*, London: Zed Books, pp. 377–403.

Raymond, E. and Hall, C.M. (2008), 'The development of cross-cultural (mis)understanding through volunteer tourism', *Journal of Sustainable Tourism*, **16**(5), 530–43.

Redclift, M. (1987), *Sustainable Development: Exploring the Contradictions*, London: Routledge.

Rist, G. (2014), *The History of Development: From Western Origins to Global Faith*, 4th edn, London: Zed Books.

Roberts, L. and Hall, D. (eds) (2001), *Rural Tourism and Recreation: Principles to Practice*, Wallingford: CABI.

Roche, M. (1992), 'Mega-events and micro-modernisation: On the sociology of new urban tourism', *British Journal of Sociology*, **43**(4), 563–600.

Rostow, W. (1967), *The Stages of Economic Growth: A Non-Communist Manifesto*, 2nd edn, Cambridge: Cambridge University Press.

Ruhanen, L. (2013), 'Local government: Facilitator or inhibitor of sustainable tourism development?', *Journal of Sustainable Tourism*, **21**(1), 80–98.

Scheyvens, R. (2002), *Tourism for Development: Empowering Communities*, Harlow: Pearson Education.

Scheyvens, R. (2015), 'Tourism and poverty reduction', in R. Sharpley and D. Telfer (eds) *Tourism and Development: Concepts and Issues*, 2nd edn, Bristol: Channel View Publications, pp. 118–39.

Seers, D. (1969), 'The meaning of development', *International Development Review*, **11**(4), 2–6.

Seers, D. (1977), 'The new meaning of development', *International Development Review*, **19**(3), 2–7.

Sen, A. (1999), *Development as Freedom*, New York: Anchor Books.

Sharpley, R. (2000), 'Tourism and sustainable development: Exploring the theoretical divide', *Journal of Sustainable Tourism*, **8**(1), 1–19.

Sharpley, R. (2002), 'The challenges of economic diversification through tourism: The case of Abu Dhabi', *International Journal of Tourism Research*, **4**(3), 221–35.

Sharpley, R. (2003), 'Tourism, modernization and development on the island of Cyprus: Challenges and policy responses', *Journal of Sustainable Tourism*, **11**(2–3), 246–65.

Sharpley, R. (2009), *Tourism, Development and the Environment: Beyond Sustainability*, London: Earthscan.

Sharpley, R. (2012), 'Responsible tourism: Whose responsibility?', in A. Holden and D. Fennel (eds) *Handbook of Tourism and the Environment*, Abingdon: Routledge, pp. 382–91.

Sharpley, R. (2015), 'Tourism: A vehicle for development?', in R. Sharpley and D. Telfer (eds) *Tourism and Development: Concepts and Issues*, 2nd edn, Bristol: Channel View Publications, pp. 3–30.

Sharpley, R. (2018), 'Responsible volunteer tourism: Tautology or oxymoron? A comment on Burrai and Hannam', *Journal of Policy Research in Tourism, Leisure and Events*, **10**(1), 96–100.

Sharpley, R. and Telfer, D. (eds) (2015), *Tourism and Development: Concepts and Issues*, 2nd edn, Bristol: Channel View Publications.

Shaw, G. and Williams, A. (1994), *Critical Issues in Tourism: A Geographical Perspective*, Oxford: Blackwell.

Sidaway, J. (2007), 'Spaces of post-development', *Progress in Human Geography*, **3**(3), 345–61.

Simpson, K. (2004), 'Doing development: The gap year, volunteer-tourists and a popular practice of development', *Journal of International Development*, **16**(5), 681–92.

Simpson, M. (2007), 'Community benefit tourism initiatives: A conceptual oxymoron?', *Tourism Management*, **29**(1), 1–18.

Sin, H. (2010), 'Who are we responsible to? Locals' tales of volunteer tourism', *Geoforum*, **41**(6), 983–92.

Sinclair, M.T. (1998), 'Tourism and economic development: A survey', *Journal of Development Studies*, **34**(5), 1–51.

Smeral, E. (2006), 'Tourism satellite accounts: A critical assessment', *Journal of Travel Research*, **45**(1), 92–8.

Smith, V. and Eadington, W. (eds) (1992), *Tourism Alternatives: Potentials and Problems in the Development of Tourism*, Philadelphia, PA: University of Pennsylvania Press.

Telfer, D. (2015), 'The evolution of development theory and tourism', in R. Sharpley and D. Telfer (eds) *Tourism and Development: Concepts and Issues*, Bristol: Channel View Publications, pp. 31–73.

Telfer, D. and Sharpley, R. (2016), *Tourism and Development in the Developing World*, 2nd edn, Abingdon: Routledge.

Telfer, D. and Wall, G. (2000), 'Strengthening backward economic linkages: Local food purchasing by three Indonesian hotels', *Tourism Geographies*, **2**(4), 421–47.

Todaro, M. and Smith, S. (2014), *Economic Development*, 12th edn, Harlow: Pearson Education.

Torres, R. (2003), 'Linkages between tourism and agriculture in Mexico', *Annals of Tourism Research*, **30**(3), 546–66.

Tosun, C. (2000), 'Limits to community participation in the tourism development process in developing countries', *Tourism Management*, **21**(6), 613–33.

Tribe, J. (2005), *The Economics of Leisure, Recreation and Tourism*, Oxford: Elsevier.

Turner, L. and Ash, J. (1975), *The Golden Hordes: International Tourism and the Pleasure Periphery*, London: Constable.

UN (2015), *The Millennium Development Goals Report 2015*, United Nations. Accessed 3 January 2018 at www.un.org/millenniumgoals/2015_MDG_Report/pdf/MDG%202015%20rev%20(July%201).pdf

UN (2017), United Nations Sustainable Development Goals. Accessed 29 December 2017 at www.un.org/sustainabledevelopment/sustainable-development-goals/

UNDP (2010), *Human Development Report 2010*, New York: Oxford University Press.

UNWTO (2005), *World Tourism Barometer 3(2)*, Madrid: UN World Tourism Organization.

UNWTO (2016), *UNWTO Tourism Highlights, 2016 Edition*, UN World Tourism Organization. Accessed 26 March 2017 www.e-unwto.org/doi/pdf/10.18111/9789284418145

UNWTO (2017a), *World Tourism Organization: What We Do*, UN World Tourism Organization. Accessed 14 December 2017 at www2.unwto.org/en#

UNWTO (2017b), *Tourism Highlights, 2017 Edition*, UN World Tourism Organization. Accessed 2 January 2018 at www.e-unwto.org/doi/pdf/10.18111/9789284419029

UNWTO (2018), *Sustainable Development of Tourism*, UN World Tourism Organization. Accessed 2 February 2018 http://sdt.unwto.org/content/about-us-5

Wall, G. and Mathieson, A. (2006), *Tourism: Change, Impacts, Opportunities*, Harlow: Pearson Education.

Wearing, S. (2001), *Volunteer Tourism: Experiences that Make a Difference*, Wallingford: CABI.

Wearing, S. and McGehee, N. (2013), 'Volunteer tourism: A review', *Tourism Management*, **38**, 120–30.

Wheeller, B. (1991), 'Tourism's troubled times: Responsible tourism is not the answer', *Tourism Management*, **12**(2), 91–6.

Williams, A. and Shaw, G. (eds) (1991), *Tourism and Economic Development: Western European Experiences*, London: Belhaven Press.

WTO (1980), *Manila Declaration on World Tourism*, Madrid: World Tourism Organization.

WTO (1998), *Tourism: 2020 Vision: Influences, Directional Flows and Key Trends*, Madrid: World Tourism Organization.

WTTC (2016), *Travel and Tourism Economic Impact 2016 World*, World Travel and Tourism Council. Accessed 2 January 2018 at www.wttc.org/-/media/files/reports/economic%20impact%20research/regions%202016/world2016.pdf

Young, G. (1973), *Tourism: Blessing or Blight?* Harmondsworth: Penguin.

Zhang, X., Song, H. and Huang, G.Q. (2009), 'Tourism supply chain management: A new research agenda', *Tourism Management*, **30**(3), 345–58.

2   A policy research agenda for tourism and development

Dianne Dredge

Introduction

The need for evidence-based policy has been vigorously discussed in a range of academic and practice forums. Equally, the advantages and disadvantages of evidence-based policy have been raised yet, despite this attention, the gap between policy and research has remained difficult to address (Head 2008, 2010; Hoppe 1999). This reflects, in part, the fact that policy makers have viewed research as irrelevant, suggesting that it is lacking in its understanding of real-world political complexities, and criticizing actions and recommendations as being naïve (Levin et al. 2012). At the same time researchers themselves have often framed their research as non-political, value-free and indifferent to political realities that shape power and resource flows and, consequently, how interests and agendas influence what happens is often backgrounded. Indeed, even within tourism studies, highly insightful explorations of the political economy of tourism target their explanations to academic audiences, but remain of little help to those working in policy practice who do not find these revelations particularly novel. It is not surprising, therefore, that researchers and policy makers remain sceptical of each other, and this remains one of the key challenges for developing a policy research agenda for tourism and development.

In previous research, Dredge and Jamal (2015) have observed that, in tourism, very few researchers have taken policy seriously by embedding policy considerations within their research as something that is entangled from beginning to end in the issues they research. These authors argue that the characteristics of the policy landscape – its structures and processes, the policy actors and practices – often underpin the issues that researchers focus on, yet these researchers rarely acknowledge how previous policy decisions and actions shape the issues at hand. Rather, they have instead opted for a simplistic view that positions policy as an outcome or recommendation from their research, often manifested in a throwaway line or two in the penultimate paragraph of their scholarly papers. Put simply, and as the key tenet of the chapter, existing policy conditions provide a baseline narrative that underpins how tourism development unfolds; it shapes the distribution of benefits and impacts, it shapes the successes and failures that emerge and it influences who wins and who loses and the balance between public and private benefit that accrues from development (Dredge & Jamal 2015; Howlett et al. 2015). It is, therefore, reasonable to claim that policy, and the nature of the political system in which tourism development takes place, ought to be taken seriously in research.

The purpose of this chapter, then, is to articulate a policy research agenda for tourism and development. Three points of departure underpin it. First, the chapter takes as its starting point the fact that the policy environment is both an important antecedent to, and has significant explanatory power over, the manner in which tourism is used as a tool for development. Second, the idea that policy is a rational, scientific and value-free process is set aside and instead, a social constructivist approach is adopted. From this perspective, the policy landscape comprises competing interests and agendas that shape ideas of what can be done and who should take responsibility. And third, we must acknowledge the political agency of both researchers and policy makers in shaping this landscape and in the role of education and information sharing, and recognize the potential change-making roles played by these actors.

In addressing the above objective, three broad questions frame this chapter:

(1) *What is policy?* This discussion reveals the dimensions of policy that provide the theoretical building blocks for policy research.
(2) *Why is a policy research agenda needed for tourism and development?* This discussion explores why deeper and more theoretically robust understandings of tourism policy are needed and how this research can inform the 'doing' of policy.
(3) *What should a policy research agenda for tourism and development include?* In responding to this question, key research questions are identified that are helpful in guiding the practices of policy making.

In setting out a policy research agenda for tourism and development, as is the aim of this chapter, a cautionary word is needed at the outset. Sustainable development and the Sustainable Development Goals (SDGs) are little mentioned in the ensuing discussion. This silence is not, however, an oversight, nor is it borne out of disinterest. Rather, the author assumes a deep commitment to sustainable development as the starting point for the development of the research agenda. This commitment is borne out of the turn towards the ethics of care and the moral responsibility that this entails for individuals to act for the good of others and for the planet. It was, therefore, decided not to reiterate the arguments for the SDGs to underpin tourism policy development, but to assume readers are already well versed in these arguments. Figure 2.1 provides the schema for the organization of the chapter.

What is policy?

Perhaps the difficulty in understanding policy in general and, therefore, the consequential low levels of research interest in tourism policy in particular stem from

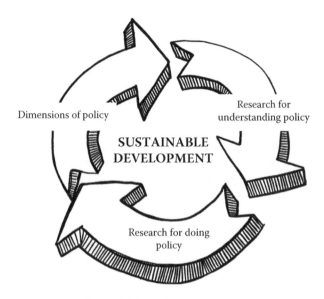

Figure 2.1   Understanding policy and doing policy research

the complex and overlapping nature of politics and policy, where it becomes just all 'too hard' to research. Aspects such as political organization, who and what constitutes the polity, roles and responsibilities of government, public interest, inclusion/exclusion, representation, power and knowledge all feature in the study of politics and policy. Moreover, these two terms, *politics* and *policy*, are not easily separated in English, while in other languages there is no distinction (Colebatch 2009). For example, *politik* in German, *política* in Spanish and *politique* in French cover both words, and it is difficult to translate the term *policy makers* into Italian. As Colebatch (2009, p. 64) explains, 'there is always an element of politics in the policy process, but the distinction between politics and policy is drawn on in shaping the action'. Very often, references are made to politics as a form of struggle and policy as an outcome (that is, policy is the result of the politics of something), but they are difficult to separate in practice because policy also involves the ongoing and dynamic negotiation within policy processes.

So, how are *policy* and related terms understood and given meaning within academic circles? Certainly, the task of defining policy has been debated at great length (Colebatch 2006), and these academic discussions have been well covered in the specific context of tourism (Dredge & Jenkins 2007). From these debates, it is evident that policy is conceptualized as a dialogical concept defined by the context in which it is being discussed; its dimensions are summarized in Table 2.1.

In an effort to balance academic definitions of policy with what policy makers understand it to be, Levin (1997) undertook a qualitative study of British politicians and officials. His research, summarized in Table 2.2, found that policy actors

Table 2.1   Policy as understood in academic literature

Dimension	Explanation
Diverse stakeholders	Policy involves government working with *stakeholders* including the private sector, a diverse third sector, community groups and the public
Action-oriented	Policy involves *action* directed toward the achievement of some desired future situation
Politics/power	Policy is *political*, and is an expression of *power*
Process	Policy most often, but not always, involves a *process*
Decisions	Policy implies *decision making*, either in a formal or informal capacity
Outcomes	Policy can (but not always) be a *tangible outcome* (e.g. a plan of written policy)
Values/interests	Policy involves the mediation of *values and interests*
Resource distribution	Policy involves an allocation or *distribution of resources* including financial and non-financial resources, expertise, in-kind resources, etc.
Diverse knowledge inputs	Policy requires the input of different kinds of *knowledge* including expertise, but may also include tacit knowledge such as lived experiences, encultured and embodied knowledge
Authority	Policy is an outcome and the *authority to undertake action*
Socially constructed/ mediated	Policy is *socially constructed*, where who is included/excluded shapes the outcome
Science/at/craft	Policy making is part *science*, part *art* and part *craft*

Table 2.2   Policy as understood by policy makers

Dimension	Explanation
Intention	Policy is a *stated intention* to undertake a particular action or bring about change
Resources	Policy is a current or past action that brings about a *redistribution of resources*
Organizational practice	Policy is an *organizational practice or response* to an issue or situation
Action	Policy denotes a *course of action* or position that has been given a formal or legitimate 'status' by government

distilled policy into four themes which are broadly consistent with the above, but which also crystallize action as a central element.

For the purposes of this chapter, then, and reflecting upon the various ideas and aspects of policy previously identified in the literature, policy is difficult to define in a single sentence or thought bubble. Indeed, the characteristics identified in Tables 2.1 and 2.2 provide some insight into the complex nature of policy and suggest that understandings of policy have moved well beyond describing that it is what governments do. Instead, policy must be understood as a process, a set of values, a negotiated practice, an outcome and an expression of power that reflects the mediation of public, private, third-sector and community values.

In the context of tourism and development in particular, the above discussion also suggests that policy is both an antecedent to the problems and challenges that might emerge in tourism and an outcome/action. However, the way tourism is valued and given meaning in policy is heavily influenced by a variety of factors, such as: the inclusion of certain (and not other) actors; the inclusion of certain (and not other) knowledge inputs; through decision making taking place in certain (and not other) forums; and through particular organizational structures and processes. In other words, a critical appreciation of tourism policy, of how it is valued and managed, and of its impacts and consequences is important if our interest is to improve the value of tourism as a development tool, especially if we take the widest possible interpretation of 'development' to include aspects such as well-being, quality of life, empowerment, equity, access to meaningful work and so on (see Chapter 1).

Why do we need a policy research agenda for tourism and development?

As noted above, the persistent gap between research and policy-making practice has been much discussed in the literature (Head 2008; Pearce & Wesselink 2014). Tourism policy is an applied area of study that draws from a range of disciplines and fields of studies including politics, studies of government, planning, geography, development studies and sociology. Yet, despite this multi-disciplinary underpinning, many researchers often assume or misinterpret policy research as a positivistic, rational scientific research endeavour concerned with what governments do, in so doing failing to appreciate the complex origins and multiple actors that contribute to the issues and emergence of problems (Dredge et al. 2011). Moreover, owing to this simplistic acceptance that policy research is very pragmatic and applied, the broader influence of social and political ideologies and assumptions are often ignored. Similarly, researchers' agency in terms of what can be done to inform or improve policy can also be overlooked (Chaperon & Bramwell 2013; Dredge & Schott 2014).

The gap between research and practice is also manifested in the decisions, actions and attitudes of policy makers. A number of studies in policy have shown that policy makers often look upon researchers as naïve and lacking in real-world understanding (Head 2010; Shergold 2011). Moreover, they see researchers as having a relatively jaundiced understanding of policy and that researchers' focus on problem formulation, justifying research processes and analytical rigour are all wrapped up in a scholarly language game that is 'lost in translation because it is inaccessible, indigestible and obscure' (Shergold 2011). Consequently, it is believed that few researchers have demonstrated the capacity to understand, let alone incorporate complex scalar thinking, political dynamics, sensitivities to power, resource flows, institutional structures and processes within their excavations of tourism policy. Moreover, the ubiquitous influence of ideological values, such as globalization and neoliberalism, that lie outside but have significant indirect influence over how tourism develops, are often considered to be overlooked. In other words, policy makers work in complex, fluid and value-laden spaces and research that fails to acknowledge these multi-layered, multi-scaled characteristics often attract disparaging remarks from policy makers. In responding to the need to address this policy research–policy practice gap, then, several areas of research engagement can be identified.

Critical attention to the influence of ideologies, interests and values

A research agenda for tourism and development can help to uncover and raise awareness of the influence of ideologies that operate at a meta-level. Foretelling the arrival of the post-truth era, Bevir et al. (2003) argue that policy is increasingly based on the subjective and bounded rationalities of the policy actors and the unquestioned ideologies that background their thoughts. They further argue that the decisions and actions of policy actors are little more than 'bubbles on the surface of political life', and that the deeper ideological drivers influencing policy need to be exposed so that we can better evaluate what is happening, and whether those directions will produce the outcomes we desire (Bevir et al. 2003, p. 195).

Moore (2017) captures this shift in the term 'Capitalocene', a new world praxis characterized by accelerated capital accumulation that has led to an increasing gap between the rich and poor. Governments have facilitated the Capitalocene through neoliberal policies that have redistributed wealth away from the commons and the public domain to private-sector interests. Two basic principles underpin policy in the Capitalocene: (1) securing cheap labour by whittling away at labour rights and protections; and (2) securing cheap nature by reducing regulatory and other barriers to access the natural resources on which the economy is based. While Europe, North America and Australia/New Zealand have been subject to sustained erosion of labour protection and natural resource restrictions, many countries in Sub-Saharan Africa, Latin America and Asia have been particularly hard hit as a result of structural adjustment policies enforced by the international agencies implementing US/European economic policy objectives (Amin 2006; Harvey 2005).

Notably, the pursuit of cheap labour and cheap nature has flowed through to tourism, and has provided the dominant ideological stance underpinning tourism development policy in both across the world since the 1990s (for example, Chin 2008; Duffy 2002). At the risk of overgeneralizing, early tourism policy was often characterized by the state allocating public resources to tourism via the provision and maintenance of physical infrastructure (for example, airports, roads, ports and visitor centres) which, in turn, facilitated private-sector growth and profit. The state also sought to open up common pool or public resources on which private-sector tourism activity could be based (for example, beaches, waterways and national parks), and it facilitated the provision of labour through investment in technical and higher education. Collectively, then, these policies emphasized governments' role in facilitating private-sector activity through both direct and indirect allocation of public resources by reducing barriers to investment and by facilitating access to cheap labour (Dredge & Jenkins 2007).

The caveat to this generalization is, of course, that in different political and social welfare systems across the world, the swing towards accelerated capitalism (i.e. the Capitalocene), neoliberalism and associated policy has been met with varying degrees of acceptance/resistance. Multiple varieties of neoliberalism have emerged to reflect the way that different social, cultural and institutional norms push back and negotiate with neoliberal forces (Brenner et al. 2010) and, in the process, certain kinds of policy approaches have come to be seen as more or less acceptable. However, these can only be understood and anticipated by appreciating social, cultural and institutional contexts. For example, in Sub-Saharan Africa, structural adjustment programmes enforced by the international agencies, such as the International Monetary Fund and World Bank, have forced governments into a hard swing towards a market economy accompanied by a retraction of social policies and public spending (Amin 2006; Hahn 2008). Such top-down austerity measures have triggered increased poverty and marginalization, whilst social and political unrest has led to a re-emergence of neo-authoritarianism and cronyism.

The underpinning rationale for this shift in prioritizing private over public interests that has been occurring over the last four decades is captured in a key principle of neoliberal ideology, namely, trickle-down economics. Trickle-down economics posits that a robust private sector, driven by growth and profit, will reinvest these profits in its workers to improve standards of living and well-being. In other words, a strong economy is the 'rising tide that lifts all boats', a concept heavily critiqued by Harvey (2005, p.64), former chief economist of the World Bank, the economist Joseph Stiglitz (1991, 2002, 2013) and others. Yet, no proof has emerged that trickle-down economics works; indeed, on the contrary, much evidence has accumulated to show that the acceleration of growth and profit only serves to enrich the top 1 per cent (Piketty 2014). Nevertheless, trickle-down economics has been widely used to justify tourism as a tool for development although, perhaps unsurprisingly, tangible results in terms of community empowerment, poverty reduction, social progress, equity, empowerment or environmental responsibility have not been forthcoming (Matarrita-Cascante 2010; Sharpley & Telfer 2014).

However, the 1980s and 1990s witnessed a shift away from policy for tourism development that sought to protect public interests, manage public and common pool resources and protect against the unintended failures or impacts of private-sector development. Specifically, the newly emerging neoliberal-inspired position was that policy should be focused almost exclusively on market development and the removal of barriers to business growth, investment, consumption and so on (UNWTO 2017). Here, another underpinning tenet of neoliberal ideology came into sharper focus – the invisible hand. Drawing upon the historical (but significantly reinterpreted) arguments of Adam Smith (1776), the invisible hand principle posits that the markets will address market failures that emerge from growth when these failures accumulate to the point that the markets are negatively affected to the extent that demand starts to decline. In other words, markets supposedly self-regulate to avoid the negative impacts of overdevelopment, overexploitation of resources, exploitation of labour and so on. Again, however, the doctrine of the invisible hand has been disproved (Stiglitz 1991) and in tourism in particular, the clearest evidence that the invisible hand does not work is found in the renewal of interest in the way tourism exploits local communities and resources in a vicious cycle (Duffy 2002; Russo 2002).

The above discussion provides a brief illustration of the ideologies, interests and values that can have a profound influence on policy development but that are often not clearly articulated, acknowledged or addressed in the framing of policy research. In this discussion, there are a number of overlapping lines of inquiry that a research agenda for tourism and development could usefully address which are crystallized in the paragraphs below. These lines of inquiry seek to go beyond the pragmatic and practical concerns of policy making to better understand the deeper currents of interest that flow through and underneath policy development.

Public versus private interests

As suggested earlier, policy has long been considered to be 'what governments do' (Dye 1978), and modernist twentieth-century traditions have upheld the idea that *public* policy should aim to protect *public* interests. However, and based on the above discussion, it is perhaps more accurate these days to conceptualize policy as a public–private response to diverse but predominantly private-sector interests. That is, protecting public interests and safeguarding citizens from the failures generated by the private sector, such as environmental impacts, resource exploitation, violations of labour rights and so on, is no longer a central concern of policy making. Instead, the idea that governments should make policy to protect public interests has been replaced by the notion that governments should protect the interests of the private sector, its profitability and its access to resources and labour (Harvey 2005). Hence, a research agenda for tourism and development could usefully explore public interests in tourism and development. Although public interest has been explored to some extent in the research (Pal & Maxwell 2004; Richter 1987, 1989), the diversity of public interests and the impacts of shifting ideological commitments to neoliberalism and the Capitalocene on current and future generations mean that understandings are fragmented and little understood.

Understanding policy as the redistribution of resources

The discussion above has drawn attention to the role of policy in the allocation of public resources and, in particular, to the reallocation of resources away from the public towards support for private-sector activity. Policy research should, therefore, be concerned with researching the effects of the redistribution of resources as a result of policy, not least because, under the current neoliberal ideological climate the accumulation of capital under the *Capitalocene* is manifested in an accelerated redistribution of resources in the top 1 per cent (Moore 2017; Piketty 2014). Tourism policy researchers could, therefore, usefully turn their attention to questions that examine and monitor the effects and consequences of the (re) distribution of resources that result from policies. A question to be asked, for example, is: what are the real benefits and consequences of tourism infrastructure projects, such as cruise terminals, airports or national park infrastructure, on the communities that are said to be empowered by the resulting tourism activity? Such infrastructure projects often rely on international loans and provide access to cheap resources and labour. However, little is known about the extent to which local communities benefit when taking into account longer-term effects of these tourism-related policies on foreign debt, capital flows, accumulation and so on. Hence, a better understanding of the nature of resource (re)distribution, and who wins and who loses over time, are important questions for a research agenda in tourism and development.

Securing diverse value

It has been emphasized above that tourism policy is framed within a narrative of dominance of economic development wherein the flows and power of capitalism are treated as the dominant and all-encompassing force. According to Cave and Dredge (2018), other kinds of transactions, as well as economic spaces and non-monetized resources, are rendered invisible as a result of this focus. By excavating alternative spaces of exchange, it is possible to identify other kinds of transactions (for example, unpaid labour, in-kind transactions, gifting, sharing, collaboration and so on) and alternative economic practices (for example, informal economies, commons platforms or community cooperatives) that also take place in tourism, and that can generate significant value for some actors. Within this framing of tourism policy there are diverse kinds of value created by tourism that have often been overlooked, including social, cultural, environmental and political value. The point that emerges from this observation is that it is important to 'zoom out' and enhance understanding of the diverse economic practices, forms of exchange and different types of value generated in tourism in order to better identify and evaluate future directions for tourism policy. A research agenda for tourism and development therefore needs to acknowledge diverse economic practices and value-creation opportunities beyond the economic, and how tourism policies might more effectively pursue blended value.

Representation, inclusion and exclusion in policy making

Tourism policy also produces a range of intended and unintended effects on communities, on different cohorts of actors, on common pool and public resources and so on. Yet who speaks for the environment? Who speaks for the people, the labour force and for the future generations not present at the policy table? How are these interests represented, and what power do they have in the tourism policy-making process, in decision making and in the formulation of actions? What are the rights of nature in policy making (Dredge 2018)? In short, issues of representation in policy making and associated concerns about social and environmental justice, fairness, transparency and trust provide additional questions that policy research must therefore address. Drawing on reflections on governance in the Anthropocene, Dredge (2018) stretches this imperative further by calling for representation of both humans and nature in governance and policy making, arguing that present vulnerabilities of our social and ecological systems are interlinked and cannot be treated separately, as has been the case to date.

A policy research agenda for tourism development responds to the previously discussed need to address a broader and more inclusive development agenda than the one set out by neoliberal ideology. It is becoming increasingly obvious that neoliberal concerns for development that prioritizes private-sector interests is taking us towards politically unstable territory. As previously discussed, winners and losers are emerging, the gap between the two camps is widening and the pace of social marginalization or exclusion is accelerating.

Issue identification and problem structuring

There is an old idiom: 'a problem is not a problem until it is seen to be a problem'. The point is that many issues only come to be raised as policy problems after a long incubation period. Often this incubation goes unnoticed, and it is only after issues coalesce and feed off each other and after they create discernible negative impacts or costs to some stakeholders that they become visible problems. Dredge et al.'s (2016) case examining the regulatory environment associated with Airbnb in Paris, Berlin, Amsterdam and Barcelona is a good example of a wicked policy problem that, left untreated, resulted in a political and policy fiasco of global proportions. In this case, the effects of housing policies, tourism growth policies, investment policies and social welfare policies accumulated over time to create a perfect storm and a rising tide of frustration amongst diverse stakeholders from incumbent accommodation industry actors, community groups and welfare advocates. These policy failures empowered an urban tourism-resistance movement which has, in turn, fed into growing global concerns about so-called overtourism.

An issue becomes a problem because the cluster of policy failures associated with it has coalesced and become politicized; the contemporary increasing incidence of overtourism is seen as a policy fiasco framed by multiple stakeholders in diverse ways and affecting them all differently. Interestingly, Bovens and 't Hart (1998) distinguish policy fiascos by the political folly that surrounds them, but overtourism is not a new phenomenon; it can be traced back through different theoretical framings of limits or capacity, such as limits of acceptable change, the psychology of overcrowding, environmental thresholds and political limits such as Doxey's tourism irridex. Howlett et al. (2015) argue that the persistence of such problems is best understood by examining the range of factors within and beyond the subsystem, in this case tourism. In most cases, these authors argue, the persistence of the problem, as well as its visibility and politicization, mask other ongoing social, political and economic problems.

But perhaps too much emphasis has been placed on understanding policy failure; it is also important to understand why policy succeeds and the conditions for its success (Bovens & 't Hart 2016). Understanding the key characteristics of problems, how they are linked together, what kind of policy design alternatives are available and the selection of the most appropriate policy instruments provides important insights to assist in successful policy formulation (Hoornbeek & Peters 2017). Research into tourism and development could benefit from analysing the policy-related dimensions of the problem, including the identification of issues, the historical evolution of these issues and how they are linked, who the key actors are and processes of politicization. Moreover, deeper and more sophisticated knowledge about issue identification, problem structuring and framing can contribute to researchers realizing that the problem that is the focus of their research is indeed a result of persistent policy failures. Identifying these failures is important in addressing the tourism research–tourism policy gap and formulating more effective policy.

Effects and consequences of policy along different registers of value and benefit

Following on from the above discussion of policy failures and successes, tourism policy research should focus on the consequences and effects of policy on different actors. In other words, the policy-making process is not the only aspect to be better understood; the effects and consequences of policy also need to be better understood in order to facilitate policy learning. Tourism policy often focuses on, and is evaluated in terms of, its intended consequences on tourism development, where 'development' is often interpreted uncritically as an economic imperative. More recently, however, it has become clearer that a broader range of metrics and registers of value produced or created by tourism policy (both positive and negative) need to be understood. More pointedly, the focus of evaluation is often narrowed down to the economic effects of policy actions to the exclusion of social, political, ecological, environmental, cultural and other impacts. Moreover, the reduction of the effects of policy to a single (frequently economic) unit of measurement is also problematic.

Marilyn Waring (1999) argued this point in her seminal work exploring the way that the outcome of policies needs to be valued quite differently by, for example, men and women. Questioning the taken-for-granted practice of environmental accounting wherein environmental performance was traditionally measured in terms of a single measure (usually economic) to facilitate comparison and determine net loss of gain, she countered:

> Is he really saying that 'rational man' does not have the conceptual capacity to deal with more than one indicator, that this abstract male character maximizing his self-interests in daily trade-offs can manage such an exercise if all his options are expressed in the same unit? Most women I know make these multidimensional judgements, and many of them, every day. (Waring 1999, p. xxxv)

Waring's powerful argument about the way men and women value things differently, when translated into policy, suggests that greater effort needs to be placed on valuing the different types of outcomes, effects and consequences that emerge from tourism policy. Of course, over the last decades, a range of researchers have argued this point, suggesting that we need a more nuanced set of measures and valuation mechanisms and frameworks that attend not only to gender but also diverse populations (Higgins-Desbiolles 2006, 2010). More recently, it has also been noted that policy makers are often blind to the unintended consequences and effects of tourism policy on non-human interests and the effects of policy on those non-human interests that are not represented (Dredge 2018). This is, arguably, a future line of policy research for tourism and development of utmost importance.

Knowledge needs for policy
Questions also need to be addressed that surround the knowledge needs required to make good policy and the way that ideological factors influence values, policy approaches, information and expertise inputs. The knowledge that contributes to the process, whether it is fit for purpose and its quality and trustworthiness, especially in a post-truth world, are all significant factors determining the identification of policy options, the quality of the deliberation process and decision making. Accordingly, a research agenda could also examine the knowledge needs for informed policy development and action. Such a research theme could usefully explore aspects including the knowledge dynamics of policy making, the type, quality of evidence required, the dialogical spaces in which information is transmitted, learning takes place and possible actions are evaluated and decided upon.

The future
Tourism policy is a future-oriented activity. It addresses questions of what kind of tourism is desirable and how it can be achieved. A policy research agenda for tourism and development should also anticipate and adopt a future orientation that alerts us to potential problems and issues before small issues become big problems. The recent discourse around overtourism, for example, previously captured by Russo's notion of the 'vicious cycle' or Dredge et al.'s (2016) depiction of 'the perfect storm', are good illustrations. The different issues, including housing shortages, the cost of housing, the growth in cruise tourism, the growth in low-cost air carriers and economic stimulus by governments in infrastructure and so on have synergized to create a more complex and far-reaching wicked problem set that is more difficult to address than any of the issues on their own (Dredge et al. 2016). A research agenda for tourism and development that examines the future using different research approaches and methodologies, from trend analysis to scenario building and foresight studies, would provide useful insights.

What should a policy research agenda for tourism and development include?

In the above discussion, nine key themes of potential research enquiry have been identified that help to develop critical understanding of the multi-scalar, multi-actor, multi-interest landscape in which policy making takes place, and its effects and consequences on diverse human and non-human actors. These themes are as follows:

- the influence of ideologies, interests and values
- public versus private interests
- understanding policy as the redistribution of resources
- securing diverse values
- representation, inclusion and exclusion in policy making
- issue identification and problem structuring
- effects and consequences of policy along different registers of value and benefit
- knowledge needs for policy making
- the future of tourism (desirable/viable/feasible).

However, understanding alone is insufficient, and brings little insight to policy practitioners. Research efforts within these nine areas still need to be oriented towards generating useful insights, knowledge and understanding for policy actors, and producing research outputs of use in policy making. In other words, theoretical knowledge alone is insufficient, and a pragmatic appreciation of policy making, decision making and contextualized political sensitivity is also required. Here, the notion of phronesis – or practical wisdom – becomes relevant (Dredge 2011; Flyvbjerg 2001).

Discussions of phronesis within the tourism literature are not new. Inspired by Aristotle's *Nicomachean Ethics*, phronesis posits that scientific knowledge (*episteme*) and technical knowledge (*techne*) are brought together to produce a kind of practical wisdom or prudence which is necessary to reflect, understand and act in a manner that is consistent with good actions. In Aristotle's view, both *episteme* and *techne* could be taught, but phronesis comes from mindfulness, maturity and experience. Phronesis can be difficult to codify (Abizadeh 2002) and requires reflection, political sensitivity and awareness of self and others (Maguire 1997). In support of this phronetic agenda in supporting good actions and decision making in tourism and development, Table 2.3 presents a typology of policy research for tourism planning and development that addresses a number of key questions regularly posed by policy practitioners.

Conclusions

We now return to the three broad questions that have framed this chapter, attending to each in turn. First, what is policy? Traditionally, policy has been assumed to be what governments do, and the complexity of understanding policy, politics and power, and how these aspects link with governance, policy-making processes, interests, agendas and outcomes, and has been put in the 'too hard' basket for many researchers. As a consequence, there are few researchers who have sought to engage in a genuine theoretical manner with tourism policy. That said, in this chapter the case has been made for this to change, and a policy research agenda for tourism and development has been proposed.

Table 2.3 A policy research agenda for tourism and development

Research focus	Key policy questions	Line of inquiry	Practical policy knowledge
Descriptive	Why is this issue a problem? How has the problem come to be?	The influence of ideologies, interests and values on policy. Public versus private interests. Issue identification and problem structuring. Knowledge needs for policy	Problem identification. Problem formulation/ emergence. Policy issues and agenda
Normative/ prescriptive	What kind of tourism do we want? What is desirable/ undesirable? What ought to be done? Who ought to do it? How should policy decisions be made?	Securing diverse values. Knowledge needs for policy. The future (desirable/ viable/feasible)	Models, frameworks. Principles. Measures and benchmarks
Distributive	Who are the winners and losers? Is this distribution of resources desirable (and to whom/what)?	Understanding policy as the redistribution of resources. The future. Public versus private interests	Redistributive effects of policy. Diversity and gender implications of policy
Procedural	How should the policy-making process be? How did this policy-making process happen?	The influence of ideologies, interests and values. Representation, inclusion and exclusion in policy making	Policy cycles and processes. Knowledge dynamics
Predictive	What do we want tourism to be like in the future? What knowledge is needed to plan? What policy actions can lead us there?	The future (desirable/ viable/feasible). Knowledge needs for policy	Foresight and futures studies. Scenarios. Trend analysis
Evaluation	Is the policy a success/ failure? Were the political objectives achieved?	Securing diverse values. Effects and consequences of policy along different registers of value and benefit. Knowledge needs for policy	Monitoring and evaluation. Impacts and consequences for human/non-human actors

Table 2.3   (continued)

Research focus	Key policy questions	Line of inquiry	Practical policy knowledge
Relational	How are the policy relations? How can relationships be managed?	Representation, inclusion and exclusion in policy making	Network analysis Governance structures/ processes Relationships with nature Relationships between actors
Reflexive	What is the role of the researcher and how can research make a difference in practice?	Knowledge needs for policy Influence of ideologies, interests and values	Social and environmental justice

For the purpose of this chapter, policy can be seen as a process, a set of values, a negotiated practice, an outcome, an expression of power that reflects the mediation of public, private and third sectors and community values. It has been argued that a critical appreciation of tourism policy, how it is valued and managed, and its impacts and consequences is important if our interest is to improve the value of tourism as a development tool, especially if we take the widest possible interpretation of 'development' to include aspects such as well-being, quality of life, empowerment, equity, access to meaningful work and so on.

The second question addressed by this chapter was 'why is a policy research agenda needed for tourism and development?' In addressing this question, it was argued that there is a need for 'deep' policy research approaches that engage in the practical work of policy making, inclusive participation and decision making; indeed, this has been well argued in the literature (Dredge 2011; Flyvbjerg 2001; Peck 2000). The challenge is, however, to better understand, share knowledge and provide practical guidance on some of the deeper challenges of contemporary tourism policy making. These challenges include the need to better understand the impact of macro-factors that are often neither explicit nor recognized, such as the power of ideological forces (for example, neoliberalism or globalization) for which we need 'deep, engaged and incisive research as opposed to shallow superficial and sweeping' meta-narratives (Peck 2000, p. 256). Such research can help to reveal power relations, and assist policy actors in responding in thoughtful and locally meaningful ways. Nine key themes of potential research enquiry, listed above, were identified. It is suggested that these would help to develop critical understanding of the multi-scalar, multi-actor, multi-interest landscape in which policy making takes place, and its effects and consequences on diverse human and non-human actors.

However, these lines of theoretically driven policy inquiry have to be matched with a pragmatic appreciation of policy making and decision-making practices, and contextualized within the political sensitivities of policy-making practices. Here Aristotle's notion of phronesis – or practical wisdom – was brought into relevance, helping to answer the third and final question: 'What should a policy research agenda for tourism and development include?' In answering this question, it is important to return back to the key questions that policy makers regularly ask in their policy making, questions which concern the descriptive, normative, distributive, procedural, predictive, evaluative, relational and reflexive dimensions of policy. The research agenda outlined in Table 2.3 excavates a range of issues that researchers could usefully explore, and it poses questions that can illuminate the key concerns that policy makers are interested in. The research agenda presented is context free, providing researchers with the opportunity to contextualize and exca-vate within their particular political, social, economic and institutional systems. When brought together, research into the two realms of understanding policy and doing policy should provide more robust insights and directions for tourism policy development in the future.

References

Abizadeh, A. (2002), 'The passions of the wise: Phronesis, rhetoric, and Aristotle's passionate practical deliberation', *Review of Metaphysics*, **56**(2), 267–96.

Amin, S. (2006), 'The millennium development goals: A critique from the South', *Monthly Review*, **57**(10), 1–15.

Bevir, M., Rhodes, R. and Weller, P. (2003), 'Comparative governance: Prospects and lessons', *Public Administration*, **18**(1), 191–210.

Bovens, M. and 't Hart, P. (1998), *Understanding Policy Fiascoes*, London: Taylor & Francis.

Bovens, M. and 't Hart, P. (2016), 'Revisiting the study of policy failures', *Journal of European Public Policy*, **23**(5), 653–66.

Brenner, N., Peck, J. and Theodore, N. (2010), 'After neoliberalization?', *Globalizations*, **7**(3), 327–45.

Cave, J. and Dredge, D. (2018), 'Reworking tourism: Diverse economies in a changing world', *Tourism Planning and Development*, **15**(5), 473–7.

Chaperon, S. and Bramwell, B. (2013), 'Dependency and agency in peripheral tourism development', *Annals of Tourism Research*, **40**, 132–54.

Chin, C. (2008), 'Labour flexibilization at sea', *International Feminist Journal of Politics*, **10**(1), 1–18.

Colebatch, H. (2006), *The Work of Policy: An International Survey*, Oxford: Lexington Books.

Colebatch, H. (2009), *Policy*, 3rd edn, Buckingham: Open University Press.

Dredge, D. (2011), 'Phronetic tourism planning research: Reflections on critically engaged tourism plan-ning research and practice', paper presented at *IV Critical Tourism Studies Conference: Tourism Futures: Creative and Critical Action*, Cardiff: Welsh Centre for Tourism Research.

Dredge, D. (2018), 'Governance, tourism and resilience: A long way to go?', in J. Saarinen and A. Gill (eds) *Resilient Destinations: Governance Strategies of Tourism in the Transition towards Sustainability*, Abingdon: Routledge, pp. 48–66.

Dredge, D. and Jamal, T. (2015), 'Progress in tourism planning and policy: A post-structural perspective on knowledge production', *Tourism Management*, **51**, 285–97.

Dredge, D. and Jenkins, J. (2007), *Tourism Planning and Policy*, Milton: John Wiley and Sons.

Dredge, D. and Schott, C. (2014), 'Academic agency and leadership in tourism higher education', in D. Prebežac, C. Schott and P. Sheldon (eds) *The Tourism Education Futures Initiative: Activating Change in Tourism Education*, Abingdon: Routledge, pp. 36–60.

Dredge, D., Jenkins, J. and Whitford, M. (2011), 'Stories of practice', in D. Dredge and J. Jenkins (eds) *Stories of Practice: Tourism Policy and Planning*, Farnham: Ashgate, pp. 37–46.

Dredge, D., Gyimóthy, S., Birkbak, A., Jensen, T.E. and Madsen, A.K. (2016), *The Impact of Regulatory Approaches Targeting Collaborative Economy in the Tourism Accommodation Sector: Barcelona, Berlin, Amsterdam and Paris*, Impulse Paper No. 9, European Commission, Brussels.

Duffy, R. (2002), *A Trip Too Far: Ecotourism, Politics, and Exploitation*, London: Earthscan.

Dye, T. (1978), *Understanding Public Policy*, 3rd edn, Englewood Cliffs, NJ: Prentice Hall.

Flyvbjerg, B. (2001), *Making Social Science Matter: Why Social Inquiry Fails and How It Can Succeed Again*, Cambridge: Cambridge University Press.

Hahn, N.S.C. (2008), 'Neoliberal imperialism and pan-African resistance', *Journal of World-Systems Research*, 8(2), 142–78.

Harvey, D. (2005), *A Brief History of Neoliberalism*, Oxford: Oxford University Press.

Head, B. (2008), 'Three lenses of evidence-based policy', *Australian Journal of Public Administration*, 67(1), 1–11.

Head, B. (2010), 'Public management research', *Public Management Review*, 12(5), 571–85.

Higgins-Desbiolles, F. (2006), 'More than an "industry": The forgotten power of tourism as a social force', *Tourism Management*, 27, 1192–208.

Higgins-Desbiolles, F. (2010), 'In the eye of the beholder?', in P. Burns, C. Palmer and J.-A. Lester (eds) *Tourism and Visual Culture*, Wallingford: CABI, pp. 98–106.

Hoornbeek, J. and Peters, G. (2017), 'Understanding policy problems: A refinement of past work', *Policy and Society*, 36(3), 365–84.

Hoppe, R. (1999), 'Policy analysis, science and politics: From "speaking truth to power" to "making sense together"', *Science and Public Policy*, 26(3), 201–10.

Howlett, M., Ramesh, M. and Wu, X. (2015), 'Understanding the persistence of policy failures: The role of politics, governance and uncertainty', *Public Policy and Administration*, 30(3–4), 209–20.

Levin, K., Cashore, B., Bernstein, S. and Auld, G. (2012), 'Overcoming the tragedy of super wicked problems: Constraining our future selves to ameliorate global climate change', *Policy Sciences*, 45(2), 123–52.

Levin, P. (1997), *Making Social Policy: The Mechanisms of Government and Politics and How to Investigate Them*, Buckingham: Open Universivy Press.

Maguire, S. (1997), 'Business ethics: A compromise between politics and virtue', *Journal of Business Ethics*, 16(12/13), 1411–18.

Matarrita-Cascante, D. (2010), 'Beyond growth', *Annals of Tourism Research*, 37(4), 1141–63.

Moore, J.W. (2017), 'The Capitalocene, Part I: On the nature and origins of our ecological crisis', *Journal of Peasant Studies*, 44(3), 594–630.

Pal, L. and Maxwell, J. (2004), *Assessing the Public Interest in the 21st Century: A Framework*, Ottawa: Canadian Policy Research Network, paper prepared for the External Advisory Committee on Smart Regulation. Accessed 12 October 2018 at http://citeseerx.ist.psu.edu/viewdoc/download?doi=10.1.1.5 82.613&rep=rep1&type=pdf

Pearce, W. and Wesselink, A. (2014), 'Evidence and meaning in policy making', *Evidence and Policy*, 10(2), 161–5.

Peck, J. (2000), 'Jumping in, joining up and getting on', *Transactions of the Institute of British Geographers*, 25, 255–8.

Piketty, T. (2014), *Capitalism in the 21st Century*, Cambridge, MA: Belknap Press of Harvard University Press.

Richter, L. (1987), 'The political dimensions of tourism', in J.R.B. Ritchie and C.R. Goeldner (eds) *Travel Tourism and Hospitality Research*, New York: John Wiley & Sons, pp. 215–28.

Richter, L. (1989), *The Politics of Tourism in Asia*, Honolulu, HI: University of Hawaii Press.

Russo, A.P. (2002), 'The "vicious circle" of tourism development in heritage cities', *Annals of Tourism Research*, **29**(1), 165–82.

Sharpley, R. and Telfer, D. (2014), *Tourism and Development: Concepts and Issues*, 2nd edn, Clevedon: Channel View Publications.

Shergold, P. (2011), 'Seen but not heard', *The Australian*, 4 May.

Smith, A. (1776), *An Inquiry into the Nature and Causes of the Wealth of Nations*, with Preface by Edwin Cannan, 1904, London: Methuen & Co.

Stiglitz, J. (1991), *The Invisible Hand and Modern Welfare Economics*, National Bureau of Economics Research Working Paper (3641), 1–48.

Stiglitz, J. (2002), 'Joseph Stiglitz: There is no invisible hand'. Accessed 10 May 2015 at www.theguardian.com/education/2002/dec/20/highereducation.uk1

Stiglitz, J. (2013), *The Price of Inequality*, London: Penguin.

UNWTO (2017), 'Tourism: Growth is not the enemy; it's how we manage it that counts', *UN World Tourism Organization Press Release*, August. Accessed 12 October 2018 at http://media.unwto.org/press-release/2017-08-15/tourism-growth-not-enemy-it-s-how-we-manage-it-counts

Waring, M. (1999), *Counting for Nothing: What Men Value and What Women Are Worth*, 2nd edn, Toronto: University of Toronto Press.

3 The tourism-development nexus from a governance perspective: a research agenda

Emmanuel Akwasi Adu-Ampong

Introduction

Tourism is expanding across many developing-country destinations, where the promotion and rapid uptake of tourism is based on the widespread belief that it can contribute to both (local) economic development in general and to the alleviation of poverty in particular. More broadly, tourism is seen in principle as a viable economic development strategy with the potential to improve livelihoods through increased foreign exchange earnings, income generation, job creation and the conservation of biodiversity. In practice, however, this commonly perceived positive relationship between tourism and economic development (henceforth referred to as the tourism-development nexus) has also been shown to generate uneven outcomes in many destinations and that, at least in some destinations, the effects tend to be negative. Hence, attention has increasingly been focused on the need to understand the wider governance context of a given country in order to identify and comprehend the constraints to the realization of the tourism-development nexus.

The purpose of this chapter, then, is to establish a research agenda into tourism and development from a governance perspective, specifically seeking to demonstrate how such a perspective may offer new insights into the extent to which tourism can contribute to local economic development and poverty reduction. To accomplish this, the chapter begins with a brief overview of historical and contemporary research into the relationship between tourism and development. It goes on to present a thematic review of the conceptual and empirical limitations of existing governance research in tourism studies and, finally, explores the way forward by proposing a future research agenda for the tourism-development nexus that, in essence, takes governance seriously. In other words, governance, in its multivariate forms, is now commonly accepted to be a key dependent variable in shaping wider economic development outcomes within any country. Therefore, in order to enrich our understanding of how and to what extent tourism can contribute to (local) economic development and poverty reduction, there is a need to embrace new thinking from the general governance literature and from the field of development studies.

A brief history of the tourism-development nexus

Recent decades have witnessed extensive and increasing research into the positive and negative impacts of tourism on development (Ashley et al. 2000; Britton 1982; Bryden 1973; Holden 2013; Lea 1988; Meyer 2007; Mowforth & Munt 2009; Pleumarom 1994; Scheyvens 2011; Schilcher 2007; Sinclair & Tsegaye 1990; Turner 1976). Much of the earlier work, however, particularly from the late 1960s up until the early 1980s, was shown by both de Kadt (1979) and Britton (1982) to have been divorced from the historical and political processes that shape development in any given country. Consequently, from the mid-1980s and into the 1990s, there was a move towards a more critical reflection on the role of tourism in development. More specifically, this period witnessed tourism's role in economic development increasingly being placed within the political economy of international development, with a number of studies that critiqued the arguably overly positive tone of earlier research into tourism's role in development (see also Chapter 1). Notably, these studies highlighted the negative impacts of tourism and called for a more cautious approach in utilizing tourism as a tool for economic development (Britton 1982; Brohman 1996; Harrison 2008; Pleumarom 1994).

On the cusp of the new millennium, the debate on tourism's role in economic development then shifted, moving from a consideration of tourism's role in economic development more generally to a more direct focus on how tourism contributes to poverty reduction in particular. Specifically, in January 1999 the UK's Department for International Development (DFID) commissioned Deloitte and Touche (Oliver Bennett), the International Institute for Environment and Development (Dilys Roe) and the Overseas Development Institute (Caroline Ashley) to conduct a study with the overall objective of providing an overview of the international development work that was related to the links between poverty and tourism in developing countries (Bennett et al. 1999). It was in their final report submitted to DFID titled 'Sustainable Tourism and Poverty Elimination Study' that the term 'pro-poor tourism' (PPT) was first used. PPT referred to 'tourism that generates net benefits for the poor (benefits greater than costs)' (Bennett et al. 1999, p. iii). As Scheyvens (2007) thus observes, it was a shift within the international development industry during the 1990s to make poverty a top priority that broadly inspired the concept of PPT. Scheyvens (2007) also points out that the focus on pro-poor policies was a direct response to the effects of the structural adjustment programmes of that period. These were major economic restructuring projects which, reflecting the prevailing neo-classical political-economic agenda, encouraged developing countries to diversify their economies from overdependence on commodity exports into such services as tourism. To summarize, then, the DFID report suggested that tourism was already contributing to poverty alleviation in poor countries and that there was more to achieve with a specific focus on the poor. The authors were nonetheless cautious in their conclusions, noting that whether tourism is or is not pro-poor is a question that can only be addressed in context and assessed on a case-by-case basis before tourism is promoted for poverty objectives. In their view, however, the most useful and pressing question was not if but how tourism could become more pro-poor (Bennett et al. 1999; also Ashley et al. 2000).

The emergence of the concept of PPT precipitated research into PPT and resulted in a burgeoning number of case studies typically based upon consultancy projects exploring how to leverage tourism's potential for poverty reduction. These were followed, however, by several critiques and counter-critiques concerning the contribution made by PPT studies to our understanding of tourism's role in economic development and poverty reduction (Chok et al. 2007; Goodwin 2008; Harrison 2008; Scheyvens 2007; Schilcher 2007; Spenceley & Meyer 2012). As a consequence, throughout the 2000s the relevant literature featured both optimistic and cautious perspectives on tourism's economic development role. Within this context, Sharpley and Telfer (2015) argue that a conceptual leap was being made between tourism and development. That is, they suggest that much of the relevant research during this period failed to situate tourism's role in economic development within the political and socio-economic processes of other sectors that collectively shape a particular country's development outcomes. In a sense, therefore, this conceptual leap can be seen as a response to the lack of attention in tourism studies to insights from the field of development studies and, specifically, from the governance-development literature.

By contrast, however, attention is now increasingly focused on the dynamic relationship between tourism and the development process more generally (Mowforth & Munt 2009; Scheyvens 2011; Sharpley & Telfer 2015; Spenceley & Meyer 2012; Telfer & Sharpley 2016). As noted above, the 'new poverty' agenda that came to underline research into tourism's role in economic development and poverty reduction brought a new focus on the need to enhance state institutions and governance. This new focus has shifted the debate from reductionist conclusions that portray tourism simply as a force for good or for evil, to representing a focus on tourism as 'a powerful social force that needs to be better understood in order to connect it more effectively to development agendas that go beyond purely economic considerations' (Spenceley & Meyer 2012, p. 301; see also Scheyvens 2011). This view argues that tourism development takes place within a wider governance and overall socio-economic development context. It is, therefore, imperative to understand this context to identify the enabling and constraining factors to the tourism-development nexus. In short, this shift within the research into the tourism-development nexus has largely been an explicit manifestation of the 'institutional turn' and 'good governance' agenda that came to dominate the development studies field from the late 1990s onwards.

Nevertheless, although previous research has highlighted the importance of governance in enhancing the tourism-development nexus, such studies remain relatively rare (Brohman 1996; Holden 2013; Konadu-Agyemang 2001; Rogerson 2014; Scheyvens 2007). Moreover, only a few attempts have been made to conceptualize the tourism-development nexus within a governance framework. One notable example is Holden (2013), who argues that the effective future use of tourism for poverty reduction will depend on good governance, which is characterized by 'increased citizen participation and improved accountability of public officials' (Holden 2013, p. 155). This is in contradistinction to bad or poor governance distinguished by 'corruption and the abuse of public office for private gain . . . [which] undermines the legitimacy of government and reduces the availability and quality of public services' (Holden 2013, p. 156). Similarly, Scheyvens (2007, p. 248) suggests 'there is a need for effective governance structures if tourism is to maximize benefits for the poor'. Generally, however, the issue of governance within the tourism-development nexus has more typically enjoyed only a passing mention, rather than being considered a key explanatory variable in understanding the relationship between tourism and development. This, in turn, has been the result of limited theorizing of governance within tourism research in general and the slow integration of insights from governance studies with tourism research in particular.

The state of governance research in tourism

In much of the social sciences, governance as an empirical phenomenon and as a set of theories used to *explain* this empirical phenomenon has been in vogue since the turn of the millennium (Pierre 2000; Pierre & Peters 2000; Rhodes 1996; Stoker 1998). Nevertheless, a consideration of governance is yet to be fully established within the tourism literature (Erkuş-Öztürk 2011). This is a curious (under)development or omission in the research, particularly as tourism is often considered an interesting context in which to study governance (Ruhanen 2013), not least because the tourism sector sits at the intersection of public, private, civic, civil and community interests. Put differently, tourism as a socio-economic and political activity is recognized as a highly complex and dynamic system that comprises a multitude of actors and stakeholders (Britton 1982; Hall 1998, 2000; Ioannides & Debbage 1998; Mosedale 2011; Slocum & Backman 2011). The intersection of these numerous and diverse actors and their interests, which may not always be compatible, thus requires the key features of governance, such as the application and allocation of power, resources and rules, as well as the coordination of actors more generally (Bramwell 2011).

Indeed, in tourism research the term governance is used much less frequently than such related terms as politics, policy and planning (Bramwell & Lane, 2011). At the same time, much existing research tends to focus on such case study-based issues as public-private partnerships (Bramwell & Sharman 1999; Zapata & Hall, 2012), policy networks (Dredge, 2006; Cooper et al. 2009; Scott et al. 2008) and so on. Moreover, in most cases where tourism governance is specifically studied, it is usually from the perspective of sustainable tourism (Bramwell 2011; Sofield & Li 2011) and destination competitiveness (d'Angella et al. 2010; Ritchie & Crouch 2003). By contrast, assessments of the role of tourism governance in the context of the tourism-development nexus are generally neglected.

There are, however, interesting dichotomies in research that do exist on tourism governance. The first set of dichotomies consists of research that originates from, on the one hand, the perspective of corporate management and, on the other hand, from the political science perspective (Pechlaner et al. 2014; Ruhanen

2013). Following these, a further set of dichotomies consists of a policy-science perspective versus a political-economy perspective of governance (Erkuş-Öztürk, 2011). These sets of dichotomies tend to overlap, with the corporate management perspective research viewing governance in terms of policy, while the political science perspective adopts a political-economy approach to governance. Research from each of these sets of dichotomies offers some insights into understanding tourism governance, notwithstanding some limitations in the literature. Hence, an understanding of existing research on tourism governance in general may provide a foundation on which to chart a future research agenda on a governance perspective for the tourism-development nexus.

Destination governance à la corporate management

The starting point for research on destination governance from a corporate management perspective is a well-defined geographical tourism destination consisting primarily of tourist firms (Beritelli et al. 2007). From such a starting point, a destination is seen as an amalgamation of tourism products which collectively provide an integrated experience to visitors. Such a conceptualization posits the need for destination management organizations (DMOs) tasked with the planning and marketing of the destination within the overall strategic objective of enhancing competitiveness.

Destination governance as a concept grew from earlier works on destination planning and destination management (Beritelli 2011). In the early 1990s, research on tourism planning emphasized tourist destinations as competitive units with a diversity of stakeholders and interests (Inskeep 1988). As a consequence, tourism planning came to focus on how to plan destinations to integrate the interests of various stakeholders with a view to increasing the destination's competitiveness (Ritchie & Crouch 2003). Within this paradigm, the tourism destination as a unit of analysis was taken as a given and the fragmented nature of the supply of tourist products in a destination was not critically assessed.

Subsequent research then established the need to move from simply planning the destination to the process of destination management to improve the coordination of the activities of stakeholders (Bramwell & Sharman, 1999; Hall 1999). However, much of this research was, and continues to be, undertaken from a primarily business management perspective which concerns itself with destination management and marketing in purely business terms (Buhalis 2000; Pechlaner et al. 2009; Pechlaner & Tschurtschenthaler 2003). Hence, destination management is considered to be 'the processes of tourism planning, managing and coordination that take place in tourist destinations, usually carried out by a destination management organisation' (Smith et al. 2010, p. 40). The main unit of analysis within this perspective is the DMO, with tourist numbers and business revenues being indicators of its success. In the literature, case studies identified the key challenges faced by DMOs in effective destination management and planning; in particular, difficulties in establishing collaborative efforts (Jamal & Getz 1995; Lovelock 2001) and differences in performance outcomes of DMOs (d'Angella & Go 2009) pointed to the need to unpack and explore in greater depth numerous issues within destination management that were taken as given. Amongst others, these included the processes of collaboration, coordination and stakeholder interaction, and the opening up of these concepts to critical analysis paved the way to a greater understanding of the process of destination planning and management.

Studies attempting to consider these issues within destination management now come under the rubric of destination governance which, according to Beritelli (2011), is concerned with identifying and conceptualizing the specificity of destination management processes and the factors that shape outcomes. For the most part, research on destination governance follows two main lines of enquiry: first, how to define and conceptualize destination governance and, second, how to identify the various modes of governance to be studied (Pechlaner et al. 2011). However, owing to its roots in business management, research into destination governance is ultimately geared towards enhancing destination competitiveness to the benefit of organizations and businesses in the tourism sector. This is mainly accomplished through offering concepts and models that can help effective destination (corporate) planning and management (Beritelli 2011).

The concepts and processes of corporate governance largely inform the conceptualization of destination governance (Beritelli et al. 2007; d'Angella et al. 2010; Pechlaner et al. 2011, 2012). As a consequence, the unit of analysis within destination governance research remains DMOs and their management structure. Because of this (over)reliance on ideas rooted in corporate governance, destination governance has come to be explained largely in terms of the firm – that is, DMOs – and so the work on destination governance is essentially focused on the internal effectiveness and efficiency of DMOs as organizations and how DMOs foster cooperation and collaboration (Pechlaner et al. 2012).

Interestingly, however, the focus of more research on destination governance has moved from the study of organizations and institutions as key variables to elite individuals or key players within tourism destinations. Thus, the unit of analysis has now become the managers of DMOs and how their leadership styles affect destination governance and management (Beritelli & Bieger 2014; Pechlaner et al. 2014). As such, this represents a classic case of methodological individualism which has been much criticized in the tourism literature. Bianchi (2002), for instance, notes that focusing on the creativity and innovation of individual leadership styles does not offer any sustained analysis of how existing power relations and structures constrain the success of DMO leadership.

To summarize, then, research on destination governance à la corporate governance undoubtedly provides interesting insights into the processes that render destinations competitive. There are, however, key deficiencies within this literature. Indeed, Beritelli et al. (2007, p. 107), conclude that 'further research in the field of destination governance must address the integration of other theories . . . (for example, the political economy)'. More specifically, the lacuna in existing research reflects the failure to critically assess the wider role of DMOs in destination management and planning. That is, by depending on corporate governance theory or, in other words, overlooking the potential contribution of theories from political economy, research on destination governance tends to prioritize tourist firms (DMOs) over and above other stakeholders, including residents. Put differently, by overemphasizing rationality and focusing on overt decision-making processes in a tourism destination (Bianchi 2002), research undertaken from the corporate governance perspective downplays power relations and the processes through which various actors bargain within the tourism development process. Only a few studies examine how destination governance processes affect the tourism-development nexus whilst, in particular, several frameworks of destination governance have been developed and tested, but only in the context of developed country destinations, where poverty reduction through tourism is not a pressing or relevant issue. The need thus exists for future research that broadly explores the connection between destination governance practices and the tourism-development nexus in a variety of destination contexts in both the Global North and the Global South.

Destination governance à la political science theory

There is a sizeable literature on tourism governance that draws on theories of political science (Bramwell 2011; Erkuş-Öztürk 2011; Göymen 2000; Hall 2011a, 2011b). Such discussions are premised on the assumption that 'tailored and effective governance is a key requirement for implementing sustainable tourism' (Bramwell & Lane 2011, p. 411). In this sense, governance is understood as opening up tourism planning and decision-making processes to the participation of a variety of actors as well as the use of appropriate policy instruments to achieve sustainable development. It should be noted here that while notions of sustainable tourism development have been increasingly adopted in academic, business and government policy, discourses remain rigorously contested and debated (Hall 2011b; Sharpley 2009).

Tourism governance cuts across different sectors, spans a range of policy domains and involves a diverse group of actors. The state is considered central to any explanation of tourism governance. Indeed, as Bramwell (2011) maintains, even though the state has been pushed back by private agencies and (quasi-)markets in the tourism sector, it retains a significant influence, not least because it is still the site of policy making and is thus well positioned to coordinate the actions of diverse groups of actors in the tourism policy domain. Thus, in cases where partnerships are formed between the public and private sectors, the state can control the direction of such partnerships. Whereas in approaches in tourism inspired by corporate governance literature the central focus is the firm or DMO, those based on a political science perspective locate the state at the centre of their analysis.

In other words, it is recognized that the curtailing of the state's regulatory capacity and service provision for the tourism sector is intricately linked with the neo-liberal reforms that commenced in the 1980s and continued into the 1990s (Mosedale

2011; Pastras & Bramwell 2013; Shone & Memon 2008), a transformation that provides the foundational basis for the use of a political-economy approach in analysing tourism governance. Bianchi (2002), for example, suggests that while the prescriptive and technical analysis of tourism provides a quantitative view of the value of tourism, it offers insights into the dynamics of the tourism sector. By contrast, a political-economy approach to tourism governance is normatively concerned with 'an analysis of the social relations of power which condition the unequal and uneven processes of tourism development, which are reinforced through particular configurations of ideologies and institutions' (Bianchi 2002, p. 266).

Although not extensively adopted in the field of tourism, the political-economy approach has been applied by a number of researchers (for example, Bianchi 2002; Dieke 2000; Mosedale 2011). In these cases, the use of the political-economy approach is more typically in the broader context of tourism development, though some studies focus specifically on tourism governance. For example, Bramwell (2011) explores the applicability of a strategic-relational approach to political economy to tourism governance for sustainability. In so doing, he identifies a number of distinctive research themes and perspectives that are easily transferable to the study of tourism governance. These include the focus of the strategic-relational approach on the state's role in regulating the economic and political system, its concern with structure and agency, its holistic focus on dialectics and relational perspective, and an emphasis on how the state adapts at various spatial scales. He applies this approach to five country case studies, aiming to understand the state's role in tourism development and sustainability. This research highlights important lessons that can inform future research on the tourism-development nexus from a governance perspective, especially when utilized through a case study, where the design allows a clear focus on how structural processes and contingent forces shape the actions of actors and, ultimately, the governance of the tourism-development nexus. This makes it possible to analytically move back and forth between the initial theoretical explanations and the empirical data, thus enabling theories to be challenged while explanations are revised along the way.

A more recent example of the political-economy approach to tourism governance is found in Pastras and Bramwell (2013), where again a strategic-relational approach is utilized in a study of tourism governance in Athens, Greece. This study highlights the need to examine the relationship between formal institutional arrangements, informal cultural practices and ideas about beliefs and values in tourism governance research. The specific focus of this paper is on how this relationship has shaped governments' role in the creation of tourism marketing policies and activities. The use of the strategic-relational approach facilitated a focus on how institutions and actors in the public and the private sector interact, and accounted for changes and continuities in the evolution of institutions, their practices and values. Such a strategic-relation approach to the study of tourism governance has the potential to shed light on how processes and outcomes of tourism policies are affected by individual actors, events, changes in contexts and the upward and/or downward rescaling of governance authority to new tiers of government. These are important elements that can enable a better understanding of how new forms of governing processes are shaping the tourism-development nexus.

New avenues for future research on the tourism-development nexus from a governance perspective

Studies in tourism governance that are informed by social theories in general and political-economy approaches in particular offer much promise. A political-economy approach allows tourism governance research to move from descriptive analysis to more analytical and theoretically informed work; in other words, the all too frequent static account of governance in tourism research is avoided when the research draws on ideas and concepts of political economy, thereby enhancing the analysis and understanding of causality and processes of change (Bramwell 2011). Despite the merits of this approach, much existing research focuses mainly on tourism governance typologies, their implications for policy analysis (Hall 2011a, 2011b) and the relationship of tourism governance and sustainability or, more precisely, sustainable tourism development (Bramwell 2011; Sofield & Li 2011). Consequently, there remains a surprising lack of in-depth research into the relationship between tourism governance at the general level and the tourism-development nexus. Moreover, where research focuses on governance and sustainable tourism development, there tends not to be a direct focus on the poverty alleviation potential of tourism. Future research will need to bridge this gap by relating tourism governance to the specific outcomes of the tourism-development nexus.

There is a clear need to integrate research on tourism's role in poverty reduction into work on tourism governance. Research in the field of development studies and such allied fields as public policy, public management and public administration has established the key role of governance variables in explaining development/poverty-reduction outcomes – especially in developing countries. An integration of ideas from these debates into a (re)conceptualization of the tourism-development nexus from a political-economy governance approach would be a viable and logical option. Certainly, analysis of the tourism-development nexus must incorporate rigorous political analysis, and will be embedded in various place-based socio-economic interventions. The emphasis thus needs to be on governance mechanisms through which overall socio-economic development occurs at the destination level and this, in turn, requires a focus on the central role of the state in the governing process. As Amore and Hall (2016, p. 114) have argued, 'much of the work related to governance in tourism has managed to define the state out of governance processes or at least minimize its role in comparison to emphasizing markets (business), network (voluntary self-organization) or community (local) approaches'. In short, to set out a future agenda for the tourism-development nexus from a governance perspective requires that the state needs to be (re)defined back into the centre of the governance process.

Interactive governance perspective and tourism-development nexus outcomes

Two specific areas within governance studies that offer promising avenues for future research are an interactive governance perspective and stakeholder governance capacity. As noted earlier, up to the early 2000s, research on the tourism-development nexus failed to take sufficient account of core debates within the field of development studies (Sharpley & Telfer 2002, 2015). Since then, this situation has changed little, and future research needs to situate tourism within its wider socio-economic and political context. Consequently, researchers need to pay attention to debates within development studies, theory and thought. In particular, there is a need to take account of local political particularities, as a politically informed governance approach can provide dynamic accounts of the effects of global and local forces on the outcomes at the destination level. To this end, a governance perspective offers a useful prism through which to view the interaction of actors and stakeholders in the fragmented tourism sector and, importantly, interactions within the wider socio-economic and political context.

In relation to the governance literature, there are as many definitions of governance as there are people who write about the topic. These definitions range from governance as, 'governing with and through networks' (Rhodes 2007, p. 1246) or 'the tools, strategies and relationship used by governments to help govern' (Bell & Hindmoor 2009, p. 2) to governance as 'the processes and institutions, both formal and informal, that guide and restrain the collective activities of a group' (Keohane & Nye, 2000, p. 12). However, a key point is that governance involves a process in which a multitude of actors come together with the aim of achieving some collective goals. Thus, Grindle (2017, p. 17) has recently argued that, when applied to the public sector, governance 'encompasses notions of how political and administrative decisions get made, how governmental systems work, and why both formal and informal institutions matter in how things get done and how states relate to societies'. Governance, then, is essentially about interactions between actors and such a conceptualization has important implications for studying and understanding the tourism-development nexus.

Put differently, to fully understand the tourism-development nexus from a governance perspective, it is necessary to integrate a governance framework that makes interaction between and within the public, private and civil society sectors central to its conceptualization. The tourism sector operates within a larger political-economic setting and, hence, the effectiveness of the tourism-development nexus will largely depend on state policy and governing directives which span a multitude of institutions across a variety of governance levels (Adu-Ampong 2018; Rogerson 2014; Scheyvens 2007; Slocum & Backman 2011; Spenceley & Meyer 2012). As noted by Harrison when discussing PPT (2008, p. 863), 'as in development matters generally, the impact of any PPT projects, even if on a large scale, is likely to be limited unless a state's entire tourism strategy is constructed around the aim of poverty alleviation. In effect, PPT requires a developmental state.' Thus, future research on tourism governance needs to relocate the state as central to the governance process. It then becomes possible to assess how far attempts to use tourism to bring about poverty reduction and, more widely, development, are in tune with overall state socio-economic governance priorities in a given destination.

There is also a place in future research for an historical approach that examines the tourism-development nexus vis-à-vis national economic development governance and planning. More specifically, an historical approach can help identify how changing national governing activities affect the priority accorded to the tourism-development nexus in economic planning. In a recent paper, for example, Adu-Ampong (2018) examines the historical conception of tourism development in Ghana as found in successive national economic development plans since 1957. A key finding from this study is that national economic development policy and planning frameworks provide an insight into understanding the tourism-development nexus and the governance processes involved in utilizing tourism as a tool for economic development and poverty reduction.

An historical approach to the governance of the tourism-development nexus means that we can understand the contemporary state of a destination's tourism development status, as situated within the changes and continuities in overall socio-economic development governance. This is because overall national development plans act as a framework within which resources become available for sectors such as tourism. National governing activities are not static but are subject to varying degrees of change owing to both internal and external pressures. Consequently, it is important for future research to trace the changing intellectual trends regarding the tourism-development nexus, and to examine the historical and contemporary changes in the perceived and actual role of state governance stakeholders in the tourism-development nexus.

A potentially useful conceptual basis for future research is the so-called interactive governance perspective (Bavinck et al. 2013; Kooiman 1999, 2000, 2003; Kooiman et al. 2005, 2008), defined as 'the whole of public as well as private interactions taken to solve societal problems and create societal opportunities; including the formulation and application of principles guiding those interactions and care for institutions that enable them' (Kooiman et al. 2005, p. 17). Such a definition offers a useful starting point for exploring and explaining the governing processes around tourism-development nexus initiatives and projects. This conceptualization points not only to interaction within a given sector, such as tourism, but also requires an analytic focus on the wider socio-economic and political context. It can also act to 'provide a language and frame of reference through which reality can be examined and lead theorists to ask questions that might not otherwise occur' (Judge et al. 1995, p. 3). The value of the interactive governance perspective is that it offers an organizing framework for understanding changing processes of governing and helps to identify important questions (Stoker, 1998) in relation to the tourism-development nexus. However, notwithstanding ongoing changes, the state maintains a central role in the governing interactions in which policy decisions are made because it maintains control of key resources (Peters & Pierre 2016; Pierre & Peters 2000, 2005; Torfing et al. 2012). This leads to a number of interesting research questions for future research on the governance of the tourism-development nexus, including:

- To what extent does the state still play a key role in directing tourism development?
- How does the form of interaction between state and societal actors enable/ constrain the implementation of tourism-development nexus projects and initiatives?
- What is the historical relationship between tourism and the governance of national economic development planning in a given destination?

Stakeholder governance capacity and the tourism-development nexus

The need for collaboration and coordination in tourism is established in the tourism literature. Moreover, it has been suggested that collaborative tourism planning is most crucial in developing-country destinations, which tend to depend on foreign direct investment for tourism development (Pansiri 2013). The importance of collaboration and coordination within tourism, however, goes beyond the simple need to attract investment. If tourism is to contribute significantly to national and local economic development, there must be adequate levels of collaboration and coordination among the various stakeholders involved in tourism development. Previous research has established that some benefits of collaboration within the tourism sector include the cost effectiveness arising from the pooling resource (Aas et al. 2005; Bramwell & Sharman 1999; Jamal & Getz 1999; Ladkin & Bertramini 2002; Lovelock 2001; Pansiri 2013; Tosun 2000). These benefits notwithstanding, however, collaborative theories as used in tourism research continue to fail to deal adequately with systematic constraints within tourism destinations that hinder collaboration – especially in relation to improving the tourism-development nexus. Tosun (2000), for example, has argued that operational, structural and cultural limits vis-à-vis existing power structures tend to be ignored in research on tourism collaborations. One way of overcoming such systematic constraints in tourism collaboration research in relation to the tourism-development nexus is to take a more situated approach and consider the wider socio-economic and political context within which stakeholders operate and engage in governing activities.

If governance of the tourism-development nexus is conceptualized as interactive, it is important to consider how far interacting stakeholders can effect the desired changes, and research into stakeholder governance capacity offers a promising avenue for providing much needed insights into governance issues. The inherently fragmented nature of the tourism sector calls for a concerted effort to pool resources of different stakeholders to plan, manage and govern tourism development. However, such a pooling of resources is made more difficult by the number of diverse stakeholders and actors within the tourism sector at global, national, regional and local levels, and the outcomes of any initiative, project or investment to increase the positive outcomes of the tourism-development nexus cannot be systematically guaranteed. Tourism is a social force (Spenceley & Meyer 2012); its outcomes depend on the depth and extent of stakeholder interactions in the planning and implementation process, and therefore require further research.

The uneven nature of the resources available to tourism stakeholders in their quest to build governing capacity requires an examination of the allocation and application of resources, rules and decision-making power (Bramwell 2011) within the tourism sector. This is particularly relevant for the tourism-development nexus in that the level of stakeholder governance capacity has a bearing on the extent tourism can be leveraged for poverty-reduction purposes (Slocum & Backman 2011). It is through interaction that conflicting interests are negotiated, coalitions built and tourism development activities coordinated among stakeholders across multiple governance levels. It has been argued that at the most basic level, stakeholder capacity is about the 'extent to which a given stakeholder or set of stakeholders have at their disposal the tools and the ability to effect desired change' (Adu-Ampong, 2016, p. 27). Thus, future research on the tourism-development nexus should explore the tools available to – and the ability of – tourism and non-tourism stakeholders in their quest to leverage tourism for developmental and poverty-reduction purposes. A clear understanding of the allocation of power, tools and other resources across the range of stakeholders will provide the basis of understanding how the tourism-development nexus can be effectively governed for desired outcomes. The following questions are starting points for future research in this area:

• What are the various visions held by stakeholders regarding the tourism-development nexus and how do they make these explicit in their governing interactions?
• How do stakeholders identify, develop and deploy new governing instruments in achieving their governing vision for the use of tourism in development and poverty-reduction purposes?
• How do existing power relations within a destination enable and/or constrain the ability, authority and legitimacy of tourism stakeholders in their governing interactions with other stakeholders?

Conclusion

The tourism-development nexus has received renewed attention across a multitude of international development agencies and national governments. Indeed, in three of the new set of 17 Sustainable Development Goals there is an explicit reference to tourism: in Goal 8: economic growth and employment; Goal 12: sustainable consumption and production; and Goal 14: conserve and sustainably use the oceans, seas and marine resources for sustainable development. As tourism continues to be seen as key to development, it is important for future research on the tourism-development nexus to consider the wider socio-economic and governance context that shapes overall development within any given destination. This chapter has made the case for a new research agenda on the tourism-development nexus from a governance perspective. In its various forms, governance is about how stakeholders interact, develop capacity and make use of resources to achieve desired end goals. It is, therefore, essential to apply a variety of governance perspectives and, in particular, attention needs to be paid to the past, present and future governing arrangements that enable and constrain the use of tourism in national and local economic development planning strategies.

The concept of governance – as both an empirical phenomenon and as a set of theories – is now in vogue across much of the social science disciplines, including tourism studies. There remains, however, some misunderstanding with regards to the concept and its usage in a variety of contexts. These can sometimes appear contradictory. Nonetheless, at the most basic level, governance is about bringing together a multitude of actors of different types towards some collective goal (Peters & Pierre 2016) whilst, at the same time, it is also about political and social communication between stakeholders. It is such an understanding of governance that makes it an essential concept in exploring the tourism-development nexus, and while it may no longer have the ultimate monopoly over governing activities, the state still maintains a strong leading role in this process of political and social communication. It is this communicative turn in governance that highlights the importance of increased interaction between the state and other stakeholders in the policy-making process (Allmendinger & Tewdwr-Jones 2002; Healey 2006). This is particularly pertinent for understanding the tourism-development nexus and should shape the areas for future research identified in this chapter.

A future research agenda needs to start from a conceptualization of governance as interaction in order to explore ways in which the multitude of tourism stakeholders collaborate and coordinate their activities. An interactive governance perspective offers a way to (re)define the state back into tourism governance and helps to identify the historical ways in which state governance activities continue to shape the tourism-development nexus. Such an approach helps in raising questions about the governance capacity of stakeholders involved, and while it is very worthy to recommend stakeholder collaboration and coordination as an avenue for enhancing the tourism-development nexus, it is also important to examine and establish the interactional *capacity* of stakeholders, and the power dynamics which characterize the context of their interaction. In this regard, a political-economy approach to governance research within tourism studies offers more insights for the tourism-development nexus compared to tourism governance research from a management perspective. And unlike the latter, the former will take politics seriously.

References

Aas, C., Ladkin, A. and Fletcher, J. (2005), 'Stakeholder collaboration and heritage management', *Annals of Tourism Research*, 32(1), 28–48.

Adu-Ampong, E.A. (2016), 'Governing tourism-led local economic development planning: An interactive tourism governance perspective on the Elmina 2015 Strategy in Ghana', unpublished PhD Thesis, Department of Urban Studies and Planning, University of Sheffield.

Adu-Ampong, E.A. (2018), 'Tourism and national economic development planning in Ghana, 1964–2014', *International Development Planning Review*, **40**(1), 75–95.

Allmendinger, P. and Tewdwr-Jones, M. (eds) (2002), *Planning Futures: New Directions for Planning Theory*, London: Routledge.

Amore, A. and Hall, C.M. (2016), 'From governance to meta-governance in tourism? Re-incorporating politics, interests and values in the analysis of tourism governance', *Tourism Recreation Research*, **41**(2), 109–22.

Ashley, C., Boyd, C. and Goodwin, H. (2000), 'Pro-poor tourism: Putting poverty at the heart of the tourism agenda', *Natural Resource Perspectives*, **51**, 1–12.

Bavinck, M., Chuenpagdee, R., Jentoft, S. and Kooiman, J. (2013), *Governability of Fisheries and Aquaculture: Theory and Applications*, Dordrecht: Springer.

Bell, S. and Hindmoor, A. (2009), *Rethinking Governance: The Centrality of the State in Modern Society*, Cambridge: Cambridge University Press.

Bennett, O., Roe, D. and Ashley, C. (1999), *Sustainable Tourism and Poverty Elimination Study*, London: Department for International Development.

Beritelli, P. (2011), *Tourist Destination Governance through Local Elites: Looking beyond the Stakeholder Level*, unpublished cumulative postdoctoral thesis, University of St Gallen, Institute for Systemic Management and Public Governance Center for Tourism and Transport.

Beritelli, P. and Bieger, T. (2014), 'From destination governance to destination leadership defining and exploring the significance with the help of a systemic perspective', *Tourism Review*, **69**(1), 25–46.

Beritelli, P., Bieger, T. and Laesser, C. (2007), 'Destination governance: Using corporate governance theories as a foundation for effective destination management', *Journal of Travel Research*, **46**(1), 96–107.

Bianchi, R. (2002), 'Towards a new political economy of global tourism', in R. Sharpley and D. Telfer (eds) *Tourism and Development: Concepts and Issues*, Clevedon: Channel View Publications, pp. 265–99.

Bramwell, B. (2011), 'Governance, the state and sustainable tourism: A political economy approach', *Journal of Sustainable Tourism*, **19**(4–5), 459–77.

Bramwell, B. and Lane, B. (2011), 'Critical research on the governance of tourism and sustainability', *Journal of Sustainable Tourism*, **19**(4–5), 411–21.

Bramwell, B. and Sharman, A. (1999), 'Collaboration in local tourism policymaking', *Annals of Tourism Research*, **26**(2), 392–415.

Britton, S.G. (1982), 'The political economy of tourism in the Third World', *Annals of Tourism Research*, **9**(3), 331–58.

Brohman, J. (1996), 'New directions in tourism for third world development', *Annals of Tourism Research*, **23**(1), 48–70.

Bryden, J. (1973), *Tourism and Development: A Case Study of the Commonwealth Caribbean*, Cambridge: Cambridge University Press.

Buhalis, D. (2000), 'Marketing the competitive destination of the future', *Tourism Management*, **21**(1), 97–116.

Chok, S., Macbeth, J. and Warren, C. (2007), 'Tourism as a tool for poverty alleviation: A critical analysis of "pro-poor tourism" and implications for sustainability', *Current Issues in Tourism*, **10**(2–3), 144–65.

Cooper, C., Scott, N. and Baggio, R. (2009), 'Network position and perceptions of destination stakeholder importance', *Anatolia*, **20**(1), 33–45.

d'Angella, F. and Go, F. (2009), 'Tale of two cities' collaborative tourism marketing: Towards a theory of destination stakeholder assessment', *Tourism Management*, **30**(3), 429–40.

d'Angella, F., De Carlo, M. and Sainaghi, R. (2010), 'Archetypes of destination governance: A comparison of international destinations', *Tourism Review*, **65**(4), 61–73.

de Kadt, E. (ed.) (1979), *Tourism: Passport to Development? Perspectives on the Social and Cultural Effects of Tourism in Developing Countries*, Oxford: Oxford University Press.

Dieke, P. (2000), *The Political Economy of Tourism Development in Africa*, New York: Cognizant Communication Corp.

Dredge, D. (2006), 'Policy networks and the local organisation of tourism', *Tourism Management*, **27**(2), 269–80.

Erkuş-Öztürk, H. (2011), 'Modes of tourism governance: A comparison of Amsterdam and Antaly', *Anatolia*, **22**(3), 307–25.

Goodwin, H. (2008), 'Pro-poor tourism: A response', *Third World Quarterly*, **29**(5), 869–71.

Göymen, K. (2000), 'Tourism and governance in Turkey', *Annals of Tourism Research*, **27**(4), 1025–48.

Grindle, M. (2017), 'Good governance, RIP: A critique and an alternative', *Governance: An International Journal of Policy, Administration and Institutions*, **30**(1), 17–22.

Hall, C.M. (1998), 'The institutional setting: Tourism and the state', in D. Ioannides and K.G. Debbage (eds) *The Economic Geography of the Tourist Industry: A Supply-Side Analysis*, London: Routledge, pp. 199–219.

Hall, C.M. (1999), 'Rethinking collaboration and partnership: A public policy perspective', *Journal of Sustainable Tourism*, **7**(3–4), 274–89.

Hall, C.M. (2000), 'Rethinking collaboration and partnership: A public policy perspective', in B. Bramwell and B. Lane (eds) *Tourism Collaboration and Partnerships: Politics, Practice and Sustainability*, Clevedon: Channel View Publications, pp. 143–58.

Hall, C.M. (2011a), 'Policy learning and policy failure in sustainable tourism governance', *Journal of Sustainable Tourism*, **19**(4–5), 649–71.

Hall, C.M. (2011b), 'A typology of governance and its implications for tourism policy analysis', *Journal of Sustainable Tourism*, **19**(4–5), 437–58.

Harrison, D. (2008), 'Pro-poor tourism: A critique', *Third World Quarterly*, **29**(5), 851–68.

Healey, P. (2006), *Collaborative Planning: Shaping Places in Fragmented Societies*, 2nd edn, Basingstoke: Palgrave Macmillan.

Holden, A. (2013), *Tourism, Poverty and Development*, Abingdon: Routledge.

Inskeep, E. (1988), 'Tourism planning: An emerging specialization', *Journal of the American Planning Association*, **54**(3), 360–72.

Ioannides, D. and Debbage, K. (1998), *The Economic Geography of the Tourist Industry: A Supply-Side Analysis*, London: Routledge.

Jamal, T. and Getz, D. (1995), 'Collaboration theory and community tourism planning', *Annals of Tourism Research*, **22**(1), 186–204.

Jamal, T. and Getz, D. (1999), 'Community roundtables for tourism-related conflicts: The dialectics of consensus and process structures', *Journal of Sustainable Tourism*, **7**(3–4), 290–313.

Judge, D., Stoker, G. and Wolman, H. (1995), 'Urban politics and theory: An introduction', in D. Judge, G. Stoker and H. Wolman (eds) *Theories of Urban Politics*, London: SAGE, pp. 1–13.

Keohane, R. and Nye, J. (2000), 'Introduction', in J. Nye and J. Donahue (eds) *Governance in a Globalizing World*, Washington, DC: Brookings Institution, pp. 1–41.

Konadu-Agyemang, K. (2001), 'Structural adjustment programmes and the international tourism trade in Ghana, 1983–99: Some socio-spatial implications', *Tourism Geographies*, **3**(2), 187–206.

Kooiman, J. (1999), 'Social-political governance', *Public Management Review*, **1**(1), 67–92.

Kooiman, J. (2000), 'Societal governance: Levels, modes and orders of social political interaction', in J. Pierre (ed.) *Debating Governance: Authority, Steering and Democracy*, Oxford: Oxford University Press, pp. 138–64.

Kooiman, J. (2003), *Governing as Governance*, London: SAGE.

Kooiman, J., Bavinck, M., Jentoft, S. and Pullin, R. (2005), *Fish for Life: Interactive Governance for Fisheries*, Amsterdam: Amsterdam University Press, Centre for Maritime Research.

Kooiman, J., Bavinck, M., Chuenpagdee, R., Mahon, R. and Pullin, R. (2008), 'Interactive governance and governability: An introduction', *Journal of Transdisciplinary Environmental Studies*, 7(1), 1–11.

Ladkin, A. and Bertramini, A. (2002), 'Collaborative tourism planning: A case study of Cusco, Peru', *Current Issues in Tourism*, 5(2), 71–93.

Lea, J. (1988), *Tourism and Development in the Third World*, London: Routledge.

Lovelock, B. (2001), 'Inter-organisational relations in the protected area – tourism policy domain: The influence of macro-economic policy', *Current Issues in Tourism*, 4(2–4), 253–74.

Meyer, D. (2007), 'Pro-poor tourism: From leakages to linkages. A conceptual framework for creating linkages between the accommodation sector and "poor" neighbouring communities', *Current Issues in Tourism*, 10(6), 558–83.

Mosedale, J. (2011), *Political Economy of Tourism: A Critical Perspective*, Abingdon: Routledge.

Mowforth, M. and Munt, I. (2009), *Tourism and Sustainability: Development, Globalisation and New Tourism in the Third World*, 3rd edn, Abingdon: Routledge.

Pansiri, J. (2013), 'Collaboration and partnership in tourism: The experience of Botswana', *Tourism Planning and Development*, 10(1), 64–84.

Pastras, P. and Bramwell, B. (2013), 'A strategic-relational approach to tourism policy', *Annals of Tourism Research*, 43, 390–414.

Pechlaner, H. and Tschurtschenthaler, P. (2003), 'Tourism policy, tourism organisations and change management in alpine regions and destinations: A European perspective', *Current Issues in Tourism*, 6(6), 508–39.

Pechlaner, H., Raich, F. and Fischer, E. (2009), 'The role of tourism organizations in location management: The case of beer tourism in Bavaria', *Tourism Review*, 64(2), 28–40.

Pechlaner, H., Raich, F. and Kofink, L. (2011), 'Elements of corporate governance in tourism organizations', *Tourismos: An International Multidisciplinary Journal of Tourism*, 6(3), 57–76.

Pechlaner, H., Herntrei, M., Pichler, S. and Volgger, M. (2012), 'From destination management towards governance of regional innovation systems: The case of South Tyrol, Italy', *Tourism Review*, 67(2), 22–33.

Pechlaner, H., Kozak, M. and Volgger, M. (2014), 'Destination leadership: A new paradigm for tourist destinations?', *Tourism Review*, 69(1), 1–9.

Peters, B.G. and Pierre, J. (2016), *Comparative Governance: Rediscovering the Functional Dimension of Governing*, Cambridge: Cambridge University Press.

Pierre, J. (2000), *Debating Governance: Authority, Steering and Democracy*, Oxford: Oxford University Press.

Pierre, J. and Peters, G.B. (2000), *Governance, Politics, and the State*, New York: St Martin's Press.

Pierre, J. and Peters, B.G. (2005), *Governing Complex Societies: Trajectories and Scenarios*, Houndmills: Palgrave Macmillan.

Pleumarom, A. (1994), 'The political economy of tourism', *Ecologist*, 24(4), 142–9.

Rhodes, R. (1996), 'The new governance: Governing without government', *Political Studies*, 44(4), 652–67.

Rhodes, R. (2007), 'Understanding governance: Ten years on', *Organization Studies*, 28(8), 1243–64.

Ritchie, J.R.B. and Crouch, G. (2003), *The Competitive Destination: A Sustainable Tourism Perspective*, Wallingford: CABI.

Rogerson, C. (2014), 'Strengthening tourism-poverty linkages', in A. Lew, C.M. Hall and A. Williams (eds) *The Wiley Blackwell Companion to Tourism*, Oxford: Wiley Blackwell, pp. 600–10.

Ruhanen, L. (2013), 'Local government: Facilitator or inhibitor of sustainable tourism development?', *Journal of Sustainable Tourism*, 21(1), 80–98.

Scheyvens, R. (2007), 'Exploring the tourism-poverty nexus', *Current Issues in Tourism*, 10(2–3), 231–54.

Scheyvens, R. (2011), *Tourism and Poverty*, Abingdon: Routledge.

Schilcher, D. (2007), 'Growth versus equity: The continuum of pro-poor tourism and neoliberal governance', *Current Issues in Tourism*, **10**(2), 166–93.

Scott, N., Baggio, R. and Cooper, C. (2008), *Network Analysis and Tourism: From Theory to Practice*, Clevedon: Channel View Publications.

Sharpley, R. (2009), *Tourism Development and the Environment: Beyond Sustainability*, London: Earthscan.

Sharpley, R. and Telfer, D. (eds) (2002), *Tourism and Development: Concepts and Issues*, Clevedon: Channel View Publications.

Sharpley, R. and Telfer, D. (eds) (2015), *Tourism and Development: Concepts and Issues*, 2nd edn, Bristol: Channel View Publications.

Shone, M. and Memon, P. (2008), 'Tourism, public policy and regional development: A turn from neoliberalism to the new regionalism', *Local Economy*, **23**(4), 290–304.

Sinclair, M.T. and Tsegaye, A. (1990), 'International tourism and export instability', *Journal of Development Studies*, **26**(3), 487–504.

Slocum, S. and Backman, K. (2011), 'Understanding government capacity in tourism development as a poverty alleviation tool: A case study of Tanzanian policy-makers', *Tourism Planning and Development*, **8**(3), 281–96.

Smith, M., MacLeod, N. and Robertson, M.H. (2010), *Key Concepts in Tourist Studies*, London: SAGE.

Sofield, T. and Li, S. (2011), 'Tourism governance and sustainable national development in China: A macro-level synthesis', *Journal of Sustainable Tourism*, **19**(4–5), 501–34.

Spenceley, A. and Meyer, D. (2012), 'Tourism and poverty reduction: Theory and practice in less economically developed countries', *Journal of Sustainable Tourism*, **20**(3), 297–317.

Stoker, G. (1998), 'Governance as theory: Five propositions', *International Social Science Journal*, **155**, 17–28.

Telfer, D. and Sharpley, R. (2016), *Tourism and Development in the Developing World*, 2nd edn, Abingdon: Routledge.

Torfing, J., Peters, B., Pierre, J. and Sorensen, E. (2012), *Interactive Governance: Advancing the Paradigm*, Oxford: Oxford University Press.

Tosun, C. (2000), 'Limits to community participation in the tourism development process in developing countries', *Tourism Management*, **21**(6), 613–33.

Turner, L. (1976), 'The international division of leisure tourism and the Third World', *Annals of Tourism Research*, **4**(1), 12–24.

UN (1992), United Nations Sustainable Development, Agenda 21. Accessed on 28 May 2019 at https://sustainabledevelopment.un.org/content/documents/Agenda21.pdf

Zapata, M. and Hall, C.M. (2012), 'Public-private collaboration in the tourism sector: Balancing legitimacy and effectiveness in local tourism partnerships. The Spanish case', *Journal of Policy Research in Tourism, Leisure and Events*, **4**(1), 61–83.

4 NGOs, tourism and development

Helene Balslev Clausen

Introduction

Over recent decades, non-governmental organizations (NGOs) have taken a prominent role in promoting tourism to generate wider development. More specifically, NGOs have increasingly been seen to integrate tourism into policies and processes relating to the strengthening of communities and their livelihoods as an alternative path to enhance sustainable development. It is not surprising, therefore, that significant debate has surrounded the role, activities and influence of NGOs in tourism-related development. The intention of this chapter is to reflect critically on NGOs operating at the intersection between tourism and development to achieve political, socio-cultural or economic ends and, in particular, to propose avenues for further research so that their role in creating more responsible futures through tourism is better understood.

NGOs may be defined essentially as non-state actors possessing the main characteristics of being private in form though public in nature, and of adopting a non-profit orientation in its objectives and activities (Salamon & Anheier 1996, 1998). Collectively, they are generally understood to be autonomous, relatively permanent or institutionalized (but not always voluntary) intermediary organizations, staffed by professionals or the educated elite (Bebbington & Hickey 2006). Their foundations and purpose can be conceptualized as located within the development as opposed to a purely business and market paradigm; nevertheless, they are often the manifestation of private initiatives. While some have been established to serve members, most function as intermediaries or brokers between resource providers and those in populations whose ill-being or disadvantage justifies the organizations' existence and provides the NGOs with legitimacy. In addition, NGOs are typically thought of as somewhat homogenous; that is, they are generally considered to be similar in their roles and activities. However, their participation in development has increasingly come to constitute a more heterogeneous collection of actors and alliances. At the same time, whilst they continue to largely limit their interaction with traditional aid actors, NGOs have increasingly come to represent an important part of the tourism industry (Simpson 2008; Wearing & Wearing 2006) but appear to have moved – consciously or unconsciously – towards a pro-market and technology-oriented agenda. However, this chapter argues that NGOs not only continue to be relevant in the tourism and development arena, but also constitute a viable alternative to create transformations in communities. In the following sections, several approaches are summarized and examined in the context of tourism and development.

The growth of the NGO sector and tourism

Since the 1950s, NGOs have become an important and vocal platform for the involvement of civil society in public affairs in general; moreover, they have increasingly come to play a pivotal role in the formulation as well as the implementation of development policies in particular, thereby becoming key actors in the political economy of development (Bebbington et al. 2008). This expanding influence of NGOs is similarly traceable through their specific history of engagement with the United Nations (UN). Indeed, in 1997, in response to their growing influence, the UN Security Council held its first meeting with NGOs and, having been represented at such important UN conferences as the 1992 Earth Summit, NGOs became incorporated in the UN system (Sharpley & Telfer 2015), thus becoming increasingly integrated into global decision-making processes.

Equally, tourism as a specific socio-economic activity was recognized at the 1992 Earth Summit (the UN Conference on Environment and Development in Rio de Janeiro) as a possible contribution to community development (United Nations 1992). This theme was taken up and expanded upon by a variety of organizations, including the UN Development Program (Mowforth & Munt 1998; Sharpley & Telfer 2002). Since then, a multiplicity of new actors, including tourism companies, diaspora groups, philanthropic foundations and celebrities, have entered the development field as legitimate development actors who configure and shape the ideas for and financing of development. These new actors are involved in what used to be such typical 'development cooperation issues' as poverty, water, conservation of biodiversity, health care or education and, as a consequence, traditional actors in the field of international development have been losing their monopoly. More specifically, sources of development finance from 'outside' the traditional development agencies have been increasingly shaping the funding and agenda of development and, consequently, NGOs have been obliged to position themselves in alternative ways by turning to donations, contract work and fees for services as sources of funding. This of course raises important questions about the role of NGOs' alliances and networks – where boundaries between public and private realms are blurred – as well as how and by whom development is pursued and practised.

The acronym NGO is applied to many forms of organization. These range from small NGOs working to enhance the livelihood conditions of the marginalized in the Western hemisphere, large Northern-based charities – primarily focused on the global South, working on advocacy, education and raising awareness in the Western hemisphere about marginalized people and their poor livelihood conditions in the South – to South-based local organizations typically working to meet the aim of improving the quality of life in their communities. Clearly, the highly contested and dichotomous idea of the North–South divide masks socio-political and cultural diversity and conflicting economic and environmental interests amongst all nations and societies. It is, however, beyond the scope of this chapter to enter into this fundamental debate, which is elaborated on in the theoretical framework *Epistemologies of the South* proposed by Santos (2014) as a means of recognizing other, different perspectives on understanding development, and where a variety of non-Western views about our existence are proposed (discussed further in Escobar 2011, 2014, 2016).

However, the point is that NGOs must collaborate with a range of different actors, from national governments to local committees and associations, in the growing belief that they may offer alternative models of development and play a key role in processes of development and democratization. NGOs are a key part of civil society, sometimes to the extent that they are actually conflated *with* civil society, a move that appeals to tourists since it permits them to fund or participate in the activities of NGOs. For example, they may act as volunteers (see, amongst others, Butcher & Smith 2010; Wearing 2001) or participate as development tourists (Baptista 2011; Spencer 2018) and then claim to be supporting civil society.

Generally, then, some argue that the neoliberal economic agenda in the global South and the commencement of the poverty agenda have thus begun to shift the funding of development in ways that strengthen some roles and create new dilemmas for NGOs (Butcher & Smith 2010; Scheyvens 2015). A myriad of examples can be found of tourism development projects that have been poorly designed because no one thought about, or knew how to communicate with, those most immediately affected – the local community. As a result, most projects now insist – at least in their terms of reference – upon consultation with the local communities in which the NGO operates. Moreover, several socio-political issues are regarded as sensitive and the NGO world itself is not free from issues of corruption (the recent scandal surrounding aid workers being allegedly involved in sexual exploitation being a notable example – see Dearden 2018), whilst problems of legitimacy and downward accountability are becoming more evident (Butcher 2006; Antlöv et al. 2006). Nevertheless, research has established that the multifaceted approaches to inform public sentiment with regards to the role and activities of NGOs also contribute to processes of conservation and empowerment of local communities (among others, Higgins-Desboilles 2003; Strauss 2015).

NGOs and Sustainable Development Goals

It is widely acknowledged that the inclusion of the NGO sector, as well as the diversity of approaches by which it is characterized, in the processes and management of tourism initiatives can bring about more sustainable and prolonged benefits to communities (Brockington & Scholfield 2010; Jamal & Getz 1995; Murphy 1998; Strauss 2015). Moreover, acceptance of the role of NGOs in tourism-related development projects rests on the notion that they seek to empower individuals and communities to take responsibility for their own (sustainable) development in ways that will make future funding unnecessary (Mowforth & Munt 2008). In other words, the premise is that sustainable development processes must constitute a form of 'help for self-help' that will transform aid recipients into becoming self-reliant and self-activating.

Despite being applied to innumerable processes and objectives, and also being the focus of continuing debate (Telfer & Sharpley 2016), the concept of sustainable (tourism) development can still be considered relevant, not least because of the implementation of the 17 Sustainable Development Goals (2015–30) that succeeded the Millennium Development Goals programme (UN, n.d.). Amongst other things, the goals seek to end poverty, fight inequality and injustice and tackle climate change by 2030. To date, they have been adopted by more than 100 governments, multilateral institutions and international organizations, but achieving them remains a complex task.

In response, and irrespective of whether the focus is on the global North or South, governments, the private sector and NGOs are all reframing their actions towards empowering communities to become change agents; that is, to become leaders and stewards of their own future wellbeing. Of particular relevance to this chapter, NGOs do not perceive tourism in particular to be just an industry; instead, they promote and engage with tourism to affect new and positive attitudes, values and actions in the tourist and host community (Spencer 2010). The commitment to sustainability is derived from methods of participatory development that helped place 'local knowledge' and 'local solutions' on the agenda (Mtapuri & Giampiccoli 2016; Peredo & Wurzelmann 2015; Zahra & McGehee 2013). Although participatory development was once seen as a radical critique of aid practice, it has since become a fundamental element of NGOs' development policies and strategies (Butcher 2007; Cooke & Kothari 2001; Cornwall & Brock 2005), where social and economic problems are addressed by empowering local actors to make 'responsible' choices. For this reason, tourism is often promoted as a tool to improve wellbeing, create better livelihood opportunities and underpin development. More specifically, the emphasis of the Sustainable Development Goals on specific elements and targets of development enables NGOs to embrace tourism, for instance, by including volunteer programmes in their work.

The main challenge, however, is that NGOs' sustainable tourism projects often have a limited lifespan or, because of a lack of funding, are obliged to close down (Butcher 2006). In either case, the outcome can be the disempowerment of the community because NGOs play an essential bridging role between different important stakeholders. Hence, although the presence of NGOs in tourism development projects is assumed – indeed, almost required – to be transitory, it is recognized that instead of implementing projects themselves, NGOs should empower local structures through facilitating 'local actors' with a permanent presence to take on the implementation role. Nevertheless, serious doubts remain as to how far NGOs in the North are able to address the structural societal challenges in their host countries. In addition, serious questions are raised about the ability of NGOs in the South to fulfil their role because, as well as facing constraints that arise from funding decisions and the ever more restrictive conditions linked to such decisions, they are often obliged to operate in sensitive political-economic environments.

As a consequence, some NGOs, for example, Tourism Concern (Barnett 2008) and the Center for Responsible Travel (see www.responsibletravel.org), have adopted an alternative approach. Recognizing that focusing on development education may never bring about significant changes in the global dynamics of tourism, particularly in the face of increased liberalization and such international trade agreements as the General Agreement on Trade in Services (Barnett 2008), they are becoming advocacy organizations. In addition, a significant number of NGOs now also dedicate resources to lobbying power brokers in industry and government, both nationally and internationally, through public campaigns, research and publications on different media platforms. At the same time, they are increasingly utilizing discursive and experiential strategies in trying to foster awareness of development issues and global responsibility. Specifically, they are seeking to address global injustice through raising public awareness and generating action at the local level in the global North to lobby governments and to promote global action. They attempt to do so by tapping into cosmopolitan moral relationships of mutual respect between individuals (Spencer 2010).

Thus, overall, international NGOs have been building up knowledge and experience in setting up and operating tourism initiatives designed to deliver benefits to communities. For example, the Ibn Albaytar Organization (in Morocco), Oxfam and the International Alliance of Indigenous Peoples have all embarked on capacity-building support and community-development initiatives involving tourism, and have actually taken equity and invested in research, advocacy and campaigning.

NGOs crafting national policies

Ashley and Jones (2001) and Strauss (2015) suggest that NGOs operating in a community setting typically play a key role as facilitators in both community development and partnership building, where they can transform a destructive conflict among stakeholders into a constructive dialogue through stakeholder empowerment, especially community members and their representatives. Nevertheless, Clausen and Gyimóthy (2015) stress that, although external entities, including NGOs, can assume the role of facilitators, the role of government remains essential during a sustainable tourism development initiative.

Arguably, because they are more cognizant of what is happening 'on the ground', NGOs can help governments craft more appropriate policies and regulations than would otherwise have been the case. More specifically, as Strauss (2015) clearly demonstrates, they can play a vital role in building civil accountability, undertaking consultancy and providing full spectrum alliances (increased networking, resource sharing and deep engagement). At the same time, and depending on their structure and public sensitivity, NGOs can take on responsibilities and create additional areas of responsibilities to benefit local society.

Economic growth and the expansion of tourism, in particular in the global South, have led NGOs to use local, bottom-up approaches. These participatory approaches are widely recognized as the preferred way to engage local communities in tourism projects. Often, tourism NGOs fill in public-sector gaps that result from a lack of governmental regulations and programmes, or a lack of government resources, to meet their public responsibilities (among others, Clausen 2012; Mitchell & Reid 2001; Timothy 2002). For example, the Moroccan NGO, Ibn Albaytar Organization, has turned the classical approach to initiate environmental sustainable (tourism) projects upside down by converting the ecological problem into an economic opportunity, that is, tourism. The NGO set out to protect a species long considered able to provide an effective 'green curtain' against the desert, thus combating desertification. However, with a lack of support and resources from the government, they turned to the International Development Research Centre in Canada to organize the marginalized, local Berber women into fair-trade cooperatives and to produce argan products for sale to tourists in cooperatives and to more distant consumers, promoting the argan products as 'doing good development'. The NGO inscribes the cooperatives into the development discourse as it also requires women working in the cooperative to attend reading and writing classes, as most are illiterate. As a consequence, the activities of the Ibn Albaytar Organization have been central to improving the local actors' livelihood conditions, and have been instrumental in the crafting of the recent Moroccan national development policy and tourism strategy. This example thus demonstrates that NGOs can bring in novel ways to rethink sustainable regional development and attract more distant consumers (Clausen forthcoming).

Clearly, where government lacks presence or resources, NGOs' knowledge of and interest in the locality gives them considerable advantages. They are also popular in government circles and local communities because they are considered administratively flexible, able to access the poor through their work at the grassroots level, innovative in problem solving, adaptable to the local context and more cost-effective than corresponding state partners. Moreover, their grassroots representation brings legitimacy and community mobilization to programmes and projects.

The following section explores how NGOs work in different types of tourism, for example, eco-tourism (Jamal et al. 2007; Romero-Brito et al. 2016), poverty/pro-poor tourism (PPT) (Hall 2007; Scheyvens 2011, 2015), volunteer tourism (Wearing 2001; Butcher & Smith 2010; Wearing 2010) and humanitarian tourism (Mostafanezhad 2013; Richey & Ponte 2014). These are some of the most significant and most heavily contested types of tourism in which NGOs participate, along with justice tourism and responsible tourism, although such involvement breeds a complex myriad of cultural, societal, political, economic and environmental challenges.

NGOs and ecotourism

Successful ecotourism projects are amongst the most common in which NGOs are assuming an important role through formal and informal political lobbying, buying or covenanting land for conservation and forming partnerships to undertake specific conservation and ecotourism projects (Jamal et al. 2007; van Wijk et al. 2015). At the same time and more generally, the increasingly important environmental role of NGOs has been witnessed at the Bali Climate Summit in 2007 and the UN Climate Conference in Copenhagen in 2009. In environmental struggles, these NGOs are factors to be reckoned with by government in decision making. As Gould (2017) notes, for instance, Belize has a highly developed ecotourism sector, but the threat of oil development on the largest barrier reef resulted in the significant political mobilization of both national and international NGOs. As a consequence, the Belize government had to withdraw permission to several extractive oil industries in July 2018. Gould also suggests that the case of Belize shows that environmental NGOs can serve as a political barrier against environmentally destructive development options, even though economic conditions shift in favour of less sustainable development projects.

Romero-Brito et al.'s (2016) study of 240 global cases where NGOs use ecotourism with a conservation aim suggests that the proportion of successful ecotourism projects is higher when both international and local NGOs are involved. Whereas international NGOs can generally mobilize more funds, offer broader expertise and wield greater political power, local NGOs generally have greater knowledge of local circumstances and enjoy better connections and rapport with local communities and other stakeholders (Stronza & Pegas 2008; Wearing & McDonald 2002). Other authors have suggested that NGOs in the global North prefer to operate ecotourism enterprises themselves, or form partnerships with government agencies in tourism policy and management for protected areas (Spencer 2010). By contrast, in the global South, NGO ecotourism projects commonly combine nature conservation with poverty alleviation, often in challenging political circumstances. Tactics include the establishment of community-based ecotourism projects and campaigns to create and promote social pressure to end unsustainable development (Romero-Brito et al. 2016).

In the academic literature, an element often overlooked is the ethical basis of NGO behaviour in host communities. When the former acts as an intermediary between tourists and local residents, the agreement on benefit sharing, with the promise of implementing some market-based ecotourism community-development programmes for the locals, may often be exploitative and unethical. By contrast, there is interesting research to be carried out on projects at destinations prioritizing just, responsible and indigenous tourism (Higgins-Desboilles 2003; Jamal & Camargo 2014).

NGOs and volunteers/volunteer tourism

Within the context of the so-called 'tourism–development dilemma' (Telfer & Sharpley 2016), volunteer tourism shows that tourism's potential to bring about the equal distribution of benefits, or stimulate social and economic development, often fails to materialize, and may entail significant costs to local communities. Indeed, at the core of the tourism–development dilemma is how far tourism can contribute to most acute development issues at a local level (Sharpley & Telfer 2015).

Significant efforts have been made to understand the complexities of volunteer tourism and, not surprisingly, perceptions of its impacts range from it being potentially beneficial (Higgins-Desboilles 2003; Wearing & Wearing 2006; Zahra & McGehee 2013) to it being the main cause of negative impacts and the disempowerment of the recipients of volunteers' work, even to the extent of destroying decades of development work (Mowforth & Munt 2008). Nevertheless, participation in volunteer tourism has steadily increased over the last two decades, not least reflecting the growing demand, particularly among young adults searching for their individual identity through volunteer experiences (Butcher & Smith 2010; Sin 2009; Wearing & McGehee 2013). Volunteer tourism tries to answer the demand of a modern tourist; that is, to be doing 'meaningful work' in different environments and experience deeper immersion with local people when working side by side with them on conservation, humanitarian or community projects (Spencer 2008). Indeed, volunteer tourism is perceived by some as a responsible form of tourism, closely linked to altruistic and benign volunteer work and far from exploitative forms of mass tourism (Raymond & Hall 2008). In this vein, a study by Zahra and McGehee (2013) suggests that volunteer tourism may even foster different forms of community capital in the host community, ranging from social and personal to financial and built capital.

Nevertheless, the concept of volunteer tourism has attracted significant criticism, particularly with regards to the extent volunteer tourists have either altruistic or ego-centric motives. Indeed, some consider volunteer tourism to be an oxymoron (see Sharpley 2017), a tourist experience that contrasts directly with more established international volunteering programmes.

Volunteer NGOs often work on assisting communities in the global South and remote regions by carrying out or assisting in such tourism projects as environmental education, fostering attitudes and behaviour conducive to maintaining natural and social environments and empowering host communities (Wearing & McDonald 2002). As pointed out by Palacios (2010), NGOs should consider providing opportunities for the volunteer tourist to contribute to a just and equitable space, avoiding neocolonialism. Relying on volunteers as frontline workers is presented as sustainable because they are 'always there' and because their willingness to volunteer reflects their commitment to 'do good'. However, it is difficult for many NGOs to rely on volunteer tourists, as they are often young and non-skilled, and tend to stay for short periods, thus contributing to projects' lack of sustainability. A similarly harsh critique suggests that volunteer tourism reflects, sustains and confirms recurring geopolitical discourses of North–South relations that naturalize political, economic and social inequality (Mostafanezhad 2013; Richey & Ponte 2014). Moreover, some even argue that the very foundation of volunteer tourism exists in a commodified environment and serves as a stronghold for the privileged (Raymond & Hall 2008). In this regard, Simpson (2004) highlighted the dangers of overreliance on volunteer tourism as a prescription for international development, mainly because inherent issues of power in relations between volunteers and the recipients of 'aid' could jeopardize decades of work by experienced NGOs and empowered communities.

In recent years, then, there has been growing public and academic disquiet about whether volunteering is ethical (Mowforth & Munt 2003; Palacios 2010). If we are to understand the limits to the NGOs' aim to foster structural transformations to alleviate poverty and create better livelihood conditions for the marginalized and the poor, there is a need to engage critically with the discourses and practices underlying NGOs' relationships with volunteers and address the ethical dimensions at a much deeper analytical level than has hitherto occurred.

NGOs, pro-poor, fair-trade and celebrity tourism

Intimately related to the above discussion is the issue of NGOs integrating volunteers into tourism projects related to PPT, a practice queried by Hall (2007) and Scheyvens (2007), who query the identity of the beneficiaries. NGOs face significant constraints and contradictions in their ability to alleviate poverty because of their weak roots in society, the pressures they face to be non-political and to be upwardly accountable to funding organizations (rather than 'downward' to beneficiaries) and their focus on short-term projects rather than long-term structural change. Certainly, many NGOs work directly with poor communities, assisting them to develop alternative livelihood strategies (Scheyvens 2015). In particular, fair-trade tourism, which has emerged from some of the fundamental tenets of ecotourism and PPT, reveals an alternative path proposed by NGOs to create sustainable practices. Fair trade ensures, or seeks to ensure, the benefits from tourism for the local community through mutually beneficial and equitable partnerships between national and international tourism stakeholders (Tourism Concern 2017). More specifically, fair-trade tourism aims at fair wages and working conditions, the fair distribution of benefits and ethical business practices for cultures, human rights and the environment (Boluk 2011). However, this represents a fruitful area of further research, for there have been few attempts to ascertain whether or not fair trade actually addresses poverty, and if tourism has benefitted the marginalized.

NGOs offer positions to volunteers, providing them with the opportunity to 'do good development' while experiencing other parts of the world. A recent trend is for NGOs to systematically engage celebrities to become an essential component for branding their organizations in a competitive field (Mostafanezhad 2013; Richey & Ponte 2014), reflecting a rising general interest in more 'sophisticated' and calibrated marketing techniques to attract volunteers. Several studies demonstrate that celebrities can not only attract attention, but also generate some surplus value or benefit from the fact of being well known. Capitalizing on such celebrities as George Clooney and Bono, and denoting them as spokespeople, there is thus a focus on advocacy, which includes raising awareness and meeting with policy-makers in the North. Conversely, Madonna, Sean Penn, Oprah Winfrey and Matt Damon's organizations emphasize grant making, regranting funds and implementing programmes in the global South (Mostafanezhad 2013; Richey & Ponte 2014). These new alliances between NGOs and spatially distant tourists/consumers to 'do good development' are scarcely researched and tap into the debate about how market logics shape and influence tourism development projects.

Challenges facing NGOs

Many argue that NGOs in the global North and South have suffered from an increasing emphasis on cost recovery, needing to charge for services, and from the professionalization of staff relationships and increasing competition. Such transformations, which may be collectively described as the 'pro-market diversification' of NGO relations, may ultimately erode the ability of NGOs to foster social and political change. However, there are also potentially zero benefits and negative effects in misguided and ill-judged collaboration among stakeholders, who may have contradictory agendas, and disputes among them are not uncommon (Hall 1999; Liburd 2004).

More specifically, NGOs participating in tourism initiatives have often been criticized for their lack of transparency, lack of commitment and their excessive focus on self-promotion. Additional critiques suggest they focus primarily on the symptoms rather than the root causes of development problems. Rather than promoting radical, deep-rooted changes, they are often accused of preserving the status quo by setting up systems of patronage that undermine and depoliticize social movements and other grassroots organizations (see, among others, Brennan & Allen 2001; Gardner & Lewis 1996). In other words, rather than empowering 'local structures', in practice most function as professional project implementers. These same NGOs can also present problems within a community, altering the existing power balance and triggering a range of other factors that challenge the economic, environmental and socio-cultural sustainability of the community (Clausen 2012; Mowforth & Munt 2008; Swarbrooke 1999). Yet, if NGOs' abilities to act politically or engage in institutional change are inherently constrained, it makes sense to focus on specific problems, where small, positive steps may be possible, even if the ensuing reforms are likely to be incremental rather than extensive. Put differently, NGOs might be encouraged to apply 'best fit' approaches to specific countries and institutions, rather than trying to import 'best practices' which may not apply to the local context.

Another challenge NGOs have to address is the risk of resources and opportunities being misused or hijacked by powerful members of the community, and the nature of the state is absolutely central to the role they can play in national development. It is governments that give NGOs the space and autonomy to organize, network and campaign. Of course, it is difficult to generalize about state–NGO relations, as local political networks are always diverse, but most NGOs working in tourism are constrained by capitalist market conditions if they are to support local initiatives or to create benefits to the communities in which they operate. However, this is rarely in collaboration with the state; rather, NGOs' resources may exceed those of local authorities and create parallel structures to the government (Clausen 2012).

Many citizens of the USA and Canada living in villages in Mexico, for example, have initiated several non-profit NGOs. These expatriates often run their own tourism business and, in addition, set up an NGO to solve social issues in their villages. Examples of these include *Amigos de Educacion* (an NGO that provides scholarships and school materials for poor and marginal families) and *Comadres* (which provides food baskets to marginalized single mothers). These NGOs alleviate poverty and provide access to education which, in principle, are services that local authorities should provide. Such expatriate communities or transnational second homeowners are not only consumers, but also producers of innovative social development projects. The NGO projects they instigate to solve social issues have far more applicants among the Mexicans than the government's social services, for Mexicans know the authorities lack resources. As a consequence, NGOs alter local governmental structures and create parallel structures, which might be problematic as it will be the NGOs which decide who is to be categorized as poor and marginalized (Clausen 2012, forthcoming).

Northern-based NGOs also face challenges over the extent and nature of their Southern links, which are meant to provide practical experience and technical expertise in their field of operation. However, while local civil society organizations have indeed become increasingly capable of owning processes of change, the working methods, distribution of tasks and the balance of power between the North and South have essentially remained unchanged (Mowforth & Munt 2008). Despite the prevailing rhetoric, Northern NGOs continue to make key decisions in a top-down manner. However, the example from Morocco, introduced earlier in this chapter, reveals how knowledge providers are Southern-based. The issue here is the lack of knowledge within the academic literature about the capacities of these NGOs.

Despite the increasing presence and importance of Southern-based NGOs in tourism, their exact impact is difficult to measure as there currently are no objective criteria or methods for measuring their success or failure. Millions of dollars are going into host communities all over the world through donations and grants (as well as services rendered), much of which is untraceable and unrecorded by any consistent method. As this is so little studied, urgent research needs to be undertaken on the impacts of tourism NGOs in the communities in which they work (Kennedy & Dornan 2009). Moreover, it has been argued that Northern NGOs are becoming more like agencies than non-governmental partners and, indeed, some within these organizations express similar sentiments (Banks et al. 2015), as also do some involved in large Southern NGOs. In this funding climate, NGOs have struggled to adapt, and many spend considerable time chasing money that is not very useful to them, especially if they lack the necessary financial skills to make the most of the situation and to competently and successfully pursue an alternative agenda.

Tourism NGOs as catalyst for alternative development?

NGOs have increasingly collectively become a transnational community, one which overlaps with other transnational networks and institutions (Townsend 1999). These linkages and networks spread new forms of development discourse and modes of governance as well as resources throughout the global South, and some Southern NGOs have begun to gain their own footholds in the North, with outposts in Brussels, Washington and elsewhere (including, for example, the Grameen Foundation and Breadline Africa). Consequently, transnational NGO networks are not necessarily as characterized by uneven North–South relations as might be assumed. Rather, as the more horizontal experiences of Slum Dwellers International (a network of community-based organizations of the urban poor in 33 countries in Africa, Asia and Latin America) show, the spatial networking of development has increased opportunities for the voices of socially excluded groups to be heard. Moreover, some NGOs are working with such groups to increase the representation of these voices.

Such change generated by tourism is multifaceted. On the one hand, NGOs initiating sustainable tourism projects possess the potential to bring benefits to communities, acting as a catalyst or a social agent of change (Mowforth & Munt 2008). On the other hand, the same NGOs can also present problems within a community, triggering an array of economic, environmental and socio-cultural factors. Nonetheless, it remains essential to understand NGOs – as well as states, markets and civil societies – in the context of these transnational relations and flows. NGOs are present in, are part of, even when trying to be apart from, the political economy – and the workings of this political economy are transnational in nature and global in reach. If NGOs are to regain a sense of being and offering alternatives, it is critical that they reconsider themselves in relation to struggles over development as an underlying and increasingly globalized form of social change – and not simply in relation to the state or market (Banks et al. 2015). The growing capacity of a strong Southern civil society has emerged and has become increasingly capable of owning processes of change, working methods and the distribution of tasks. Recent research suggests that NGOs might not have the capacity to be change makers or social agents of change, in the sense of transforming root causes and meeting the structural societal challenges of inequality and poverty. Nevertheless, they may still be considered to be of utmost importance in bringing innovative transformation and alternative modes of exchange and development within sustainable tourism.

NGOs and tourism creating responsible futures?

NGOs have the creative ability to bring in ways of arranging micro-finance for project planning in tourism development and service delivery as an alternative means of intervening in social change and development. The key issue for the future, however, is whether or not – and how – NGOs will adapt to global changes currently under way. If they are to be efficient, they have constantly to link with local and global agendas, and they will increasingly be forced to learn from and adapt to changing demands and opportunities. Returning briefly to Santos (2014) and Escobar (2016), it is argued that avenues for future research must focus on NGOs at the intersection of the global South and North if frameworks for social change are to emerge. Interestingly, Kennedy and Dornan (2009) demonstrate that there are thousands of NGOs in the world, and that the most successful partnerships seem to be those between NGOs based in the Western Hemisphere and local Southern-based NGOs. These partnerships are a key element to alternative forms of tourism development. Additionally, when considering the liaison and communication between and within the different actors involved in tourism projects, NGOs always hold an essential position in facilitating collaboration among the multiple social actors involved in tourism projects. Thus, these environments need to be in the fore to detect 'best practice' in order to achieve benefits for communities associated with tourism (Hall 1999; Jamal & Getz 1995). Gaining insights from development studies, NGOs using tourism as a tool for improving human wellbeing and livelihood conditions for marginalized people, aligned with the Sustainable Development Goals, could consider dedicating more resources to advocacy, increasing staff time and establishing departments devoted to research and lobbying (Jepson 2005). Tourism NGOs could gain further importance and, especially at present, when tourism is considered an essential tool to alleviate poverty, create growth and pave the way for education and democracy as an integrated part of the strategies of several global organizations, for example, the Inter-American Development Bank and Oxfam. Thus, further research is needed into the fundamental components of best practice to determine how tourism NGOs can generate most benefits to the community.

Possible avenues for future research

As is evident from the literature on NGOs, tourism and development, the role of tourism as a tool for sustainable development is controversial. In this section, three new agendas are suggested, which may clarify some of the problems. First, in order to expand the horizons of the scholarly literature on NGOs, tourism and development, it is necessary to move beyond the traditional traits of the North–South divide. Instead, future research needs to examine South–South-based NGO relations to see how they engage with economic realities and ideological values and, as a consequence, how they might contribute to innovative ideas, stories and development models which are profoundly different from Western models. These, in turn, could yield important insights into responsible, sustainable development, as seen, for example, in the Moroccan case.

The second significant theme for future research is the ethical and political framework within which NGOs position themselves and the implications thereof. This is related to the basic aim of NGOs, where the focus is on how NGOs can continue to succeed in service delivery and, at the same time, engage strongly with the root causes of poverty and inequality. Specifically, research is required into the impact of NGO activities and how these are influenced by the ethical and political framework within which they operate. And finally, a research agenda should cast light on the significant role played by NGOs at the intersection of the state and the market, especially by examining the context in which ideas and what passes for knowledge about sustainable tourism development emerge and are subsequently implemented.

Can NGOs deliver what is expected of them? While it must be recognized that they operate in very different contexts, a gap seems to be emerging between rhetoric and practice, and it is becoming increasingly necessary to ask how their involvement in sustainable tourism projects can be monitored and evaluated, to what extent their behaviour is legitimated and how far they are accountable. However, despite growing interest in evaluation, over the last decade only limited research has been undertaken into the role of NGOs in effecting social change. If this is indeed to occur, focus needs to be redirected to specific histories, differences in assumptions, organizational cultures and patterns of social interaction, none of which are captured in binary categorizations of Northern or Southern NGOs (see, among others, Escobar 2016).

A pivotal societal role of tourism NGOs is to raise important issues, for instance, tourism's relationship to the environment, its impacts on human wellbeing, awareness of the downside of globalization and the need for commitment to participation, human rights and issues of climate change. However, tourism NGOs and, indeed, NGOs more generally have not identified ways of changing systems that perpetuate poverty or in redistributing benefits arising from tourism. Nor have they become transparent or accountable. Nevertheless, it is imperative that NGOs continue to experiment in ways of bringing about social transformation and development, and that their attempts to organize themselves differently and promote alternative approaches to sustainable tourism development are identified, monitored and assessed. Most importantly, perhaps, they need to continually reflect on their role in promoting tourism as a development tool.

References

Antlöv, H., Ibrahim, R. and van Tuijl, P. (2006), 'NGO governance and accountability in Indonesia: Challenges in a newly democratizing country', in L. Jordan and P. van Tuijl (eds) *NGO Accountability: Politics, Principles and Innovation*, London: Earthscan, pp. 147–63.

Ashley, C. and Jones, B. (2001), 'Joint ventures between communities and tourism investors: Experiences in Southern Africa', *Journal of Tourism Research*, 3(5), 407–23.

Banks, N., Hulme, D. and Edwards, M. (2015), 'NGOs, states, and donors revisited: Still too close for comfort?', *World Development*, 66, 707–18.

Baptista, J. (2011), 'The tourists of developmenttourism: Representations "from below"', *Current Issues in Tourism*, 14(7), 651–66.

Barnett, T. (2008), 'Influencing tourism at the grassroots level: The role of NGO Tourism Concern', *Third World Quarterly*, 29(5), 995–1002.

Bebbington, A. and Hickey, S. (2006), 'NGOs and civil society', in D. Clark (ed.) *The Elgar Companion to Development Studies*, Cheltenham, UK and Northampton, MA, USA: Edward Elgar Publishing, pp. 417–22.

Bebbington, A., Hickey, S. and Mitlin, D. (2008), *Can NGOs Make a Difference? The Challenge of Development Alternatives*, London: Zed Books.

Boluk, K. (2011), 'Fair trade tourism South Africa: Consumer virtue or moral selving?', *Journal of Ecotourism*, **10**(3), 235–49.

Brennan, F. and Allen, G. (2001), 'Community-based ecotourism, social exclusion and the changing political economy of KwaZulu-Natal, South Africa', in D. Harrison (ed.) *Tourism and the Less Developed World: Issues and Case Studies*, Wallingford: CABI, pp. 203–21.

Brockington, D. and Scholfield, K. (2010), 'The work of conservation organizations in Sub-Saharan Africa', *Journal of Modern African Studies*, **48**(1), 1–33.

Butcher, J. (2006), 'A response to building a decommodified research paradigm in tourism: The contribution of NGOs in Stephen Wearing, Matthew McDonald and Jess Ponting', *Journal of Sustainable Tourism*, **13**(5), 424–55.

Butcher, J. (2007), *Ecotourism, NGOs and Development: A Critical Analysis*, New York: Routledge.

Butcher, J. and Smith, P. (2010), 'Making a difference: Volunteer tourism and development', *Tourism Recreation Research*, **35**(1), 27–36.

Clausen, H.B. (2012), 'Power and nonprofit organizations: North American charity organizations in a Mexican town in the border region', in H.B. Clausen, N. Bjerre-Poulsen and J. Gustafsson (eds) *Projections of Power*, Abingdon: Routledge, pp. 225–45.

Clausen, H.B. (forthcoming), 'The bargaining power of argan: Social entrepreneurship and sustainable development models – transforming Moroccan rural economies', *Tourism Planning and Development*.

Clausen, H.B. and Gyimóthy, S. (2015), 'Seizing community participation in sustainable development: Pueblos Mágicos of Mexico', *Journal of Cleaner Production*, **111**, 318–26.

Cooke, B. and Kothari, U. (eds) (2001), *Participation: The New Tyranny?*, London: Zed Books.

Cornwall, A. and Brock, K. (2005), 'What do buzzwords do for development policy? A critical look at "participation", "empowerment" and "poverty reduction"', *Third World Quarterly*, **26**(7), 1043–60.

Dearden, L. (2018), 'Aid sector guilty of "complacency verging on complicity" over sexual abuse by staff, MPs find', *Independent*, 31 July. Accessed 4 September 2018 at www.independent.co.uk/news/uk/h ome-news/oxfam-sex-abuse-haiti-aid-sector-charities-complicity-open-secret-report-committee-m ps-a8470401.html

Escobar, A. (2011), *Encountering Development: The Making and Unmaking of the Third World*, Princeton, NJ: Princeton University Press.

Escobar, A. (2014), *Sentipensar con la tierra: Postdesarrollo y diferencia radical*, Medellín: Universidad Autónoma Latinoamericana.

Escobar, A. (2016), 'Sentipensar con la tierra: Las luchas territoriales y la dimensión ontológica de las epistemologías del sur', *Revista de Antropología Iberoamericana*, **11**(1), 11–32.

Gardner, K. and Lewis, D. (1996), *Anthropology, Development and the Post-Modern Challenge*, London: Pluto Press.

Gould, K. (2017), 'Ecotourism under pressure: The political economy of oil extraction and cruise ship tourism threats to sustainable development in Belize', *Environmental Sociology*, **3**(3), 237–47.

Hall, C.M. (1999), 'Rethinking collaboration and partnership: A public policy perspective', *Journal of Sustainable Tourism*, **7**(3), 274–89.

Hall, C.M. (ed.) (2007), *Pro-Poor Tourism: Who Benefits? Perspectives on Tourism and Poverty Reduction*, Clevedon: Channel View Publications.

Higgins-Desbiolles, F. (2003), 'Reconciliation tourism: Tourism healing divided societies', *Tourism Recreation Research*, **28**(3), 35–44.

Jamal, T. and Camargo, B. (2014), 'Sustainable tourism, justice and an ethic of care: Toward the just destination', *Journal of Sustainable Tourism*, **22**(1), 11–30.

Jamal, T. and Getz, D. (1995), 'Collaboration theory and community tourism planning', *Annals of Tourism Research*, **22**(1), 186–204.

Jamal, T., Kreuter, U. and Yanosky, A. (2007), 'Bridging organisations for sustainable development and conservation: Paraguayan case', *International Journal of Tourism Policy*, **1**(2), 93–110.

Jepson, P. (2005), 'Governance and accountability of environmental NGOs', *Environmental Science and Policy*, **8**, 515–24.

Kennedy, K. and Dornan, D. (2009), 'An overview: Tourism non-governmental organizations and poverty reduction in developing countries', *Asia Pacific Journal of Tourism Research*, **14**(2), 183–200.

Liburd, J.J. (2004), 'NGOs in tourism and preservation democratic accountability and sustainability in question', *Tourism Recreation Research*, **29**(2), 105–9.

Mitchell, R. and Reid, D. (2001), 'Community integration: Island tourism in Peru', *Annals of Tourism Research*, **28**(1), 113–39.

Mostafanezhad, M. (2013), 'Getting in touch with your inner Angelina: Celebrity humanitarianism and the cultural politics of gendered generosity in volunteer tourism', *Third World Quarterly*, **34**(3), 485–99.

Mowforth, M. and Munt, I. (1998), *Tourism and Sustainability: New Tourism in the Third World*, London: Routledge.

Mowforth, M. and Munt, I. (2003), *Tourism and Sustainability: Development and New Tourism in the Third World*, 2nd edn, London: Routledge.

Mowforth, M. and Munt, I. (2008), *Tourism and Sustainability: Development, Globalisation and New Tourism in the Third World*, 3rd edn, Abingdon: Routledge.

Mtapuri, O. and Giampiccoli, A. (2016), 'Towards a comprehensive model of community-based tourism development', *South African Geographical Journal*, **98**(1), 154–68.

Murphy, P. (1998), 'Tourism and sustainable development', in W. Theobald (ed.) *Global Tourism*, 2nd edn, Oxford: Butterworth Heinemann, pp. 173–90.

Palacios, C. (2010), 'Volunteer tourism, development and education in a postcolonial world: Conceiving global connections beyond aid', *Journal of Sustainable Tourism*, **18**(7), 861–78.

Peredo, B. and Wurzelmann, S. (2015), 'Indigenous tourism and social entrepreneurship in the Bolivian Amazon: Lessons from San Miguel del Bala', *International Indigenous Policy Journal*, **6**(4). Accessed 23 March 2018 at https://ir.lib.uwo.ca/cgi/viewcontent.cgi?article=1261&context=iipj

Raymond, E.M. and Hall, C.M. (2008), 'The development of cross-cultural (mis)understanding through volunteer tourism', *Journal of Sustainable Tourism*, **16**(5), 530–43.

Richey, L. and Ponte, S. (2014), 'New actors and alliances in development', *Third World Quarterly*, **35**(1), 1–21.

Romero-Brito, T., Buckley, R. and Byrne, J. (2016), 'NGO partnerships in using ecotourism for conservation: Systematic review and meta-analysis', *PLoS ONE*, **11**(11), e0166919. doi:10.1371/journal.pone.0166919

Salamon, L. and Anheier, H. (1996), *The Emerging Nonprofit Sector: An Overview*, Manchester: Manchester University Press.

Salamon, L. and Anheier, H. (1998), 'Social origins of civil society: Explaining the nonprofit sector cross-nationally', *International Journal of Voluntary and Nonprofit Organizations*, **9**(3), 213–248.

Santos, B. (2014), *Epistemologies of the South: Justice against Epistemicide*, Boulder, CO: Paradigm Publishers.

Scheyvens, R. (2007), 'Exploring the tourism–poverty nexus', *Current Issues in Tourism*, **10**(2–3), 231–54.

Scheyvens, R. (2011), *Tourism and Poverty*, New York: Routledge.

Scheyvens, R. (2015), 'Tourism and poverty reduction', in R. Sharpley and D. Telfer (eds) *Tourism and Development: Concepts and Issues*, 2nd edn, Bristol: Channel View Publications, pp. 118–39.

Sharpley, R. (2017), 'Responsible volunteer tourism: Tautology or oxymoron? A comment on Burrai and Hannam', *Journal of Policy Research in Tourism, Leisure and Events*. doi:10.1080/19407963.2017.1362798

Sharpley, R. and Telfer, D. (2002), *Tourism and Development: Concepts and Issues*, Clevedon: Channel View Publications.

Sharpley, R. and Telfer, D. (2015), *Tourism and Development: Concepts and Issues*, 2nd edn, Bristol: Channel View Publications.

Simpson, K. (2004), '"Doing development": The gap year, volunteer-tourists and a popular practice of development', *Journal of International Development*, **16**(5), 681–92.

Simpson, M. (2008), 'Community benefit tourism initiatives: A conceptual oxymoron?', *Tourism Management*, **29**(1), 1–18.

Sin, H.J. (2009), 'Volunteer tourism: Involve me and I will learn?', *Annals of Tourism Research*, **36**(3), 480–501.

Spencer, R. (2008), 'Lessons from Cuba: A volunteer army of ambassadors', in K. Lyons and S. Wearing (eds) *Journeys of Discovery in Volunteer Tourism: International Case Study Perspectives*, Wallingford: CABI, pp. 36–47.

Spencer, R. (2010), *Development Tourism: Lessons from Cuba*, Farnham: Ashgate.

Spencer, R. (2018), 'Development tourism in Cuba: Experiential learning and solidarity in the development tourism encounter', *Tourism Planning and Development*, **15**(3), 277–92.

Strauss, S. (2015), 'Alliances across ideologies: Networking with NGOs in a tourism dispute in northern Bali', *Pacific Journal of Anthropology*, **15**(2), 123–40.

Stronza, A. and Pegas, F. (2008), 'Ecotourism and conservation: Two cases from Brazil and Peru', *Human Dimensions of Wildlife*, **13**(4), 263–79.

Swarbrooke, J. (1999), *Sustainable Tourism Management*, Wallingford: CABI.

Telfer, D. and Sharpley, R. (2016), *Tourism and Development in the Developing World*, 2nd edn, Abingdon: Routledge.

Timothy, D.J. (2002), 'Tourism and community development', in R. Sharpley and D. Telfer (eds) *Tourism and Development: Concepts and Issues*, Clevedon: Channel View Publications, pp. 149–64.

Tourism Concern (2017), *Annual Report and Accounts*. Accessed 2 February 2018 at www.tourismconcern.org.uk/wp-content/uploads/2014/06/Annual-Report-201617-web.pdf

Townsend, J. (1999), 'Are non-governmental organizations working in development of a transnational community?', *Journal of International Development*, **11**(4), 613–25.

UN (n.d.), *Sustainable Development Goals*, United Nations. Accessed 13 June 2018 at www.un.org/sustainabledevelopment/sustainable-development-goals/

van Wijk, J., Lamers, M. and van der Duim, R. (2015), 'Promoting conservation tourism: The case of the African Wildlife Foundation's tourism conservation enterprises in Kenya', in R. van der Duim, M. Lamers and J. van Wijk (eds) *Institutional Arrangements for Conservation, Development and Tourism in Eastern and Southern Africa*, Dordrecht: Springer, pp. 203–18.

Wearing, S. (2001), *Volunteer Tourism: Experiences that Make a Difference*, Wallingford: CABI.

Wearing, S. (2010), 'A response to Jim Butcher and Peter Smith's paper "Making a Difference": Volunteer tourism and development', *Tourism Recreation Research*, **35**(2), 213–15.

Wearing, S. and McDonald, M. (2002), 'The development of community-based tourism: Re-thinking the relationship between tour operators and development agents as intermediaries in rural and isolated area communities', *Journal of Sustainable Tourism*, **10**(3), 191–206.

Wearing, S. and McGehee, N. (2013), 'Volunteer tourism: A review', *Tourism Management*, **38**, 120–30.

Wearing, S. and Wearing, M. (2006), '"Rereading the subjugating tourist" in neoliberalism: Postcolonial otherness and the tourist experience', *Tourism Analysis*, **11**(2), 145–62.

Zahra, A. and McGehee, N. (2013), 'Volunteer tourism: A host community capital perspective', *Annals of Tourism Research*, **42**, 22–45.

5 Travel philanthropy and development

Amy Scarth and Marina Novelli

Introduction

The global North is shifting from compassion for distant suffering towards a growing desire to act across those distances, to alleviate suffering directly (Korf 2007) and to achieve physical and personal encounters with beneficiaries or 'distant others', whilst creating in-lifetime legacies (Silk 2004). As such, it appears that the end of the 'armchair philanthropist' has been reached as, after all, seeing is believing, and travel can connect people from across the globe in a far more accessible manner (Bertini et al. 2014) and facilitate a more direct and interactive way of engaging in philanthropy.

This chapter presents critical research on the relationship between philanthropy, travel and tourism and explores the emerging concept of travel-related philanthropy, most widely referred to both in academic and industry material as 'travellers' philanthropy' or 'travel philanthropy', the latter being used as the preferred term in this chapter. Arguably a multifaceted and ambiguous term, accompanied by a theoretically nascent discourse (Novelli et al. 2015; Novelli 2016), travel philanthropy will be discussed here primarily from an African perspective and contextualization. The ultimate purpose of this chapter is to provide food for thought on the fast-evolving practice of travel philanthropy and, in particular, identifying, justifying and explaining future research needs and directions.

Philanthropy, tourism and development

Over the last two decades, private philanthropy for international development has snowballed, comprising large numbers of relatively smaller donations (Atkinson 2009) and with US citizens being identified as the most active in such practice (Partzsch & Fuchs 2012). Let's say that there is a scale for this with, at one end, the world's wealthiest individuals, such as Bill Gates and Warren Buffett, sharing their private fortunes (Clifford 2017), directly intervening to address African socio-economic development and conservation (Wilson 2016), and, at the other end, a somewhat long tail of private philanthropists and donors of charitable funds determined to address the challenges posed by global inequalities, particularly those affecting the African continent. While, on one hand, Atkinson (2009) argues that public policy should pay more attention to this private willingness to make charitable transfers overseas, on the other hand, the international aid chain is widely critiqued for its weak connections and financial wastage of up to 30 per cent (Pettit & Beresford 2009). At the same time, we are witnessing a growth in travellers who are donating money or in-kind handouts to specific causes while travelling or on their return, at times inspired by an alternative approach to institutionalized foreign aid (Korf 2007) or the effect of greater geographical proximity to an overseas cause provided by the act of travel (Harrow & Jung 2016).

It is argued that with aid budgets under pressure, global philanthropy is becoming more important with philanthropists often being commended for their new approaches (Bertini et al. 2014). Philanthropy has been differentiated from 'charity' (Bertini et al. 2014) and praised for its potential to be more impactful and sustainable than government foreign aid, owing to characteristics of innovation, unnecessary political accountability and reduced aid budgets' funds. However, while Bertini et al. (2014) highlight the evolution of new approaches and mechanisms within philanthropy, such as 'venture philanthropy', and renewed interest in old ideas, such as collaborative giving, McGoey and Thiel (2018) critique the lack of governance and hidden political agendas of, for example, high net-worth private individual donors referred to as philanthrocapitalists.

Sub-Saharan Africa (SSA), globally infamous for statistically including 22 of the 29 'poorest' or lowest-income countries in the world, received USD 24 billion net bilateral overseas development assistance in 2015 (OECD 2016). The image of the African continent is consumed across the world, curated and moderated by politicians, the media, celebrities and campaigners, including a proportion of the tourism industry, who foster international compassion for Africa's miseries (Ayittey 2015) and influence people's values and inclination to intervene in order to make the world a better place (Harrison 2013; Hüncke & Koot 2012; McDonald & Scaife 2011). At the same time, tourism in SSA is one of the fastest growing and potentially one of the most advantageous economic sectors, with a reported increase in arrivals of 8 per cent during 2017 (UNWTO 2018) and an economic value chain that can reach some of the most remote rural communities. Within this growth, an increasing number of SSA countries are becoming popular destinations targeted by individuals interested in travel-related philanthropy.

Tourism in SSA remains dominated by tour operator-led wildlife safari leisure products, although the last ten years have witnessed a considerable growth in travel and tourism products shaped around philanthropy-focused activities, such as volunteering or voluntourism (for example, African Impact and GVI); altruistic travel (Singh 2002; Wanderink 2013); adventure philanthropy (Michelson 2013); compassionate, transformative, meaningful and charity tourism (Coghlan & Filo 2013; Nankervis 2009; UNWTO 2016); philanthropic journeys (Fernandez 2010); and social tours (Burgold & Rolfes 2013). For instance, tour operators such as Elevate Destinations (2012) divide philanthropic-related travel into three targets: donor travel – aimed at committed philanthropists who travel for that purpose; private travel – aimed at those who may dig deeper in terms of community exchange, but may have different interests besides philanthropic engagements; and urgent service travel – targeting volunteers for humanitarian emergencies and/or natural disaster zones. Other philanthropy-related experiences include compassionate by-products to a wildlife safari, such as visits to orphanages and/or local charities. Technology, values, wealth and contemporary needs are just some factors shaping how, why and where people give, and the rise in travel driven by similar factors has contributed to the evolution of the travel philanthropy product (Bertini et al. 2014). Notably, however, whilst travel philanthropy associated with financial donations to destinations has existed for years (Ardoin et al. 2016), the extent and impact of such practice remain unrecorded.

Philanthropy and gift giving are increasingly intertwined with tourism in SSA, with practices ranging from individuals purposely travelling to identify or support a cause in person or incidental acts of giving to the allocation of donations on the spot to tourism companies' corporate social responsibility (CSR) initiatives or other chosen beneficiaries. Travel to destinations affected by specific environmental issues or areas inhabited by less fortunate communities appears to stimulate philanthropy amongst consumers (Ardoin et al. 2016) and creates the belief that a difference can be made by giving back (Goodwin et al. 2009), even just through the donation of 'spare change'. In this instance, Honey (2011, p. 3) shares a more comprehensive vision that 'travellers philanthropy is not just about collecting loose change for charities' but, rather, helping tourism businesses become involved as 'good citizens' in the destinations where they work. In other words, it assists local projects with a 'hand up', not a 'hand out', by promoting social empowerment, education and entrepreneurship in an effort to foster longer-term sustainable conservation and development of destinations. At the same time, it also enriches the travel experience for visitors through 'meaningful, culturally sensitive, and productive interactions with people in host communities' (Honey 2011, p. 3).

Questioning the conceptual boundaries of travel philanthropy

The relatively new and arguably problematic concept of 'travel philanthropy' is a fuzzy domain that involves a multitude of stakeholders. Yet it is a term seemingly recognized by a growing range of academics and practitioners (Ardoin et al. 2016; Bertini et al. 2014; Honey 2011; Novelli 2016; Novelli et al. 2015) that is stimulating morally charged debates. Nevertheless, such a multifaceted term is charged with conceptual ambiguity and suffers inconclusive practical or, most recently, academic weight.

Sources questioning its definition are very rare, yet broad-brush issues surrounding the presumed concept are not. Despite the advocacy, and critique, many efforts are proceeding with limited theoretical understanding of the entire concept and, therefore, remain anecdotal or conceptual (see Ardoin et al. 2016). A handful of organizations, such as the Centre for Responsible Travel (CREST) and Sustainable Travel International, have produced guidelines specifically for 'travellers' philanthropy' (see Global Giving 2014 and Sustainable Travel International 2008). There also exist handbooks (Honey 2011) that assemble descriptive case studies or practitioner accounts, whilst three international symposiums about travel-related philanthropy have, to date, been hosted by CREST. In the meantime, the practices of gift giving in SSA, where it is a seemingly growing phenomenon, continue unabated.

Although CREST's good intentions to raise awareness about 'travellers' philanthropy' amongst the media, governments and development agencies have had some impact, the need remains for more clarity and in-depth critical research about the concept, its ethics and practical implications, not least because few attempts have been made to critically assess travel philanthropy beyond the more specific practice of volunteer tourism (Novelli et al. 2015; Novelli 2016). More specifically, Honey (2011) has argued for the need to deepen, enrich and embolden the concept of travel philanthropy in order to raise its profile, but her claims that travellers' philanthropy has become more widespread and professional over the last ten years remain based upon a concerning lack of evidence. Indeed, there remains both conceptual confusion and practical dilemmas about the 'dos' and 'don'ts' of travel philanthropy and, therefore, before we can be clear about what exactly we are referring to, questions need to be raised about the meaning, the value and the direction of travel philanthropy. Putting it another way, it is simply impossible to measure or improve something without an agreed understanding of what is to be measured. Moreover, without clear definitions and perhaps standards, the risk of a 'greenwashing' effect through travel philanthropy remains as it does, for example, as a result of the overuse and loose application of the term ecotourism, leading to limited environmental or socio-economic significance and, in some cases, negative ecological and social implications (Biggs 2008).

Defining travel(lers') philanthropy

Michael Seltzer is most commonly referenced to have coined the term 'travellers' philanthropy' in 2001 to encompass the '3 T's of support – time, talent and treasure – to host communities' (Seltzer & Spann 2004). A review of the literature suggests that although this is the most commonly used term, it is not sufficiently explained or consistently used with a range of other terms emerging, such as the one used in this chapter ('travel philanthropy') and 'travel-related philanthropy'.

Put simply, 'travel(ler) philanthropy' is made up of two words: 'travel(ler)' and 'philanthropy'. First, no literature has clearly defined what the term 'travel(ler)' specifically incorporates, leaving the meaning of 'travel' and/or 'traveller' in the context of 'travel(lers') philanthropy' open to interpretation. And second, 'philanthropy' is an equally contested concept also argued to be sitting in a loose field of theorizing (Liket & Simaens 2015) across a wide-ranging spectrum of debates (Harrow & Jung 2016). Indeed, a substantial body of knowledge is available in the social sciences domain on philanthropy and research appears across different disciplines, including marketing, economics, social psychology, biological psychology, neurology and brain sciences, sociology, political science, anthropology, biology and evolutionary psychology (Bekkers & Wiepking 2011). The tourism sector must, therefore, reflect on this long-established phenomenon and strive to understand its significance within the sustainable travel and tourism context.

The most conventional modern definition of philanthropy understands it as private initiatives for public good, aimed at fostering a better quality of life (Bertini et al. 2014), an inner ideal or disposition of human nature that motivates outward acts of benevolence (Sulek 2010). More recent studies have focused on why people give and their motives, such as loyalty and entrepreneurialism (Bekkers & Wiepking 2011; Etang et al. 2012; Goldfarb 2011; McDonald & Scaife 2011; Mickiewicz et al. 2016; Nickel & Eikenberry 2009; Harbaugh 1998), and attention to these have attracted particular interest partly because non-profit organizations face more financial constraints these days (Goldfarb 2011).

Typically, academic work on the subject of philanthropy has generally been conducted outside the tourism context, focusing in particular on the characteristics of those who engage in it and how intentions are influenced (Bekkers & Weipking 2011); hence, there is still very little knowledge with regards to how it may be manifested differently in the travel and tourism context (Ardoin et al. 2016). Ideas such as the 'warm glow' have emerged around the power of donor emotions in gift giving and the 'public good' versus the personal benefit derived from the act of giving (Atkinson 2009; Harbaugh 1998; Null 2011). Weaver and Jin (2016) emphasize that in tourism, the focus usually returns to transitory tourism experiences related to the attainment of selfish goals, and that compassion has been neglected in the tourism literature, lacking empirical investigation. Sulek (2010) similarly argues that a well-thought-out definition of philanthropy which specifies boundaries between motives, meanings and objectives that are truly philanthropic and those that are not is still required.

In terms of conceptual boundaries, while Spalding (2011) questions if the term refers to giving back to the host community, collecting donations, enhancing the traveller experience, voluntourism or actually effective strategic philanthropy, Novelli et al. (2015) provide the only deeper insight into travel philanthropy in the context of values and practices of traditional, modern and post-modern philanthropy. Whilst recognizing the potential for benefits, they question the reality of the ethics and impacts of related projects beyond the majority of the debate, calling upon much needed further research and leaving space for more accurate definitions of travel philanthropy.

Travel philanthropy as a concept thus currently remains framed by inconsistent perspectives and based on an interchangeable and perhaps inadequate use of terms. In an attempt to understand potential boundaries, we therefore now provide a brief helicopter view on terminologies associated with travel philanthropy.

Tourist donations

Travel philanthropy has been associated with a donation by a traveller on-trip or post-trip (Talladay 2011), which is a (voluntary) contribution in addition to the cost of the trip already purchased (Maathai 2011), and an amount which generates a new flow of cash, goods and volunteer services beyond what is generated through the normal tourism business (Bertini et al. 2014; Honey 2011). However, the term 'normal' has been undefined and lacking critique. From this perspective, it appears that travel philanthropy simply means that the tourism operator receives a donation from the traveller. How and where that is spent is therefore, in this understanding, a separate issue.

Donations from tourists and tourism businesses

Other authors consider not only concrete contributions from the 'traveller' but also from both the traveller and tourism business (Bertini et al 2014; Crouch 2011; Honey 2011). Crouch (2011, p. 117), for example, refers to travellers' philanthropy as 'providing contributions from your company and your guests to communities in tourism destinations' and includes funds raised from the company, travellers, foundation/grants and other fundraising activities, therefore changing the emphasis from the 'travellers' to fundraising from any source by the tourism operators.

What is emerging, therefore, is that travel philanthropy would not be accurately represented if the focus is only on travellers' direct donations to specific recipients in a destination or to a tourism company. Rather, it also often includes practices associated with what is more widely known as corporate philanthropy or CSR, in that funds raised by a tourism company, whether through their fundraising practices and/or a proportion of their business profit, is used to support specific causes. However, this blurs somewhat the boundaries between a growth in private philanthropic giving by travellers with more traditional CSR or corporate philanthropy evident in other industries.

'Corporate philanthropy' and CSR have been evolving in recent years. This is evidenced by an emerging literature on concepts such as: 'strategic CSR' (Baron 2001; Burke & Logsdon 1996; Luo 2005) aimed at simultaneously driving business competitiveness and social responsibility; 'shared value' (Smith 1994) also for competitiveness, moving beyond products and services not harming society to creating products that link to social and environmental gain (Porter & Kramer 2011; Valente & Crane 2010); 'altruistic CSR' (Lantos, 2001) or 'philanthropic responsibility' (Carroll 1991) with no business gain intended; cause-related marketing, contributing a percentage of sales revenue to an adopted cause (Kotler & Lee 2005); and corporate volunteering (Smith & Sypher 2010).

Corporate philanthropy in tourism may well be on the increase, as illustrated through examples such as Thomas Cook who reported more than $7.7 million in travel-related donations between 2005 and 2009, or a collectively estimated $249 million in philanthropic donations raised by just 39 companies in this manner (Goodwin et al. 2009, cited in Ardoin et al. 2016). Whilst this scale is unlikely as an average across an entire industry made up of predominantly fragmented small players, it is indicative of tourism's potential contribution beyond 'normal' business. However, it remains unclear how CSR is manifested differently within the travel and tourism context or, indeed, if it is part of travel philanthropy.

CSR through price increases

It has been suggested that CSR is lagging in tourism compared to other sectors (Ashley et al. 2007). Consequently, some recommend that it should therefore become mandatory for tourism operators to donate in the destinations in which they operate, achieved by levying a kind of tax to consumers (Blanco et al. 2012) by way of a non-voluntary contribution on top of a client's trip price. In her Tanzanian study amongst tour operators, Wolff (2011) reports a consensus amongst tour operators who would prefer the government to create a formal requirement for all operators to provide financial support to communities and conservation projects through a proportion of corporate earnings. McLachlan and Binns (2014) similarly support this in their Zambia case study whilst, in practice, there are some operators around the world voluntarily adding an additional obligatory fee to the cost of the trip per traveller, openly adding an amount to the sum of the holiday, such as $100 charged per person for a trip of four or more days (for example, Lets Go Travel Kenya 2011). Therefore, if this is essentially an involuntary contribution with the customer having no choice but to pay, it poses the question whether donations in this context would sit within travel philanthropy, CSR or an effective pricing strategy aimed at generating an additional revenue stream to pay a mandatory fee to a destination. As many operators are small and predominantly not eager to sacrifice their often small profit margins, it also raises the question of whether travel philanthropy is becoming a clever means or useful term for the industry to maintain their social licence in return for public cultural and natural assets under the banner of good works funded by others.

Hence, it is unclear if obligatory donations (through increased pricing) or corporate donations raised from profit share are to be considered part of travel philanthropy, or if these should be based on a 'voluntary' act by the travellers to qualify as travel philanthropy.

Serving consumer demand for philanthropy

That travellers contribute voluntarily to different causes is a fact; indeed, a significant proportion of the relevant literature focuses on the role of tourism operators in maximizing travellers' donations. Moreover, according to Crouch (2011), travellers are often actively looking for ways to make a difference in the world and are waiting to be shown or asked. Similarly, Jamieson et al. (2004, p. 9) highlight the growth in tourists seeking to improve the conditions of the destinations they visit and argue 'the tourist must be provided with opportunities to directly participate in the poverty reduction process'.

More specifically, Bertini et al. (2014, p. 20) suggest that project visits create a 'virtuous cycle of deeper commitment that leads to more donations' because, as mentioned earlier, 'seeing is believing'. Other authors also tend to agree, noting that travel experiences will naturally emotionally 'move' and spur people on to find additional ways to benefit the places they have visited (Exquisite Safaris 2010). Market research has demonstrated that consumers are increasingly taking social impact into account when designing their trips (Ashley et al. 2007), whilst Ham (2011) highlights that travel philanthropists are usually driven by personal satisfaction and the perhaps naïve belief that a place is better off because they visited it.

Therefore, many travel companies have embraced the business potential of this demand and marketed philanthropy-related products with Phocuswright (2015), for example, recommending four steps to successful travel philanthropy programmes, as follows: (1) creating CSR initiatives; (2) educating and informing travellers about giving programmes; (3) arranging site visits; and (4) facilitating interactions with local communities.

Strategic product development and innovation

In order to achieve the so-called 'best wins' and to 'lure' tourist donations, travel philanthropy is widely discussed in the context of travel product innovation. Although according to Honey (2011), travellers' philanthropy spans the market and is associated with a diverse range of travel and product types, Burns and Barrie (2005, p. 469) reluctantly state that the 'much needed social and economic development [is turned] into a "holiday experience"'. Small-scale tour operators, non-governmental organization (NGO) aid projects, as well as luxury travel companies, such as Abercrombie & Kent, are all increasingly facilitating tourists' trips to development projects, centred around the notion of 'ethical consumption' under labels of social, community or volunteer tourism (Burgold & Rolfes 2013).

Some products are indirectly centred around giving and are designed in such a way that the traveller is tempted to give, such as in the case of a South African 'social tour', during which giving is induced as a result of 'philanthropic impulses' resulting from being immersed in 'poverty', rather than being the core focus of the holiday (Burgold & Rolfes 2013). Consequently, some argue that tourism operators are capitalizing on the vulnerability of some destinations in which they operate (Dawson et al. 2011) – and arguably, of tourists – and that they often promote a 'dual mandate' by drawing people to an authentic homogeneous group whilst also supposedly promoting real development goals amongst indigenous peoples (Hüncke & Koot 2012). Hence, Nickel and Eikenberry (2009) argue that owing to the marketization of philanthropy, its transformative potential is increasingly lost in the market-based discourse of philanthropy that includes the consumption of products.

There are a range of debates tackling the 'time' and 'talent' aspects of travel philanthropy including the manufacturing of volunteer programmes for the donor (Fernandez 2010). Whilst Seltzer and Spann (2004) list 'time' and 'talent' as two of their three Ts, the volunteer tourism literature constitutes a clearly separate set of undertakings, most of which ignore the links to 'philanthropy' in general and travel philanthropy in particular. For example, Honey (2011, p. 208) states that 'some travel companies have philanthropy or voluntourism as their central mission', thus suggesting that volunteerism and philanthropy do not fall under the same banner.

Although this chapter does not focus on the issue of *volunteering*, it is worth noting that volunteer tourism is arguably the most debated form of travel philanthropy. Wearing and McGehee (2013) provide a detailed review of volunteer tourism literature, most of which has appeared in the last decade. They outline the evolution to have shifted from definitions, idealisms and advocacy to cautionary stances from the mid- to late 2010s which continue today.

Beyond fundraising

Honey (2011) also states that travellers' philanthropy includes making corporate donations as well as soliciting contributions from guests for specific community or conservation projects. This perspective points to the practice of both collecting donations as well as allocating resources, with travellers' philanthropy often defined as an actual 'giving programme' through which donations are given to specific projects (Honey 2011). Beyond fundraising, therefore, there is evidence that travel companies are also channels of compassion (Lambert & Lester 2004). In a similar vein, Western (2011), whilst highlighting the 'personal contribution' within his definition, also emphasizes the role of the travel company to 'marshal' positive community development and conservation through this 'form of charity'. However, the legitimacy of tourism operators to manage such charitable funds opens up yet another debate.

Travel is viewed as a means to advance philanthropy (Sustainable Travel International 2008) and also as 'a powerful medium' and a legitimate solution for social justice, economic development, biodiversity conservation, environmental protection and cultural preservation (UNWTO 2016, p. 3), as well as 'a mechanism for stewardship of the Earth and its people' (Bertini et al. 2014, p. 52). Travellers' philanthropy has, in parallel, been titled a 'progressive development strategy', a 'cost-effective means of delivering social and conservation services' (Honey 2011 pp. 207–8) and the three Ts 'flowing from the travel industry and travellers into host communities' (Honey 2011, p. 3).

More often than not, travel philanthropy is commonly associated with a formal 'programme' established and managed by a tourism operator. These include small-scale local programmes run by individual lodging businesses to global programmes and destination-wide funds (Honey 2011). Thomas (2014, p. 370), conversely, refers to 'the implementation of programmes generated by travellers' philanthropy', with 'generated by' suggesting that travellers' philanthropy does not refer to the actual programmes at all. Thus, in some cases, programmes are considered to be only a channel for funds, though in other cases a form of charity claiming improvements in healthcare, education, local livelihoods and environmental stewardship (Honey 2011). Therefore, it is critical to recognize and understand the boundaries and the role of tourism companies if the travel philanthropy concept is to progress theoretically and practically.

Ashley et al. (2007) go further, arguing that tourism companies are not development agencies and rarely have the choice or desire to prioritize development over profit. Indeed, that tourism does not exist to primarily benefit the poor (Song et al. 2013) is part of a long-standing debate, with Krippendorf (1987, p.137) overtly reiterating that 'tourism is a business not a charity'. Nevertheless, an increasing number of tourism operators, as channels of compassion, have begun to formalize their channels, with some creating hybrid models and becoming formally recognized charities, thereby entering into the development aid and community development arena. Examples of this include Wilderness Safaris' association with the Wilderness Wildlife Trust and Basecamp Explorer having a sister Basecamp Foundation operation.

Owing to the complex ecosystem and heterogeneity of tourism, operators have however been warned not to uniformly implement travel philanthropy initiatives or programmes into travel businesses (Sustainable Travel International 2008). Whilst it is recognized that the partnership of charities and tour operators can be symbiotic, and that there exists a long history of this with charities benefitting from the experience of tour operators in fundraising expeditions and tour operators benefitting from positive public relations by association with the charity (Turner et al. 2001), the distinction between tourism operators' commercial objectives and the development objectives associated with their charity arms becomes blurred. Hence, rather than a more traditional partnership existing between a tourism operator and an external/separate charity, there is an increasing trend towards tourism operators engaging in both roles.

Unmanaged giving by travellers

What if travelling philanthropists are not drawn towards a formal programme? Certainly, travel philanthropy-related to donations that do not involve the tourism operator is a widespread phenomenon. However, anecdotal evidence has raised the concern that no matter how small the amounts of philanthropic giving by tourists directly channelled into the hands of individuals or specific community groups, the risk emerges of creating a handout or dependency mentality or boosting the power of corrupt leaders, especially where previously negative occurrences of this kind have been identified. 'Impulse charity by travellers and/or contributions by travel operators or hotels to meet what they perceive as local needs and priorities' is a thing of the past (Spalding 2011, p.19), suggesting that direct donations or handouts by tourists may have detrimental effects (Novelli et al. 2015).

Travel philanthropy and tourism for development: origins, impacts and assumptions

In its broader senses, travel philanthropy has also been welcomed as a positive development emerging from the responsible and sustainable tourism movements (Pollock 2016), representing a shift in these movements towards the 'integration of tourism company and visitor support for local communities into the core definition of responsible travel' (Bertini et al. 2014, p. 51). Indeed, Spalding (2011) explains travel philanthropy as the new form of responsible tourism, evolving in a similar manner to how ecotourism businesses and their guests responded, out of either compassion or guilt, to the needs they saw in host communities. Consequently, it is also emphasized by some that philanthropic motivations have been found to be particularly in evidence in the context of ecotourism and nature-based travel (Ardoin et al 2016; Barnes & Eagles 2004).

Having said this, it appears to be widely assumed that giving through travel is 'responsible', yet what such behaviour entails has been neither defined nor considered in detail. Rather, it is sometimes simply referred to as providing a 'hand-up', not a 'hand-out' (Honey 2011, p. 2). Moreover, no empirical evidence exists within published research or industry discussions that demonstrates the impact of so-called philanthropic activities in host destinations – and with the evidence we have to work with, it is overly ambitious to claim that travel philanthropy is a form of sustainable or responsible tourism.

More broadly, as intimated above, there has been a noticeable transformation in the travel philanthropy discourse from a focus on fundraising towards tourism operators as channels for donations and, beyond that, towards the responsibility for socio-economic or environmental impacts from those funds, aligning with what was previously expected from the eco, responsible and sustainable tourism movements and pro-poor tourism strategies. Reflecting this, some authors have shaped their definition of travel philanthropy around using donations effectively (Spalding 2011) and being part of the solution for the sustainability of destinations (Bertini et al. 2014). Examples include 'improvements to the environmental and social conditions in the destinations they serve' (Sustainable Travel International 2008, p. 11), '[to] support and maintain the unique communities/environments travellers want to visit' or 'to further the wellbeing of local communities and conservation in travel destinations' (Bertini et al. 2014, p. 51). Ardoin et al. (2016) and Brightsmith et al. (2008) similarly suggest that travel philanthropy is often, or could be, designed to contribute directly to meeting the needs of destinations. As such, travellers' philanthropy can be understood as a means of strengthening local support for tourism activities, thereby providing a welcoming environment for tourists by building greater happiness through tackling welfare needs (UNWTO 2016).

Does this, then, mean that travel philanthropy is a development initiative beyond the practices of fundraising or passing on donations to local charities? If this is the case, then the role of and relationship between travel philanthropy and tourism for development undoubtedly requires further critical analysis, not least because globally, there is an increasing expectation that the private sector should engage more deeply in development. That is, it has been highlighted that it is necessary to differentiate between corporations as an 'actor in development' – a tool of immanent development through creating jobs, investing in infrastructure and so on – and corporations as a 'development actor'; that is, taking responsibility for the outcomes of its 'intentional' programmes (Blowfield & Dolan 2014).

Some studies are optimistic about the financial contributions of tourism businesses in destinations. For example, McLachlan and Binns' (2014, p.104) research in Livingstone, Zambia, explored the 'proactive', 'active' and 'reactive' behaviours of tourism operators in terms of CSR and revealed overwhelmingly positive outcomes. Similarly, Burns and Barrie (2005, p.483) analyse the activities of CCAfrica and the Africa Foundation, positioning them as an 'excellent example of corporate responsibility', though querying whether or not they were promoting colonial-style behaviours.

Nevertheless, Pollock (2016) has urged the sector to 'stop using CSR and philanthropic practices to justify ignoring some of the structural and systemic flaws of the current system', arguing that the industry needs to stop overlooking such a lack of mutually beneficial linkages with local communities and, instead, hiding behind philanthropic practices. She goes on to argue that 'a far better philanthropic outcome will only occur when success is re-defined from the growth of enterprises and volume of visitors to enhanced qualitative social, environmental and personal development' (Pollock 2016). Ashley et al. (2007) also suggest that tourism businesses should go beyond making donations and invest in doing business differently. They observe that 'community economic development is viewed as a philanthropic cause rather than a core business risk or source of opportunity' (Ashley et al. 2007, p.14) and that most tourism businesses still lie at the philanthropic end of the spectrum. They also address the critical question of whether tourism businesses are forming sufficient linkages between local economies and their actual business practices, thus helping to drive a pro-poor approach to the sector, going on to suggest that there is a need to distinguish philanthropic donations from adapted business practice and to identify if it is 'integrated into business practice or is a stand-alone activity' (Ashley et al. 2007, p.268). They argue that, over time, the net increase in local income can outweigh philanthropic spend.

There is a burgeoning literature that assumes and supports the role of tourism businesses in the development of 'poor' communities in general whilst the travel philanthropy-related literature in particular provides substantial advice or recommendations as to how tourism enterprises, big and small, might act more like charitable organizations (for example, Crouch 2011). However, it should still be questioned whether articles such as those published by Crouch (2011) are actually missing the critical point of the travel philanthropy concept. That is, whilst generally acknowledging that travel businesses are not charities, they appear to suggest that these companies can make a direct difference to the poorest in society and, therefore, provide advice on behaving like an NGO/charity.

At the same time, travel philanthropy is often unreservedly assumed to involve a 'partnership' between community projects, tourism business and travellers (Spalding 2011) and, hence, it is argued that tourism organizations may play a role in development aid superior to that of more traditional NGOs. This assertion is based on claims that the tourism sector is able, through the development of partnerships, to provide direct support at a local level through grassroots organizations 'on the front line' (Honey 2011). More specifically, Lindkvist (2011, p. 124), a representative of Basecamp, also suggests that 'one of the absolutely unique aspects of travel philanthropy is that it has the potential for long term planning', arguing that tourism businesses are likely to be around for longer than traditional NGOs. He does, however, also accept that tourism can be volatile, thereby challenging the sustainability of destinations.

Generally, then, and as Honey (2011) explains, there has been a shift from charity and handout philanthropy models to sustainable development projects. Yet, although many suggest that tourism operators are now not only fundraising and channelling funds but are also playing a more direct role in contributions to social and environmental sustainability in the destination, there remains no empirical evidence to evaluate the veracity of such claims.

Travel philanthropy legitimacy and meaningful measurement of its impact

The reality of philanthropy in tourism is that, typically, the traveller leaves and the money or gift of some sort remains in the destination; that is, many donors think their job is simply to make a gift or donation. However, although charitable giving may be simple to carry out, alleviating poverty is a significantly complex task (Ashley et al. 2007). Specifically, tourists do not necessarily take responsibility for the short- or longer-term impacts of their gift giving. For instance, travel philanthropists may lack the time or ability to fully understand a problem or solution (Brest 2015); they are, perhaps, encouraged or obliged to think within the timescale of their trip and, as a result, behave instinctively and emotionally rather than making a more logical, considered and deliberate attempt to understand the root cause of the problem (Abernethy 2011; Brest 2015). Certainly, the understanding of travel-related giving amongst tourists remains under-researched, and the need exists to question what, how and where to give or, indeed, whether to give at all.

In this context, Abernethy (2011) notes a dilemma often facing the tourist, notably, to whom the gift should be given, in the limited time they have at a particular destination, to maximize the ethical value of the contribution. Whilst not taking into account emotion and individual encounters, he outlines three options for channelling donations through: (1) a travel supplier or intermediary, such as a hotel or tour operator; (2) a village member with recognized status, such as the village chief; and (3) a local organization with close ties to the village, such as the village council or an NGO. He goes on to argue that it is the responsibility of the tour operator as a moral obligation to identify legitimate local projects, thereby reducing spontaneity and enhancing the legitimacy and sustainability of philanthropic activities. Zijlma (2018) similarly recommends that travellers should always donate via an operator, whilst Bertini et al. (2014) emphasize the importance of making donations through someone known and trusted. This perspective is supported by Fernandez (2010), who also suggests that it is the responsibility of the service provider (the tourism operator) to encourage clients (the traveller) to make purposeful observations of the impact of the beneficiary organization. It is argued that with tour operators commonly being foreign and white, the tourist tends to trust 'my kind of people', believing that they can leverage and incentivize the operator to manage the money well (Abernethy 2011).

Although it is recognized that fundraising can be achieved through tourism, beyond a handful of isolated and (arguably) misleading case studies there is no evidence of either positive or negative consequences (Honey 2011; Novelli et al. 2015). Indeed, evidence from the perspective of the intended beneficiaries is particularly lacking. Despite recurring themes of 'done well', 'if carried out well' and the 'successful execution of travellers' philanthropy' for win–win outcomes for the destination, which suggest travel businesses and travellers themselves have ambitions to improve (UNWTO 2016), very limited research has been undertaken into the actual impact of cash or in-kind donations via the tourism industry to host destinations, or to develop an understanding of what this may constitute. A few references have been made to the challenges resulting from personal contributions (Western 2011), and there have been calls for a shift towards 'ethical traveller philanthropy', supported with a checklist to help improve consequences (Abernethy 2011), but the effects of such giving remain largely unknown.

Consequently, the ambiguity surrounding travel philanthropy suggests that it cannot be claimed to be accountable and transparent; as Honey (2011) suggests, it may provide hands-on experiences and contact with recipients, but claims of its benefits unfortunately remain unfounded. For example, through his interest in the tourism value chain, Thomas (2014) recognizes that programmes 'generated by travellers' philanthropy' are not well organized and generally go unrecorded in the context of pro-poor impact from the tourism sector. In his Mali-based research he reports the philanthropic outputs from the combined donations of 10,000 tourists, such as schools, ambulances and tons of donated food, but argues other qualitative returns may exist, though only the tangible output is recorded. Similarly, Wolff (2011) highlights the role of travel philanthropy in safari-based tourism but, whilst her analysis identified the level of financial and in-kind donations at the destination (one of very few attempts to analyse such activity at the destination level), her report measured inputs rather than any subsequent outcomes; that is, the amounts donated rather than their impacts, tangible or intangible, positive or negative.

Nevertheless, Western (2011) acknowledges that philanthropy is important in destinations because the travel industry cannot tackle sustainability challenges with fees alone, but warns of the risks of dependency on donor money, thus highlighting the need to manage the actual impact of travel philanthropy, an issue typically considered theoretically rather than empirically. Equally, although it is suggested that 'the future of travel philanthropy is bright [as a] third of travellers expect to increase their travel-related giving in the next two years' (Phocuswright 2015, p. 11), Novelli (2016) questions whether travel philanthropy is just mirroring the mistakes of more traditional aid models. Either way, the impacts that are likely to emerge will require considerable research.

Alternatively, Macy (2011) discusses the potential issue of 'unwanted philanthropy' and the widely discussed 'paint syndrome' associated with flocks of young volunteers travelling to paint schools in remote areas of the world. At the same time, increasing attention has been paid to controversies surrounding orphanage tourism that have emerged over the past few years. More generally, Butcher (2003) discusses the moralization of tourism and the complexities associated with ethical consumption and cultural sophistication which, in turn, may lead to fundamental reflections on travel philanthropy versus ethical consumption.

Generally speaking, however, the travel philanthropy literature is based on the assumption that giving is good – yet, with only few exceptions (Novelli et al. 2015; Novelli 2016), the actual impacts of such transitory gift giving are rarely debated, especially in the context of tourism. Others have touched upon the paradoxes for development in the context of travel philanthropy (Burns & Barrie 2005) but again, the geographies of generosity influenced by travel, fuelled by compassion and emotions, rich in moral motivations (Silk 2004), cannot be assumed positive for the 'addressee' (Korf 2007). That is, research has demonstrated that giving gifts can create a superior 'self' and a passive receiving 'other'. In the 'Resource Transfer Paradigm' proposed by Silk (2004), the notion of Northern actors as carers who are active and generous, and Southern actors as cared for, passive and grateful recipients, raises moral debates; Silk (2004) emphasizes that such North–South encounters lack the effort of listening to the poor and are, rather, defined by donors choosing to give and what to give.

In a similar vein, Pollock (2016) argues that 'much is made of the human right to travel and turn up on another's door step unannounced or without adequate preparation for the consequences, yet very little is said of the right of a destination community to say either "no thanks" or to try to shape the kind of visitation that ensues'. And as Carlson (2012) emphasizes, no one wants to think their generosity hurts people, but there is a need to learn from debates within the international development and aid literature, which have raised complex issues around dependency, sustainability, power relations and other implications of gift giving, and to consider the right of the recipient community to shape the activity of travel philanthropy. More specifically, gift relations in the aid chain need to be considered with regards to the issues of dignity, respect and lack of recognition for the recipient (Korf 2007).

Millions of dollars are expected to go into the host communities all over the world through donations and grants as well as through voluntary services, but will remain predominantly untraceable and unrecorded by any consistent method. According to the United Nations Environment Programme (cited in WTTC 2016), just $5 of each $100 spent by a tourist from a developed country travelling in a developing country destination remains in the local economy. This does not include philanthropic donations. As the industry jumps on opportunities to promote philanthropic activities, and projects become tangible through poverty and deprivation having 'real faces' (Crouch 2011), the potential to generate additional funds is clearly enormous. However, whilst it is important to measure the monetary value, it is also crucial that research does not focus only on economic 'benefits' in any measurement development framework because, as Biggs (2008) exemplifies, although ecotourism might benefit a community economically, it may well result in damage to social and cultural life.

Overall, then, the impact of travel philanthropy has not been thoroughly investigated and remains unclear. Intervention in SSA development traverses an immensely complex terrain and rather than debating which public good is better than another, a theme in the CREST handbook (Honey 2011), focus should be on understanding what actually constitutes the 'public good' in this context. As Goldfarb (2011) argues, it is likely to be complex and multifaceted, and fundamental considerations centre on who decides on what, how, where and why to give. A glaring gap in the literature is meaningful measurement – both the extent of travel philanthropy and its impact. However, as established in this chapter, continuing with blurred definitions of travel philanthropy runs the risk of following the 'ecotourism' and 'responsible travel' labels which are, at times, criticized for having failed to live up to their promised local impacts.

Final considerations

Emerging from a relationship between philanthropy, travel and tourism, travel(lers') philanthropy is effectively a form of aid in Africa (and elsewhere) of which the general level of understanding is extremely limited and the foundations of which to expand meaningful debates are arguably very weak too. The review of the literature in this chapter suggests that 'travel philanthropy' as a term and concept remains fuzzy, with definitions varying from author to author, and in practice is manifested variously amongst fundraising organizations, CSR programmes, product development, formal charitable programmes, direct conservation and development interventions, unmanaged handouts by tourists, as well as responsible and sustainable aspects of tourism. Other than a few isolated examples indicating the extent of donations for specific cases, this chapter has identified a critical lack of data (both qualitative and quantitative) concerning the extent of this phenomenon on a wider more representative scale for Africa (and beyond), and the actual impacts of such financial or in-kind donations and associated practices. We seem to continue with the unquestioned assumption that fundraising and giving is good, and that tourists and tourism businesses are not only legitimate stakeholders in Africa's 'development', but claim some superiority to traditional development organizations delivering aid. Research is in its nascent stages of understanding travel(lers') philanthropy as a theoretical concept. Without streamlining our debates, standing back, opening our eyes to the bigger picture and approaching its issues with far more sophistication, we risk (albeit unintended) short- and long-term consequences for communities of tourism destinations in Africa and for the tourism sector itself, and also miss the opportunity to transform this peripheral form of aid into a valued part of the Sustainable Development Goals.

References

Abernethy, D. (2011), 'Engaging travelers in travelers' philanthropy: Unintended consequences of the traveler's best intentions', in M. Honey (ed.) *Travelers' Philanthropy Handbook*, Washington, DC: Centre for Responsible Travel, pp. 179–90.

Ardoin, N., Wheaton, M., Hunt, A., Schuh, J. and Durham, W. (2016), 'Post-trip philanthropic intentions of nature-based tourists in Galapagos', *Journal of Ecotourism*, 15(1), 21–35.

Ashley, C., De Brine, P., Lehr, A. and Wilde, H. (2007), *The Role of the Tourism Sector in Expanding Economic Opportunity*, Cambridge, MA: John F. Kennedy School of Government, Harvard University.

Atkinson, A.B. (2009), 'Giving overseas and public policy', *Journal of Public Economics*, 93(5–6), 647–53.

Ayittey, G. (2015), 'Post-MDGs and Africa's development conundrum', *Journal of International Development*, 27(3), 345–61.

Barnes, M. and Eagles, P. (2004), 'Examining the relationship between ecotourists and philanthropic behavior', *Tourism Recreation Research*, 29(3), 35–8.

Baron, D. (2001), 'Private politics, corporate social responsibility and integrated strategy', *Journal of Economics and Management Strategy*, 10(1), 7–45.

Bekkers, R. and Wiepking, P. (2011), 'A literature review of empirical studies of philanthropy: Eight mechanisms that drive charitable giving', *Nonprofit and Voluntary Sector Quarterly*, 40(5), 924–73.

Bertini, I., Malone, C. and Revell, T. (2014), *Sustainable Philanthropy*, 2nd edn, Lincoln: Simon Leadbetter. Accessed 10 September 2018 at www.scrt.scot/wp-content/uploads/2015/12/Sustainable-Philanthropy-guide-2014.pdf

Biggs, G. (2008), *Ecotourism as a Conservation Strategy for Funders*, New York: Environmental Grantmakers Association.

Blanco, E., Lopez, M. and Coleman, E. (2012), 'Voting for environmental donations: Experimental evidence from Majorca, Spain', *Ecological Economics*, 75, 52–60.

Blowfield, M. and Dolan, C. (2014), 'Business as a development agent: Evidence of possibility and improbability', *Third World Quarterly*, 35(1), 22–42.

Brest, P. (2015), 'Strategic philanthropy and its discontents', Stanford Social Innovations Review. Accessed 11 February 2019 at https://ssir.org/up_for_debate/article/strategic_philanthropy_and_its_discontents

Brightsmith, D., Stronza, A. and Holle, K. (2008), 'Ecotourism, conservation biology, and volunteer tourism: A mutually beneficial triumvirate', *Biological Conservation*, 141(11), 2832–42.

Burgold, J. and Rolfes, M. (2013), 'Of voyeuristic safari tours and responsible tourism with educational value: Observing moral communication in slum and township tourism in Cape Town and Mumbai', *Die Erde: Journal of the Geographical Society of Berlin*, 144(2), 161–74.

Burke, L. and Logsdon, J. (1996), 'How corporate social responsibility pays off', *Long Range Planning*, 29(4), 495–502.

Burns, P. and Barrie, S. (2005), 'Race, space and "Our own piece of Africa": Doing good in Luphisi Village?', *Journal of Sustainable Tourism*, 13(5), 468–85.

Butcher, J. (2003), *The Moralisation of Tourism: Sun, Sand and Saving the World*, London: Routledge.

Carlson, D. (2012), 'Why you should consider cancelling your short-term mission trips', *Gospel Coalition*, 18 June. Accessed 12 September 2018 at www.thegospelcoalition.org/article/why-you-should-consider-cancelling-your-short-term-mission-trips

Carroll, A. (1991), 'The pyramid of corporate social responsibility: Toward the moral management of organizational stakeholders', *Business Horizons*, **34**(4), 39–48.

Clifford, C. (2017), 'These 14 billionaires just promised to give away more than half of their money like Bill Gates and Warren Buffett', *CNBC*, 31 May 2017. Accessed 7 June 2018 at www.cnbc.com/2017/05/31/14-billionaires-signed-bill-gates-and-warren-buffetts-giving-pledge.html

Coghlan, A. and Filo, K. (2013), 'Using constant comparison method and qualitative data to understand participants' experiences at the nexus of tourism, sport and charity events', *Tourism Management*, **35**, 122–31.

Crouch, J. (2011), 'Engaging communities and local organizations in travelers' philanthropy. How to manage interaction with community projects', in M. Honey (ed.) *Travelers' Philanthropy Handbook*, Washington, DC: Center for Responsible Travel, pp. 115–22.

Dawson, J., Johnston, M., Stewart, E., Lemieux, C., Lemelin, R., Maher, P. and Grimwood, B. (2011), 'Ethical considerations of last chance tourism', *Journal of Ecotourism*, **10**(3), 250–65.

Elevate Destinations (2012), 'What is travel philanthropy?', *Huffpost Travel*, 13 April. Accessed 26 March 2018 at www.huffingtonpost.com/elevate-destinations/what-is-travel-philanthro_b_1405994.html

Etang, A., Fielding, D. and Knowles, S. (2012), 'Giving to Africa and perceptions of poverty', *Journal of Economic Psychology*, **33**(4), 819–32.

Exquisite Safaris (2010), 'Understanding travelers philanthropy: Defining philanthropy's role in travel'. Accessed 12 September 2018 at https://travelmatters.wordpress.com/

Fernandez, M. (2010), '6 questions to ask before planning a philanthropic trip', *Philanthropy Indaba*. Accessed 25 February 2019 at https://philanthropyindaba.wordpress.com/2009/12/03/6-questions-to-ask-before-going-on-a-philanthropic-trip-part-1/

Global Giving (2014), *Global Giving Tools and Training Blog*. Accessed 11 February 2019 at http://tools.blog.globalgiving.org

Goldfarb, N. (2011), 'Josiah Royce's philosophy of loyalty as philanthropy', *Nonprofit and Voluntary Sector Quarterly*, **40**(4), 720–39.

Goodwin, H., McCombes, L. and Eckardt, C. (2009), *Advances in Travel Philanthropy: Raising Money Through the Travel and Tourism Industry for Charitable Purposes*, London: World Travel Market.

Ham, S. (2011), 'The ask – or is it the offer?', in M. Honey (ed.) *Travelers' Philanthropy Handbook*, Washington, DC: Center for Responsible Travel, pp. 141–9.

Harbaugh, W. (1998), 'What do donations buy? A model of philanthropy based on prestige and warm glow', *Journal of Public Economics*, **67**(2), 269–84.

Harrison, G. (2013), 'Campaign Africa: Exploring the representation of Africa and its role in British identity', *British Journal of Politics and International Relations*, **15**(4), 528–47.

Harrow, J. and Jung, T. (2016), 'Philanthropy and community development: The vital signs of community foundation?', *Community Development Journal*, **51**(1), 132–52.

Honey, M. (ed.) (2011), *Travelers' Philanthropy Handbook*, Washington, DC: Center for Responsible Travel.

Hüncke, A. and Koot, S. (2012), 'The presentation of Bushmen in cultural tourism: Tourists' images of Bushmen and the tourism provider's presentation of (Hai//om) Bushmen at Treesleeper Camp, Namibia', *Critical Arts*, **26**(5), 671–89.

Jamieson, W., Goodwin, H. and Edmunds, C. (2004), 'Contribution of tourism to poverty alleviation: Pro-poor tourism and the challenge of measuring impacts', Transport Policy and Tourism Section, Transport and Tourism Division, UN ESCAP. Accessed 10 September 2018 at http://haroldgoodwin.info/resources/povertyalleviation.pdf

Korf, B. (2007), 'Antinomies of generosity: Moral geographies and post-tsunami aid in Southeast Asia', *Geoforum*, **38**(2), 366–78.

Kotler, P. and Lee, N. (2005), *Corporate Social Responsibility: Doing the Most Good for Your Company and Your Cause*, Hoboken, NJ: Wiley.

Krippendorf, J. (1987), *The Holiday Makers: Understanding the Impact of Leisure and Travel*, Oxford: Butterworth-Heinemann.

Lambert, D. and Lester, A. (2004), 'Geographies of colonial philanthropy', *Progress in Human Geography*, **28**(3), 320–41.

Lantos, G. (2001), 'The boundaries of strategic corporate social responsibility', *Journal of Consumer Marketing*, **18**(7), 595–632.

Lets Go Travel Kenya (2011), 'Travellers philanthropy: Giving back to our communities'. Accessed 16 April 2018 at http://letsgotravelkenya.blogspot.ug/2011/09/travellers-philanthropy-giving-back-to.html

Liket, K. and Simaens, A. (2015), 'Battling the devolution in the research on corporate philanthropy', *Journal of Business Ethics*, **126**(2), 285–308.

Lindkvist, L. (2011), 'Working with donors in travel-based philanthropy: Lessons from basecamp', in M. Honey (ed.) *Travelers' Philanthropy Handbook*, Washington, DC: Center for Responsible Travel, pp. 123–37.

Luo, X. (2005), 'A contingent perspective on the advantages of stores' strategic philanthropy for influencing consumer behaviour', *Journal of Consumer Behaviour*, **4**(5), 390–401.

Maathai, W. (2011), 'Foreword', in M. Honey (ed.) *Travelers' Philanthropy Handbook*, Washington, DC: Center for Responsible Travel, pp. 1–2.

Macy, P. (2011), 'Unwanted philanthropy', in M. Honey (ed.) *Travelers' Philanthropy Handbook*, Washington, DC: Center for Responsible Travel, pp. 177–8.

McDonald, K. and Scaife, W. (2011), 'Print media portrayals of giving: Exploring national "cultures of philanthropy"', *International Journal of Nonprofit and Voluntary Sector Marketing*, **16**(4), 311–24.

McGoey, L. and Thiel, D. (2018), 'Charismatic violence and the sanctification of the super-rich', *Economy and Society*, **47**(1), 111–34.

McLachlan, S. and Binns, T. (2014), 'Tourism, development and corporate social responsibility in Livingstone, Zambia', *Local Economy*, **29**(1–2), 98–112.

Michelson, E. (2013), *Adventure Philanthropist: Great Adventures Volunteering Abroad*, Dubai: emCon LLC.

Mickiewicz, T., Sauka, A. and Stephan, U. (2016), 'On the compatibility of benevolence and self-interest: Philanthropy and entrepreneurial orientation', *International Small Business Journal*, **34**(3), 303–28.

Nankervis, A. (2009), 'Vulnerability analysis and sustainability in tourism: Lessons from Phuket', in C. Pforr and P. Hosie (eds) *Crisis Management in the Tourism Industry*, Farnham: Ashgate Publishing, pp. 93–106.

Nickel, P. and Eikenberry, A. (2009), 'A critique of the discourse of marketized philanthropy', *American Behavioral Scientist*, **52**(7), 974–89.

Novelli, M. (2016), *Tourism and Development in Sub-Saharan Africa: Current Issues and Local Realities*, Abingdon: Routledge.

Novelli, M., Morgan, N., Mitchell G. and Ivanov, K. (2015), 'Travel philanthropy and sustainable development: The case of the Plymouth Banjul Challenge', *Journal of Sustainable Tourism*, **24**(6), 824–45.

Null, C. (2011), 'Warm glow, information, and inefficient charitable giving', *Journal of Public Economics*, **95**(5–6), 455–65.

OECD (2016), 'Development aid in 2015 continues to grow despite costs for in-donor refugees', *Organisation for Economic Co-operation and Development*, Paris, 13 April. Accessed 10 September 2018 at www.oecd.org/dac/stats/ODA-2015-detailed-summary.pdf

Partzsch, L. and Fuchs, D. (2012), 'Philanthropy: Power with in international relations', *Journal of Political Power*, **5**(3), 359–76.

Pettit, S. and Beresford, A. (2009), 'Critical success factors in the context of humanitarian aid supply chains', *International Journal of Physical Distribution and Logistics Management*, **39**(6), 450–68.

Phocuswright (2015), *Good Travels: The Philanthropic Profile of the American Traveler*. Accessed 23 June 2018 at https://static1.squarespace.com/static/54de6549e4b054179782boeb/t/5602foofe4bo449 3f84b6c74/1443033103345/TC-Good-Travels-Whitepaper-092215.pdf

Pollock, A. (2016), 'Time has come to rethink travel philanthropy', *Conscious Travel*, May. Accessed 12 September 2018 at https://conscioustourism.wordpress.com/2016/05/19/time-has-come-to-re-think -travel-philanthropy/

Porter, M. and Kramer, M. (2011), 'Creating shared value: How to reinvent capitalism – and unleash a wave of innovation and growth', *Harvard Business Review*, **89**(1/2), 62–7.

Seltzer, M. and Spann, J. (2004), 'Traveler's philanthropy: Helping communities build economic assets and sustain environmental and cultural resources in an era of rapid globalization', in *Travelers' Philanthropy Conference Proceedings*, Palo Alto, CA: Stanford University.

Silk, J. (2004), 'Caring at a distance: Gift theory, aid chains and social movements', *Social and Cultural Geography*, **5**(2), 229–51.

Singh, T. (2002), 'Altruistic tourism: Another shade of sustainable tourism', *Tourism (Zagreb)*, **50**(4), 361–70.

Smith, C. (1994), 'The new corporate philanthropy', *Harvard Business Review*, **72**, 105–16.

Smith, J. and Sypher, B. (2010), 'Philanthropy in the workplace: How a financial institution communicates charitable giving values', *Southern Communication Journal*, **75**(4), 370–91.

Song, H., Liu, J. and Chen, G. (2013), 'Tourism value chain governance: Review and prospects', *Journal of Travel Research*, **52**(1), 15–28.

Spalding, M.J. (2011), 'What is successful philanthropy?', in M. Honey (ed.) *Travelers' Philanthropy Handbook*, Washington, DC: Center for Responsible Travel, pp. 19–24.

Sulek, M. (2010), 'On the modern meaning of philanthropy', *Nonprofit and Voluntary Sector Quarterly*, **39**(2), 193–212.

Sustainable Travel International (2008), 'Best practices in travel philanthropy manual V1: Tour operator sector'. Accessed 11 February 2019 at https://voluntourismgal.files.wordpress.com/2009/04/ sti_bp.pdf

Talladay, J. (2011), 'Why travelers become philanthropists: Donor motivations', in M. Honey (ed.) *Travelers' Philanthropy Handbook*, Washington, DC: Center for Responsible Travel, pp. 193–6.

Thomas, F. (2014), 'Addressing the measurement of tourism in terms of poverty reduction: Tourism value chain analysis in Lao PDR and Mali', *International Journal of Tourism Research*, **16**(4), 368–76.

Turner, R., Miller, G. and Gilbert, D. (2001), 'The role of UK charities and the tourism industry', *Tourism Management*, **22**(5), 463–72.

UNWTO (2016), *The Transformative Power of Tourism: A Paradigm Shift towards a More Responsible Traveller*, Affiliate Members Global Report, Vol. 14, Madrid: United Nations World Tourism Organization.

UNWTO (2018), *UNWTO Tourism Highlights 2018*, UN World Tourism Organization. Accessed 12 September 2018 at http://mkt.unwto.org/publication/unwto-tourism-highlights-2018

Valente, M. and Crane, A. (2010), 'Public responsibility and private enterprise in developing countries', *California Management Review*, **12**(3), 52–78.

Wanderink (2013), 'Saving the world, one trip at a time: Different responsible travels'. Accessed 22 June 2018 at www.wanderink.com/archives/saving-the-world-one-trip-at-a-time-different-responsible- travels/

Wearing, S. and McGehee, N.G. (2013), 'Volunteer tourism: A review', *Tourism Management*, **38**, 120–30.

Weaver, D. and Jin, X. (2016), 'Compassion as a neglected motivator for sustainable tourism', *Journal of Sustainable Tourism*, **24**(5), 657–72.

Western, D. (2011), 'Travelers' philanthropy and the good Samaritan', in M. Honey (ed.) *Travelers' Philanthropy Handbook*, Washington, DC: Center for Responsible Travel, pp. 13–18.

Wilson, T. (2016), 'Buffett's son funds hydropower plant to help save Congo gorillas', *Bloomberg*, 7 April. Accessed 7 June 2018 at www.bloomberg.com/news/articles/2016-04-06/congo-park-builds-hydro power-plants-to-protect-mountain-gorillas

Wolff, J. (2011), 'Survey of tour operators in Arusha, Tanzania', in M. Honey (ed.) *Travelers' Philanthropy Handbook*, Washington, DC: Center for Responsible Travel, 2011, pp. 150–8.

WTTC (2016), *Tourism for Tomorrow Newsletter September 2016*, World Travel and Tourism Council. Accessed 10 June 2018 at www.wttc.org/tourism-for-tomorrow-awards/newsletter/2016/september -2016/

Zijlma, A. (2018), 'Gift and donation tips for visitors to Africa', *TripSavvy*, 9 January. Accessed 12 September 2018 at www.tripsavvy.com/giving-tips-for-africa-visitors-1454151

6 Tourism and poverty

David Harrison and Stephen Pratt

Introduction

It has long been believed in 'development' circles that tourism has the potential to reduce poverty. Indeed, from the time of domestic mass tourism in the mid-nineteenth century, it came to be felt that tourism would, almost inevitably, reduce poverty in those regions that were fortunate enough to attract visitors. The emergence of mass international tourism after the Second World War simply seemed to confirm that tourism's benefits to 'host' societies would be extended to the developing world. Such a laissez-faire approach, described by Hall (2008, p. 54) as boosterism, 'a simplistic attitude that tourism development is inherently good and of automatic benefit to the hosts', remains a position held by many of those who place themselves on what Jafari (1989, p. 22) has described as tourism's 'advocacy' platform.

As international tourism grew exponentially, other 'platforms' emerged, warning against unquestioned acceptance of international tourism and, in line with more critical approaches to the nature of 'development', pointed to all kinds of environmental, social and cultural 'problems' that, at least to some extent, might offset tourism's economic benefits. Nevertheless, despite such theoretical debates, often shifting focus to the nature of international capitalism, modernization, globalization and dependency, tourism's contribution to economic growth and, *ipso facto*, to development and poverty alleviation, in at least *some* of its variants, by and large seems to be accepted as a proper basis for development policies in both developing and developed society destinations. Put differently, tourism is generally felt to contribute to development by promoting economic growth and thus, at least potentially, to contribute to the alleviation of poverty.

As indicated elsewhere (Willis 2005, pp. 93–115), the links between economic growth and poverty alleviation (and, more widely, 'development') have figured in numerous theoretical and policy frameworks, including 'bottom-up', 'basic needs' and 'participatory' approaches emanating from a wide range of development institutions, including the United Nations (and its promotion of the Millennium Development Goals) and international non-government organizations. Indeed, a recent authoritative restatement of human development approaches, while reiterating the importance of economic growth, also highlights the vital role played by social institutions and organizations in advancing human development (Stewart et al. 2018).

Such approaches have been applied directly to tourism's role in development and poverty alleviation (Harrison 2008), ranging from de Kadt's (1979) early but still relevant query as to how far tourism is 'a passport to development' to the emergence in the late 1990s of what, for a while, seemed a separate pro-poor tourism (PPT) 'school' (Harrison 2008) and the Sustainable Tourism – End Poverty (ST-EP) initiative of the United Nations World Tourism Organization, launched in 2002 at the World Summit on Sustainable Development in Johannesburg.

Defining poverty

The association of poverty reduction, development and tourism is, however, beguilingly simplistic. In practice, even defining poverty is problematic. Perhaps the most basic approach is to try to produce an objective minimum level of income, either as an exact figure or as some kind of average income, below which basic needs cannot be met. This can then be applied across or within countries. In 2015, for instance, the World Bank proposed a global, extreme poverty line of US $1.90 per day, with correspondingly higher daily poverty lines for lower-middle-income countries (US $3.20), upper-middle-income countries (US $5.50 per day) and high-income countries (US $21.70 per day) (Weller 2017). Many individual countries also produce their own poverty lines, which are then used to assess local or national levels of poverty and the progress made in reducing it.

Poverty lines can be useful but they are limited. As Gordon (2006, p. 45) notes, they tend to be arbitrary and are crude measures of inequality. Differences in the life experience, for instance, of someone on a poverty line and another who is 10 cents above the line are likely to be minor, and yet one is defined as 'poor' and the other – like an individual earning several times the basic amount – as 'non-poor'. Furthermore, because they vary according to levels of national development, and because prices of goods vary from one country to another, they are not usually comparable, and subjectivity is involved in identifying 'basic needs': what is deemed 'basic' in one country might not be considered so in another.

An alternative approach is to focus on how people themselves define 'poverty'. However, individual perceptions vary widely. In a survey of 55 households conducted by Harrison in 2004, in the village of Don Det Tok, Laos, for example, no less than 17 different definitions of poverty were provided, and while the lack of rice and inability to be self-sufficient were the most mentioned, other criteria included old age, financial uncertainty, illness, a lack of labour, having only a small boat, an unpredictable income, an inability to meet social obligations and being alone. Compared to the official poverty measure, which assessed 20 per cent of the villagers as poor (as based on their annual income), 60 per cent of respondents defined themselves as living in poverty (Harrison & Schipani 2007, pp. 217–18). Similarly, unpublished research in Ban Pha Thao, another village in Laos, revealed that villagers strongly disputed official poverty statistics which indicated only eight households were poor. Rather, they argued, most households were self-sufficient in rice (a common measure of self-sufficiency), only because children had to be taken out of school to assist with the harvest, a requirement they felt was indicative of another feature of poverty.

Laotian villagers are not alone in focusing on the multi-dimensionality of poverty. Similarly, but in quite a different context, while introducing *Poverty and Social Exclusion in Britain*, Gordon (2006, p. 31) notes the relative nature of the United Nations definitions of absolute and overall poverty, where the former is 'severe deprivation of basic human needs, including food, safe drinking water, sanitation facilities, health, shelter, education and information' and the latter is 'lack of income and productive resources to ensure sustainable livelihoods; hunger and malnutrition; ill health; limited or lack of access to education and other basic services; increased morbidity and mortality from illness; homelessness and inadequate housing; unsafe environments and social discrimination and exclusion'. He continues: 'These are clearly *relative* definitions of poverty in that they all refer to poverty not as some "absolute basket of goods" but in terms of the minimum acceptable standard of living applicable to a certain member state and within a person's own society' (Gordon 2006, p. 31).

Indeed,

> in scientific terms, a person or household in Britain is 'poor' when they have both a low income *and* a low standard of living. They are 'not poor' if they have a low income and a reasonable standard of living or if they have a low standard of living but a high income. Both low income and low standard of living can only be accurately measured relative to the norms of the person's or household's society. (Gordon 2006, p. 39)

At the same time, Gordon himself has proposed seven criteria against which basic need satisfaction can be measured and where absolute poverty can be considered present when two or more criteria are not met, namely:

(1)   severe food deprivation, as measured in body mass index
(2)   severe water deprivation
(3)   severe deprivation of sanitation facilities
(4)   severe health deprivation
(5)   severe shelter deprivation
(6)   severe education deprivation
(7)   severe information deprivation, with no access to newspapers and other information sources. (Gordon 2005)

Again, the criteria are useful but, as with the United Nations Development Programme's Human Development indices, we have moved from a single income criterion to a multi-dimensional definition of deprivation, which inevitably incorporates millions more people than those on low income alone. Put differently, the emphasis has shifted from poverty as defined by low income to poverty as a multi-faceted phenomenon.

The multi-dimensional criterion of poverty can also be seen from Sen's work and his capabilities approach (Sen 1999). Capabilities refer to an individual's ability to function, to have the freedom to make choices, to have agency and seize opportunities (Croes 2012). Well-being and, by extension, poverty are determined, for example, by such extrinsic factors as quality of education, life expectancy, income levels, employment and discrimination, and by such intrinsic factors as memory, ethics, common sense and reason.

In sum, poverty has been defined in absolute terms, where individuals or households are considered 'poor' if they fall below a certain income threshold, and in relative terms, where a household or whole population is considered 'poor' if household income falls below the mean or median income of a specific percentage of the population or the distribution of income of the population (Bourguignon 2006).

Generally speaking, scholars have increasingly used multi-dimensional criteria for case studies and micro-level studies, while the criterion of single income is the norm for macro-level studies. As with any indicator, there are advantages and disadvantages, but scholars have tended to use the poverty indicator that is most appropriate or convenient.

Macro-economic perspectives

The contribution of the tourism sector(s) to gross domestic product (GDP) is a common but blunt measure to assess tourism's impact on poverty. The World Travel and Tourism Council (WTTC) (2017) reports that in 2016, travel and tourism generated US$7.6 trillion and 292 million jobs, the equivalent to 10.2 per cent of global GDP and approximately one in ten jobs worldwide, and that travel and tourism comprised 6.6 per cent of total global exports. How much of that contributes to alleviating poverty, though, is a matter for debate and academic research, much of which remains to be done. At the most basic level, of the top 25 countries most dependent on tourism, as measured in its contribution to GDP, none is classified by the UNDP as of low development (Harrison 2008, p. 862). Furthermore, among the 30 countries most dependent on tourism as a percentage of GDP, there is a predominance of islands, and in many small island states tourism has become the backbone of the economy, often when there is little other economic activity (Pratt 2015). In the Caribbean, for example, as Croes notes (2006), tourism is the single largest earner of foreign exchange in 16 of the 30 countries in the region, but research is urgently needed as to how far income from tourism 'trickles down' the social scale.

Clearly, tourism can be a pathway to prosperity for a host region or country (Mihalič 2002; Mitchell & Ashley 2010). It is an important source of foreign earnings, generating employment opportunities, fostering new investment and infrastructure projects and providing an important source of government revenue through taxes and visa fees. However, for any contribution of tourism to poverty alleviation to occur, what tourists spend must remain in the host destination. The mere fact they visit and spend in the destination does not necessarily mean their expenditure will reach the poor or low-income families. Rather, the 'tourist dollar' may leak from the economy, or trickle down only to non-poor members of society. More technically, tourism's contribution to the host economy depends on the size of different multipliers, which reveal the amplifying effect of the initial injection of new demand as tourists' expenditure circulates throughout the host economy. In turn, as Pratt (2011) notes, the size of the multiplier depends on the prevailing leakages in the economy and the linkages of the tourism-oriented sectors with other sectors in the economy. By way of example, Pratt (2015) estimates the economic contribution of tourism to the economies of seven small island developing states (SIDS). He finds that, on average, for every tourist dollar spent in these island states, only US$0.69 stays in the local economy and that tourism income multipliers range from US$0.44 for American Samoa to US$0.91 for Fiji.

Recent attempts to measure the relationship between tourism and poverty are based on various methodologies and use a range of methods (Mitchell & Ashley 2010). Jiang et al. (2011), for example, examine the correlations between tourism intensity and several proxy measures for poverty, namely the Human Development Index, Under Five Mortality rates, and GDP per capita for SIDS. Their conclusion, that those SIDS in Africa, the Caribbean and the Asia-Pacific region with high tourism intensities have higher GDP per capita, higher Human Development Indices and lower Under Five Mortality rates, is useful, but this demonstrates correlation rather than causality.

Other scholars have tended to use two methods to empirically investigate the relationship between tourism and poverty. One is impact analysis, often using computable general equilibrium models which are constructed of the economy being analysed. Simulated increases in tourism are then introduced, to observe their impact on different household income levels.

One of the earlier such macro-economic studies to examine how tourism affects poverty was by Blake et al. (2008). The distributional effects of a simulated 10 per cent increase in tourism expenditures in Brazil show that tourism benefits the lower-income households of Brazil and has the potential to reduce income inequality. However, the main beneficiaries are the low- (but not the lowest) income households. There may be structural reasons for this situation. The lowest-income households, which are characterized by relatively low educational achievement and few employment opportunities, for example, might not directly interact with tourists. Similarly, in Thailand, Wattanakuljarus and Coxhead (2008) find that increased international tourism demand raises aggregate household income but also widens income distribution. They show that while tourism growth benefits all household income groups, the high-income and non-agricultural households gain most. In part, this is because inbound tourism expenditures draw resources away from the tradable sectors, notably the agricultural sector, toward domestic-oriented production. The increase in demand for tourism means that tourism businesses need more labour and capital to satisfy that demand. Depending on the availability of these resources, tourism businesses may offer higher wages to attract labour from other sectors. A growth of tourism also increases the demand for local currency, as tourists exchange their foreign currency for local currency, thus putting upward pressure on the exchange rate, and any appreciation of the exchange rate results in a decrease in competitiveness of other export sectors.

Similar findings have been reported from Indonesia (Mahadevan et al. 2017), Belize (Banerjee et al., in press), Thailand (King & Dinkoksung 2014) and Kenya (Njoya & Seetaram 2018). Mahadevan et al. (2017) find that while increased tourism leads to a reduction in poverty, it also increases income inequality in both urban and rural regions in Indonesia: the greater the reduction in poverty, the more income inequality increased. Similarly, Banerjee et al. (in press) simulate, together and separately, an increase in international tourism demand and an increase in government investment in tourism-related infrastructure. Noting that tourism and tourism investment have positive impacts on the national and local economies of Belize, they suggest that the distribution of benefits depends on socio-economic and institutional factors. More specifically, increased income inequality follows the skill requirements needed to fill employment positions created as a result of the investment. Such findings are replicated in the village of Ban Pa-Ao, Thailand, where tourism prompted the emergence of numerous local entrepreneurs who were able to double the income they obtained from agriculture. However, 'these rewards are highly concentrated. Only a small number of households participate in each activity' (King & Dinkoksung 2014, p.696). By contrast, at a macro level, Njoya and Seetaram (2018) note that in Kenya, increased demand by international tourists for local currency puts pressure on the exchange rate, which appreciates and consequently makes imports less expensive, thus leading to a worsening of the balance of payments. Hence it is the agricultural sector, and by association the rural regions, which tend to suffer. This provides an uncomfortable trade-off for tourism policymakers; tourism development comes at a cost, and decisions must be made whether to promote more tourism and grow the overall economy or attempt to improve and narrow income distribution.

The second method of investigating the relationship of tourism with poverty derives from econometrics and several recent studies, some of which are reviewed below, have used this approach to test the relationship and causality between tourism and poverty. Using a data set from 1991 to 2012 of 49 developing countries, Alam and Paramati (2016) find that tourism actually increases income inequality. With the Gini coefficient as a measure of income inequality, they suggest that the predominantly oligopolistic nature of many tourism service suppliers (especially hotels and transportation) means that service provision in developing countries is dominated by several large suppliers, often a few transnational corporations. As a consequence, the benefits of tourism accrue to owners, investors and senior management of these large companies. By contrast, few benefits go to frontline staff whose earnings may be on or near the minimum wage. Furthermore, small to medium-sized local tourism service providers cannot compete with these large transnational enterprises, resulting in increased income inequality. Bartik (1991) too considers tourism may increase income inequality, as increased demand arising from tourism leads to inflation, including in property values.

The level of causality between national income (usually measured by GDP) and tourism has been the subject of much research (Bilen et al. 2017). Researchers often seek to test the Tourism-Led Growth Hypothesis (TLGH), which states that an expansion in international tourism paves the way for economic growth because international tourism increases foreign exchange earnings that contribute to capital goods, which can further stimulate economic growth and employment (Brida et al. 2016). Alternatively, economic growth can stimulate tourism income, the so-called Growth-Led Tourism Hypothesis. This can occur where a growing economy can create tourism-related business opportunities, or where economies of scale, due to economic growth, decreases costs for the tourism sector, thus making it more competitive (Bilen et al. 2017). The above-mentioned hypotheses are usually tested using Granger's approach to causality (Granger 1969), which assesses the significance of the lagged values of the independent variable (tourism in the case of the TLGH) on an autoregressive model of a dependent variable (income/GDP in the case of the TLGH). If the lagged tourism variables are significant, tourism is said to 'Granger cause' economic growth.

Using Nicaragua as a case study, Croes and Vanegas (2008) sought to show the links between tourism development, economic growth and poverty reduction. They find that tourism 'Granger causes' economic expansion and poverty reduction, and suggest there is a bidirectional causal relationship between economic expansion and poverty reduction. Later, extending the TLGH by using poverty headcount instead of income, Croes (2014) finds that tourism can help alleviate poverty, provided there is a high incidence of extreme poverty, a lower level of economic development and tourism is at a developing stage. Consequently, Croes finds tourism is better at alleviating poverty in Nicaragua because tourism receipts are more important to the poor, and tourism creates jobs in the informal sector and provides vending opportunities for poor households (Croes 2014). By contrast, in Costa Rica there were fewer opportunities as it already had a higher level of economic development than Nicaragua. Croes surmises that tourism growth in Costa Rica generates fewer jobs overall, and that most of what it does create goes to the better educated and foreign workers, rather than the poor.

In short, there is evidence that international tourism brings overall benefits, though the extent to which it contributes to economic growth, poverty reduction and long-term development varies according to economic, environmental, socio-cultural and institutional factors and the linkages between them (Banerjee et al., in press).

It seems clear, too, that international tourism *also* contributes to social inequality. If this is indeed the case, it is reasonable to ask whether or not increased inequality inevitably accompanies poverty alleviation (another appropriate matter for research) and how much the association *matters*. The latter question, perhaps, is more an ethical than a social scientific issue; put simplistically, if a family has been recently relieved from hunger, it is surely legitimate to ask whether or not it matters if, at the same time, their neighbours have gained an extra slice of cake.

Processes of poverty alleviation through tourism

Conventionally, economists describe tourism's economic impacts on destination economies as occurring through the operation of the market. Visitors arrive at a destination and their expenditure on a range of goods and services – stereotypically accommodation, travel and attractions – injects income into the destination which, through the operation of the income multiplier, percolates through the local economy and creates further income for residents. However, there are also leakages, as goods and services required by tourists are imported from outside the local or regional economy, payment for which is thus removed from the destination economy and helps, in turn, to bolster the income of people resident elsewhere.

While the economic mechanisms through which tourism creates income and, at least, potentially alleviates poverty are straightforward, they operate through quite different circumstances and through the agency of a wide variety of social institutions and organizations. In this chapter, we suggest five different scenarios, often involving different types of tourism, and all require further research on tourism's role in poverty alleviation.

Coincidental poverty alleviation

The most common (and most researched) way of considering tourism's role in poverty alleviation is perhaps to see it as a by-product of the normal operation of all those industries that together comprise the travel and tourism sector. According to the WTTC, in 2017 travel and tourism contributed an estimated 11.4 per cent of global GDP and 11.1 per cent of total global employment (WTTC 2017, p. 1). Simply by carrying out their everyday business activities in providing accommodation and all the products and services required by tourists, countless tourism organizations, operating primarily for profit, create income and employment and, thus, alleviate poverty in destination areas. Arguably, tourism entrepreneurs are primarily in business to make a profit. They are not philanthropists although, like other business people, they frequently maintain that in carrying out their business they are also providing a public service in creating employment and income. Indeed, it can be argued that such activities can be hugely beneficial even if promoted by employers with less than strict adherence to good working conditions and minimum wage rates.

Supplementary poverty alleviation

Another form of poverty alleviation from tourism occurs when secondary tourism enterprises, especially those operated by community and/or civil society organizations, take advantage of their association with private-sector tourism enterprises and develop ancillary products and services. Examples from Fiji (experienced by both authors of this chapter) are, for example, activities and services arranged for hotel guests or cruise ship passengers, including village visits and cultural shows, shell markets, treks and taxi tours and the hire of kayak and water skis. Individuals and organizations offering such additions to the tourism 'product', often grouped together as forms of community-based tourism, may include small-scale tour operators and entrepreneurs, as well as individual families and clan groups, and women's and youth groups, often operating with little or no experience of capitalist enterprise.

Policy-focused poverty alleviation

This category refers primarily to tourism enterprises especially developed or targeted to enhance the income of the poor. They include approaches formulated by governments and international organizations, including international aid agencies and international non-government organizations, sometimes in conjunction with local non-government organizations and the private sector, and are most likely to be small-scale, community-based operations that depend on continuous funding from external agencies. Overall, this approach is characteristic of what has been described as pro-poor tourism (PPT) (Harrison 2008) although it is recognized, even by PPT's proponents, that such targeted interventions are unlikely to benefit the poorest in the community who lack skills and cultural and social capital and are, thus, unable to take up the opportunities provided by the PPT initiatives (Ashley 2006, p. 10; Department for International Development 1999, p. 1). Similarly, community-based tourism projects, which are not necessarily identical to PPT projects, are known to have generated few incentives for conservation and have contributed but little to poverty reduction (Harrison 2008, p. 863). By contrast, it needs to be recognized that all kinds of tourism, including mass tourism, function to alleviate poverty and are thus, at least potentially, 'pro-poor'.

Corporate social responsibility/strategic alleviation

Corporate social responsibility (CSR) is both a movement and a business approach. As a movement, it serves to encourage companies to behave more ethically and to consider the impact of their business on society; as a business approach, it aims to contribute to sustainable development by delivering economic, social and environmental benefits for all stakeholders (Financial Times Lexicon, n.d.).

The involvement of business in wider community issues, apparently going beyond simply economic matters, is not new. As indicated elsewhere, nineteenth-century initiatives, ranging from Robert Owen's experiments in New Lanark, contributing to the cooperative movement and, later, the humanistic development of chocolate manufacture at Bournville, near Birmingham, UK, by the Cadbury family, were all predecessors of what is now known as CSR (Harrison 2004, p. 249). More recently, from the 1990s, stakeholder approaches have increasingly concentrated on the need to satisfy wider interest groups than immediate shareholders and, in the USA, such companies as IBM and the Body Shop led the way in developing and publicizing ethical trading practices (Harrison 2004, p. 250). As Harrison notes, the US-based network Business for Social Responsibility was started in 1992 and, in the UK, at the end of the 1990s, the Ethical Trading Initiative, an association of companies, trade unions and non-government organizations (including the Fair Trade Federation), was formed 'to identify and promote good practice in the implementation of codes of labour practice'. Also, in the UK in 1996, the Institute for Social and Ethical Accountability emerged to strengthen 'the social responsibility and the ethical behaviour of the business community and non-profit organisations' (Harrison 2004, p. 250).

Within the tourism sector, there is increasing recognition of the role both large and small companies can play in alleviating social problems in the wider community, though the topic remains relatively little researched. Nevertheless, CSR is considered by the WTTC to be vital to tourism's future, as it should 'help ensure thriving, attractive and welcoming destination communities that will draw visitors, the basis for long term growth and profitability' (WTTC 2002, p. 5) and, in the same publication, such luminaries as Abercrombie and Kent, Accor, Avis, British Airways and Tui are cited as role models for good and sustainable business practice, contributing variously to numerous social projects to assist local communities, protecting the physical environment, countering global warming and supporting projects to expand health treatment, better hygiene, the availability of potable water and affordable housing in poorer communities (WTTC 2002, pp. 7–17). Others who refer more specifically to the active and potential contributions of smaller tourism enterprises in developing sustainable tourism and poverty alleviation include Mitchell and Ashley (2010, pp. 58–60), who discuss philanthropic flows of income to communities arising from tourism as an example of one pathway to prosperity, Cleverdon and Kalisch (2000, pp. 183–4), who discuss the potential of the fair trade movement in tourism to alleviate poverty, Kalisch (2002), who focuses on the role of tour operators, Scheyvens and Russell (2010), Scheyvens and Hughes (2014, 2015 and 2016) and Hughes and Scheyvens (2018), who emphasize CSR and tourism in the Pacific, as do Harrison and Prasad (2013) and Harrison (1999 and 2004), who examine the CSR policies of a specific Pacific island resort in Fiji. By contrast, Henderson has discussed the reaction of hotel companies in Phuket, Thailand, after the 2004 Indian Ocean tsunami (2007).

CSR is not unproblematic. At a general level, the *business case* for it is not universally accepted (Prahalad & Porter 2003; Hardyment 2015) and, in an extensive review of the literature on CSR in tourism, Coles et al. (2013) note that such research is derivative from (and perhaps less advanced than) mainstream studies of CSR in other business and industry sectors. In both, there are problems in actually defining CSR, which is too commonly seen as a homogeneous activity, whereas in fact it covers a wide range of business activities. Furthermore, it is often difficult to ascertain whether or not claimed CSR policies are being implemented, how such activities can be measured and, given the different approaches to CSR in tourism, how to compare their implementation across companies. And while Mitchell and Ashley (2010, pp. 58–60) take a very positive view of philanthropic transfers from tourism businesses to local communities, others point to the promotion and publicity of CSR by tourism companies as examples of cosmetic and inconsequential 'greenwashing', often intended to divert attention (and government legislation) from the damaging social and environmental effects of their operations (Mowforth & Munt 2009, pp. 198–9). At an even more basic level, doubt has been cast on the idea – crucial in promoting CSR – that there is a good business case for it (Hardyment 2015; Prahalad & Porter 2003).

While some such criticisms are justified, case studies have shown that CSR, even carried out for solely business reasons, can bring benefit to communities in destination areas (Harrison 2004). However, whether practised by large corporations or small and medium-sized tourism enterprises, most such activities are carried out on an *ad hoc* basis, with little consistency over time or across the tourism sector, and are on a small scale. Opportunities undoubtedly exist for a more consistent approach (Hughes & Scheyvens 2018) but, so far, despite the importance of tourism in the global economy, the *overall* contribution of CSR by tourism enterprises to poverty alleviation and, more widely, sustainable tourism development is relatively insignificant (and relatively unresearched).

Culturally situated alleviation

Within this category, which overlaps in some respects with that of supplementary alleviation (where smaller enterprises 'piggy back' on the supply of tourists from larger hotels and tour operators) and policy-focused alleviation (including PPT initiatives), we include enterprises which may be defined as quasi-capitalistic. Such tourism enterprises, which are not fully incorporated into a capitalistic tourism economy, are operated by individual or collective owners to make money, for example, by offering hospitality at or running tour operations to 'traditional' villages and other 'cultural' as well as 'natural' attractions. However, the primary purpose of obtaining funds is not to maintain or develop the business. Rather, such funds are used to meet daily and/or traditional financial obligations, for example, payment of school fees, or for such life-cycle events as weddings and funerals. When compared to conventional and more commercial tourism, these enterprises, often run by indigenous communities, are very much in the minority, and failure to reinvest often means they survive only a few years. In fact, their sustainability may depend on several factors, including the absolute number of residents involved, the level of consensus within the community, the extent communities can control the exploitation of their natural resources and the degree of support they receive from outside agencies, including non-government organizations and the private sector (Hinch & Butler 1996, p. 17; Harrison & Price 1996, pp. 5–14). Nevertheless, as

already indicated, this range of small-scale, community-owned and (often) indig-
enously owned initiatives can alleviate poverty, evidence of which can be found in a
wide range of case studies from the South Pacific (Harrison & Price, 1996; Movono
et al. 2015, pp. 101–17; Gibson 2015), Africa (Manyara & Jones 2007; Snyman 2012;
Tucker & Boonabaana 2012) and elsewhere (Harrison & Price 1996; Suntikul et al.
2009; Wang et al. 2010).

Conclusion and directions of future research

In this chapter, we have argued that tourism can indeed improve the lives of residents of destination areas. However, much research remains to be done on how far
this happens in practice, the social institutions and organizations involved, and on
social, economic and other barriers to tourism as a successful tool for development.
Macro-economic data, for example, are frequently inadequate. There is much talk
about multipliers and leakages, but all too often the data are insufficient to arrive
at sensible conclusions. And when macro-economic data *are* adequate, it is still
difficult to gauge the socio-economic impact of tourism at national, regional and
community levels. The strong evidence that non-poor residents may benefit at
least as much, if not more, as the poor from increased tourism raises important
ethical issues. Sometimes, at least, equality may have to be sacrificed for growth,
and democratically orientated researchers may easily err in assuming an inbuilt
tendency towards equality even (or especially) at village level.

Secondly, while tourism has a positive role in poverty alleviation, there is little
comparative research (and equally little agreement) on what *types* of tourism are
most effective. As argued elsewhere (Harrison 2008, pp. 863–4), PPT tends to have
been most closely associated with small-scale community-based tourism, while the
role of mass tourism has been largely ignored. In practice, though, the very positive
correlation of high GDPs in SIDS with a reliance on mass tourism suggests, at the
very least, that mass tourism's role in poverty alleviation is worthy of investigation.
So far, though, the necessary research has not been carried out. We simply do not
know which type of tourism is most successful at alleviating poverty, when and in
what conditions.

Thirdly, comparative research is urgently required on the role in tourism alleviation
of such key stakeholders as tourists, government and transnational tourism enterprises in both developed and developing societies. Some research has been carried
out on how far tourists themselves are willing to pay *extra* for worthy conservation or welfare causes but good intentions are rarely translated into acceptance
of higher prices (Antouskova 2015; Kazeminia 2016; Pulido-Fernandez & Lopez-
Sanchez 2016), and what tourists say they will do and what they actually do can be
quite different (see also Chapter 8). At a more formal, institutional level, important
roles can be played by pressure groups, such as hotel associations or trade unions,
which may help or hinder governments in taxing tourism enterprises and redistributing income to the poorest members of society, either directly or indirectly,

by providing better roads, schools, electricity and potable and accessible water. The latter projects are examples of poverty alleviation. So, too, are some of the activities of transnational tourism enterprises, which not only provide employment (often at rates higher than those paid by local companies), but also (as indicated above) engage in a wide range of *ad hoc* activities that come under the vague heading of CSR.

Like 'development' generally, international tourism does not occur in a vacuum. Tourists come and go, and as they travel they spend. Who benefits from this expenditure, though, depends on the type of tourism involved, the prevailing economic, political and social structure at the destination and the overall ability and commitment of governments to extend tourism's benefits as widely as possible. In this chapter, it has been argued that tourism undoubtedly has the potential to alleviate poverty and bring about 'development'. How far it has successfully done so, and when, where and how, is an appropriate matter for research.

References

Alam, M.S. and Paramati, S.R. (2016), 'The impact of tourism on income inequality in developing economies: Does Kuznets curve hypothesis exist?' *Annals of Tourism Research*, **61**, 111–26.

Antouskova, M. (2015), 'Willingness to pay', in C. Cater, B. Garrod and T. Low (eds) *The Encyclopaedia of Sustainable Tourism*, Wallingford: CABI, p. 536.

Ashley, C. (2006), 'Participation by the poor in Luang Prabang tourism economy: Current earnings and opportunities for expansion', Working Paper 273, London: Overseas Development Institute.

Banerjee, O., Cicowiez, M., Morris, E.J. and Moreda, A. (in press), 'Boosting tourism's contribution to growth and development: Analysis of the evidence', *Review of Development Economics*. doi:10.1111/rode.12385

Bartik, T.J. (1991), *Who Benefits from State and Local Economic Development Policies?* Kalamazoo, MI: W.E. Upjohn Institute for Employment Research.

Bilen, M., Yilanci, V. and Eryuzlu, H. (2017), 'Tourism development and economic growth: A panel Granger causality analysis in the frequency domain', *Current Issues in Tourism*, **20**(1), 27–32.

Blake, A., Arbache, J.S., Sinclair, M.T. and Teles, V. (2008), 'Tourism and poverty relief', *Annals of Tourism Research*, **35**(1), 107–26.

Bourguignon, F. (2006), 'From income to endowments: The difficult task of expanding the income poverty paradigm', in B. Grusky and D. Kanbur (eds) *Poverty and Inequality*, Stanford, CA: Stanford University Press, pp. 76–102.

Brida, J.G., Cortes-Jimenez, I. and Pulina, M. (2016), 'Has the tourism-led growth hypothesis been validated? A literature review', *Current Issues in Tourism*, **19**(5), 394–430.

Cleverdon, R. and Kalisch, A. (2000), 'Fair trade in tourism', *International Journal of Tourism Research*, **2**(3), 171–87.

Coles, T., Fenclova, E. and Dinan, C. (2013), 'Tourism and corporate social responsibility: A critical review and research agenda', *Tourism Management Perspectives*, **6**, 122–41.

Croes, R. (2006), 'A paradigm shift to a new strategy for small island economies: Embracing demand side economics for value enhancement and long term economic stability', *Tourism Management*, **27**(3), 453–65.

Croes, R. (2012), 'Assessing tourism development from Sen's capability approach', *Journal of Travel Research*, **51**(5), 542–54.

Croes, R. (2014), 'The role of tourism in poverty reduction: An empirical assessment', *Tourism Economics*, **20**(2), 207–26.

Croes, R. and Vanegas, M. (2008), 'Cointegration and causality between tourism and poverty reduction', *Journal of Travel Research*, **47**(1), 94–103.

de Kadt, E. (ed.) (1979), *Tourism: Passport to Development?* New York: Oxford University Press.

Department for International Development (1999), *Tourism and Poverty Elimination: Untapped Potential*, London: DFID.

Financial Times Lexicon (n.d.), 'Definition of corporate social responsibility'. Accessed 26 February 2018 at http://lexicon.ft.com/Term?term=corporate-social-responsibility--(CSR).

Gibson, D. (2015), 'Community-based tourism in Fiji', in S. Pratt and D. Harrison (eds) *Tourism in Pacific Islands: Current Issues and Future Challenges*, Abingdon: Routledge, pp. 118–33.

Gordon, D. (2005), *Indicators of Poverty and Hunger*, Expert Group Meeting on Youth Development Indicators, United Nations Headquarters, New York, 12–14 December. Accessed 22 February 2018 at www.un.org/esa/socdev/unyin/documents/ydiDavidGordon_poverty.pdf

Gordon, D. (2006), 'The concept and measurement of poverty', in C. Pantazis, D. Gordon and R. Levitas (eds) *Poverty and Social Exclusion in Britain: The Millennium Survey*, Bristol: Policy Press, pp. 29–68.

Granger, C.W.J. (1969), 'Investigating causal relations by econometric models and cross-spectral methods', *Econometrica*, **37**(3), 424–38.

Hall, C.M. (2008), *Tourism Planning: Policies, Processes and Relationships*, 2nd edn, Harlow: Pearson Education.

Hardyment, R. (2015), 'Back to the future: Harvard ditches the business case'. Accessed 4 June 2018 at https://ccbriefing.corporate-citizenship.com/2015/01/27/back-future-harvard-ditches-business-case/

Harrison, D. (1999), *A Cultural Audit of Turtle Island, Fiji*, Fiji: Turtle Island.

Harrison, D. (2004), 'Working with the tourism industry: A case study from Fiji', *Social Responsibility*, **1**(1–2), 249–70.

Harrison, D. (2008), 'Pro-poor tourism: a critique', *Third World Quarterly*, **29**(5), 851–68.

Harrison, D. and Prasad, B. (2013), 'The contribution of tourism to the development of Fiji Islands and other Pacific island countries', in C. Tisdell (ed.) *A Handbook of Tourism Economics*, Singapore: World Scientific Publishing, pp. 741–61.

Harrison, D. and Price, M. (1996), 'Fragile environments, fragile communities? An introduction', in M. Price (ed.) *People and Tourism in Fragile Environments*, Chichester: John Wiley & Sons, pp. 1–18.

Harrison, D. and Schipani, S. (2007), 'Lao tourism and poverty alleviation: Community-based tourism and the private sector', *Current Issues in Tourism*, **10**(2–3), 195–230.

Henderson, J. (2007), 'Corporate social responsibility and tourism: Hotel companies in Phuket, Thailand, after the Indian Ocean Tsunami', *International Journal of Hospitality Management*, **26**(1), 228–39.

Hinch, T. and Butler, R. (1996), 'Indigenous tourism: A common ground for discussion', in R. Butler and T. Hinch (eds) *Tourism and Indigenous Peoples*, London: International Thomson Business Press, pp. 3–19.

Hughes, E. and Scheyvens, R. (2018), 'Development alternatives in the Pacific: How tourism corporates can work more effectively with local communities', *Tourism Planning and Development*. doi:10.1080/21568316.2018.1478881

Jafari, J. (1989), 'Sociocultural dimensions of tourism: An English language literature review', in J. Bystrzanowski (ed.) *Tourism as a Factor in Social Change, Vol. 1: A Sociocultural Study*, Vienna: European Coordination Centre for Research and Documentation in Social Sciences, pp. 17–60.

Jiang, M., DeLacy, T., Mkiramweni, N.P. and Harrison, D. (2011), 'Some evidence for tourism alleviating poverty', *Annals of Tourism Research*, **38**(3), 1181–4.

Kalisch, A. (2002), *Corporate Futures: Social Responsibility in the Tourism Industry*, London: Tourism Concern.

Kazeminia, A. (2016), 'Willingness to pay', in J. Jafari and Honggen Xiao (eds) *Encyclopedia of Tourism*, Cham, Switzerland: Springer, pp. 1021–2.

King, R. and Dinkoksung, S. (2014), 'Ban Pa-Ao, pro-poor tourism and uneven development', *Tourism Geographies*, **16**(4), 687–703.

Mahadevan, R., Amir, H. and Nugroho, A. (2017), 'Regional impacts of tourism-led growth on poverty and inequality: A dynamic general equilibrium analysis for Indonesia', *Tourism Economics*, **23**(3), 614–31.

Manyara, G. and Jones, E. (2007), 'Community-based tourism enterprises development in Kenya: An exploration of their potential as avenues of poverty reduction', *Journal of Sustainable Tourism*, **15**(6), 628–44.

Mihalič, T. (2002), 'Tourism and economic development issues', in R. Sharpley and D.J. Telfer (eds) *Tourism and Development: Concepts and Issues*, Clevedon: Channel View, pp. 81–111.

Mitchell, J. and Ashley, C. (2010), *Tourism and Poverty Reduction: Pathways to Prosperity*, London: Earthscan.

Movono, A., Pratt, S. and Harrison, D. (2015), 'Adapting and reacting to tourism development: A tale of two villages on Fiji's Coral Coast', in S. Pratt and D. Harrison (eds) *Tourism in Pacific Islands: Current Issues and Future Challenges*, Abingdon: Routledge, pp. 101–17.

Mowforth, M. and Munt, I. (2009), *Tourism and Sustainability: Development, Globalisation and New Tourism in the Third World*, 3rd edn, London: Routledge.

Njoya, E.T. and Seetaram, N. (2018), 'Tourism contribution to poverty alleviation in Kenya: A dynamic computable general equilibrium analysis', *Journal of Travel Research*, **57**(4), 513–24.

Prahalad, C.K. and Porter, M. (eds) (2003), *Harvard Business Review on Corporate Responsibility*, Cambridge, MA: Harvard Business Publishing.

Pratt, S. (2011), 'Economic linkages and impacts across the TALC', *Annals of Tourism Research*, **38**(2), 630–50.

Pratt, S. (2015), 'The economic impact of tourism in SIDS', *Annals of Tourism Research*, **52**, 148–60.

Pulido-Fernandez, J.I. and Lopez-Sanchez, Y. (2016), 'Are tourists really willing to pay more for sustainable destinations?', *Sustainability*, **8**(12), 1240. doi:10.3390/su8121240

Scheyvens, R. and Hughes, E. (2014), 'Prospects for sustainable development in the Pacific: A review of corporate social responsibility in tourism', *Journal of Pacific Studies*, **35**(1), 47–65.

Scheyvens, R. and Hughes, E. (2015), 'Tourism and CSR in the Pacific', in S. Pratt and D. Harrison (eds) *Tourism in Pacific Islands: Current Issues and Future Challenges*, Abingdon: Routledge, pp. 134–47.

Scheyvens, R. and Hughes, E. (2016), 'Corporate social responsibility in tourism post-2015: A development first approach', *Tourism Geographies*, **18**(5), 469–82.

Scheyvens, R. and Russell, M. (2010), *Sharing the Riches of Tourism in Fiji: Summary Report*, Palmerston North, New Zealand: Massey University.

Sen, A. (1999), *Development as Freedom*, Oxford: Oxford University Press.

Snyman, S.L. (2012), 'The role of tourism employment in poverty reduction and community perceptions of conservation and tourism in southern Africa', *Journal of Sustainable Tourism*, **20**(3), 395–416.

Stewart, F., Ranis, G. and Samman, E. (2018), *Advancing Human Development: Theory and Practice*, Oxford: Oxford University Press.

Suntikul, W., Bauer, T. and Song, H. (2009), 'Pro-poor tourism development in Viengxay, Laos: Current state and future prospects', *Asia Pacific Journal of Tourism Research*, **14**(2), 153–68.

Tucker, H. and Boonabaana, B. (2012), 'A critical analysis of tourism, gender and poverty reduction', *Journal of Sustainable Tourism*, **20**(3), 437–55.

Wang, H., Yang, Z., Chen, L., Yang, J. and Li, R. (2010), 'Minority community participation in tourism: A case of Kanas Tuva villages in Xinjiang, China', *Tourism Management*, **31**(6), 759–64.

Wattanakuljarus, A. and Coxhead, I. (2008), 'Is tourism-based development good for the poor? A general equilibrium analysis for Thailand', *Journal of Policy Modeling*, **30**(6), 929–95.

Weller, C. (2017), 'The World Bank released new poverty lines – find out where your country stands'. Accessed 21 February 2018 at http://uk.businessinsider.com/world-bank-released-new-poverty-lines-see-where-your-country-falls-2017-10

Willis, K. (2005), *Theories and Practices of Development*, London: Routledge.

WTTC (2002), *Corporate Social Leadership in Travel and Tourism*, London: World Travel and Tourism Council.

WTTC (2017), *Travel and Tourism Economic Impact 2017: World*, London: World Travel and Tourism Council.

7 Community-based tourism and 'development'

*Tazim Jamal, Christine Budke and Ingrid Barradas-Bribiesca**

Introduction

One area that has attracted a great deal of attention in the context of tourism development is community-based tourism (CBT). Reflecting the trend towards alternative, grassroots approaches that began to arise as a counter to mass tourism in the 1970s, CBT has been advocated as a means of enhancing tourism-related benefits through local control and resident participation in tourism development, as well as poverty alleviation in the context of international development (for example, Ashley et al. 2000). Yet, definitions of CBT remain vague and its principles continue to be debated and discussed, along with the meaning of both 'community' and 'development.'[1] Additionally, critical questions arise about the success of CBT approaches in today's globalized landscape and the privatization of commerce and trade (i.e. neoliberal globalization). Subsequent to four major development paradigms that dominated development thinking in the twentieth century (modernization, dependency, neoliberalism and alternative/sustainable development), the 1990s onwards has witnessed the emergence of post-development critiques and the rejection of Western notions of 'development' as being neocolonial and driven by large institutional and corporate interests (see Sachs 2010; Sharpley & Telfer 2016).

This chapter explores the complicated landscape in which CBT finds itself today in search of clarity and new perspectives to inform some of the contestation and confusion over the notion of CBT. Our view is partial, as the topic is rich and deserving of collaborative engagement by tourism-related researchers, community practitioners and those who stand to be most impacted by our research – local residents (their visitors being an important stakeholder but a secondary one). The next section commences with a short discussion of some favoured CBT principles, followed by a critical look at notions of 'development'. Two paradigm shifts are offered for consideration: a 'One Health' perspective and a post-development approach that embraces a plurality of worldviews beyond the modern – a 'pluriverse' of cultural values and ways of being and relating to each other and to nature (Escobar 2016, 2018).[2] This is then followed by a case study of rural endogenous 'development' in Mexico, where a local microfinance non-governmental organization (NGO) is facilitating women's empowerment and involvement in local and social enterprise (see, for example, Agarwal 2016, on microfinance and poverty alleviation).[3] The final section summarizes a few considerations for researchers willing to take up a post-development research stance in a neoliberalized local-global landscape of travel and tourism.

A critical look at CBT

Alternative approaches to mass tourism, broadly referred to as alternative tourism, typically emphasize the development of local, small-scale tourism initiatives, local control, resident involvement in planning and decision making, gender equity, environmental conservation, capacity building and social benefits to the local community. Among examples cited here with a CBT-related focus are pro-poor tourism (PPT), fair trade tourism and volunteer tourism (McGehee 2012). PPT is a community-based approach oriented towards strategies that enhance benefits and opportunities for the poor. It is generally focused on grassroots development, poverty alleviation, gender equality and income equity, local empowerment and participation.[4] Alternative approaches that adopt a sustainable livelihoods perspective aim to use tourism to diversify livelihood options and support environmental conservation. Community-based natural resource management (CBNRM), for instance, aims to promote sustainable livelihoods, local participation in wildlife management and resource use rights of the local communities. It is based on the principle that rural communities will feel greater stewardship over their environments and support conservation if they derive economic benefits from natural resource use (e.g. Mbaiwa & Stronza 2010).

In all cases, CBT lays claim to some common principles such as *local ownership* of tourism-related enterprises, *local control* over tourism development and the local commons (natural and cultural) and *local economic and social benefits* including capacity building, enabling gender equity and women's empowerment, facilitating social capital (social relationships, social bonds, reciprocity) and community agency (see Borlido & Coromina 2018; Matarrita-Cascante et al. 2010). *Resident participation* in the development, planning and management of CBT, *organizational forms* and *institutional structures* are then needed that enable local ownership, conservation and stewardship, as well as equity and fairness in the distribution of the costs and benefits of tourism development. Local approaches to economic development can include collaborative networking, community-based enterprise, social enterprise and social entrepreneurship, microcredit NGOs and cooperatives, as well as individual business enterprises within the community (Dredge 2006; Manyara & Jones 2007). Mansuri and Rao (2004, pp. 1–2) offer valuable insight into this crucial political (and cultural) issue by carefully distinguishing *community-driven* development from *community-based* development: 'Community-based development is an umbrella term for projects that actively include beneficiaries in their design and management, and community-driven development refers to community-based development projects in which communities have direct control over key project-decisions, including management of investment funds'. However, challenges arise quickly, particularly when notions of community and land tenure are unclear.

Taylor (2017) points out that the community-based Indigenous tourism project development in Ek'Balam, a rural Maya village in the Yucatan, Mexico, has been praised for its ecological, economic and social sustainability, particularly owing to resident participation in the project design and management. However, lack of differentiation of the meaning of 'community' in relation to the *ejido* land tenure system resulted in a few kin groups dominating the CBT project and corralling the majority of the benefits. Elite domination (elite capture) and lack of attention to the sociopolitical landscape of the 'community' were two crucial inhibiters of CBT:

> The existing social relationships and power structures contained within a community are exactly why the use of community as a defining category over which development initiatives can be superimposed is so troublesome . . . In Ek'Balam, as in most small, rural, Indigenous communities in the literature, the rhetoric of benefits shared among the community can be realized as a reality only when the development trajectory is slow, focused, and based in careful use of existing local knowledge. (Taylor 2017, p. 444)

Palmer and Chuamuangphan (2018, p. 320) similarly discover that governance 'in the sense of social order, social coordination, social practices – is identified as having a key influence upon the ways in which participation in tourism occurs at a local level'. They highlight social status, legitimacy and power as areas for future research to better understand the dynamics of CBT development. By contrast, Movono and Dahles (2017) argue that despite patriarchal structures in Indigenous Fijian society along the Coral Coast of Fiji, Indigenous Fijian women in Vatuolalai village have adapted to benefit from tourism. Getting involved in the village tours that brought visitors, they became successful as small-scale business operators and influential drivers of sociopolitical changes. The Vatuolalai women's group, known as the Soqosoqo Vakamarama or Women's Development Committee, that they formed enabled them to act on community-wide issues since the 1980s, facilitating social and political empowerment. Movono and Dahles (2017) thus argue that direct participation and enterprise ownership through tourism-based entrepreneurship has facilitated economic as well as psychological, social and political empowerment (following Scheyvens' 1999 empowerment framework).

Power relations and conflict influence CBT constructively in the above case, aided by the reflexivity and determination of the women. Crucial to success were collaborative organizational structures that enabled the women to direct and manage communal and social issues. Local control over development and planning relate closely to governance and policy, and institutional structures need to be carefully assessed and enacted (see Dredge 2006). Ruiz-Ballesteros and Brondizio (2013) offer a detailed study of a participatory multi-level, local to regional governance system to define and control CBT development and tourism operations in the island community of Floreana, located within Galápagos National Park (GNP) in the Galápagos Islands. It required a new model for managing common pool resources (CPR) with tourism use and the crafting of new institutions. Governance, again, is an important dimension. At the local level, rule crafting included creation of a 'governing board in the community tourism organization' (Ruiz-Ballesteros

& Brondizio 2013, p. 328). The authors also note the diverse stakeholders at the regional and local levels. For example, CPRs at the local level are associated with the canton government, the community assembly, local groups (e.g. kinship and agricultural association), local tourism entrepreneurs and the general population. The NGOs, local government and GNP participate at both levels.

Ruiz-Ballesteros and Brondizio (2013) also identify a complex landscape of world-views including 'environment first' (privileging conservation) and 'humans first' (socioeconomic development for local residents through tourism, but with an environmental sensibility), plus a worldview of non-participating regional tourism entrepreneurs based on market logic and governance influenced by market-based competition. The market vision is also present among tourism entrepreneurs at the local level. Duffy (2009) and others have similarly noted how CBNRM is affected by external stakeholders and by market mechanisms that do not coincide with local values and practices related to land and nature. These worldviews, conflict-ing values and their relationship to governance are not well explored, despite the obvious merit of ensuring a culturally appropriate approach to CBT and govern-ance. This relationship is examined below, leading to a call for a more holistic, non-patriarchal, culturally situated *pluralistic* approach to development and CBT.

Decentring modernist 'development' towards cultural pluralism

Hills and Lundgren's (1977) core-periphery analysis of Caribbean tourism was a classical illustration of the impacts of mass tourism that led to a growing call for alternative approaches to and forms of tourism. From the 1970s, responsible tour-ism and ecotourism, followed by sustainable tourism development, CBT and, more recently, PPT have emerged. A number of studies have attempted to address the lack of resources, management and marketing knowledge and capacity building needs of CBT in poorer regions (e.g. Ashley et al. 2000). Yet, how well do these economic and business (managerial) discourses relate to the sociocultural and historical context of the community under study? The above discussion indicates that much greater thought has been given to the ontological and epistemological assumptions and worldviews driving approaches to tourism development and CBT emanating from the Global North, so are the plethora of CBT principles generaliz-able and universal? These principles and the motives and interests that drove them merit greater scrutiny, which we attempt to do below.

In the context of *international* development, CBT has been closely linked to issues of economic leakage, dependency and domination of external stakeholders. The controlling and integrating forces in international tourism include large trans-national organizations engaged in transportation, hospitality and entertainment services, such as international airlines, all-inclusive resorts and large tour operators that offer a diverse array of packaged tours to facilitate the movement of large numbers of travellers for 'mass tourism'. Under the neoliberal market conditions that became entrenched in the twentieth century, national, transnational and global economic policies and regulations continue to facilitate the profitability and success of these organizations, while the destination countries struggle to control their economic dependency on visitors, expertise and financing from the 'West'. Neoliberal approaches emphasize the efficiency of large-scale free market capitalism, limited government involvement (other than to facilitate free trade interests regionally and globally) and economic growth (seen as 'development') to resolve trade deficits and national debt (Telfer 2009). Structural adjustment programmes (SAPs) and debt repayment related to large development projects that benefited primarily external stakeholders and domestic elites locked poorer countries in a vicious cycle of debt repayment that exacerbated poverty and extreme disparities and inequities in wealth and income (Holden 2013). SAPs consisted of loans provided by the World Bank and International Monetary Fund that were tied closely to 'free market' policy reforms. The costs of 'development' were high in terms of destination vulnerability, social and economic inequalities, high leakage of tourist expenditures back to the core generating regions, and continued dependency and underdevelopment (Britton 1982; see also Mosedale 2011).

A growing stream of post-colonial and ecofeminist critiques continue to challenge and shift the dominant Eurocentric, modernist values that have driven 'development' and entrenched a discourse of relentless growth and consumption that is needed to drive capital market expansion globally. Ecofeminist and feminist perspectives offer the opportunity to identify and redress key omissions (like the loss of intangible cultural and heritage relationships with land and nature), develop counter-discourses to domination and further inform critical perspectives such as political ecology (see Shiva 1988; Salleh 1984). They also offer valuable insights for resituating the missing gendered, diverse body in tourism, reintroducing intangibles such as emotions (e.g. love, concern, friendship). They call us to pay attention to human–environmental and other cultural relationships, as well as to intangible, oppressive and exploitative economic structures and unequal power relationships in a local-global domain. As ecofeminist Vandana Shiva describes, 'economic globalization as we are seeing it unfold is not a process of ever widening circles of inclusion. It is a process of ascending hierarchies that concentrate power and exclude people from participating in the political and economic life of their societies' (Shiva 1997, p. 22). She goes on to state that ecological feminism 'sees in the current trend the ultimate concentration of capitalist patriarchy and its violence against nature and women' (Shiva 1997, p. 24).

Post-development advocates like Gustavo Esteva and Arturo Escobar call for a paradigm shift to a holistic, post-development approach to CBT that incorporates a cultural, relational, autonomous approach for communal well-being (see various entries in Sachs 2010; Kothari et al. 2019). Others such as Karst (2017) have drawn on Indigenous worldviews like *Buen Vivir* (good living) to examine culture–spiritual–nature relationships and notions of well-being in CBT and ecotourism. *Buen Vivir* recognizes the rights of nature and its rich concept encompasses social-cultural and spiritual relationships, reciprocity and communality, self-determination and autonomy. It also translates into a political ontology, resisting modernist notions of development to celebrate Indigenous well-being and ways of being (Escobar 2018).

Collaborative governance and cultural-historical justice

Community-based collaboration between scientific experts, government, the tourism industry and local residents is essential to bring scientific knowledge, Indigenous knowledge and local knowledge (including citizen science) to bear on issues related to resource conservation, climate change, social equity and poverty alleviation.[5] The question is how to facilitate thoughtful, inclusive dialogue and negotiation of different worldviews, values and interests, and to take the historical and cultural context into consideration, in order to enable good governance, collaborative planning and control over CBT at the local level.

Co-management of Indigenous land that had been appropriated into protected areas was one such approach, such as in Kakadu National Park (KNP), Australia, which is co-managed by the KNP Traditional Owners and the federal Australian Nature Conservation Agency. Inclusion of traditional knowledge, respect for traditional values and ancestral relationships with the land and equitable sharing of tourism income are key to effective co-management. Addressing land, nature and culture holistically in governance is a vital principle that helps to address injustices that affect the success of CBT in post-colonial destinations. For instance, examining the post-colonial context of tourism development and poverty alleviation in Tanzania reveals historically embedded challenges and conflicts over land tenure, wildlife revenues and access to tourism benefits in northern Tanzania (Nelson 2012; see also Akama et al. 2011 for a post-colonial critique of safari tourism and Indigenous exclusion in Kenya). 'The development of explicitly rights-based approaches to tourism that emphasize tenure and devolved governance would aid the implementation of poverty alleviation strategies, as would research into the political economy of tourism and its governance' (Nelson, 2012, p. 359).

However, more than a rights-based approach is needed if governance is to effectively devolve to the local level. Using an emic perspective and culturally appropriate methodology, including informal *talanoa* (discussions), Farrelly (2011) examined community-based ecotourism management (CBEM), Indigenous governance and decision making in Boumā National Heritage Park, Fiji. Exploring the roles of kin groups, village spokesmen and clan systems, and their relationship with Western business decision-making practices, she argues for greater attention to local systems of governance and empowerment as part of tourism development (not an outcome of it). Importantly, she examines the core Fijian cultural concept of vanua as a way of life, involving interrelated social, ecological and spiritual elements – the 'vanua way' conflicted with Western forms of community-based enterprise until the Boumā people adapted CBEM to their core values. 'They call this the "business va'avanua" or business the vanua way: a hybrid of western-based entrepreneurship and Boumā's moral economy', explained Farrelly (2011, p. 825).

The above example also speaks to a post-development narrative. An important point that arises here is how Indigenous and local communities 'gently' resist dispossession and expropriation of traditional ancestral lands, neocolonialism and

Western values of modernization and market capitalism that accompany CBEM and CBT models introduced externally. Recognizing they are unable to fully extract themselves from these, they adapt them to their own needs and values, mediating economic benefits, conservation and cultural relationships for their own well-being (for an example of Andean campesino community engagement with protected areas and conservation-related displacement to seek 'historical justice', see Rasmussen 2018). One of the crucial priorities as CBT progresses into the twenty-first century will be to attend to the plurality of meanings and ways of being and relating, and design new, holistic ways to embrace such a 'pluriverse' as Escobar (2018) describes. We outline below one example of such a holistic, relationship approach, focusing on sustainability and health.

One Health and sustainability: towards a holistic approach to CBT

> Sustainable development in the Anthropocene: 'Development that meets the needs of the present while safeguarding Earth's life-support system, on which the welfare of current and future generations depends'. (Griggs et al. 2013a, p. 306)

As climate change and other sustainability challenges gather increasing urgency on global policy agendas, one aspect that merits greater attention in CBT research and practice is tourism's role in relation to sustainability and health. A holistic, relational approach to health at the community level would include understanding and addressing human–environmental relationships; that is, the health focus is not merely with respect to diseases, but also attends to social and cultural relationships with land and nature. Multi-fold issues arise here, such as control over the commons, stewardship of natural and cultural resources, social bonds and *communal well-being* that are interrelated with spiritual relationships and *cultural survival of* minority ethnic groups who face discrimination and oppression, or whose values do not coincide with those of a dominant group. Ecological justice issues also arise here; both Fennell (2014) and Holden (2018) point out a major gap in tourism studies related to animal welfare and nature's rights, respectively.

Human activities are important drivers of change (including climate change) on a global scale and poverty alleviation is a crucial goal for overall planetary health and well-being of its inhabitants. In anticipation of the new Sustainable Development Goals (SDGs) that were to replace the existing Millennium Development Goals (MDGs), Griggs et al. (2013a, 2013b) argued that sustainable development in the Anthropocene must put the Earth's life-support systems alongside the key goals of the MDGs, making planetary support and poverty alleviation (a key focus of the MDGs) twin priorities of the new SDGs. Drawing on a complex systems approach, they offered a 'unified framework' containing a new 'paradigm' whereby economy and society are nested within Earth's life-support systems, and where environmental health and poverty alleviation are viewed as being interrelated. Combining the sustainability requirements in their framework with the MDG targets (updated and extended for 2030), they proposed six SDGs (along with provisional targets for 2030):

- thriving lives and livelihoods
- sustainable food security
- sustainable water security
- universal clean energy
- healthy and productive ecosystems
- governance for sustainable societies.

Their unified framework and the six core SDG goals they proposed correspond well with the 17 SDGs that now replace the MDGs (see www.un.org/sustainabledevel opment/sustainable-development-goals/). We argue here that while Griggs et al.'s scientific framework offers valuable guidance towards an integrated paradigm for sustainable development, sustainable tourism and CBT, it needs to be inclusive of more than a Western, scientific and modernist paradigm. The discussion in the previous section lends support for an argument for collaborative, *community-driven* approaches to sustainable tourism development that embrace human–environmental and cultural relationships and is attentive to historical context (colonialism's legacies included) and gendered perspectives that pave the way for new sensitivities, feminine concerns and intangible values like emotion, love, care and health to help address the SDGs.

One potential avenue of investigation for such an inclusive paradigm, particular to the rural CBT context, is a holistic, embodied approach to health that encompasses micro–macro interrelationships of human health and environmental health (ecosystems and animals included, see Figure 7.1) and tackles historical, social and cultural injustices such as economic and gender inequality, social inequities and

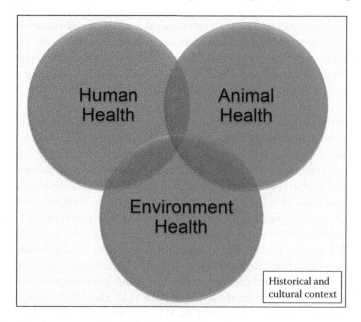

Figure 7.1   Visual representation of the One Health concept

cultural racism. A fruitful area of future investigation may be the emerging global paradigm of 'One Health', which can be adapted to address complex social dynamics, human–environmental relationships (ethical, cultural, social and psychological), and human–animal interactions (e.g. disease transmission, food and health hazards, human–animal bonds).

One Health originated at the local level in relation to human–livestock health and disease issues in East Africa in the 1970s. The term has been attributed to Calvin Schwabe (he in fact used the term 'One Medicine'), but it has been argued that the foundation of the One Health concept can be traced back to the time of Hippocrates and later to the likes of Virchow and others (Schwabe 1968, 1984). Health, holistically, rather than economy is the crux of a One Health approach. According to the World Health Organization, '[h]ealth is a state of complete physical, mental and social well-being and not merely the absence of disease or infirmity'.[6] Its scope, scale and significance have expanded since then into a holistic approach to health that jointly addresses human health and environmental sustainability with concrete policies and actions.[7] As such, it represents a significant paradigm shift in the way knowledge, attitudes and actions are initiated in relation to environmental conservation and sustainable development (for more detail, see Jamal et al. 2014).

On a global level, the human–animal–environment health model emerged as a means to address human–animal interactions that result in emerging and re-emerging zoonotic diseases. Animals are also closely linked to the livelihood and socioeconomic stability of millions of people around the world, including small-scale agriculturalists, pastoralists and those that rely on healthy wildlife to attract tourism dollars to their communities, including community-based conservation programmes such as CBNRM. Public health, food safety, food security and bio-terrorism/defence are all imbricated in this local-global picture of human health. Generalized systems dynamic frameworks of One Health such as that forwarded by Zinsstag et al. (2011), therefore, approach health within social-ecological systems. In this model, ecosystem health entails human health, animal health, plant health and environmental health interacting as a system. The social-cultural-economic-political determinants and outcomes of health include governance, infrastructure, education, public and animal health systems, livelihoods, access, resilience, equity and so on. The ecological determinants and outcomes of health involve 'sustainability', resilience and adaptive management.

Drawing from the previous sections, it could be argued that sustainable development in the Anthropocene would be better served by a holistic, health-based approach *and* a cultural lens sensitive to cultural relationships and 'other' worldviews than those entrenched by modernization, colonialization and market capitalism. A One Health perspective is one possible example that focuses on the interrelatedness of environment, animal health and human health (Figure 7.1). Following a post-development, culturally sensitive perspective, these overlapping circles within Figure 7.1 would be embedded in the cultural and historical context of the community. Understanding the historical land-related relationships does matter; ethical and effective CBT and CBNRM would necessarily have to deal with human rights issues and cultural injustices related to the past, such as through exclusion from traditional grazing lands due to the formation of protected areas, or land expropriation through settler colonialism that continues to disadvantage and displace Indigenous populations (Zips & Zips-Mairitsch 2007).

This embodied health paradigm would holistically address emotional and psychological health, intangible relationships (e.g. human–environmental and human–animal bonds) and development that is ethically gendered, embracing feminine values such as care, and confronting gendered inequalities, sexist discourses and so on. It could be further enhanced by post-development critiques and movements towards *solidarity, communality* and *relationality* – a culturally situated approach which hence must consider political ontology as well (Escobar 2016). These principles would help to inform the importance of a culturally situated, community-driven approach to CBT. The next section presents a case study to help explore the importance of an integrated, relational approach to CBT where well-being encompasses health in the holistic sense above, and a post-development sensibility – facilitating human–environmental and human–cultural relationships and alerting the changes brought about by modernization and market-based economic development. Such an approach is, arguably, of critical importance in rural endogenous settings.

Case study: Indigenous well-being in Cudilla, Mexico

Cudilla (a pseudonym to protect the community's privacy) is a transitional community with Otomi heritage, rich cultural traditions, human–environmental relationships and two community-based cooperatives, one of which is a women's embroidery cooperative that a small, locally based microcredit NGO helped to set up. The NGO leader is a young man who was born and raised in the rural district of San Miguel de Allende. He is self-educated, having studied microfinance through books he obtained. The impetus for establishing the NGO was to assist the local impoverished communities with rural economic and social development. He and the NGO staff who lived in the same area as the communities they worked with are regarded with great respect. They work closely with residents on capacity building for health management (e.g. teaching local families to grow vegetables and tend family-owned gardens to supplement their diet) and offer microcredit loans to start new local enterprises.

Approaching the rural endogenous study

This case is part of an ongoing research project near the historic city of San Miguel de Allende (a UNESCO-designated World Heritage Site in the state of Guanajuato, Mexico). The main purpose of this preliminary study was to commence an exploratory investigation of health, cultural heritage and microcredit-facilitated women's enterprise in the community of Cudilla, using participant observation in the city and local market, informal and formal conversations with local residents and

Figure 7.2a   Compound dotted with mesquite trees

two focus group meetings. The discussion below draws on a four-day structured research trip in December 2012 where the NGO leader was present at each focus group meeting. Two subsequent informal meetings with the microfinance NGO were held in San Miguel in 2015/16 to discuss training programmes and other support being provided to communities in their programme.

Informal discussions plus two focus group meetings took place on a cool December day (2012) in an open space within the village that was dotted with trees and other vegetation (Figure 7.2a). One of the three researchers was a Guanajuato resident; she facilitated the focus group meetings (in Spanish). Plastic chairs were organized in a sunny area in which two focus groups were convened, one in the morning, the other in the early afternoon, in order to facilitate participation and work schedules. Time was budgeted between and after the focus group meetings to walk to the small historic church nearby (badly in need of repair; Figure 7.2b), talk informally with local residents, view the embroidered napkins and cloth they displayed for sale and further examine various tools (primarily food preparation and creating spinning yarn for the embroidery) that had been shown to us during the focus group meetings. On a different day, we visited the market in San Miguel where we spoke to the women at the stand where they sold their embroidered items and observed their interactions with visitors to the market.

Figure 7.2b   Historic church near the community

Six women and one young man participated in the morning focus group (Group 1) (as well as a few *perros* – domesticated dogs wandered around the village). Doña Celia was in her mid–late 60s, a midwife since the age of 14 with traditional medicinal knowledge.[8] Her father had been a carpenter. Her daughter-in-law Delilah was born in the community. Asha was an elderly woman in her 60s, she came with her daughter, Ala, who was born in Cudilla. Doña Celia's daughter, Marta, was around 30 years old, born in the community; she arrived with a baby. Julio, who was 24 years old, was Doña Celia's son and had suffered from severe bone disease (better now). Magda was 20 years old. Doña Celia was clearly a matriarch in the community, she facilitated a number of responses, brought out tools and materials to show us and seemed to be respected and liked by the others.

The afternoon group (Group 2) was comprised of three elderly women, four younger women, two young children (one male, the other female), two even younger children (4–5 years old) plus a toddler. The women in this meeting explained they were also members of a cooperative that produced toiletries from traditional plants. Towards the end of this group meeting, we were speaking to only two women (several children hung around) as the rest departed for a cooperative meeting. Like Doña Celia in the morning session, there was a clear leader in Group 2 (Doña Carmen) who played an active, affirmative role, shared a meal with us and invited us to return. In both sessions, the women seemed confident and friendly, conversed easily, laughing and smiling.

An Otomi community in transition

Located 20 km from the town of San Miguel, Cudilla (population 1,000) is a small rural community of approximately 200 Indigenous Otomi families, many with Otomi heritage. The small residential dwellings consist of adobe or stone wall housing with corn husk roofs. It also has a small (two-person) hair-dressing salon plus a small stationery shop, in addition to a small convenience store. Livestock sales (pigs, cows, sheep, chicken, turkeys, goats) have provided the bulk of income. One local inhabitant sold milk. The community is currently attempting a transition from a subsistence lifestyle and low-paying agricultural jobs to a more diversified economic base. In the past, as explained to us, men generally worked the land for hacienda landlords (wheat fields surrounding the community are now replaced primarily by corn fields). Women prepared food and brought it to their husbands for lunch. They also made baskets and embroidered cloth from *manta* (thread) purchased in town. Girls learned this craft at a very young age, making and embroidering napkins that they then brought into their marriage. Both of these traditions continue today.

Attempts to diversify from dependence on subsistence agriculture are aimed at developing small individual and community-based enterprises engaged in cultural production making, for example, selling craft and products based on traditional knowledge of foods and medicinal plants, herbs, as well as a long tradition of embroidering napkins and cloth for wrapping tortillas and so on. The embroidery cooperative had been established for two years with the collaborative assistance of the microcredit NGO. Its main purpose was income generation and it now had

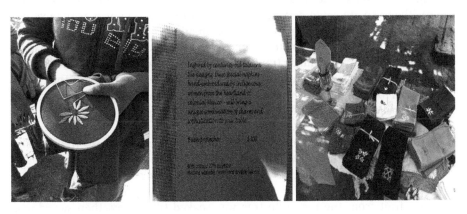

Note: Faces not shown for confidentiality.

Figure 7.3   Demonstration of embroidering by one of the young women; description; embroidered napkins

a record of accomplishments that members were proud to share. Nine women worked together to produce embroidered cloth napkins to sell to mainly American tourists visiting San Miguel de Allende (Figure 7.3). Napkins and other embroidered items were sold in the outdoor market in San Miguel on Saturdays. A set of six napkins sold for 300 pesos. The stall rental price was 70 pesos. The women also sold their napkins via special orders through the microcredit NGO and at street fairs. They explained they were now attending a course titled 'How to make my business a success' on business and money management at the microcredit NGO's location in San Miguel every Tuesday (the space was sponsored by a donor). They would graduate just before Christmas (2012). Several women attended training workshops in subsequent years, such as the following woman who attended a three two-hour business training program offered in 2013:

> I like coming to the talks because we are taught to work together and also helps me to meet people from other communities who also want to improve their lives. Sometimes I find it difficult to come to the city because I have to bring my baby but worth it because I want our embroidery shop grow. (Embroidery group participant, Cudilla, Guanajuato, Mexico).[9]

Nutrition and health: traditional knowledge and food customs in transition

Nutrition and diet in Cudilla is based on wheat, garbanzos, lentils, camotes (sweet potatoes), jicama, peaches (*duraznos*, or peach trees, were scattered around the compound) and *membrillos* (cherry-size yellow fruit, with white flesh that was used to make a potent beverage called *ponche*). They also ate *calabaza* (zucchini), *papa* (potatoes, but bought at market), *zanahoria* (carrots), *huevos* (eggs), *arroz* (rice – purchased) and so on. Doña Celia affirmed that the food they consumed was high in vitamins. Black beans (*frijoles negros*) were cooked and eaten as a *caldo* (soup). They also ate *caldo de xoconostle* (cactus fruit, also known as tuna verde) and *jicama*. *Qualite* (equivalent to *amaranto*, amaranth), is either incorporated in a soup, cooked or fried with tomatoes, chilli, coriander and garlic. *Nopalitos* (cactus leaves) and a variety of chillies (*pipil*) were a traditional part of their diet. They made tostadas and tamales with corn, eggs, *frijoles*, or meat and cheese. The cheese was made in the village compound. Traditional sweets made at home include grain-based cornballs with sugar, called *piloncello*.

Various *atoles* (drink made from local fruits and plants) were also traditionally part of their diet. The *abuelitas* (affectionate diminutive for grandmothers) made *atoles* of different types: *atole de trigo* (wheat), *atole de garbanzos* (beans), *atole de pirul* (tiny red fruit from local tree called pirul) and *atole de mesquite*. For instance, fruit from the mesquite tree was soaked till mushy, then sieved and boiled with ground corn; the fruit makes this *atole de mesquite* sweet. The *atole de pirul* has the same preparation. Traditional utensils used to prepare food and drink included: *metate* (stone slab used to grind corn), *molcajete* (stone mortar with three legs used to grind condiments for salsas and other dishes), *comal* (thin, round metal receptacle used to cook tortillas) and *cedaso* (spoon-size instrument with a fine perforated fabric to sieve flour or other ingredients). All were handmade.

Doña Celia, the midwife, also told us about the medicinal use of trees and other local plants. It appears that in addition to making *atoles,* the mesquite and pirul trees were used for healing various ailments. Tea infusions and poultices from mesquite fruit were used for gastro-intestinal (GI) health, for example, in treating ulcers or stomach upsets, as well as for diabetes and pulmonary/respiratory issues. Mesquite sap was mixed with fruit to make a tea infusion (good for lungs). Mesquite bark made into a poultice helped to control labour pains. Berries from the pirul tree can be made into a drink or mixed with alcohol and used as a poultice for easing labour pains or treating GI issues. The older women explained that the drinks made with pirul berries are very sweet, so they don't need *refrescos* (pop). To ease labour pain and aid in childbirth, they also used chocolate, *ruda* (an aromatic herb with yellow flowers), *jerbabuena* (mint) and *manzanilla* (chamomile). They also used avocado skin, onions and *rábano* (a kind of radish) for medicinal purposes, as learned from their *abuelas* (grandmothers). Doña Celia likes passing on traditional knowledge (use of plants as medicine, knowledge about midwifery). Some of her knowledge has been 'passed' along to her daughter.

But customs were changing. An elderly woman explained that traditional medicines, including *nopales, trigo* and *atole de mesquite,* used to be part of their diet, and they gathered foods from the *campo* (countryside), far away. For example, *nopalitas* were traditionally collected in the *campo,* but now are grown in their own gardens. And today, she said, they do not use the *metate* except to make *atole.* She doesn't drink coffee, and said that nowadays people in the community '*toma mucho Coca*' (drink a lot of Coke). A young woman explained she did not like *atole* made from mesquite (mesquite trees dotted the compound and were pointed out to us by the women). More meat is eaten today than in the past – including readymade cold cuts, ham, pork and sausage (*salchichas*). Milk is also a more common drink than in the past.

There is also a clear intergenerational effect in the food changes being experienced through modernization and income generation. *Marucha* (instant soup prepared by only adding hot water) is eaten today by younger people. Also, young women buy salsa in glass bottles since it is easier and faster to go to one of the shops in the community to buy these things – it was a lot of work to make their own food, they said. Older women perceived that they ate the same way as they did traditionally, but the younger people have different eating habits. The daughter of one woman mentioned that she eats *frijoles,* vegetables, sausages and ham she buys in the shops. One of the women told us that her daughter-in-law from a different rancho prefers bread, while her daughter-in-law in the United States wants tortillas. Processed food is clearly part of their diet now; a number of young children dropped into the afternoon focus group (after school), and they were munching on Cheetos (salty puffed corn, neon orange), fruit cups, cookies, wafer chocolate bars, grape Fanta and bottles of processed juice. White processed buns were also evident (soft bread).

Increasing health concerns and changing health practices

Of the concerns raised by focus group members, one woman was worried about obtaining and paying for medical care. She told us that the medication her son needed was prescription-based and very expensive. One of the problems with the newer more 'modern' foods, participants felt, was that the people who ate these foods have less energy. It makes them tired. Health concerns were also raised about kidney issues (some blamed soda replacing *atole*). Cases of gastritis, other stomach issues and diabetes were also mentioned as being observed more frequently. Doña Carmen believed that health was directly related to food and the elders generally felt there was a relation between store-bought foods and health. Another changing health tradition mentioned was related to having children: where to have children, do they need pre-natal care, whether to go to hospital for childbirth and so on. Older women indicated that going to a hospital for childbirth was not necessary for most expectant mothers, but they said the younger women want to go to the city for childbirth. Overall, not only health was changing, but also health-related customs and traditions. The One Health paradigm discussed in the previous section would be valuable to incorporate into sustainability-oriented approaches, especially the early phase of endogenous development so that traditional knowledge, traditional practices and traditional medicines are integrated into planning, policy and local residents' activities related to communal health and well-being, cultural survival and flourishing.

Cultural commodification and change

Like with food and health, cultural traditions and customs are also changing. The community practises both Indigenous and Catholic customs and traditions. They celebrated a large number of religious festivals (Canicitos, las Posadas, and Virgen de Guadalupe on 12 December were dominant in their discussions), and dances such as the Dance of the Apache, the Rattle Dance (a dance for children where hats decorated with flowers and ribbons are worn; it is not practised much, and they worry about losing this) and Danza de las plumas (Concheros). They don special clothing for the dances. The women also mentioned the two cooperatives in which several of them were involved. One stemmed from a recent state government-sponsored programme from an office in the town of San Luis de la Paz to support Indigenous resident populations by stimulating local enterprise. A community-based cooperative has been set up for the production and sale of organic cosmetics. Local products like rosemary and cactus are used to make cosmetics and skin products, which are then sold through a women's institute in San Miguel. The sta-tionery shop and the beauty (hair) salon were sponsored through this programme, providing economic and social benefit from the 'commodification' of their cultural knowledge and environmental goods.

Cultural change was also occurring with respect to the Otomi language and attire. Although the Otomi language was taught in the community school via a government-sponsored programme, it was more like one of many subjects, explained a participant, and not everyone spoke Otomi. None of the residents we encountered wore traditional clothing. As the women also explained to us, they no longer wore Indigenous (Otomi) clothing to go to town in order to avoid being assaulted or driven away.

Collaborative enterprise building

The napkins produced by the embroidery cooperative are substantially different from those that the members use at home in terms of colour, embroidery size, design and the material used. Religious symbols are common in their traditional cloth (e.g. napkins for tortilla wrapping), but not in the ones for visitors. When producing cloth for their own use they use traditional designs rather than the simple designs and stitches for the tourist market, although the actual embroidering technique has not changed. The cloth, however, has changed both for themselves and for visitors; cheaper synthetic material is used now rather than richer material that they used in the past. An expatriate advisor to the cooperative programme recommended these napkin types, explained a woman in the focus group. As the women still use original embroidery designs and stitching when making items for themselves (at home), they appeared very self-aware and comfortable about the change; one mentioned it was pleasurable to embroider for tourists, particularly American visitors (the predominant international visitors in San Miguel), as the product is simpler, takes less effort and time and contains less embroidery. Another said that she did not use the (tourist) napkins at home, not even to wrap tortillas.

Asked how the women felt about future possibilities that might engage visitors and tourism more directly, a young woman responded that it was 'okay, but there's no leadership within the community and they are not able to organize themselves; so they may not be able to organize tourism well'. As an example, she referred to a recent internal community conflict over a festival related to the Day of the Virgin of Guadalupe (Día de la Virgen de Guadalupe) holiday on 12 December, and explained she is hesitant but sees that they need more economic opportunities, hence they need to organize (though acknowledging the risks involved). However, the women's sense of self-empowerment and growing importance in the socioeconomic structure of Cudilla also opens up future possibilities for negotiating new roles in community decision making, self-determination and governance. LaPan et al.'s (2016) multi-case study of Indigenous women's engagement in cooperative tourism microenterprise showed increased self-determination and non-individual benefits, but access to credit alone was not sufficient to generate these outcomes. Such microenterprise development projects required strong cooperative social structures and engagement of men in the development process as social structures changed along with increased self-reliance and self-determination of the women (LaPan et al. 2016).

The microcredit NGO's role in collaborative enterprise building

The microcredit NGO that supports the embroidery cooperative plays an instrumental role in facilitating community development and working towards economic and social sustainability, not only in Cudilla but also in approximately 20 additional communities. Poverty alleviation through income-producing strategies is a primary goal. The NGO also contributes to health issues by collaborating with other local NGOs like 'Feed the Hungry' (which focuses on nutrition and children) and 'CASA' (that provides childbirth services, along with other health-related services). Assisted by local NGOs, Doña Celia (who couldn't read and write until recently) completed primary school and then took a certificate course in midwifery. She was able to transcend a violent, abusive past and is happy to see her daughters-in-law in healthier relationships. She also provides advice to any community member seeking her wisdom and experience.

It should be noted that the women's embroidery cooperative in Cudilla was not a PPT project; the focus of this project was not tourism development, but, rather, *income generation* and *capacity building* (skill building and training). Thus, in addition to tourists at the local market in San Miguel, or visitors who might stop at the village on their way to another destination, the target market includes area-based residents and consumers farther away (reached via other distribution channels being developed). The conversations described above reflect a gradual change in women's agency and awareness of not only the physical health challenges (in terms of diet and food, use of traditional medicines and medicinal knowledge), but also the overall health and well-being of their community.

Economic and social empowerment: striving towards gender equity

The women's embroidery cooperative was clearly a crucial event in the women's gradual transition from subsistence lifestyles towards aiming at sustainable livelihoods and social empowerment. The reflexive, self-aware stance of the women toward their traditional craft is evident in how they manage the 'performing' of the craft (making and selling napkins on site at the village and at the weekly outdoor market frequented by visitors) and in relationships with traditional embroidery in their home world (maintaining traditional embroidery for the home as much as possible).

In Cudilla, changing performativities are also evident as the women working in the two cooperatives gained both economic and social empowerment, as well as new skills and knowledge, such as managing a microenterprise. A younger woman who was part of the embroidery group told us that her husband helps her a lot with her son and the household, recognizing that through her work the family has some extra income. Another young woman also said that her husband supported her efforts. He does not do household chores, she said, but he helps her with their child and encourages her to be part of the embroidery group. However, it was also mentioned that the local men were pressured by other men if they tried to be more supportive of their women. Moreover, many of the women worked in San Miguel as there was no work in the community for either men or women; a number of the men do not like women working so far away (about 20 km). A young woman in a baseball cap felt that the embroidery work gave women more power and balance in their relationships with men. Related to cooperative activities, younger women went to town to buy materials and were learning about the world.

While attempts to diversify the economy through microenterprises were viewed as encouraging to help younger people stay in the community (rather than migrating), a number of social issues concerned the women to whom we spoke. In the semi-arid region of San Miguel, for example, access to water is a major concern, and the women mentioned concern about water availability (rivers were running dry and the weather was changing, as their *abuelas* (grandparents) had predicted, they said). A more general worry was getting good education for the children (one woman said she sends her little boy, 9 years old, to a church school in San Miguel de Allende). Alcohol, drugs and violence among the younger generation were major issues in the community, said the women. The changing behaviour of their children was also a significant concern. As one woman explained: 'In the past, parents were respected and traditions continued through the children, but today, respect is being lost so traditions are at risk. They don't do what they are asked to do, they talk back to their parents, the girls are going out and hanging out with boys at night.' And, unlike in the past, young men and women were tending to live together rather than getting married first. While some of this change is driven by the economic diversification and activities noted above, racism also plays a part. General education overall was voiced as a concern and a development priority by more than one woman.

Empowerment through collaborative enterprise

Cudilla illustrates the closely interwoven relationships between women, environment and economy as the women negotiate changing environmental and cultural relationships and social reconfiguration and strive to diversify into sustainable livelihoods and better futures for their children and community. *Psychological empowerment* (increased self-confidence, pride, etc.) and *social empowerment* (in relation to family and community) through *economic empowerment* (via participation in the cooperative) are beginning to emerge, and correspond with community empowerment dimensions that Scheyvens (1999) proposed in the context of ecotourism development: economic empowerment, psychological empowerment, social empowerment and political empowerment (see also Scheyvens 2002). Her empowerment framework is useful to consider here, even though her focus was on ecotourism-related empowerment. The changes being identified in Cudilla are occurring in the early phases of endogenous development and they are closely related to changes in health and relationships to traditional food and medicinal practices (human–environmental relationship, broadly), as well as changes related to the women's activities in the embroidery cooperative.

Women's participation in the embroidery cooperative set up and facilitated by the microcredit NGO illustrates not just collaborative, community-based enterprise building and *economic empowerment*, but also new learning about participating and collaborating and negotiation group dynamics. Individual and social empowerment is strong; new family and community relationships are also being negotiated, with new respect being gained and greater confidence in decision making not just for the cooperative but also for their children and family. Some signs of gender equity are also evident and social relationships are strong. But their traditional medicinal knowledge and traditional foods, ecological relationships and cultural activities such as embroidering are encountering significant change through commodification, commercialization and other modernizing influences. We argue that it is important to develop and add an *ecocultural empowerment* dimension to Scheyvens' (1999) framework that can attend to these intangible human–environmental relationships and cultural changes, and related issues of ecocultural justice and equity (Jamal & Camargo 2014). This is especially important for destinations with diverse populations and a history of institutional racism or discrimination against minority groups due to ethnicity, gender, sexual orientation, class, income inequality and so on (Jamal & Camargo 2014).

While culture is dynamic and change is inevitable (authenticity can be negotiated, emergent or staged), cultural empowerment is a crucial consideration for cultural survival and negotiating changing human–environmental relationships. This will require greater consideration of local control over cultural goods and local commons (both ecological and social-cultural). The new skills, new status and psychological as well as social empowerment being experienced by the women could be valuable precursors to *political empowerment*, but at this early stage of endogenous development, political empowerment is less evident in terms of governance and institutional structures.

Political empowerment and endogenous governance

Cudilla demonstrates rich ecocultural relationships, women's empowerment and local ownership through collaborative enterprise and support through microcredit finance. But changes are being enacted and negotiated, including cultural authenticity (the commodification of traditional embroidery practices) and social empowerment as the women gain self-esteem and recognition from their kinfolk. Culturally embedded human–environmental relationships (e.g. relationality through traditional knowledge and use of environmental goods like the mesquite and pirul trees from which they made *atole* and medical preparations) primarily lie with the older generation, women like Doña Celia who are attempting to pass on their knowledge of traditional foods and medicine use to their children. However, physical health is being impacted by the introduction of processed foods, and by intergenerational change. Will the younger generation be able to embrace traditional knowledge and foods, and continue the tradition of speaking?

The women are highly reflexive and understanding of the changes being brought about. Self-empowerment and social empowerment with strong social relations exist, and they are highly aware of the changes to their food and traditional medicine practices, as well as to the embroidery they sell. However, a missing dimension in our explorations was self-determination, autonomy and political empowerment. The women in the women's embroidery cooperative at Cudilla are at an early stage of endogenous community-based development. How will the changing roles and empowerment of women impact social relations, the community's political identity and governance (see Giovannini 2014)?[10] How can community-based, locally driven cooperatives ensure control over the use and distribution of their ecocultural goods through their local microenterprises? Cultural empowerment in the context of Cudilla should include *being able to determine for oneself what constitutes acceptable cultural change and change to human–environmental relationships*. Decision making and the governance of ecocultural goods and traditional knowledge *must* directly involve those whose cultural and environmental goods are being commodified and sold in the tourism domain.

Moving forward with CBT 'development'

Community-based enterprises like Cudilla's women's cooperative and social enterprise offer significant potential to facilitate community engagement and civic learning, local control and participatory local governance. Such endogenous development entails focusing on the local and the particular, with consideration for diverse knowledge and cultural heritage, localized and culturally informed approaches to development, financing, governance and the conservation of traditional medicines, knowledge and so on (see Schilcher 2007; Shiva 1988, 1997). However, the women and men involved in endogenous social enterprise and social entrepreneurship must be cognizant and oriented to the social and cultural 'embeddedness' of the community and the market forces at work (Curry 2003, pp. 418–19, cited in Peredo & McLean 2010, p. 613). Structures for local governance are needed and action must be oriented towards resident empowerment, economic and cultural literacy about the changes that being part of a market economy bring (see Freire et al. 2018), and local control over the local commons and their natural and cultural heritage. Public–private-sector partnerships and collaborative capacity building with the help of NGOs, such as the microfinance organization working with Cudilla, can help facilitate poverty alleviation and reduce income and gender inequities, but greater attention is needed to local governance tailored to the context and setting, so that 'development' is attentive to dependency issues and post-development critiques of modernization and the monopolizing of neoliberal capitalism. Among other things, it means developing collaborative governance structures for equitable and inclusive participation of the men and the women so that the needs and interests of all community members can be met.

Local institutional structures enabling Indigenous governance for Indigenous communities are crucial so that there is autonomy to participate in a 'pluriverse' of relational ontologies and different ways of being – living well in natural and cultural relationships to land, nature and each other, in the sense of *Buen Vivir* (Escobar 2018). Political empowerment is vital to address inequality and facilitate redistributive strategies that benefit the poor and enable steady, systemic change oriented towards equity and collaborative governance, not a one-world modernist view but a post-development, pluralistic sensibility to other ontological and epistemological approaches particular to the local community or cultural groups within it (see Escobar 2018; see also Jamal, 2019). From a methodological perspective, CBT requires 'embedded' community researchers (Dredge et al. 2013) and in the post-colonial and Indigenous context, decolonizing methodologies (Denzin et al. 2008; Lincoln & González y González 2008; Smith 1999; see also Humberstone 2004) and Indigenous-driven research, insofar as it is invited and serves to benefit the Indigenous peoples (Holmes et al. 2016). Among other things, it involves the following considerations: (1) critical reflexivity that is written into the research design and methodological approach, that is, reflecting on relationships between self and the 'other', critically evaluating the discourses influencing one's own ontological and epistemological assumptions and, hence, how these shape our research designs and methods, as well as implementation, interpretations and sharing of results; (2) methods oriented to critical engagement and reflexivity, for instance, participatory (action) research, social action research, thoughtful auto-ethnography; (3) appropriate (often extended) research time in the community context, directly involving those who stand to be most impacted by the research; and (4) in the post-colonial and Indigenous context, facilitating Indigenous-led research attentive to Indigenous epistemologies and/or knowledges (for example, concepts of *Buen Vivir*, well-being), with Indigenous methodologies enabling engagement and accountability to the community (see critique by Hardbarger 2018).

NOTES
* Our sincere appreciation and thanks to the microfinance NGO and the women and other residents of Cudilla, for their time and support of our work. We would also like to thank the Greenline Institute for permission to incorporate material from our conference paper (Jamal et al. 2016).

1 See Dangi & Jamal 2016 for a review of definitions and principles of CBT. This is an open access article so we do not rehash these here.

2 Problematizing the notion of 'development' as various post-development critics have done with respect to international development raises red flags over the use of terms like 'developed countries', 'developing nations', 'lesser developed' and 'underdeveloped' countries. We refer here instead to the Global North and the Global South, popularized in post-development discourse (see Kothari et al. 2019). The Brundtland Commission also evoked the North–South divide in discussing the inequitable distribution of the benefits and burdens of industrialization and modernization of countries in the North versus the South in their report on sustainable development, *Our Common Future* (United Nations World Commission on Environment and Development 1987).

3 While Cudilla has historically been an Indigenous Otomi community, it is in a transitional stage and not all residents speak Otomi.

4 See Shen et al. (2008) for a discussion on approaching sustainable livelihoods in a more holistic way than through tourism as a development tool.

5 An early seminal paper that addressed citizen involvement in local planning and governance is Arnstein's (1969) ladder of participation. It influenced an emerging movement toward new models for collaborative planning and shared decision making. See also Tosun (2000) and Choi and Sirakaya (2006).

6 This definition has not been amended since 1948, see Preamble to the Constitution of the World Health Organization as adopted by the International Health Conference, New York, June 19–22, 1946; signed on 22 July

1946 by the representatives of 61 states (Official Records of the World Health Organization, no. 2, p.100) and entered into force on 7 April 1948.

7 See, for example, the 2004 Manhattan Principles on 'One World, One Health', and the One Health Commission based in Ames, Iowa, USA. Accessed 10 June 2013 at www.onehealthcommission.org/en/resources/health__ecosystems_anal ysis_of_linkages_heal/

8 Pseudonyms are used to protect the identity of the focus group participants. The name of the microcredit NGO is not shared for the same reason.

9 Apoyo a Gente Emprededora A.C., Microfinance newsletter November 2013, San Miguel de Allende, Gto. Accessed 25 October 2018 at www.apoyoemprededores.wordpress.com

10 Peredo and Chrisman (2006) sketch a concept of 'community orientation' to capture the social organization of Indigenous communities in the Andes on which their study focuses. The more 'community oriented' a society is, the more its members experience their membership as resembling the life of parts of an organism, the more they will feel their status and well-being is a function of the reciprocated contributions they make to their community (Peredo & Chrisman, 2006, p.313; cited in Peredo & McLean, 2010, p.606).

References

Agarwal, Y. (2016), 'Microfinance and poverty alleviation', *Imperial Journal of Interdisciplinary Research*, **2**(11), 1575–7.

Akama, J.S., Maingi, S. and Camargo, B. (2011), 'Wildlife conservation, safari tourism and the role of tourism certification in Kenya: A postcolonial critique', *Tourism Recreation Research*, **36**(3), 281–91.

Arnstein, S. (1969), 'A ladder of citizen participation', *AIP Journal*, July, 216–24.

Ashley, C., Boyd, C. and Goodwin, H. (2000), 'Pro-poor tourism: Putting poverty at the heart of the tourism agenda', *Natural Resource Perspectives*, No. 51, London: Overseas Development Institute.

Borlido, T. and Coromina, L. (2018), 'Social capital as cause and consequence of rural touristic development: The case of Lindoso (Portugal)', *European Journal of Tourism Research*, **19**, 71–85.

Britton, S.G. (1982), 'The political economy of tourism in the Third World', *Annals of Tourism Research*, **9**(3), 331–58.

Choi, H. and Sirakaya, E. (2006), 'Sustainability indicators for managing community tourism', *Tourism Management*, **27**, 1274–89.

Curry, G.N. (2003), 'Moving beyond postdevelopment: Facilitating Indigenous alternatives for "development"', *Economic Geography*, **79**(4), 405–23.

Dangi, T. and Jamal, T. (2016), 'An integrated approach to sustainable community-based tourism', *Sustainability*, **8**(5), 475. doi:10.3390/su8050475

Denzin, N.K., Lincoln, Y.K. and Tuhiwai Smith, L. (eds) (2008), *Handbook of Critical and Indigenous Methodologies*, Los Angeles: SAGE.

Dredge, D. (2006), 'Networks, conflict and collaborative communities', *Journal of Sustainable Tourism*, **14**(6), 562–81.

Dredge, D., Hales, R. and Jamal, T. (2013), 'Community case study research: Researcher operacy, embeddedness and making research matter', *Tourism Analysis*, **18**(1), 29–43.

Duffy, R. (2009), 'Global-local linkages: The meaning of CBNRM in global conservation policies', in B. Mukamuri, J. Manjengwa and S. Anstey (eds) *Beyond Proprietorship: Murphree's Laws on Community-Based Natural Resource Management in Southern Africa*, Ottawa: Harare Weaver Press, pp.58–72.

Escobar, A. (2016), 'Thinking-feeling with the earth: Territorial struggles and the ontological dimension of the epistemologies of the south', *AIBR Revista de Antropologia Iberoamericana*, **11**(1), 11–32. Accessed 12 February 2019 at https://doi.org/10.11156/aibr.110102e

Escobar, A. (2018), *Designs for the Pluriverse: Radical Interdependence, Autonomy, and the Making of Worlds*, Durham, NC: Duke University Press.

Farrelly, T. (2011), 'Indigenous and democratic decision-making: Issues from community-based eco-tourism in the Boumā National Heritage Park, Fiji', *Journal of Sustainable Tourism*, **19**(7), 817–35.

Fennell, D. (2014), 'Exploring the boundaries of a new moral order for tourism's global code of ethics: An opinion piece on the position of animals in the tourism industry', *Journal of Sustainable Tourism*, **22**(7), 983–96.

Freire, P., Ramos, M.B., Macedo, D.P. and Shor, I. (2018), *Pedagogy of the Oppressed. 50th Anniversary Edition*, translated by Myra Bergman Ramos with an introduction by Donaldo Macedo and an afterword by Ira Shor, New York: Bloomsbury Academic.

Giovannini, M. (2014), 'Indigenous community enterprises in Chiapas: A vehicle for buen vivir?' *Community Development Journal*, **50**(1), 71–87.

Griggs, D., Stafford-Smith, M., Gaffney, O., Rockström, J., Öhman, M.C., Shyamsundar, P., Steffen, W., Glaser, G., Kanie, N. and Noble, I. (2013a), 'Sustainable development goals for people and planet', *Nature*, **495**, 305–7.

Griggs, D., Stafford-Smith, M., Gaffney, O., Rockström, J., Öhman, M.C., Shyamsundar, P., Steffen, W., Glaser, G., Kanie, N. and Noble, I. (2013b), 'Rethinking sustainable development in the Anthropocene', *Anthropocene Journal*. Accessed 12 February 2019 at https://anthropocenejournal.wordpress.com/2013/03/24/rethinking-sustainable-development-in-the-anthropocene/

Hardbarger, T. (2018), 'The medicine of peace: Indigenous youth decolonizing healing and resisting violence (Jeffrey Paul Ansloos)', *Transmotion*, **4**(1), 165–7.

Hills, T. and Lundgren, J. (1977), 'The impact of tourism in the Caribbean', *Annals of Tourism Research*, **4**(5), 248–67.

Holden, A. (2013), *Tourism, Poverty and Development*, Abingdon: Routledge.

Holden, A. (2018), 'Environmental ethics for tourism: The state of the art', *Tourism Review*. Accessed 12 February 2019 at https://doi.org/10.1108/TR-03-2017-0066

Holmes, A., Grimwood, B., King, L. and Lutsel K'e Dene First Nation (2016), 'Creating an Indigenized visitor code of conduct: The development of Denesoline self-determination for sustainable tourism', *Journal of Sustainable Tourism*, **24**(8–9), 177–93.

Humberstone, B. (2004), 'Standpoint research: Multiple versions of reality in tourism theorizing and research', in J. Phillimore and L. Goodson (eds) *Qualitative Research in Tourism: Ontologies, Epistemologies and Methodologies*, London: Routledge, pp. 119–36.

Jamal, T. (2019), *Justice and Ethics in Tourism*, Abingdon: Routledge.

Jamal, T. and Camargo, B. (2014), 'Sustainable tourism, justice and an ethic of care: Towards the Just Destination', *Journal of Sustainable Tourism*, **22**(1), 11–30.

Jamal, T., Budke, C.M. and Barradas-Bribiesca, I. (2014), 'A (One) Health based paradigm shift to sustainable development', in H. Clausen, V. Andersson and S. Gyimóthy (eds) *Global Mobilities and Tourism Development: A Community Perspective*, Copenhagen: Aalborg University, pp. 169–96.

Jamal, T., Budke, C.M. and Barradas-Bribiesca, I. (2016), 'Eco-cultural empowerment, gender equity and collaborative enterprise in La Cuadrilla, Mexico', in S. Lira, A. Mano, C. Pinheiro and R. Amoêda (eds) *TOURISM 2016: Proceedings of the International Conference on Global Tourism and Sustainability*, Barcelos, Portugal: Green Line Institute, pp. 211–20.

Karst, H. (2017), '"This is a holy place of Ama Jomo": Buen vivir, Indigenous voices and ecotourism development in a protected area of Bhutan', *Journal of Sustainable Tourism*, **25**(6), 746–62.

Kothari, A., Salleh, A., Escobar, A., Demaria, F. and Acosta, A. (2019), *Pluriverse: A Post-Development Dictionary*, Delhi, Authors Upfront.

LaPan, C., Morais, D.B., Wallace, T. and Barbieri, C. (2016), 'Women's self-determination in cooperative tourism microenterprises', *Tourism Review International*, **20**(1), 41–55.

Lincoln, Y. and González y González, E. (2008), 'The search for emerging decolonizing methodologies in qualitative research', *Qualitative Inquiry*, **14**(5), 784–805.

Mansuri, G. and Rao, V. (2004), 'Community-based and-driven development: A critical review', *World Bank Research Observer*, **19**(1), 1–39.

Manyara, G. and Jones, E. (2007), 'Community-based tourism enterprises development in Kenya: An exploration of their potential avenues of poverty reduction', *Journal of Sustainable Tourism*, **15**(6), 628–44.

Matarrita-Cascante, D., Brennan, M.A. and Luloff, A.E. (2010), 'Community agency and sustainable tourism development: The case of La Fortuna, Costa Rica', *Journal of Sustainable Tourism*, **18**(6), 735–56.

Mbaiwa, J. and Stronza, A. (2010), 'The effects of tourism development on rural livelihoods in the Okavango Delta, Botswana', *Journal of Sustainable Tourism*, **18**(5), 635–56.

McGehee, N. (2012), 'Oppression, emancipation, and volunteer tourism: Research propositions', *Annals of Tourism Research*, **39**(1), 84–107.

Mosedale, J. (ed.) (2011), *Political Economy of Tourism: A Critical Perspective*, Abingdon: Routledge.

Movono, A. and Dahles, H. (2017), 'Female empowerment and tourism: A focus on businesses in a Fijian village', *Asia Pacific Journal of Tourism Research*, **22**(6), 681–92.

Nelson, F. (2012), 'Blessing or curse? The political economy of tourism development in Tanzania', *Journal of Sustainable Tourism*, **20**(3), 359–75.

Palmer, N.J. and Chuamuangphan, N. (2018), 'Governance and local participation in ecotourism: Community-level ecotourism stakeholders in Chiang Rai province, Thailand', *Journal of Ecotourism*, **17**(3), 320–37.

Peredo, A.M. and Chrisman, J.J. (2006), 'Towards a theory of community-based enterprise', *Academy of Management Review*, **31**(2), 309–28.

Peredo, A.M. and McLean, M. (2010), 'Indigenous development and the cultural captivity of entrepreneurship', *Business and Society*, **52**(4), 592–620.

Rasmussen, M.B. (2018), 'Paper works: Contested resource histories in Peru's Huascarán National Park', *World Development*, **101**, 429–40.

Ruiz-Ballesteros, E. and Brondizio, E. (2013), 'Building negotiated agreement: The emergence of community-based tourism in Floreana (Galápagos Islands)', *Human Organization*, **72**(4), 323–35.

Sachs, W. (2010), *The Development Dictionary: A Guide to Knowledge as Power*, 2nd edn, London: Zed Books.

Salleh, A.K. (1984), 'Deeper than deep ecology: The eco-feminist connection', *Environmental Ethics*, **6**(4), 339–45.

Scheyvens, R. (1999), 'Ecotourism and the empowerment of local communities', *Tourism Management*, **20**(2), 245–9.

Scheyvens, R. (2002), *Tourism for Development: Empowering Communities*, Harlow: Prentice Hall.

Schilcher, D. (2007), 'Growth versus equity: The continuum of pro-poor tourism and neoliberal governance', *Current Issues in Tourism*, **10**(2–3), 166–93.

Schwabe, C.W. (1968), 'Animal diseases and world health', *Journal of the American Veterinary Medical Association*, **153**(12), 1859–63.

Schwabe, C.W. (1984), *Veterinary Medicine and Human Health*, 3rd edn, Baltimore, MD: Williams and Wilkins.

Sharpley, R. and Telfer, D. (2016), *Tourism and Development in the Developing World*, 2nd edn, Abingdon: Routledge.

Shen, F., Hughey, K. and Simmons, D. (2008), 'Connecting the sustainable livelihoods approach and tourism: A review of the literature', *Journal of Hospitality and Tourism Management*, **15**(1), 19–31.

Shiva, V. (1988), *Staying Alive: Women, Ecology, and Development*, London: Zed Books.

Shiva, V. (1997), 'Economic globalization, ecological feminism and sustainable development', *Canadian Woman Studies*, **17**(2), 22–7.

Smith, L.T. (1999), *Decolonizing Methodologies: Research and Indigenous Peoples*, London: Zed Books.

Taylor, S.R. (2017), 'Issues in measuring success in community-based Indigenous tourism: Elites, kin groups, social capital, gender dynamics and income flows', *Journal of Sustainable Tourism*, **25**(3), 433–49.

Telfer, D. (2009), 'Development studies and tourism', in T. Jamal and M. Robinson (eds) *The SAGE Handbook of Tourism Studies*, London: SAGE, pp. 146–65.

Tosun, C. (2000), 'Limits to community participation in the tourism development process in developing countries', *Tourism Management*, **21**, 613–33.

United Nations World Commission on Environment and Development (1987), *Our Common Future*, New York: Oxford University Press.

Zinsstag, J., Schelling, E., Waltner-Toews, D. and Tanner, M. (2011), 'From "one medicine" to "one health" and systematic approaches to health and well-being', *Preventive Veterinary Medicine*, **101**, 148–56.

Zips, W. and Zips-Mairitsch, M. (2007), 'Lost in transition? The politics of conservation, Indigenous land rights and community-based resource management in Southern Africa', *Journal of Legal Pluralism and Unofficial Law*, **39**(55), 37–71.

8 Tourism, development and the consumption of tourism

Richard Sharpley

Introduction

Tourism is, fundamentally, a social phenomenon. It is about people, tourists, who in increasingly large numbers travel within their own countries or overseas, staying in other places and interacting with other people. In so doing, they spend often significant sums of money on a variety of goods and services, including transport, accommodation, food and beverages, souvenirs, entertainment and so on, that collectively comprise the tourist experience. And it is that spending that underpins tourism's potential role in stimulating economic and social development in destination areas. In other words, tourism is an expenditure-driven activity and, as outlined in Chapter 1, the economic benefits arising from that expenditure, such as income, employment and government revenues, are the principal reason for tourism's widespread adoption as an agent of development.

Inevitably, then, the economic benefits of tourism to a great extent reflect tourists' expenditure patterns, although of course a variety of other factors, widely considered in the literature (Mihalič 2015; Vanhove 2018; Wall & Mathieson 2006), also come into play. Nevertheless, it has long been argued for example that, on the one hand, so-called 'enclave' tourism or all-inclusive resorts bring relatively limited economic benefits to the destination, with little if any out-of-pocket expenditure occurring outside the resort (Freitag 1984; Naidoo & Sharpley 2016). Similarly, the economic benefits of cruise tourism accrue primarily to cruise operators rather than to the destinations they visit (Wilkinson 2017); indeed, the negative consequences of cruise tourism for destinations frequently outweigh any economic advantage, hence the recent policy in Dubrovnik, for example, to drastically reduce the number of cruise passengers permitted into the city (Morris 2017). Yet, significant and increasing demand exists for both all-inclusive and cruise tourism (Sharpley 2017). On the other hand, alternative (to mass) forms of tourism development, such as ecotourism or community-based tourism, are claimed to optimize the economic and other benefits of tourism for destination communities (see Chapter 1); not only do local communities, in principle, retain control of (and the profits from) tourism, but greater opportunities exist for out-of-pocket expenditure by tourists amongst the local community. And again, such forms of tourism have become increasingly popular, with the growth in participation in ecotourism in particular being demand rather than supply led (Perkins & Grace 2009).

Inevitably, the extent to which the economic benefits of tourism do in fact reflect the character and scale of tourism development and, hence, tourist expenditure patterns not only varies by context but also remains the focus of debate. The point, however, is that an intimate relationship exists between the demand for or consumption of tourism and the wider economic and social development of a destination. In other words, the role of tourists or, more precisely, their behaviour (including their spending) as consumers of tourism experiences cannot be ignored when considering tourism's role in development, both at the macro and micro levels. For example, at the wider macro level, trends in international tourism flows, reflecting both short- and longer-term forces and influences, have a direct impact (both positive and negative) on destination development. Thus, increasing prosperity in the Asia and Pacific region, specifically in China, has underpinned rapid tourism-related development in the region whilst particularly in Europe, the evolution and increasing popularity of low-cost airlines has brought additional tourist flows and significant economic benefits to both new and established destinations (Donzelli 2010; Dunne et al. 2010; Rey et al. 2011). At the same time, transformations in tourist demand at the micro-destinational level, such as the increasing popularity of all-inclusive holidays, also impact on local development.

Therefore, and as has long been recognized, comprehensive knowledge and understanding of the nature of and trends in the consumption of tourism is considered to be of fundamental importance to both the planning and management of tourism in particular and to local and national development policy-making more generally. Indeed, it is not surprising that not only was much of the earliest research in tourism concerned with its social aspects – the motives, demands and behaviours of tourists (Dann & Parrinello 2009) – but significant attention continues to be paid to tourism consumption and the tourist experience (Sharpley 2016). Importantly, however, this research is predominantly tourism-centric; that is, it is primarily concerned with understanding (and predicting) tourist behaviour and experiences or, more broadly, how tourists consume tourism as a basis for informing the more effective planning and marketing of tourism. In contrast, much less attention has been paid to exploring the relationship between tourism consumption and development, specifically how patterns and trends in the demand for tourism can and will influence its developmental role. Hence, the purpose of this chapter is to propose ways in which knowledge of that relationship might be enhanced; that is, to identify and justify those areas and issues relevant to the relationship between tourism consumption and the socio-economic development of destinations that deserve further investigation. To do so, however, it is first necessary to review briefly the scope of extant research into the consumption of tourism in order to highlight where gaps in knowledge exist.

Tourism consumption research: key themes

Simplistically speaking, tourism is a product (or more precisely, an experience) that people purchase and consume like any other. Consequently, it might be suggested, equally simplistically, that tourists follow a process of 'acquiring and organising information in the direction of a purchase decision and of using and evaluating products and services' (Moutinho 1987, p. 5). That is, unless acting on impulse, tourists seek out travel experiences that best suit their needs and that reflect budgetary and other constraints and, following that experience, they evaluate this as a basis for informing future travel decisions.

In reality, however, the consumption of tourism is a complex, dynamic and multidimensional process (Sharpley 2018, p. 125). Typically, it is neither a one-off event and nor does it necessarily follow a unidirectional, circular demand process from one experience to the next. That is, throughout their lifetime tourists may progress up a 'travel career ladder' (Pearce & Caltabiano 1983); not only do they become more experienced as tourists but also their values, attitudes and lifestyle factors may all evolve and transform, consequently influencing their consumption decisions, including those related to tourism. Moreover, the consumption of tourism does not occur in a socio-cultural vacuum. As it has become democratized (Urry 2002), tourism has become both an accepted and expected social activity, to the extent that it has been described both as a habit (Henning 2012) and an irrational form of consumption (Ryan 1997, p. 3). Equally, it is but one of innumerable objects of consumption in (post)modern societies that are, according to some, defined by a prevailing consumer culture whereby products and experiences are consumed not only for utilitarian reasons but also because they 'act as meaningful markers of social relationships' (Lury 1996, p. 11; also Appadurai 1988). In other words, although some goods and services are purchased simply out of necessity to fulfil a particular function, such as petrol for a car (see Lodziak 2002 for a discussion of the myth of a consumer culture), people attach social and cultural significance to many of the products they consume, primarily for the purpose of establishing self-identity – a role that the consumption of tourism has long fulfilled (Munt 1994). Consequently, therefore, tourism as a form of consumption can be usefully summarized as 'discretionary, episodic, future oriented, dynamic, socially influenced and evolving' (Pearce 1992, p. 114).

Despite this inherent complexity of the consumption of tourism, a number of early attempts were made to describe or model what can be described as the tourism demand process. Goodall (1991), for example, outlined a five-stage decision process commencing with problem identification, through information search, evaluation and purchase decision to feedback informing subsequent travel choices. More specifically, Gilbert (1991) identified four elements of the process, namely energizers, filterers and affectors of demand and the role of the tourist, whilst a similar set of influences had earlier been built into a more complex model proposed by Schmoll (1977). Since then, both understanding of the consumption of tourism and also the variety of perspectives adopted in studies of it have expanded significantly, particularly with regards to the travel experience dimension. Indeed, such is the breadth and variety of research into the consumption of tourism that it is impossible here to note all the specific issues and topics addressed in the literature, let alone consider them in any depth. Nevertheless, for the purposes of this chapter, a number of key themes can be identified; these are now introduced and briefly reviewed under three broad, but by no means definitive, headings.

Motivation

The significance of motivation in the consumption of tourism has long been recognized; it represents, in effect, the why, where, when and how of tourism or, putting it another way, 'the importance of motivation in tourism is quite obvious. It acts as a trigger that sets off all events in travel' (Parrinello 1993, p. 233). It is, not surprising, then, that not only is it considered 'one of the most basic and indispensable subjects in tourism studies' (Wahab 1975, p. 44) but also that much attention is paid to it in the literature. Nevertheless, the observation made by Jafari (1987, p. 152) some 30 years ago that no 'common understanding' of tourist motivation had yet emerged remains apposite; moreover, the diversity of perspectives on and disciplinary approaches to its study – and, not least, debates surrounding the psychological and sociological roots of motivation (Iso-Ahola 1982) – suggests that such consensus remains unachievable.

In a widely cited review, Dann (1981) identifies seven distinct perspectives that have been adopted within the research into tourist motivation. These provide a useful framework for summarizing the main conceptual approaches and topics addressed, as well as highlighting some potential gaps in the research. It should be noted that much of the work remains conceptual; empirical studies that attempt to verify theories of tourist motivation remain relatively rare, perhaps reflecting the fact that tourists themselves are unable (or unwilling) to recognize or identify their true motives (Krippendorf 1987; Mill & Morrison 1985). Nevertheless, attempts have been made to reveal the motives of particular types of tourists and/or tourism, such as backpackers (Chen et al. 2014; Ross 1993), nature tourism (Luo & Deng 2008) or beach tourism (Prebensen et al. 2010).

Travel as a response to what is lacking yet desired

Crucially, tourist motivation translates needs into goal-oriented travel behaviour. In other words, it is the process by which an individual recognizes a need and subsequently engages in travel-related behaviour to satisfy that need or, as Dann (1981, p. 205) proposes, 'a meaningful state of mind which adequately disposes an actor or group of actors to travel'. Often, the need exists to experience something that is lacking in tourists' home culture and environment; it may, for example, be a physical or tangible need (for example, a warmer climate), or it may be emotional or psychological, such as the need for love and affection or, related to Cohen's (1979) phenomenology of tourist experiences (see 'Motivational typologies' below), a need to achieve a personal meaning or identity.

Destinational pull in response to motivational push

Much of the research focuses broadly on the distinction between so-called destinational pull and motivational push; the former relates to what Goodall (1991, p. 59) describes as 'destination-specific attributes' which pull a tourist towards choosing that destination, the latter to the motivations which 'push' choosing a particular destination. And it is within this context that much of the relevant research is located. Focusing primarily on those factors that create the need that stimulates travel-related responses, both extrinsic, or socially determined, and intrinsic, psychological factors are explored in depth in the literature (see Sharpley 2018).

Motivation as fantasy

'Escape' has long been considered one of the two principal factors underpinning tourism motivation; as van Rekom (1994, p. 22) observes, 'a central need which has been revealed time and time again in empirical research is the "escape" notion'. That escape may be from the reality of the everyday, hence the theme of fantasy in motivation research; tourists may, for example, have the need to engage in 'ludic' behaviour not normally acceptable in their home environment (Lett 1983), to temporarily live a life of luxury (Gottlieb 1982) or even to regress to a child-like existence (Dann 1996). Equally, tourism has been considered, like consumption more generally, as the pursuit of fantasy, feelings and fun (Holbrook & Hirschman 1982).

Motivation as classified purpose

Commonly but arguably erroneously, some studies equate motivation (that is, a need of satisfaction) with the purpose or, indeed, outcome of the trip. McIntosh and Goeldner (1990, p. 131), for example, propose four 'basic' motivators: physical, cultural, interpersonal and status and prestige motivators which, typically, refer to goal-oriented behaviour that is a response to a felt need rather than the actual motive. More specifically, and of particular relevance here, numerous studies have addressed the motivation for participation in ecotourism, a form of tourism that might be motivated by or at least influenced by an awareness of its potential developmental benefits. However, both early (Eagles 1992; Silverberg et al. 1996) and also more recent research identify not ecotourists' motives, but their purposes or desired experiences. For instance, Kamri and Radam (2013), in a study of (eco) tourists' motives for visiting Bako National Park in Sarawak, found four dominant 'motives': having a challenging experience, social interaction, going on a nature tour and getting away from it all, all of which are quite evidently not motivations but manifestations of goal-oriented behaviour. This points to a more general gap in the research, discussed in more detail later in this chapter, regarding tourists' understanding of and responses to the developmental potential of different forms of tourism.

Motivational typologies

A popular strand of research frequently linked to motivation is that of tourist typologies. Essentially, such typologies attempt to categorize tourists within some form of conceptual framework as a means of explaining and predicting the consumption behaviour of different tourists. Best known, perhaps, is Cohen's (1972) early typology based on a familiarity-strangerhood continuum; tourists, he suggested, are more or less able or willing to seek out the unfamiliar whilst, along similar lines, Plog's (1977) widely cited study categorized tourists according to their degree of aversion to risk. Since then, numerous typologies have been proposed, including some based on consumer lifestyles and values (Dalen 1989; Madrigal & Kahle 1994) but, perhaps with the exception of Cohen's (1979) phenomenology of tourists, most are descriptive and do not reveal tourists' motivations. Indeed, returning to the context of ecotourism, Weaver (2002) identified the category of 'hard-core' ecotourists who displayed biocentric tendencies towards ecotourism, yet whose motives were more ambivalent or unclear. Equally, no attempts have been made to create a typology based upon tourists' awareness or understanding of tourism's developmental role, and their subsequent behaviour, arguably a notable gap in the extant research.

Motivation and tourist experience

According to Dann (1981), motivation in tourism can be linked to the expected experience or, indeed, to the anticipation of a particular experience (Parrinello 1993) – that is, anticipating or looking forward to a holiday may provide as much fulfilment (or need satisfaction) as the actual holiday experience. More specifically, from what Witt and Wright (1992) refer to as an expectancy theory perspective, tourists will be motivated by the extent to which a particular choice of action may lead to desired outcomes. Such an approach may be of particular pertinence in understanding the motives and behaviour of those participating in development-related tourist activities, such as volunteer tourism (see also Chapter 6). Although an increasingly popular and, from a destination community perspective, potentially valuable form of tourism, debate surrounds the role and intent of volunteer tourists, particularly the extent to which they are driven by altruism or self-interest (Wearing & McGehee 2013). Yet, this question has attracted surprisingly little academic attention and, again, is deserving of more rigorous research.

Motivation as auto-definition and meaning

The final theme in tourist motivation research identified by Dann (1981) relates to studies which seek to explore how tourists define or make sense of particular touristic situations and experiences. In essence representing a phenomenological approach, the link between 'auto-definition' and motivation may in fact be difficult to establish, whilst the distinction between this and the expectancy approach discussed above might be considered fuzzy. Nevertheless, it highlights a particular issue that is important in understanding the relationship between tourism and development, namely, the meaning or significance of tourism as a contemporary manifestation of consumption. Putting it another way, understanding how people make sense of tourism as an accepted, arguably expected and, typically, relatively expensive form of consumption may provide a cultural framework in general for considering how tourism's role in or contribution to development might be perceived and responded to by tourists in particular.

Demand factors

Demand factors can be thought of collectively as the forces and influences that determine travel choices. In other words, if tourism consumption is considered (albeit simplistically) as a process commencing with motivation (need recognition or push), followed in response by information collection and evaluation and a subsequent travel decision, that decision will be subject to a variety of factors that determine the eventual choice. Moreover, such demand factors can be loosely categorized under two headings: first, pull factors, or the tourist's knowledge and image of a destination or experience and, second, what Gilbert (1991, p. 79) refers to as 'filterers' of demand, or the variety of demographic, socio-economic and other factors that either enable or constrain particular choices.

With regards to the former, much of the research is concerned broadly with destination image, or 'the sum of beliefs, ideas, and impressions that a person has of a destination' (Crompton 1979, p. 18). This is unsurprising; the image of a destination, as well as the specific attributes it offers, have long been recognized as being directly influential on consumer behaviour prior to, during and, indeed, following the stay at the destination (Tasci & Gartner 2007). More specifically, those destinations that enjoy a positive image are likely to prosper, whilst those with negative or unfavourable images may struggle (Sirakaya et al. 2001). Hence, significant attention has been paid to how destination image is formed in general (Beerli & Martin 2004; Echtner & Ritchie 1993; Gartner 1994; Govers et al. 2007; Gunn 1988), and to how specific factors such as risk (Lepp & Gibson 2008) or loyalty (Zhang et al. 2014) impact on destination image in particular.

Destination image is evidently related to development; social and economic development is likely (though not necessarily) to be enhanced in destinations with a positive image and, hence, a thriving tourism sector. However, of greater relevance to the present discussion, a simpler and more direct relationship exists between tourism and development in the context of those 'filterers' of demand that act as drivers or barriers of tourism demand. In other words, as suggested earlier in this chapter, the nature, scale and direction of tourist flows may have a direct bearing on tourism's developmental contribution. Hence, an understanding of not only those factors in principle but also trends and transformations in those factors in practice may be considered essential to both tourism planning and management in particular and to development policy more generally.

For example, since the mid-nineteenth century, the evolution and growth of tourism has been and continues to be driven by three well-known demand factors:

increases in free time, increases in disposable income and technological advances, particularly in transport. Of course, other factors have also been influential, not least the emergence of a diverse and innovative travel and tourism 'industry' which has facilitated continuing growth in participation in tourism, as well as the digital information revolution which has significantly empowered the role of tourists themselves in the tourism demand process (see below). Nevertheless, without sufficient temporal and financial resources and increasingly efficient, safe and fast means of transport, people would not have been able to participate in tourism (both domestic and international) to the extent witnessed today. Hence, given its rapid socio-economic development over the last two decades, the emergence of China as the world's largest international tourism market has been entirely predictable.

At the same time, other social and demographic 'filterers' impact upon destination and/or experience choice, many of which have been considered in the literature. For example, family lifecycle constraints, ageing (Glover & Prideaux 2009: Sedgley et al. 2011), disabilities (Small & Darcy 2011) and sexual orientation (for example, Waitt & Markwell 2006) may constrain or direct travel choices. However, with the exception of ageing, the implications of these factors are relatively short term and of most relevance to the tourism sector; in contrast, local, national and indeed international development may, in the longer term, need to take into account population growth and transformations in the socio-economic structures and characteristics of populations. Yet, as discussed shortly, relatively little attention has been paid to these in the tourism literature.

Tourist roles and experiences

The third and, undoubtedly, largest and most diverse research theme related to the consumption of tourism falls under the broad heading of tourist roles and experiences. Even to simply identify all the specific topics and issues explored in the relevant literature, let alone to review them in any detail, would be an impossible task; indeed, much of the academic study of the tourist, from seminal works such as MacCannell's (2013) *The Tourist: A New Theory of the Leisure Class* or Urry's (2002) *The Tourist Gaze* (also Urry & Larsen 2011) to more specific studies addressing particular forms of tourism or tourist practices, could be categorized under this heading.

Nevertheless, much of the research can be located within one of two broad subthemes, the first of which can be referred to as conceptual approaches to understanding the tourist experience. These include research into the nature or meaning of tourism, embracing in particular the perennial debates surrounding the authenticity of tourist experiences and tourism as a sacred or spiritual experience, as well as progressive studies into the manner in which tourist experiences are created, from the notion of the so-called experience economy (Andersson 2007; Pine & Gilmore 1998, 1999) to the more recent concept of the co-creation of tourist experiences (Binkhorst & Den Dekker 2009). In addition, discussions of tourism within the broader framework of postmodern consumer culture fall into this category (Pretes 1995; Sharpley 2018).

Of these, the concept of authenticity and, in particular, the suggestion that contemporary tourists seek authenticity in their experiences is perhaps of most relevance to the tourism–development relationship. Specifically, since Boorstin (1964) claimed that tourists are satisfied with inauthentic, 'pseudo' experiences, countered by MacCannell's (2013) thesis that, living in an alienated modern society, people seek authenticity through tourism in other times and other places, extensive research has focused on issues such as the meaning and construction of authenticity (Wang 1999), staged authenticity (MacCannell 1973, 2013), the marketing of authenticity (Silver 1993) and the relationship between authenticity and the commoditization of places, cultures and tourist experiences (Cohen 1988). The relevance of this work to development is twofold. First, it is argued that to be perceived as authentic, places and cultures should be seen as traditional or pre-modern, yet to develop is, in a broad sense, to become modern. Hence, tourism that is built on a search for (or the provision of) authentic experiences is, arguably, counterproductive; that is, it militates against the very purpose of tourism, namely, development. And second, the inevitable commoditization of cultural forms, whether inanimate objects such as artworks that are mass produced as souvenirs (often referred to as 'airport art') or events or rituals performed for tourist consumption, as they are accorded a monetary value and produced to meet the needs of tourists means they not only lose their inherent cultural meaning but also that their significance to the producers/performance is also diluted, as suggested in Greenwood's (1989) widely cited study. Putting it another way, one recognized objective of development is to affirm and strengthen a society's cultural identity, yet the commoditization process in tourism may serve to achieve the opposite, although as some suggest, this may not always be the case (Cole 2007; McKean 1989).

Interestingly, however, few attempts have been made to verify empirically the claim that tourists do indeed seek authenticity, to explore the extent to which a perceived lack of authenticity diminishes (if at all) the tourist experience or if, indeed, in the alleged era of the so-called 'post-tourist' (Feifer 1985), in which tourism is recognized as a kind of game in which nothing is authentic, whether conceptual debates surrounding authenticity hold any practical relevance in tourism. In a similar vein, a typology of consumer behaviour (Holt 1995, adapted to the consumption tourism in Sharpley 2018) proposes that some tourists may seek to 'integrate' themselves into the destination – in effect, seeking and sharing authentic local life – but again, this concept has not benefited from empirical testing. In both cases, the lack of research is of concern; social and economic development may be enhanced by providing more appropriate services and facilities based upon better knowledge and understanding of tourists' perceptions and understanding of, and need for, authentic experiences.

The second broad sub-theme for research under the heading of tourist roles and experiences encompasses studies that focus on actual tourism experiences. Inevitably, a myriad of tourist roles, too numerous to mention here, are explored in the literature. Indeed, some forms of tourism or tourist experience are not only represented by a distinctive literature base but also benefit from dedicated academic journals, such as ecotourism/ecotourists and religious tourism/tourists, whilst other tourist roles and experiences are consistently being 'invented', often related to particular places or products. Recent examples of the latter include volcanic tourism (Erfurt-Cooper 2014) and coffee tourism (Jolliffe 2010), whilst more common and established tourist roles include adventure tourism, nature tourism, health tourism, rural tourism, wine/food tourism, literary tourism and so on. Research within this sub-theme also includes studies of tourist roles related, for example, to tourist photography (Stylianou-Lambert 2012) and the impact of digital technology, particularly smartphones, on tourist behaviour (Wang & Fesenmaier 2013). Of particular relevance here, however, is research on tourists' roles and experiences that can be more directly related to development, specifically ecotourism and volunteer tourism. Reference has already been made to these two forms of tourism earlier in this chapter when it was pointed out that although both have attracted significant academic attention resulting in greater knowledge of the behaviours and expectations of both types of tourist, there remains more limited understanding of the values and motives of such tourists, particularly with regards to the role of tourism in development. Indeed, as now discussed in the concluding section of this chapter, a broad gap exists in the literature with regards to how tourists understand tourism as a contemporary social institution, its significance within their broader life-worlds and, hence, how the roles they adopt may complement or compete with tourism's developmental objectives.

Consumption of tourism and development: knowledge gaps

It is probably true to state that what has been considered here as the consumption of tourism is one of the most researched areas in tourism studies. In other words, research into the consumption of tourism is synonymous with research into the tourist (or what might be referred to as the sociology of tourism) and, as this chapter has attempted to demonstrate, not only are there numerous perspectives on the tourist, but also there exists a long-established, diverse and substantial literature on the subject. Nevertheless, in the context of the relationship between the consumption of tourism and development, a number of issues demanding or worthy of further research have already been identified. Specifically, it has been suggested that attention should be focused on:

- tourists' understanding of and responses to the developmental potential of different forms of tourism;
- developing a typology of tourists based upon environmental awareness and/or propensity to recognize and support tourism's developmental role;
- the degree of self-interest or altruism in volunteer tourists' motives;
- exploring how tourists make sense of tourism as a contemporary form of consumption;
- attempting to verify or challenge empirically the alleged significance of authenticity in the tourist experience.

However, from the discussion in this chapter, it is evident that there are two broad areas within which further research would enhance understanding of the relationship between tourism and development, namely, demand factors and the significance of tourism as a form of contemporary consumption.

Demand factors

As noted in the introduction to this chapter, the extent to which tourism may contribute to development is fundamentally dependent on the patterns and flows of tourism demand. In other words, although a variety of political, economic and socio-cultural factors shape tourism's developmental role at the destinational level, the presence of tourists is quite obviously a prerequisite. Moreover, despite the responses of some to the challenges of so-called overtourism – for example, the authorities in Palma de Mallorca recently announced a ban on local people renting apartments to tourists (Coldwell 2018) – most destinations around the world, perhaps encouraged by the United Nations World Tourism Organization's optimistic projections, continue to seek growth in tourist arrivals. That is, there appears to be the widespread assumption amongst destination authorities that they will be competing in a continuously growing international market.

In the shorter term, this may indeed be the case. However, for development to be sustainable (in the literal sense of the word), a longer-term perspective is required. In other words, awareness and understanding of potential future transformations in tourism demand on an international scale is of fundamental importance to development policy and planning, not least because such transformations may have a major impact on development, particularly in those destinations with a relatively high dependency on tourism.

Of course, predicting future patterns and flows of tourism is fraught with difficulty. Statistics reveal that, over recent decades, tourism has been susceptible to a variety of influences and events that have had a negative impact on arrivals, though typically more locally or regionally and over the shorter term; globally, international tourism has demonstrated, by and large, consistent annual growth. However, such a trend may not be guaranteed into the future, particularly when global population dynamics are taken into account. More specifically, a number of predicted structural and demographic trends in the global population over the next half century point to some significant implications for tourism and development. For example, overall declining population growth rates and, in many countries, absolute falls in population levels combined with rapidly ageing populations, the latter 'poised to become one of the most significant social transformations of the twenty-first century, with implications for nearly all sectors of society, including labour and financial markets, then demand for goods and services . . . as well as family structures and intergenerational ties' (UN 2015, p. 1) will inevitably impact on tourism flows, as will trends in population wealth. Thus, for example, whilst China currently enjoys an increasingly dominant position as a generator of international tourism and, in all likelihood, will continue to do so in the coming years, in the longer term that position may be challenged, not least because the country's population will not only decline from 2024 onwards but also will age at twice the rate of other countries (UN 2015, 2017). Hence, those destinations that become dependent on China as their major market may eventually experience significant declines in arrivals.

There is, then, a need for research at both the national and global levels into the potential effects of population dynamics, embracing trends in population structures, ageing and per capita wealth, as well as the consequences of migration patterns resulting from political and economic pressures and, indeed, climate change. It may well be, for example, that within 50 years, tourism will return to being predominantly domestic, with all that implies for its international development role.

Tourism as a contemporary form of consumption

For more than two decades, a popular argument has been put forward in the tourism literature that tourists are becoming more responsible and more aware of their role as tourists. In particular, it is claimed that the 'new' (Poon 1993) tourist is more environmentally sensitive and proactively seeks experiences that are less impactful on the local environment and which result in positive benefits for both the tourist and the local community. In short, it is suggested that recent years have witnessed the emergence of the 'good tourist' (Popescu 2008), as evidenced by increasing demand for ecotourism, volunteer tourism and other allegedly responsible forms of tourism. That is, the assumption is made that the growth in demand for such forms of tourism is driven by tourists' environmental values, an assumption that is underpinned by numerous surveys that indicate that, for example, tourists would be happy to pay more for holidays that bring enhanced benefits to local workers (Goodwin & Francis 2003).

Equally, others have long argued that the popularity of ecotourism and other responsible forms of tourism is based not on altruistic environmental concerns but on tourists' egocentric desires, hence the notion of ecotourism being, in reality, 'ego-tourism' (Wheeller 1992), whilst more generally the motives for participating in tourism tend to take precedence over tourists' environmental values (Sharpley 2006). This explains, perhaps, the 'attitude-behaviour gap' in tourism identified by Juvan and Dolnicar (2014), whereby those who typically adopt (or claim to adopt) green consumerist behaviour at home do not do so whilst on holiday, whilst more generally it has been found that people not only remain unwilling to adopt more 'sustainable' behaviour as tourists but also that it is not their responsibility to do so (Miller et al. 2010).

These competing positions reflect a notable gap in the literature, namely, the lack of understanding of the significance of tourism as a form of consumption. Certainly, it is accepted that a value-action or attitude-behaviour gap exists in tourism; as in consumer behaviour more generally, the majority of people who claim they would purchase more 'responsible' tourism experiences or act more responsibly as consumers rarely do so, or do so for reasons other than environmental concern.

However, the question that remains unanswered is: why? What is it about tourism that separates it from other forms of consumption, so that tourists generally display more limited responsible behaviour compared with other forms of consumption? Does tourism represent not only a corporeal escape from place but also a psychological escape from responsibility? Is the consumption of tourism viewed as a reward, or do tourists – as customers paying often significant sums of money for goods and services – believe they have the right to behave as they wish? Do tourists actually understand or consider if and how their behaviour, including their spending, impacts on the destination and its development? Indeed, with the exception of those who, for example, purposefully seek out 'Fair Trade' products, it is unlikely that they do so in relation to more general consumption practices, so why should tourism consumption be any different?

Given the centrality of the role of the tourist to tourism's role in development, answers to these and other questions are vital if tourism is to be better understood as a catalyst of development. Moreover, those answers might challenge what has been described as the moralization (Butcher 2002) of tourism, offering a more pragmatic understanding of the role of the tourist in what is, in essence, a market-led capitalistic production-consumption process. And in that context, further research into the consumption of tourism as proposed in this chapter may also provide an additional perspective on the challenge of achieving more sustainable consumption more generally. In other words, more than a quarter of a century ago there were calls for more sustainable lifestyles, firmly placing the responsibility on consumers to adopt a new sustainable paradigm (IUCN 1991); in short, this called for those in wealthier, more developed countries to consume differently and, in particular, less. Current trends in tourism, as a specific form of consumption, suggest the opposite continues to occur. Hence, further research into the relationship between tourism consumption and development may serve to highlight the challenge of achieving (sustainable) development more generally, whilst also pointing towards the need for alternative and, perhaps, more interventionist policies with regards to development and resource management.

References

Andersson, T. (2007), 'The tourist in the experience economy', *Scandinavian Journal of Hospitality and Tourism*, **7**(1), 46–58.

Appadurai, A. (1988), *The Social Life of Things: Commodities in Cultural Perspective*, Cambridge: Cambridge University Press.

Beerli, A. and Martin, J. (2004), 'Factors influencing destination image', *Annals of Tourism Research*, **31**(3), 657–81.

Binkhorst, E. and Den Dekker, T. (2009), 'Agenda for co-creation tourism experience research', *Journal of Hospitality Marketing and Management*, **18**(2–3), 311–27.

Boorstin, D. (1964), *The Image: A Guide to Pseudo-Events in America*, New York: Harper and Row.

Butcher, J. (2002), *The Moralisation of Tourism: Sun, Sand and Saving the World?*, London: Routledge.

Chen, G., Bao, J. and Huang, S. (2014), 'Segmenting Chinese backpackers by travel motivations', *International Journal of Tourism Research*, **16**(4), 355–67.

Cohen, E. (1972), 'Towards a sociology of international tourism', *Social Research*, **39**(1), 64–82.

Cohen, E. (1979), 'A phenomenology of tourist experiences', *Sociology*, **13**, 179–201.

Cohen, E. (1988), 'Authenticity and commoditization in tourism', *Annals of Tourism Research*, **15**(3), 371–86.

Coldwell, W. (2018), 'Palma de Mallorca to ban residents renting apartments to tourists', *The Guardian*, 25 April. Accessed 3 May 2018 at www.theguardian.com/travel/2018/apr/25/palma-de-mallorca-spain-to-ban-residents-renting-apartments-to-tourists

Cole, S. (2007), 'Beyond authenticity and commodification', *Annals of Tourism Research*, **34**(4), 943–60.

Crompton, J. (1979), 'An assessment of the image of Mexico as a vacation destination and the influence of geographical location upon that image', *Journal of Travel Research*, **17**(4), 18–23.

Dalen, E. (1989), 'Research into values and consumer trends in Norway', *Tourism Management*, **10**(3), 183–6.

Dann, G. (1981), 'Tourist motivation: An appraisal', *Annals of Tourism Research* **8**(2), 187–219.

Dann, G. (1996), *The Language of Tourism: A Socio-Linguistic Perspective*, Wallingford: CABI.

Dann, G. and Parrinello, G. (2009), *The Sociology of Tourism: European Origins and Developments*, Bingley: Emerald Group.

Donzelli, M. (2010), 'The effect of low-cost air transportation on the local economy: Evidence from southern Italy', *Journal of Air Transport Management*, **16**(3), 121–6.

Dunne, G., Flanagan, S. and Buckley, J. (2010), 'Towards an understanding of international city break travel', *International Journal of Tourism Research*, **12**(5), 409–17.

Eagles, P. (1992), 'The travel motivations of Canadian ecotourists', *Journal of Travel Research*, **31**(2), 2–13.

Echtner, C. and Ritchie, J.R.B. (1993), 'The measurement of destination image: An empirical assessment', *Journal of Travel Research*, **31**(4), 3–13.

Erfurt-Cooper, P. (ed.) (2014), *Volcanic Tourist Destinations*, Heidelberg: Springer.

Feifer, M. (1985), *Going Places*, London: Macmillan.

Freitag, T. (1984), 'Enclave tourism development: For whom the benefits roll?', *Annals of Tourism Research*, **21**(3), 538–54.

Gartner, W. (1994), 'Image formation process', *Journal of Travel and Tourism Marketing*, **2**(2–3), 191–216.

Gilbert, D. (1991), 'An examination of the consumer behaviour process related to tourism', in C. Cooper (ed.) *Progress in Tourism, Recreation and Hospitality Management*, Vol. 3, London: Belhaven Press, pp. 78–105.

Glover, P. and Prideaux, B. (2009), 'Implications of population ageing for the development of tourism products and destinations', *Journal of Vacation Marketing*, **15**(1), 25–37.

Goodall, B. (1991), 'Understanding holiday choice', in C. Cooper (ed.) *Progress in Tourism, Recreation and Hospitality Management*, Vol. 3, London: Belhaven Press, pp. 58–77.

Goodwin, H. and Francis, J. (2003), 'Ethical and responsible tourism: Consumer trends in the UK', *Journal of Vacation Marketing*, **9**(3), 271–84.

Gottlieb, A. (1982), 'Americans' vacations', *Annals of Tourism Research*, **9**(2), 165–87.

Govers, R., Go, F. and Kumar, K. (2007), 'Promoting tourism destination image', *Journal of Travel Research*, **46**(1), 15–23.

Greenwood, D. (1989), 'Culture by the pound: An anthropological perspective on tourism as cultural commoditization', in V. Smith (ed.) *Hosts and Guests: The Anthropology of Tourism*, 2nd edn, Philadelphia: University of Pennsylvania Press, pp. 171–85.

Gunn, C. (1988), *Vacationscapes: Designing Tourist Regions*, New York: Van Nostrand Reinhold.

Henning, G. (2012), 'The habit of tourism: Experiences and their ontological meaning', in R. Sharpley and P. Stone (eds) *Contemporary Tourist Experience: Concepts and Consequences*, Abingdon: Routledge, pp. 25–37.

Holbrook, M. and Hirschman, E. (1982), 'The experiential aspects of consumption: Consumer fantasies, feelings and fun', *Journal of Consumer Research*, **9**(2), 132–40.

Holt, D. (1995), 'How consumers consume: A typology of consumption practices', *Journal of Consumer Research*, **22**(June), 1–16.

Iso-Ahola, S. (1982), 'Towards a socio-psychological theory of tourist motivation: A rejoinder', *Annals of Tourism Research*, **9**(2), 256–62.

IUCN (1991), *Caring for the Earth: A Strategy for Sustainable Living*, Gland, Switzerland: World Conservation Union.

Jafari, J. (1987), 'Tourism models: The sociocultural aspects', *Tourism Management*, **8**(2), 151–9.

Jolliffe, L. (2010), *Coffee Culture, Destinations and Tourism*, Bristol: Channel View Publications.

Juvan, E. and Dolnicar, S. (2014), 'The attitude–behaviour gap in sustainable tourism', *Annals of Tourism Research*, **48**, 76–95.

Kamri, T. and Radam, A. (2013), 'Visitors' visiting motivation: Bako national park, Sarawak', *Procedia-Social and Behavioral Sciences*, **101**, 495–505.

Krippendorf, J. (1987), *The Holiday Makers*, Oxford: Heinemann.

Lepp, A. and Gibson, H. (2008), 'Sensation seeking and tourism: Tourist role, perception of risk and destination choice', *Tourism Management*, **29**(4), 740–50.

Lett, J. (1983), 'Ludic and liminoid aspects of charter yacht tourism in the Caribbean', *Annals of Tourism Research*, **10**(1), 35–56.

Lodziak, C. (2002), *The Myth of Consumerism*, London: Pluto Press.

Luo, Y. and Deng, J. (2008), 'The new environmental paradigm and nature-based tourism motivation', *Journal of Travel Research*, **46**(4), 392–402.

Lury, C. (1996), *Consumer Culture*, Cambridge: Polity Press.

MacCannell, D. (1973), 'Staged authenticity: Arrangements of social space in tourist settings', *American Journal of Sociology*, **79**, 589–603.

MacCannell, D. (2013), *The Tourist: A New Theory of the Leisure Class*, London: University of California Press.

Madrigal, R. and Kahle, L. (1994), 'Predicting vacation activity preferences on the basis of value-system segmentation', *Journal of Travel Research*, **32**(3), 22–8.

McIntosh, R. and Goeldner, R. (1990), *Tourism: Principles, Practices and Philosophies*, New York: John Wiley & Sons.

McKean, P. (1989), 'Towards a theoretical analysis of tourism: Economic dualism and cultural involution in Bali', in V. Smith (ed.) *Hosts and Guests: The Anthropology of Tourism*, 2nd edn, Philadelphia, PA: University of Pennsylvania Press, pp. 119–38.

Mihalič, T. (2015), 'Tourism and economic development issues', in R. Sharpley and D. Telfer (eds) *Tourism and Development: Concepts and Issues*, 2nd edn, Bristol: Channel View Publications, pp. 77–117.

Mill, R. and Morrison, A. (1985), *The Tourism System*, Upper Saddle River, NJ: Prentice Hall International.

Miller, G., Rathouse, K., Scarles, C., Holmes, K. and Tribe, J. (2010), 'Public understanding of sustainable tourism', *Annals of Tourism Research*, **37**(3), 627–45.

Morris, H. (2017), 'Tourists and cruise ships could be turned away under new plans to protect Dubrovnik', *Telegraph*, 11 August. Accessed 7 April 2018 at www.telegraph.co.uk/travel/destinations/europe/croatia/dubrovnik/articles/dubrovnik-tourist-limits-unesco-frankovic/

Moutinho, L. (1987), 'Consumer behavior in tourism', *European Journal of Marketing*, **21**(1), 5–44.

Munt, I. (1994), 'The "other" postmodern tourism: Culture, travel and the new middle classes', *Theory, Culture and Society*, **11**(3), 101–13.

Naidoo, P. and Sharpley, R. (2016), 'Local perceptions of the relative contributions of enclave tourism and agritourism to community well being: The case of Mauritius', *Journal of Destination Marketing and Management*, **5**(1), 16–25.

Parrinello, G. (1993), 'Motivation and anticipation in post-industrial tourism', *Annals of Tourism Research*, **20**(2), 233–49.

Pearce, P. (1992), 'Fundamentals of tourist motivation', in D. Pearce and R. Butler (eds) *Tourism Research: Critiques and Challenges*, London: Routledge, pp. 113–34.

Pearce, P. and Caltabiano, M. (1983), 'Inferring travel motivation from travellers' experiences', *Journal of Travel Research*, **22**(2), 16–20.

Perkins, H. and Grace, D. (2009), 'Ecotourism: Supply of nature or tourist demand?', *Journal of Ecotourism*, **8**(3), pp. 223–36.

Pine, B. and Gilmore, J. (1998), 'Welcome to the experience economy', *Harvard Business Review*, July–August, 97–105.

Pine, B. and Gilmore, J. (1999), *The Experience Economy*, Boston, MA: Harvard Business School Press.

Plog, S. (1977), 'Why destination areas rise and fall in popularity', in E. Kelly (ed.) *Domestic and International Tourism*, Wellesley, MA: Institute of Certified Travel Agents.

Poon, A. (1993), *Tourism, Technology and Competitive Strategies*, Wallingford: CABI.

Popescu, L. (2008), *The Good Tourist: An Ethical Traveller's Guide*, London: Arcadia Books.

Prebensen, N., Skallerud, K. and Chen, J.S. (2010), 'Tourist motivation with sun and sand destinations: Satisfaction and the WOM-effect', *Journal of Travel and Tourism Marketing*, **27**(8), 858–73.

Pretes, M. (1995), 'Postmodern tourism: The Santa Claus industry', *Annals of Tourism Research*, **22**(1), 1–15.

Rey, B., Myro, R.L. and Galera, A. (2011), 'Effect of low-cost airlines on tourism in Spain: A dynamic panel data model', *Journal of Air Transport Management*, **17**(3), 163–7.

Ross, G. (1993), 'Tourist motivation among backpacker visitors to the wet tropics of Northern Australia', *Journal of Travel and Tourism Marketing*, **1**(3), 43–60.

Ryan, C. (1997), 'The chase of a dream, the end of a play', in C. Ryan (ed.) *The Tourist Experience: A New Introduction*, London: Cassell, pp. 1–24.

Schmoll, G. (1977), *Tourism Promotion*, London: Tourism International Press.

Sedgley, D., Pritchard, A. and Morgan, N. (2011), 'Tourism and ageing: A transformative research agenda', *Annals of Tourism Research*, **38**(2), 422–36.

Sharpley, R. (2006), 'Ecotourism: A consumption perspective', *Journal of Ecotourism*, **5**(1–2), 7–22.

Sharpley, R. (2016), 'Introduction', in R. Sharpley (ed.) *Tourist Experience*, Vol. 1, Abingdon: Routledge, pp. 1–23.

Sharpley, R. (2017), 'From holiday camps to the all-inclusive: The "Butlinization" of tourism', in D. Harrison and R. Sharpley (eds) *Mass Tourism in a Small World*, Wallingford: CABI, pp. 95–104.

Sharpley, R. (2018), *Tourism, Tourists and Society*, 5th edn, Abingdon: Routledge.

Silver, I. (1993), 'Marketing authenticity in Third World countries', *Annals of Tourism Research*, **20**(2), 302–18.

Silverberg, K., Backman, S. and Backman, K. (1996), 'A preliminary investigation into the psychographics of nature-based travellers to the south-eastern United States', *Journal of Travel Research*, **35**(2), 19–28.

Sirakaya, E., Sonmez, S. and Choi, H. (2001), 'Do destination images really matter? Predicting destination choices of student travellers', *Journal of Vacation Marketing*, **7**(2), 125–42.

Small, J. and Darcy, S. (2011), 'Understanding tourist experience through embodiment: The contribution of critical tourism and disability studies', in D. Buhalis and S. Darcy (eds) *Accessible Tourism: Concepts and Issues*, Bristol: Channel View Publications, pp. 73–97.

Stylianou-Lambert, T. (2012), 'Tourists with cameras: reproducing or producing?', *Annals of Tourism Research*, **39**(4), 1817–38.

Tasci, A. and Gartner, W. (2007), 'Destination image and its functional relationships', *Journal of Travel Research*, **45**(4), 413–25.

UN (2015), *World Population Ageing, 2015*, New York: United Nations.

UN (2017), *World Population Prospects, Vol. 2: Demographic Profiles*, New York: United Nations.

Urry, J. (2002), *The Tourist Gaze*, 2nd edn, London: SAGE.

Urry, J. and Larsen, J. (2011), *The Tourist Gaze 3.0*, London: SAGE.

van Rekom, J. (1994), 'Adding psychological value to tourism products', in J. Crotts and W. van Raaij (eds) *Economic Psychology of Travel and Tourism*, New York: Haworth Press, pp. 21–36.

Vanhove, N. (2018), *The Economics of Tourism Destinations: Theory and Practice*, 3rd edn, Abingdon: Routledge.

Wahab, S. (1975), *Tourism Management*, London: Tourism International Press.

Waitt, G. and Markwell, K. (2006), *Gay Tourism: Culture and Context*, Abingdon: Routledge.

Wall, G. and Mathieson, A. (2006), *Tourism: Change, Impacts, Opportunities*, Harlow: Pearson Education.

Wang, D. and Fesenmaier, D. (2013), 'Transforming the travel experience: The use of smartphones for travel', in L. Cantoni and Z. Xiang (eds) *Information and Communication Technologies in Tourism 2013*, Berlin: Springer, pp. 58–69.

Wang, N. (1999), 'Rethinking authenticity in tourism experience', *Annals of Tourism Research*, **26**(2), 349–70.

Wearing, S. and McGehee, N. (2013), 'Volunteer tourism: A review', *Tourism Management*, **38**, 120–30.

Weaver, D. (2002), 'Hard-core ecotourists in Lamington National Park, Australia', *Journal of Ecotourism*, **1**(1), 19–35.

Wheeller, B. (1992), 'Eco or ego tourism: New wave tourism', *ETB Insights*, Vol. 3, London: English Tourist Board, D41–44.

Wilkinson, P. (2017), 'Cruise ship tourism in the Caribbean: The mess of mass tourism', in D. Harrison and R. Sharpley (eds) *Mass Tourism in a Small World*, Wallingford: CABI, pp. 210–31.

Witt, C. and Wright, P. (1992), 'Tourist motivation: Life after Maslow', in P. Johnson and B. Thomas (eds) *Choice and Demand in Tourism*, London: Mansell Publishing, pp. 33–55.

Zhang, H., Fu, X., Cai, L.A. and Lu, L. (2014), 'Destination image and tourist loyalty: A meta-analysis', *Tourism Management*, **40**, 213–23.

9 Now everyone can sail: on the need to understand mass tourism

*Julio Aramberri**

Introduction: mass tourism is here to stay

This chapter adopts, in the context of this book, a somewhat different approach to other contributions. Specifically, it will suggest that, geopolitical shocks apart, the phenomenon of mass tourism is poised to keep on growing – and steeply – over the next ten years. This may be an unfashionable argument and, in particular, one that is contrary to what both the mainstream media and many academics who look at mass tourism with disdain might believe or hope for. Nevertheless, partiality for taste or morals aside (Butcher 2002), the existence and continuing upward drift of mass tourism – considered here to be the production and consumption of tourism on a mass scale (see Harrison & Sharpley 2017) – remains undisputable. And this is principally what this chapter will argue, in so doing leading to the conclusion that further research is necessary to understand the factors underpinning this inexorable growth and its implications for wider development.

First, however, it is necessary to define clearly the topic of enquiry. Most importantly, mass tourism is not a synonym for travel. Travel is the action of moving, journeying or roaming between two spatial – and in the 'mobilities' paradigm also cultural – points, usually located at some distance from each other. Moreover, throughout history, travel has been a significant though dynamic component of human behaviour. From earliest times, hunters and gatherers, a broad label used to refer to human societies unaffected by the Neolithic revolution, made travel a way of life. Foraging implied settling temporarily in an area, consuming available resources and moving elsewhere to start a new cycle once those resources were depleted. Relatively speaking, there were then probably many more travellers amongst hunters and gatherers than in today's complex societies, and they also travelled more frequently and for longer periods than present-day humans. However, they did so in small groups. These two features (travel as survival strategy and small absolute numbers of participants) pertain to travel in general, but not to tourism.

The subsequent introduction of agricultural practices resulted in a fundamental transformation in the character of early societies as peasants became soil-bound. Work became more productive and more predictable, but also more

168

status-dependent. Hence, although the overall number of people engaging in travel may have been greater than in the Stone Age as populations grew, travel became the preserve of elites in both Neolithic Eurasia and the Americas (Gyr 2010), establishing a social divide that would endure until the late nineteenth century. They would travel for war, trade, leisure or religious reasons and, as time went by, they developed styles of travel that can be considered as proto-tourism (Hachtmann 2007). Nevertheless, owing to threats to safe travel, primitive and time-consuming modes of transport and high costs, these early pathfinders of tourism were very limited in both absolute numbers and as a proportion of society.

Mass tourism eliminated these barriers or, more precisely, evolved as they were overcome as travel became viable, efficient, secure and cheap for an ever increasing number of humans, as travel became democratized (Urry 2002). Indeed, it is its unprecedented magnitude that distinguishes (mass) tourism from travel in general. When mass tourism commenced, however, remains a matter of some dispute, although evidence points particularly to the early twentieth century. Certainly, during the preceding nineteenth century, a new means of transportation, namely, railways, had provided the means for a rapidly expanding volume of travellers who soon numbered hundreds of thousands each year. Mass tourism, however, involves millions, indeed nowadays billions of people each year, and it was new technological innovations, including the development of cars, commercial airways and cruise ships, that made this possible. In particular, society's embracing of automobiles shaped the evolution and growth of mass tourism in the US during the first half of the twentieth century whilst the growth in car ownership, together with developments in commercial air transport, extended it to Europe during the second half of the century. These new technologies shrank the cost of travel, creating what might be described as a demand tsunami. At the same time, new food and lodging supply networks, largely based on franchises, also originated in the US, further facilitating affordable travel for the masses. In early twentieth-century America, then, and subsequently in Europe, mass tourism had come to stay.

However, it is important to point out that mass tourism would not have developed so much and so quickly but for two idiosyncratic factors that accompanied the post-Second World War evolution of capitalism: increases in discretionary income and paid vacation time. These two conditions were tangled with the unequal but, nevertheless, real expansion of the welfare state in the polities of what is often referred to as the North or, more specifically, the 36 member countries of the Organisation for Economic Co-operation and Development (OECD). In this sense, mass tourism can logically be seen as an offshoot of the Great Divergence that created a chasm between the North and the South which, in turn, partly explains the criticism directed at mass tourism in general and what many consider to be its imperialist roots in particular (Nash 1989). At the same time, academic dislike for mass tourism also harks back to the erroneous and elitist notion, propagated by late nineteenth-/early twentieth-century social commentators and perhaps most notably by Daniel Boorstin (1964), that mass tourists are a self-referential herd of consumers unable to appreciate the culture and the values of their 'tourees', epitomized in the 'tourist bubble' (Cohen 1972) metaphor. However, the development of mass tourism has followed a divergent course. New travel technologies and know-how have reduced costs; these lower costs have metastasized the demand for ever more diverse products, both broad appeal and niche, and these new, more affordable commodities have engineered a self-sustaining loop of travel opportunities. And as for the bubble, it burst when tourists took subsequent trips; even its most recent epitome – Chinese tourists – are tossing it into the recycle bin (China Real Time 2016; MGI 2018).

In this chapter, I will outline an explanation of this turn of events – the relentless growth and spread of mass tourism – through the adoption of a Great Convergence-inspired view of tourism development. This thought-provoking hypothesis can be illustrated by numerous examples from which I have selected three eventual avatars: the Majorca Compound that turned the tables in hospitality; the seismic impact of low-cost carriers (LCCs) on aviation; and the swelling niche of Croatian nautical tourism that turns rookie sailors into old salts.

The Great Convergence

A few years ago, Kenneth Pomeranz argued against the extended notion that Western European economic development was a somehow unique and exceptional episode.

> No matter how far back we may push for the origins of capitalism, *industrial* capitalism, in which the large-scale use of inanimate energy sources allowed an escape from the common constraints of the pre-industrial world, emerges only in the 1800s. There is little to suggest that western Europe's economy had decisive advantages before then, either in its capital stock or economic institutions, that made industrialization highly probable there and unlikely elsewhere. (Pomeranz 2000, p. 15)

Hence, European-style industrialization, quite limited outside of Britain until the 1860s, might well have happened in China, Japan or India, each one of them with proto-industrial foundations in place. His conclusion, however, was ultimately underwhelming. The Great Divergence, according to Pomeranz, was the result of 'a combination of inventiveness, markets, coercion, and *fortunate global conjunctures* [author's emphasis] [that] produced a breakthrough in the Atlantic world, while the much earlier spread of what were quite likely better-functioning markets in east Asia . . . instead led to an ecological impasse' (Pomeranz 2000, p. 23). Alfred P. Doolittle, of *My Fair Lady* repute, could not have agreed more with this *little bit of luck*.

Be that as it may, the Great Divergence was real, lasting and effective. In a not-so-long historical period, it completely reshaped the preceding world order: 'The ancient civilizations of Asia and the Middle East – which had dominated for four millennia – were displaced in less than two centuries by today's rich nations'

(Baldwin 2016, p. 1). In the 1820s, in the early stages of the Industrial Revolution, China and India accounted for 49 per cent of global GDP while today's industrialized nations (G7 for short, comprising the US, Germany, Japan, France, Britain, Canada and Italy) contributed just 22 per cent. The industrialization of the G7 nations, however, turned the tables in a historical blink of the eye; from the 1820s up to the 1990s, the G7's share of global GDP soared from a fifth to almost two thirds, while China and India's collective contribution share would not reach 10 per cent.

In the 1990s, however, the tide turned. The dominant global economic reality of the last three decades has been a Great Convergence. In 2014, the G7 share of global GDP declined to 46 per cent of global GDP, a 'shocking share shift', as Baldwin puts it (2016, p. 2). However, the shift was not equally spread. Only six developing nations, the so-called I6 or Industrializing Six, namely China, Korea, India, Poland, Indonesia and Thailand, accounted for most of the G7 decline. Among these, China was the main driver, growing its share of global GDP to 14.8 per cent. It should also be noted that this Great Convergence has occurred at the national GDP level; as Sachs (2008) points out, at the per capita or individual level, average income convergence is unlikely to be realized for many years. Nevertheless, there has been a fundamental shift in share of global wealth between the G7 and the I6, while the rest of the world remained largely unaffected by these changes.

Why is this the case? Baldwin takes a long detour through the 200,000 years of human economic history – globalization for short – that can be summarized as follows. For many centuries, production was inextricably linked or bundled with consumption because of the costs of moving goods (shipping), ideas (communication) and people (travel) were extremely high. Globalization can, thus, be understood as the reversal of these three constraints ('unbundling', in Baldwin's words) to production and consumption. In other words, transport technologies improved in a loop together with industrialization during the Industrial Revolution (O'Rourke & Williamson 2002, 2017) and the cost of moving these three items – goods, ideas and people – decreased, though at dissimilar speeds. Specifically, while shipping quickly became more economical (the first 'unbundling'), moving ideas and people remained expensive which, in turn, triggered significant income differences between the North and the South. For example, nineteenth-century Britons could enjoy their Chinese tea sweetened with Jamaican sugar, as product markets expanded globally. However, industries were clustered locally where innovative technologies were rooted, that is, in the North. In a few decades, the asymmetries between North and South – still existential in many areas – materialized because of differentials in the compound rate of growth. 'In short, the Great Divergence was produced by the combination of low trade costs and high communication costs' (Baldwin 2016, p. 4).

The second unbundling took place around the 1990s as a result of the information and communication technologies (ICT) revolution. ICT-led offshoring won the day by combining G7 technologies with the workforces of developing nations among massive North–South flows of know-how. Rich nations ensured that their knowledge cornucopia would remain within their production networks but, by way of restricted know-how transfers, boosted the manufacturing fortunes of some other countries that they 'cherry-picked'.

The question then to be asked is: why did the process not spread worldwide? And the answer is that the costs of moving people, as opposed to goods or ideas, remain quite high, not so much in terms of actual fares as in the time costs imposed by travel. Take, for instance, a global business such as Facebook, where the median annual salary is US$240,430 (SFC 2018). Based on 230 working days per year and eight-hour days, it can be calculated that the median Facebook worker earns an impressive US$120 hourly wage. Let us then assume that top management earns an average salary *only* 20 times higher – a massive US$2,400 per hour. If one of them takes a three-day business trip from San José International Airport to Facebook's Tokyo office, the US$15,000 first-class ticket plus three nights at a 5-star hotel on top of the 30+ hours of return travel time increase the overall cost of the trip to around US$72,000. Even financial behemoths remain parsimonious when sending their personnel abroad.

Accordingly, offshoring firms clustered their production in just a few nearby locations: 'The internationalization of production thus created Factory Asia, Factory Europe, and Factory North America – not Factory World' (Baldwin 2016, p. 132) and, as a consequence, the revolutionary changes in manufacturing enabled by ICT have therefore completely bypassed South America, Africa, the Middle East and most of Central Asia. The main exception is India because it has mostly engaged in specific service networks where face-to-face interaction can be arranged by communication technologies at nearly zero cost.

Nevertheless, despite this clustering, the Great Convergence had a broad reach. Roughly half of humanity live in the I6, so their rapid income growth created a double groundswell: (1) the booming demand for raw materials – a commodity super-cycle – that, as a knock-on effect, sparked growth in commodity-producing locales untouched by the second unbundling; and (2) rising living standards among the I6 workers and their families; that is, amongst billions of consumers.

Moreover, this new ordering has changed the way economies interact worldwide. Up until recently, the basic model for development was based on Ricardo's view of international trade, according to which productive world-economy units – nation states mostly – would manufacture items to be traded for others made elsewhere at a cheaper cost (see Dornbusch et al. 1977). The Ricardian mechanism ensured that nations would concentrate on the products that they were best at producing and exchange these for products made in other countries, so that comparative advantage was the name of the game. International trade would increasingly specialize different nations within the system, thereby creating a virtuous cycle of trade.

Ricardo's comparative advantages, however, were abstract and unexplained assumptions, hampering a comprehensive understanding of the driving forces of the Great Convergence. What happened over time was the clustering of large chunks of industry in small geographic areas (industrial cities) of each successful nation. This concentration not only allowed for economies of scale, but also enhanced the speed of innovation, as happens when many people face the same problems close to each other. Concentration came at a cost, though. Most stages of production had to be performed locally and at prevailing labour wages. Coordinating complex activities over long distances was not yet feasible; to change the equation, ideas had to be unbundled from distance.

And this is precisely what the ICT revolution empowered. Today, maintaining a continuous, two-way flow of words, images and data comes at near zero cost: 'For digitized ideas, distance truly died, or more precisely, the ICT revolution assassinated it' (Baldwin 2016, p. 133). The new communication potential meant that manufacturing stages, up till then bundled with short distance, could be dispersed internationally to places that managers and technicians might reach in one single day, as the clustering progression requires. Consequently, production stages – something less than whole production process – became scattered over a not-so-distant geographical and cultural area efficiently run by moving people within short distances. Some costly technologies developed in the old industrialized areas could be transferred offshore where they met a low-wages workforce, giving birth to global value chains (GVCs). From this perspective, offshoring – as in, for example, Apple moving factories from Texas to China – is not a case of some goods crossing borders made possible by, for instance, newly found Chinese competitiveness; it is, rather a manifestation of American technological advances and know-how combining with a low-wage Chinese workforce or, in short, a GVC.

The ICT trade revolution was asymmetric in two dimensions. First, it fostered the export of parts and the relocation of production stages more so than the relocation of the full production of final goods; and second, Southern exports of parts replaced Northern exports of totally manufactured products. As a result, those developing nations outside the new GVC-defined areas found it hard to succeed given their so-called premature deindustrialization, suffering a losing combination of low technology and low wages.

The I6, however, did not follow the previous G7 trajectory; that is, a more distinctive path appeared in their national economies. While in the past, all economies had so-called sunshine and sunset industrial sectors, nowadays the sunshine and sunset stages of production have relocated to other nations, distressing whole occupations and imposing job losses, underpinning the 'smile curve' (see Figure 9.1). In this model, increasingly more value is added by services related to manufacturing than by manufacturing itself. Thanks to the second unbundling, value addition that formerly occurred during the complete, nationally based production processes, has now amplified the role of the pre- and post-fabrication stages to the manufacture's loss. Apple, for instance, closed its last manufacturing facility in the US in 2004. Hence, nowadays the economy-wide smile curve of a nation or sector will depend on its specific combination of value added by the primary sector, manufacturing and services. Moreover, a deepening of the smile means that not only has the value

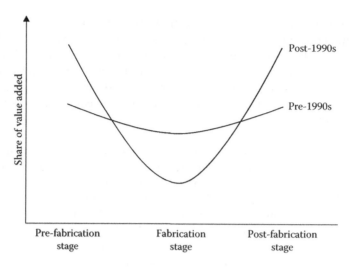

Source: Adapted from Baldwin 2016, p. 153.

Figure 9.1   The added-value smile curve

added by services grown, but also that manufacturing sectors' share in the final production has diminished its cycle. Japan, for instance, saw its smile go from a light manufacturing smirk in 1985–95 to a very deep one in the following decade as GVC-wise companies offshored their manufacturing stages.

Further discussion of Baldwin's Great Convergence thesis is unnecessary here, not least because the rest of his argument is uninteresting. As a matter of fact, it forecasts that tensions and inequality will increase more at the national than at the international level (Milanovic 2016), as many lesser-skilled G7 workers experience losses in job opportunities and income at home. Along with the equally growing competition from robots in basic occupations, their immediate future has darkened – a very disturbing trend with foreseeably ill-fated consequences for the political process in democratic societies. Baldwin's hypothesis is also not totally satisfactory as it assumes a gaping hole – that travel remains bundled. Even if one concedes the point for some kinds of business travel, as in the Facebook case above, mass tourism and the tourism industry have freed themselves from the two shackles that define bundling: high costs and no-GVC production. Indeed, there is plenty of persuasive evidence of this in both international and domestic mass tourism and, as is now contended, this is precisely why mass tourism has grown in leaps and bounds and will continue to do so, with implications for tourism's role in global development.

The Majorca Compound

Throughout the nineteenth century, Spain saw its former colonial empire melt away while the metropolis veered towards an all-time economic low. A regressive social structure along with authoritarian political institutions – the archetype of oligarchic capitalism (Baumol et al. 2007) – prevented any attempt to modernize and, as a consequence, the economy failed relentlessly (Aramberri 2009).

General Franco's dictatorship (1939–75) did not falter in its determination to sustain this oligarchic structure. The initial period of the regime, up to 1959, catered to the interests of the traditional elites, securing their privileged control of the paltry national market and stifling demands for an open economy and democracy. This autarchic period, however, came to an end in the second half of the 1950s (Salmon 1991) and in 1959, with Spain's foreign reserves pointing to bankruptcy, the government implemented a very successful stabilizing strategy. Indeed, between 1959 and 1973, '[a]mong the member states of the OECD, only Japan enjoyed faster and more sustained growth' (Harrison 1984, p.44). Specifically, the preceding vicious circle of trade deficits/low technology/underdevelopment came to an end, not because of productivity improvements in agriculture or manufacturing but, rather, thanks to an export-led take-off, as recommended by the mission of the International Bank for Reconstruction and Development (now the World Bank) that visited the country in 1961 (IBRD 1963). Foreign investment increased by a factor of 26 between 1959 and 1973.

The Spanish case had its peculiarities, not least the fact that two unconventional exports in particular solidified Spanish foreign reserves. One was cheap migrant labour turning the engine of tech-savvy manufactures in Western Europe; during the 1960s, between 1 and 2 million Spanish people migrated, with one source (Fontana & Nadal 1976) estimating that, between 1962 and 1971, remittances contributed a yearly average of 7.9 per cent to the balance-of-payments. The other largely positive item was mass tourism. Foreign investment in real estate in Spain increased sevenfold between 1965 and 1974 (Vidal Villa 1981) and a significant, though not easily quantifiable, proportion of this financed hotel and residential projects linked to tourism. Additionally, between 1951 and 1960 both the number of international visitors and the ensuing income trebled. Spain became what, after 60 years of development, it still is: Europe's beach for the European middle classes. Its coasts plus the local purchasing power parity (PPP) of the time cemented the ambitious programme recommended by the International Bank for Reconstruction and Development.

This Spanish economic 'miracle' thus owed much to the development of international tourism. Gaviria (1975), a Spanish sociologist, spoke of a two-pronged catalyst; on one hand, real-estate purchases by foreigners who wanted a permanent residence in Spain and, on the other hand, the recurrent inflows of, overwhelmingly, Western Europeans. The latter were the beneficiaries of the post-Second World War mass tourism wave, and this new demand proved to be a godsend for the small and mid-sized family-owned hotels prevalent in the Balearic Islands at the time. Up until that time, Majorca had been an unassuming destination attracting a limited Spanish honeymoon market. Taking advantage of the new tourism demand from Northern Europeans, these properties reinvented themselves as '4S' (sun, sea, sand and sex) avatars. And, as Majorcan prices were highly competitive with their French and Italian counterparts, demand grew exponentially. Existing properties filled up and new ones were badly needed.

However, most Spanish hoteliers, typically family and mid-sized companies, were unable to finance the requisite larger resorts, and Spanish banks saw no reason to extend credit to this unexperienced market. As a consequence, reflecting a Baldwin (2016) General Convergence swing, it was European tour operators who became the bankrollers of this tourism boom. They had financial resources, knew their own national markets and, since they needed beds and had ready cash, they would fund up to half the cost of the new hotels. In exchange, they signed preferential agreements with local hoteliers who provided accommodation at stable prices for between four and ten years. The deal was very attractive for both parties, helping them to plan mutual mid-term expansion. Hoteliers would soon hang *No vacancy* signs on their properties during the season while construction unleashed an upward economic cycle that, in turn, bred new resorts and new hotels to accommodate new clients. In 2016, incoming tourists, both international and domestic, to Majorca plus the other three main islands of the Balearic archipelago (Minorca, Ibiza and Formentera) reached 15.4 million (ATB 2017).

To be part of the tourism 'compound' in Majorca, the new hotels embraced the know-how provided by tour operators. Properties should be close to or directly on the beach, offer good sea views, gardens and tennis courts; eventually, golf courses also became a must. The hotels should also be near other hotels and resorts, and in the vicinity of shopping areas and night spots. Large hotels (500+ rooms) with low per-room space and good common facilities appeared, turning their clients into a captive demand during their non-beach hours for hotel bars, their commercial galleries and in-house services (hair-dressing, spas, beauty salons, foreign exchange). This new brand of hotel became par for the mass tourism markets; tour operators used to call them *convenience hotels*, but they might be better referred to as the *leisure entrepots* of industrial tourism.

Why did tour operators not take over hotel management? The simple answer is that running hotels was not their GVC part of the business; rather, their choice production stage was pre- and post-hospitality services. From their headquarters, they ran the basic and most rewarding activities (designing, pricing, marketing and advertising in their feeder markets) plus the operation of their charter fleets to transfer clients to the selected destinations. In the end, thanks to their know-how and control of foreign demand, they became the real masters of Majorcan prices. This GVC was a harbinger of what would happen in other economic sectors over the next decades.

The system had another pillar upon which its success depended, namely, a low-wage local workforce. Abundant but low on skills, local workers easily adapted to low wages and job instability; just one in three workers enjoyed permanent employment, mainly those in mid-level managing positions. The working day lasted eight hours or more and less than half of the workforce benefitted from one free day per week. Most contracts ended at the end of the season and, as the majority of employees came from the Spanish mainland, they would typically return to their hometowns for menial employment over the winter months. Their bargaining power vis-à-vis their employers was non-existent as free trade unions were illegal. From the very beginning, the Majorca Compound had a 'deep smile curve'.

Might the process have been different? Hypothetically, yes. Spanish critics of mass tourism proposed changing its inner structures to ensure a better share for the national economy through taxes and development planning. Moreover, over the years some national and local politicians also doggedly supported the idea of creating a national tour operator to replace the foreign vacation factories driving international tourism in Spain. Hypotheticals do not, however, change reality; these anti-GVC plans overlooked the fact that the know-how was in the hands of foreign tour operators who controlled an international demand that only trusted travel companies that spoke their language and understood their consumption habits.

The Majorca Compound proved reliable, resilient and suitable for all parties. Data for the 1970–2000 period are difficult to gather and compare; however, after 2002, when Spain joined the Eurozone, international and domestic tourism contributed 42–45 per cent to the Balearic Islands' GDP (MDB, 2017). In 2017 figures, it reached US$33.8 billion in total, supporting an average per capita income of US$29,115. In short, thanks to this GVC, the poor workforce of the 1970s now shares in the prosperous local lifestyle. Moreover, the successful Majorca Compound did not halt in the islands.

> The particular combination of overseas tour operators, airlines and island transport with local hotel management to produce large numbers of holidays for large numbers of people at relatively low costs but with an acceptable level of service . . . provided widespread opportunities for small hoteliers to join this process, later to experience rationalization and the emergence of a corporate sector of well-known brands. (Buswell 2011, p. 145)

For example, Barceló and Meliá, the two best-known Majorcan-born brands, transplanted this European system of low-cost holiday provision to Latin American and Asian markets as an effective and affordable Great Convergence variety, whilst many of these lessons have been well learned by many other hotel chains and tour operators worldwide.

Now everyone can fly . . .

The 1970s witnessed two momentous events in the development of mass tourism: the introduction of wide-bodied jetliners and airline deregulation (Heppenheimer 1995). Jetliners had been in use in Britain and in the US since the 1950s and, compared to piston-powered propeller-driven aircraft, they could climb faster, reach higher speeds and fly at higher altitudes. They could also accommodate more passengers – Boeing 707s for example started with 120 passengers in 1958 – and offer lower costs. However, these early jetliners were single aisle and not fit for travelling long distances. The onset of the wide-bodied planes made long-haul travel more pleasant and, because of bigger seating maps, also more affordable. Hence, since the 1970s, single-aisle jets have operated mainly on short- and medium-haul routes (a range of 1,500–4,000 km, with a maximum capacity of 295 passengers) while double-aisled aircraft cover long-haul distances (between 4,000 and 15,000 km, with a maximum capacity of 555 passengers). Since their inception, there has been an unremitting race to increase the range, bulk and fuel economy of wide-bodied aircraft.

In 1978, US President Carter signed the Airline Deregulation Act to encourage market-based, competitive air transportation. Until then, airlines had been subject to strict governmental controls on prices, routes, market entry and personnel. Further deregulatory actions followed by way of international open skies accords. This combination of technological innovation and regulatory cutbacks quickly increased the number of passengers worldwide, contributing to an upward demand curve that sloped steeply between 1970 and 2005, growing six times in 35 years. It would soon double, reaching 4 billion domestic and international passengers worldwide in 2017. Air travel thus became the means of choice for medium- and long-haul trips, with railways and automobiles dominating shorter distances.

Growth was, however, uneven, increasing at a slower rate in the North; overall, the OECD countries' air travel index climbed from 100 in 2005 to 150 in 2017, while neither in North America nor Europe specifically did it double. This reflected the fact that both regions had already developed a sizeable aviation market over the previous 35 years and, while large, increases in passenger numbers had less relative impact. At the other end of affluence, Sub-Saharan Africa could not match the gigantic leap in air passenger numbers witnessed in other regions, whereas South Asia grew the fastest (index 426). India, apparently mired forever in the languor of its colonial, overloaded and agonizingly slow trains, reached 149 million air travellers, whilst the Middle East and North Africa boasted a 409 index. Impressive expansion also occurred in East and South East Asia (Table 9.1). With the exception of isolated countries such as Brunei, Mongolia and Myanmar, along with the mature Japanese and South Korean markets, most countries in the Asia region experienced remarkable growth in air travel. Cambodia's passenger numbers, for example, increased by a factor of 6.5 although they started from a lowly position; Thailand and Malaysia, already well developed, also saw big growth, but the most remarkable advance occurred in Vietnam, with air traffic nearly eight times greater than 12 years before, the Philippines (five and a half times greater) and Indonesia (four times greater).

Correlation is not causality, but the remarkable growth of air travel occurred at the same time as LCCs were finally treading on firmer legal and financial grounds. In the mature markets of Europe and the US the older established airlines, formerly known as flag carriers and later relabelled as legacy or heirloom airlines, demonstrated more resilience in fending off fierce competition. Nevertheless, by 2017

Table 9.1   Air travel, passengers carried 2005–17, East/South East Asia and India (millions)

Country	2005	2010	2015	2017	2005 = 100
East Asia					
China	136.7	266.3	436.2	551.2	403
Hong Kong SAR, China	20.2	28.3	41.9	45.6	225
Japan	102.3	109.6	114.1	123.9	121
Korea, Rep.	33.9	36.9	66.1	84.0	247
Macao SAR, China	2.0	1.3	2.3	2.8	140
Mongolia	0.3	0.4	0.5	0.6	200
South East Asia					
Brunei Darussalam	0.9	1.3	1.1	1.2	133
Cambodia	0.2	0.3	1.1	1.3	650
Indonesia	26.8	59.4	90.0	110.2	411
Lao PDR	0.3	0.4	1.2	1.2	400
Malaysia	20.4	34.2	50.3	58.2	285
Myanmar	1.5	0.9	2.1	2.9	193
Philippines	8.1	22.6	37.0	44.1	544
Singapore	17.8	24.9	33.5	37.7	211
Thailand	18.9	28.8	56.4	71.2	376
Vietnam	5.4	14.4	29.9	42.5	787
India	27.9	64.4	98.9	139.8	501

Source: Adapted from World Bank 2017.

Ryanair, which carried fewer than 10 million passengers in the year 2000, was in a tight fight for the top spot in Europe with the Lufthansa Group, which carried 130 million passengers compared to Ryanair's 128 million. That same year, LCCs accounted for five of the eleven top European airlines (CAPA 2018).

Table 9.2 shows the penetration of LCCs in the fastest-growing markets. The South Asian case is staggering; from practically no share in the industry in 2005, LCCs provided 57.2 per cent of all available plane seats in 2017. A similar phenomenon occurred in South East Asia but, generally, LCCs grew quickly in all markets, including in Europe and the US, the only exception being China. There, despite some success stories, such as Spring Airlines, deregulation has not been implemented as the government vigorously defends the turf of state-owned legacy companies. They have adopted different names, creating the illusion of a competitive market, but in reality they are all heavily subsidized by taxes and ultimately belong to the same owner; they are state-owned companies. Private LCCs, both local and foreign, face a rigid regulatory environment that makes entry next to impossible, and such bureaucratic meddling inevitably, but unnecessarily, raises the cost of air travel for Chinese consumers. No crystal ball is needed to foresee rapid change if LCCs were allowed to operate on a level playing field in China.

Table 9.2   Low-fare seats as percentage of total

Region	Share 2016 %	Growth 2005–16 %
South Asia	57.2	+42.1
South East Asia	52.6	+32.7
East Asia	8.4	+5.8
Europe	37.9	+10.9
North America	32.7	+7.3
South America	32.2	+18.5

Source: Adapted from International Air Transport Association.

Table 9.3   Comparative costs of selected airlines, excluding fuel; LCCs in lower six rows

Company	Cost*
Air France-KLM	11.7
Lufthansa	11.1
American	10.5
Delta	10.2
United	10.1
IAG**	9.4
Southwest	8.7
EasyJet	7.9
Allegiant	6.4
Spirit	5.8
Wizz	4.1
Ryanair	3.8

Notes: * US cents per mile flown.
** International Airlines Group: British Airways, Iberia and others.

Source: Waal & Carey 2017.

As is well known, the success of LCCs depends on cost reduction and nimble operational management (Farmaki & Papatheodorou 2015; Morrell 2008), the two factors that have fulfilled Air Asia's marketing prophesy: *now everyone can fly.* Costs of LCCs are significantly lower than those of legacy airlines, as their one and only promise is basic transportation from point A to point B. Any frills are extra and, usually, their seat maps provide less legroom than legacy airlines. CASK (cost of available seats/km) differentials between the highest-cost legacy airline (Air France-KLM) and the lowest LCC (Ryanair) are 3:1 (Table 9.3). Where do these cost savings stem from? One 2013 simulation (Binggeli & Weber, 2013) showed that in two similarly arranged LCC and Legacy flights, CASK for the former would reach 4.7 US cents while the latter would reach up to 6.2 cents. Another similar

Table 9.4   Around-the-world travel costs, in US dollars

Stage	LCC*	Legacy*	Running total LCC	Running total legacy
New York–Barcelona	305	1,911	305	1,911
Barcelona–Athens	140	166	445	2,077
Athens–Singapore	307	562	752	2,369
Singapore–Kuala Lumpur	45	87	798	2,726
Kuala Lumpur–Honolulu	477	654	1,275	3,380
Honolulu–Las Vegas	228	350	1,503	3,730
Las Vegas–New York	117	147	1,620	3,877

Note: * Different LCC and legacy companies.

Source: Waal & Carey 2017.

exercise in 2017 found a respective CASK of 4.2 and 8.2 cents (Saxon & Weber 2017). As some costs (fuel, aircraft insurance, maintenance, landing fees) are equal for all aircraft, the LCC advantage in both studies harks back to nimble GVCs for sales and overhead plus lower labour costs (Doig et al. 2003). In the balance between comfort and low prices, LCC clients opt for the latter, saving themselves a significant amount of money (Table 9.4).

Cost reductions and GVCs have made air travel affordable for the billions. However, the unbundling of people and transport costs is not yet complete. LCCs will still have a tough battle to extend their reach to long-haul flights where their CASK advantage decreases due to taxes and other regulatory fees that can reach up to 80 per cent of the ticket price in some markets (Binggeli et al. 2013). Average air travel speed has remained unchanged at 900–50 km/h since jetliners started operating 60 years ago. Flying at Mach 2.04 (>2,100 km/h), Concorde reached Paris from New York in less than 3.5 hours, but it was discontinued in 2003. There has been plenty of speculation of late about hypersonic aviation and it will eventually become a reality, but for the time being speed barriers remain.

. . . and sail too

As mass tourism demand diversifies, many consumers are rejecting the former all-inclusive packages of standardized products (sun, sea and sand; city tours; winter sports), travelling for idiosyncratic purposes and seeking out niche products and experiences, from cosmetic surgery to attending religious events.

Amongst these is nautical tourism. It has been defined as 'the sum of poly-functional activities and relations that are caused by the tourist-boaters' stay within or out of the ports of nautical tourism, and by the use of vessels or other objects related to the nautical and tourist activities, for the purpose of recreation, sports, entertainment or other needs' (Luković 2012, p. 400). It therefore includes any activity undertaken on water, whether white-water rafting, kayaking, sailing, motoring, cruising or fishing. Less widely, it also embraces 'travel with the main motivation of [practising] nautical sports activities either at the selected destination or along an entire journey, using a rented boat (yacht charter) or property boat' (Payeras et al. 2011, p. 116) as opposed to cruise tourism, which typically involves rest and recreation on either round or point-to-point trips in a vessel where transportation is a secondary goal.

In 2018, mid-size leisure sailboats (10–15 metres long) from a reputable boat maker would cost around $US270,000 to purchase (baseline price, no frills), with similarly sized catamarans selling for $US320,000. In 2017, PPP adjusted, the average net monthly salary in Germany was 2,960 euros (roughly $US3,430), so buying one of those boats would take six to eight years. At such prices, boat ownership has to be mostly limited to the wealthiest social strata, a category that for US banks now starts at $US25 million of investable capital (Bloomberg 2018). Therefore, nautical tourism has traditionally been the exclusive playground of the rich and famous. This perception has, however, become outdated as new ways of enjoying yachting have made it affordable to a wider section of the population.

Nautical tourism is becoming increasingly popular in the European Union, with an estimated 36 million participants, or around 7 per cent of the European Union's population, and 6–6.5 million recreational craft including boats of all lengths, though typically smaller and cheaper in price than those referred to above. More importantly, consumers are able to charter larger craft, accommodating parties of up to 10–12 persons, for just a few days at a time. The European Boating Industry (EBI) (ICF International 2016, p. 87) estimated that in 2015, the number of charter boats in the continent totalled some 60,000 units, collectively generating 4–6 billion euros. With an expected annual growth rate of 7.1 per cent, the number could double by 2026, whilst, at present, the Mediterranean accounts for 40 per cent of the total.

Chartering is not the only income generated by nautical tourism, however, as boats, whether permanently moored or transient, have to undergo maintenance and repairs at marinas and boat yards. EBI estimates their number in Europe to be around 4,500 with an annual turnover of 3–4 billion euros and employing a workforce of between 40,000 to 70,000. Many marinas are part of GVCs that link boaters, service personnel and local suppliers of goods and services, such as restaurants, hotels and shops, to international charter companies. Once again, even in this niche market, the combination of international know-how at pre- and post-production stages with a local workforce comprising both low- and high-skilled employees (one out of three charters include local skippers) has contributed to making chartering affordable to large numbers of nautical tourists (ICF International 2016, p. 91).

Although not the biggest market for nautical tourism, Croatia is one of the fastest-growing yachting destinations in the Mediterranean. Within a distance of 420 km as the crow flies between Rijeka in the north west and Dubrovnik in the south east, Croatia boasts 5,835 km of coastline including the roughly 1,185 islands and islets that festoon it – a paradise for boaters. Besides countless secluded beaches, inlets and coves often accessible only from the sea, boaters/nautical tourists can also anchor at beautiful medieval towns packed with palaces and churches, silent witnesses of the region's complicated history and of its former share in the prosperity of Venice and its Adriatic hinterland. St Mark's lion still adorns many as a reminder of the olden times evoked by one of Croatia's marketing campaigns – 'The Mediterranean as it once was'.

In 2008, the Croatian government launched an ambitious ten-year (2009–19) development plan for nautical tourism. It projected that, by 2018, Croatian GDP would total about HRK500 billion with the income from nautical tourism contributing about HRK15 billion (Croatia 2008, pp. 19–21). In reality, total GDP reached just HRK336.8 billion in 2017, with a total direct contribution of tourism of HRK39.8 billion (WTTC 2018). As the plan's implied share of nautical tourism to GDP was 3 per cent, a contribution of about of HRK10 billion might have been expected from nautical tourism.

As usual, bureaucratic imagination overran reality. Recent statistics (CBS 2018) show that income from marinas in 2017 was just HRK855 million. Figures for charters are few and far between (Marušić et al. 2014) and are therefore difficult to compute. The 2008 plan featured 2007 charter income as HRK348 million. If charters, like marinas, had doubled their revenues since then, they would have added HRK750 million; if trebled, around HRK1.2 billion. There are no figures for sundry other items (fuel alone should represent a significant amount as motor boats are also chartered). Therefore, the most generous educated guess cannot show marinas plus charters contributing more than HRK2.1 billion in 2017, quite far from the 2008 expectation. Similar blunders were made in forecasting the number of marinas and berths of all kinds (Kovačić et al. 2015).

The structure of the Croatian nautical industry in 2017 offers a less impressive, though more credible view. Total moorings were 17,067, distributed among 140 marinas of all categories. The fleet is evenly divided between motor yachts (6,568) and sailboats (6,296); a plurality of boats fly the Croatian flag. Most berths (13,433) are occupied permanently and a majority accommodate 10–15 metre vessels that, as will be noted below, offer the best ratio of cost/occupant.

Among the few data available on the demand side (Gračan et al. 2016), in 2014 there were 4,906 vessels registered for chartering; charter passengers numbered 347,000 and made 2.4 million overnight stays. In 2015, charter companies recorded 362,589 arrivals and 2.6 million overnight stays. Most clients are foreigners but the number of Croats is also increasing. Average yacht tourists to Croatia are 45 years old and come from households with monthly incomes of 3,500+ euros; 77 per cent have a higher education degree.

Table 9.5   Skippered boat charter costs, 2018 prices in euros*

Boat type	Season	Boat charter	Moorings	Skipper	Total	Per passenger	Passenger/ day
Sailboat	High	5,400	862	1,200	7,462	746	107
	Low	3,740	383	1,200	5,323	532	76
Catamaran	High	6,850	862	1,200	8,912	891	127
	Low	4,000	383	1,200	5,583	558	78
Motorboat	High	20,000	862	1,200	22,082	2,208	315
	Low	19,300	383	1,200	20,883	2,088	298

Note: * Prices from a well-known charter company; excluding transport to destination, food and entertainment; charter trip: 7 days/10 passengers.

In 2012, they spent a daily average of 100 euros, transfers and airfares not included. Again though limited (Šipič & Najdanovič 2012), the few sources available reveal that yacht tourists spend more than any other tourism category in Croatia (Total Croatia 2016). Yet, whether boat owners hire their boats when idle to charter companies thus reducing their own yearly costs, or just charter hands, they are far from being the notional ultra-rich of conventional wisdom. On the contrary, a back-of-the-envelope estimate (Table 9.5) shows that one-week charter vacations have become affordable to middle-class tourists.

Prices vary significantly between the high (June, July and August) and low (May and September) seasons. For the ten-member parties that can be accommodated in one mid-size boat, daily costs per passenger in non-motor vessels vary between 107 and 176 euros for sailboats and 127 and 178 euros for catamarans. Such prices compare favourably with most Croatian private accommodation, including 3–4 star hotels. Moreover, charter yachts, effectively floating Airbnb-like accommodation, free their passengers from traffic jams and other hassles.

Therefore, it is not surprising that both in Croatia and in other parts of the world, GVCs that combine efficient boat-making technologies – and therefore relatively cheaper vessels – and foreign capital in the pre- and post-production stages (fleet design and financing, marketing, customer follow-up) with the local workforce (marina services, boat maintenance, skippers) have put paid to the timeworn idea of sailing as an exclusive playground for the rich and famous.

Conclusion: implications for tourism and development

The Great Convergence hypothesis is an exciting means of understanding the contemporary processes of globalization, particularly what Baldwin refers to as the 'second unbundling', or overcoming the costs imposed by distance on production and technology transfers. GVCs made it possible to perform some stages of one distinct production process in diverse international settings or, putting it another way, successfully blended know-how innovation originating in advanced societies with the low labour costs of some emerging markets. However, because of still high travel-time costs, moving highly qualified personnel between locales – the third and uncompleted unbundling – led to GVC clustering in just a small number of adjoining countries.

For unexplained reasons, however, Baldwin does not mention that this third unbundling had already impacted on the production of mass tourism from its inception over a century ago. In order to transform tourism into what the UNWTO (2018) considers to be of the world's largest export sectors, GVCs were and are created in both international and domestic travel. The three trends examined in this chapter show their influence on hospitality, air transport and the nautical tourism niche market. Their increasing popularity cannot be explained without the contribution of GVCs, that is, of a 'deep smile' at work in those sectors. They reduced the cost of travel and made it possible for billions of people to experience its joys.

However, all human ventures alloy costs and benefits and mass tourism is no exception. Its expansion goes hand in hand with entry barriers – a great chunk of mankind still cannot afford it – and hazardous and incestuous overcrowding. However, these two and many other ensuing issues need serious probing and no-bounds debates, not moral question begging nor an endless reiteration of normative mantras.

Baldwin's enticing hypothesis opens a number of research areas for those interested in the foreseeable evolution of mass tourism. Description and understanding of how the expansion of GVC networks has conditioned and, at the same time, enabled the success of tourist products, both mainstream and niche, comes first. But that would just be the beginning. More specifically: will GVCs create a permanent gaping hole between the extremes of the *smile curve* (design, development, marketing) and its centre (production)? How do they impact the globalized labour force that produces tourist services at the consumption point? Will it be doomed to just contribute low skills in exchange for stagnant wages? How does GVC expansion affect the seemingly unstoppable growth of mass tourism? And how will it shape socio-economic development at both ends of the value chains? These and related issues raised by Baldwin's views open a wide and inviting field for future research.

NOTE

*   The author would like to thank Professor Nevenka Čavlek (Zagreb University, Croatia) for her help and advice on matters of nautical tourism.

References

Aramberri, J. (2009), 'The sociology of tourism in Spain: A tale of three wise men', in G.M.S. Dann and G. Liebman Parrinello (eds) *The Sociology of Tourism: European Origins and Developments*, Bingley: Emerald, pp. 243–273.

ATB (2017), *Balearic Islands Regional Context Survey*, Agència de Turisme de les Illes Balears, Lille: Interreg Europe. Accessed 16 April 2018 at www.interregeurope.eu/fileadmin/user_upload/tx_tev projects/library/file_1508251726.pdf

Baldwin, R. (2016), *The Great Convergence: Information Technology and the New Globalization*, Cambridge, MA: Belknap Press of Harvard University Press.

Baumol, W., Litan, R. and Schramm, C. (2007), *Good Capitalism, Bad Capitalism and the Economics of Growth and Prosperity*, New Haven, CT: Yale University Press.

Binggeli, U. and Weber, M. (2013), *A Short Life in Long Haul for Low-Cost Carriers*, McKinsey & Co. Accessed 10 May 2018 at www.mckinsey.com/industries/travel-transport-and-logistics/our-insights/a-short-life-in-long-haul-for-low-cost-carriers

Binggeli, U., Dichter, A. and Weber, M. (2013), *The Economics Underlying Airline Competition*, McKinsey & Co. Accessed 10 May 2018 at www.mckinsey.com/industries/travel-transport-and-logistics/our-insights/the-economics-underlying-airline-competition

Bloomberg (2018), *Here's How Much Money You Need for Bankers to Think You're Rich*. Accessed 16 May 2018 at www.bloomberg.com/news/articles/2018-05-23/bankers-don-t-think-you-re-rich-unless-you-have-25-million

Boorstin, D. (1964), *The Image: A Guide to Pseudo-Events in America*, New York: Harper and Row.

Buswell, R.J. (2011), *Mallorca and Tourism: History, Economy and Environment*, Bristol: Channel View Publications.

Butcher, J. (2002), *The Moralisation of Tourism: Sun, Sand . . . and Saving the World?*, London: Routledge.

CAPA (2018), *Europe's Top 20 Airline Groups by Passengers 2017*, Centre for Aviation. Accessed 8 May 2018 at https://centreforaviation.com/analysis/reports/europes-top-20-airline-groups-by-passengers-2017-lufthansa-wrests-top-spot-from-ryanair-394211

CBS (2018), *Tourism*, Croatian Bureau of Statistics. Accessed 15 June 2018 at www.dzs.hr/default_e.htm

China Real Time (2016), *Tripping Point: Chinese Travelers Break Free of the Tour Bus*. Accessed 12 February 2018 at https://blogs.wsj.com/chinarealtime/2016/02/04/tripping-point-chinese-travelers-break-free-of-the-tour-bus/

Cohen, E. (1972), 'Towards a sociology of international tourism', *Social Research*, **39**(1), 64–82.

Croatia (2008), *Nautical Tourism Development Strategy: The Republic of Croatia 2009–2019*. Accessed 10 January 2018 at www.mppi.hr/UserDocsImages/Strategija%20razvoja%20nautickog%20turizma%20 ENGL%201.pdf

Doig, S., Howard, A. and Ritter R. (2003), *The Hidden Value in Airline Operations*. Accessed 16 April 2018 at www.mckinsey.com/industries/travel-transport-and-logistics/our-insights/the-hidden-value-in-airli ne-operations

Dornbusch, R., Fischer, S. and Samuelson, P.A. (1977), 'Comparative advantage, trade, and payments in a Ricardian model with a continuum of goods', *American Economic Review*, **67**(5), 823–39.

Farmaki, A. and Papatheodorou, A. (2015), 'Stakeholder perceptions of the role of low-cost carriers in insular tourism destinations: The case of Cyprus', *Tourism Planning and Development*, **12**(4), 412–32.

Fontana, J. and Nadal, J. (1976), 'Spain: 1914–70', in C. Cipolla (ed.) *Contemporary Economies: The Fontana Economic History of Europe*, Vol. 6, Part 2, London: Fontana.

Gaviria, M. (1975), *España a Go-Go: Turismo Charter y Neocolonialismo del Espacio*, Madrid: Turner.

Gračan, D., Gregorič, M. and Martinič, T. (2016), 'Nautical tourism in Croatia: Current situation and outlook', *Tourism and Hospitality Industry Congress Proceedings*, Opatja, Croatia, pp.66–79. Accessed 21 October 2018 at https://stari.fthm.hr/files/Kongresi/THI/Papers/2016/THI_April2016_66to79. pdf

Gyr, U. (2010), *The History of Tourism: Structures on the Path to Modernity*. Accessed 20 March 2018 at http://ieg-ego.eu/en/threads/europe-on-the-road/the-history-of-tourism/ueli-gyr-the-history-of-t ourism#InsertNoteID_60

Hachtmann, R. (2007), *Tourismus-Geschichte*, Göttingen: Vandenhoeck and Ruprecht.

Harrison, D. and Sharpley, R. (2017), 'Introduction: Mass tourism in a small world', in D. Harrison and R. Sharpley (eds) *Mass Tourism in a Small World*, Wallingford: CABI Publishing, pp. 1–14.

Harrison, J. (1984), *The Spanish Economy in the Twentieth Century*, New York: St Martin's Press.

Heppenheimer, T.A. (1995), *Turbulent Skies: The History of Commercial Aviation*, New York: John Wiley & Sons.

IBRD (1963), *The Economic Development of Spain*, Baltimore, MD: Johns Hopkins University Press.

ICF International (2016), *Assessment of the Impact of Business Development Improvements around Nautical Tourism: Final Report*, Brussels: European Commission.

Kovačić M., Gračan, D. and Jugović, A. (2015), 'The scenario method of nautical tourism development: A case study of Croatia', *Scientific Journal of Maritime Research*, **29**, 125–32.

Luković, T. (2012), 'Nautical tourism and its function in the economic development of Europe', in M. Kasimoglu (ed.) *Visions for Global Tourism Industry: Creating and Sustaining Competitive Strategies*, Rijeka HR: Intech, pp. 399–430.

Marušić, Z., Neven I. and Horak, S. (2014), *National Tourism within TSA Framework: Case of Croatia*, Nara, Japan: 13th Global Forum in Tourism Statistics, pp. 93–104.

MDB (2017), 'Tourism's declining contribution to GDP', *Majorca Daily Bulletin*. Accessed 26 March 2018 at https://majorcadailybulletin.com/news/local/2017/09/13/49219/tourism-declining-contribution-gdp.html

MGI (2018), *Chinese Tourists: Dispelling the Myths. An In-Depth Look at China's Outbound Tourist Market*. Accessed 14 November 2018 at www.mckinsey.com/~/media/mckinsey/industries/travel%20transport%20and%20logistics/our%20insights/huanying%20to%20the%20new%20chinese%20traveler/chinese-tourists-dispelling-the-myths.ashx

Milanovic, B. (2016), *Global Inequality: A New Approach for the Age of Globalization*, Cambridge, MA: Belknap Press of Harvard University Press.

Morrell, P. (2008), 'Can long-haul low-cost airlines be successful?', *Research in Transportation Economics*, **24**(1), 61–7.

Nash, D. (1989), 'Tourism as a form of imperialism', in V. Smith (ed.) *Hosts and Guests: The Anthropology of Tourism*, 2nd edn, Philadelphia, PA: University of Pennsylvania Press, pp. 37–52.

O'Rourke, K. and Williamson, J. (2002), 'When did globalization begin?', *European Review of Economic History*, **6**(1), 23–50.

O'Rourke, K. and Williamson, J. (2017), 'Introduction', in K. O'Rourke and J. Williamson (eds) *The Spread of Modern Industry to the Periphery since 1871*, Oxford: Oxford University Press, pp. 1–12.

Payeras, M., Jacob, M. García, M.A., Alemany, M., Alcover, A. and Martínez-Ribes, L. (2011), 'The yachting charter tourism SWOT: A basic analysis to design marketing strategies', *Tourismos*, **6**(3), 111–34.

Pomeranz, K. (2000), *The Great Divergence. China, Europe, and the Making of the Modern World Economy*, Princeton, NJ: Princeton University Press.

Sachs, J. (2008), *Common Wealth: Economics for a Crowded Planet*, New York: Penguin Press.

Salmon, K.G. (1991), *The Modern Spanish Economy: Transformation and Integration into Europe*, London: Pinter Publishers.

Saxon, S. and Weber, M. (2017), *A Better Approach to Airline Costs*. Accessed 21 June 2018 at www.mckinsey.com/industries/travel-transport-and-logistics/our-insights/a-better-approach-to-airline-costs

SFC (2018), 'Yes, median pay at Facebook really is about USD 240,000 a year', *San Francisco Chronicle*. Accessed 20 April 2018 at www.sfchronicle.com/business/networth/article/Yes-median-pay-at-Facebook-really-is-about-12870786.php

Šipič, N. and Najdanovič, F. (2012), 'Sailboat rental: Determining the price based on its attributes', paper presented at *Global Business Conference*, Zagreb: Innovation Institute, pp. 361–70.

Total Croatia (2016), 'Things are looking up for Croatian nautical tourism'. Accessed 14 May 2018 at www.total-croatia-news.com/business/2553-things-are-looking-up-for-croatian-nautical-tourism

UNWTO (2018), *Tourism Highlights 2018 Edition*, UN World Tourism Organization. Accessed 20 October 2018 at www.e-unwto.org/doi/pdf/10.18111/9789284419876

Urry, J. (2002), *The Tourist Gaze*, 2nd edn, London: SAGE.

Vidal Villa, J. (1981), 'España y el imperialismo', in R. Carballo and J. Blázquez (eds) *Crecimiento Económico y Crisis Estructural en España 1959–1980*, Madrid: Akal, pp. 293–304.

Waal, R. and Carey, S. (2017), 'How budget carriers transformed the airline industry: In 14 Charts', *Wall Street Journal*. Accessed 10 August 2017 at www.wsj.com/articles/how-budget-carriers-transformed-the-airline-industryin-14-charts-1503501624

World Bank (2017), *Air Transport, Passengers Carried*. Accessed 22 May 2018 at https://data.world-bank.org/indicator/IS.AIR.PSGR?end=2017&start=1970&view=chart

WTTC (2018), *Economic Impact 2018: Croatia*, World Travel and Tourism Council. Accessed 5 June 2018 at www.wttc.org/-/media/files/reports/economic-impact-research/countries-2018/croatia2018.pdf

10 A sustainable hospitality and tourism workforce research agenda: exploring the past to create a vision for the future

Shelagh Mooney and Tom Baum

Introduction

This chapter addresses the need for a research agenda to achieve the goal of a sustainable hospitality and tourism workforce on the global scale. Inhospitable working conditions, as well as the exploitation of vulnerable workers, are widespread in the sector across different locations and contexts (McIntosh & Harris 2012). However, the degree of attention paid to these issues remains marginal, not only in the sustainable tourism debate in particular (Baum 2018; Baum et al. 2016a) but also in other arenas of tourism development more generally. Such neglect may be attributable, in part, to the tourism academy's tendency to avoid contentious or unpalatable topics (Mooney et al. 2017a; Ram et al. 2016, p. 2010). However, it may also result from the 'disconnect' between separate avenues of research in tourism and hospitality institutions, namely, studies that focus on the tourist experience, tourism and hospitality management and critical management research, which, frequently adopting a 'problematizing' perspective, explore the employment of individuals in the sector. In particular, within the tourism management literature, extant studies tend to focus on the ways in which individuals negotiate their working lives or how particular organizations engage with their workers (Baum 2013; Baum et al. 2016b); the interactions between levels have, however, been neglected. Consequently, there have been few attempts to link the plethora of employment challenges in tourism and hospitality. These troubling issues include, *inter alia*, low pay, precarious security, poor working conditions, high labour turnover, intersectional disadvantage, occupational ghettoization and employee sexual and physical abuse that can represent a form of modern slavery. All of these need to be set in a wider social, cultural and economic context as the basis for coherent policy formulation.

This chapter seeks to fulfil an ambitious aim by suggesting a new research agenda to bridge such research gaps by adopting a selective, thematized approach. First, the current state of hospitality and tourism workforce research will be outlined, the areas examined in turn being critical hospitality studies, human resources management (HRM), strategic HR approaches, peripheral tourism workforce studies, labour geographies and diversity management in tourism and indigenous tourism.

In this examination, research into practices that foster a sustainable workforce in particular will be highlighted, whilst neglected research areas will be identified. In addition, attention will be drawn to the needs of specific groups in the workforce, such as women, younger and older workers, migrants and people with disabilities. Finally, an agenda for change will draw these strands together, indicating future directions for advancing the creation of a sustainable hospitality and tourism workforce (Baum 2018).

The current state of 'mainstream' hospitality and tourism workforce research

The approach taken in this review of the research is discursive (Paludi et al. 2014). Moreover, the literature overview is not a linear progressive account; rather, our somewhat eclectic focus is on the areas that we consider important when thinking about encouraging a more sustainable attitude to the tourism and hospitality workforce. Generally, the orientation of many studies appears to be to promote tourism as a benefactor for local communities and tourists alike and 'truth barriers' (Tribe 2010) are erected against challenging critical counter-discourses; for example, many tourism and hospitality industry conferences fail to offer tracks examining HRM in the sector.

More specifically, a disconnect exists between 'grassroots' tourism activists, who deal with specific community problems, and the tourism academy, which appears to be frequently driven by commercial interests (Higgins-Desbiolles & Powys Whyte 2014). For example, the tourism sector has long contributed to a massive growth in sex tourism and, in particular, child sex tourism (Hawke & Raphael 2016). While a consideration of this disturbing aspect of tourism is beyond the remit of this chapter, we must acknowledge that the provision of such tourism services in developing countries is driven by the move from local demand to tourist demand (Burke 2018). Economic marginalization puts women and children in developing countries at risk from sexual exploitation in their home countries; indeed, not only sexual exploitation but also the wider exploitation of the tourism and hospitality workforce is problematic in very many countries and locations, locating aspects of tourism work, particularly hospitality, within the ambit of modern slavery (Armstrong 2016; Robinson 2013). A myriad of studies reveals the prevalence of poor working conditions and the exploitation of vulnerable workers in the sector (Baum 2007, 2015; Berg & Farbenblum 2017; McIntosh & Harris 2012; Stringer 2016), yet such voices are largely ignored in the sustainable tourism debate (Baum et al. 2016a). In general, hospitality and tourism management research remains undeveloped, both in terms of scope and paradigms used.

Critical hospitality workforce research

In 2008, Morrison and O'Gorman described hospitality research, in particular, as descriptive and uncritical, a perception reiterated by Laws and Scott (2015, p. 48) in their critique of existing tourism research and what they describe as 'the proliferation of descriptive case studies and the lack of generalizable or testable hypotheses in much tourism research [which] contrasts poorly with established disciplinary fields'. More optimistic perspectives claim that tourism research has undergone what has been described as a 'hopeful tourism' reinvention (Pritchard et al. 2011). However, given Figueroa-Domecq et al.'s (2015) scathing indictment of the tourism academy's narrow vision, including its exclusion of women in academia and its privileging of Western research paradigms, the assessment of tourism as a brave new space is arguably over-optimistic. Certainly, hospitality research has long focused on hospitality management; therefore, its view has been dominated by managerial-led and commercially focused interests. This, in itself, may not be a fatal flaw in terms of adding value to research, but it has tended to keep the foci narrow at an organizational level. As Baum et al. (2016b, p.18) trenchantly observe when suggesting a new typology for hospitality and tourism workforce research, there is a need to move beyond 'a "problem solving" managerial perspective on workforce research and seek to engage with explanation'. It should be noted here that, in the field of hospitality, a new journal, *Hospitality and Society*, was launched in 2011 in order to counter the narrow management discourse that had come to define hospitality studies.

Tourism research, too, does not fully engage with studying more sociological issues, such as how the workforce accommodates tourists' needs. Veijola et al. (2014) posit that this may be because attending to the corporeal needs of guests is somehow disorderly, where tourism wishes to create a semblance of control and order. If a tourism encounter is to be 'untamed', it should be exotically or adventurously wild, not 'mundane' or domestic (Lynch 2017). Studies may address aspects of the workforce such as tour guiding or entrepreneurial approaches to business and, most recently, attention has passed to the sharing or gig economy. However, this is generally examined from a consumer or marketing perspective and, consequently, a systematic review of what effects companies such as Uber and Airbnb have on labour projections are lacking. Examples of narratives that explore this phenomenon include Dredge and Gyimóthy (2015) and Moragra (2017).

Human resources management

Given the significance of customer satisfaction to a service sector such as tourism, it is understandable that a wide range of studies have been devoted to the dimensions surrounding excellent service delivery (for example, Dedeoğlu & Demirer 2015). All testify to the crucial role played by front-line employees in delivering consistent service and HRM, therefore, should be a rewarding field for hospitality and tourism researchers and businesses. In reality, its key principles do not appear to be applied in the tourism sector and, taken from this perspective, an analysis of the application of HRM principles in the sector does not make for optimistic reading (see Baum 2007, 2015). Similarly, Kusluvan et al. (2010) soberly observe the absence of enlightened HRM practices across the sector. This neglect is set to intensify in the hospitality industry given what Solnet, Kralj and Baum (2015) consider the abandonment of HRM professionalism. In their view, HRM appears to be transitioning to an outsourced function, focused on the administration and legal compliance requirements. Likewise, Baum et al. (2016a) decry the absence of any consideration of workforce interests in the sustainable tourism debate.

One might see encouraging signs of a recognition of the importance of all stakeholders, including employees and local communities, when considering the social dimensions in the sustainable approach in the hospitality industry (for example, Legrand et al. 2016). However, very few studies explicitly provide an analysis of the financial costs and financial benefits associated with the implementation of individual sustainable practices. The pronounced lack of robust studies that would support the empirical cost/benefit measurement of specific initiatives could potentially explain the woeful absence of enlightened strategic HR practices in the tourism sector. Such studies would simultaneously enhance the financial performance of tourism and hospitality enterprises and justify sustainable HRM practices (such as stability of employment and employee development and training).

Strategic management approaches

Turning then to strategic management, Davidson and Wang (2011), when discussing sustainable HRM in Australian hotels, argued that hotels need to move beyond a cost-reduction focus and a reliance on casualized labour by adopting a more strategic approach to HRM. This short-term contingent labour model is not confined to the Asia Pacific region; it is prevalent across many jurisdictions including the United Kingdom, America, New Zealand and Canada (Baum et al. 2016b; Bernhardt et al. 2003; Davidson et al. 2006; McDowell et al. 2009; Williamson 2017). It appears that changing hotel ownership and management models have profoundly affected how hotels 'manage' their HR. In the 1990s, global hotel chains began the process of divesting themselves of their 'bricks and mortar' investments. They achieved growth in their brand portfolios across a variety of geographical locations through franchising and management contracts, selling their reservation networks, operational and marketing expertise to investment corporations and private owning companies. Therefore, wide discrepancies may exist between the pay, benefits and conditions for employees working in different hotels of the same brand, depending on the ownership of the property (Williamson 2017). This lack of consistency suggests that the traditional talent management and development policies practised by global brands are now at risk (Gannon et al. 2010) and have been eroded. This has significant implications for the training, talent development and working conditions of individual employees.

To an increasing extent in some destinations (although these appear to be global brands), properties are owned by offshore interests, divorced from local conditions and interests and only delivering value or loyalty to family interests or shareholders. Mooney's (2016) study of New Zealand hotel HR practices provided insights into the frustrations of executives over the unwillingness of overseas investment companies to increase wages for casual workers, even by a very small proportion. She found that supervisors were paid only marginally more than inexperienced workers who were on minimum wage arrangements. More generally in the hospitality sector, contingent or precarious labour appears to be regarded as the most cost-effective way to respond to scholastic demand (Williamson 2017) and there are obviously short-term advantages for organizations who are no longer responsible for what were once regarded as 'welfare' benefits, such as medical care for workers. Although some researchers (for example, Kusluvan et al. 2010), may regret the lack of value placed on strategic HRM in the sector, it appears that hospitality and tourism research deficiencies may have contributed to the neglect of the more positive HRM strategies implemented in other business sectors.

It would appear to be counter-intuitive that the hospitality sector does not practise a strategic HRM approach when the benefits are so clear. In their overview of strategic HRM management research in the tourism and hospitality sector, Madera et al. (2017) postulate that studies show a positive correlation between strategic HRM practices and superior firm performance. Effective selection, training and development and reward systems affect employees at the individual level and enhance firm performance. However, Madera et al. identify similar gaps to those that have been observed in other areas of hospitality research – for example, in sustainable tourism enterprises and diversity management – such as the failure to isolate the costs associated with specific initiatives or to measure causal outcomes. Their summary of strategic HRM research in hospitality highlights 'glaring' gaps and 'room for improvement' (Madera et al. 2017, p. 60). In their view, the first gap is that few studies measure firm performance using direct financial measures, such as assets, return on equity, market return and sale growth; rather, they focus on individual-level or organizational-level indirect performance outcomes. The second gap is that the majority of strategic HRM studies focus on the individual, not organizational level, measuring managers' perceptions of HRM rather than measuring the effects of HRM strategies at organization level at the pinnacles of firm hierarchies. They identify a third gap as the failure to implement conceptual models that are commonly found in the general management literature. The final gap, they posit, is the absence of multi-level studies – a blind spot also observed by Baum et al. (2016b) – and the failure to examine how organizational-level processes modify behaviour and attitudes at the individual level, which then feeds through into productivity levels and ultimately moderates firm performance.

In another critical review which empirically mapped the 'intellectual structure' of research into HR in hospitality and tourism management, García-Lillo et al. (2018, p. 1752) decry the neglect of 'the human aspect [including] . . . human capital [and] . . . complex social behaviours and interactions'. Madera et al. (2017, p. 49) also remark on this deficiency, referring to the 'black box' of factors that mediate the effect of HRM systems on performance, such as human and social capital and motivation. García-Lillo et al. (2018, p. 1752) argue that HR is a critically important element in a hospitality or tourism firm's competitive advantage. Therefore, they believe that without effective HRM strategies, hospitality and tourism businesses are unable to change quickly enough in response to threats and opportunities.

Digital disruption

In her prediction of future challenges facing a dynamic tourism and hospitality sector, Christensen Hughes (2018) reiterates the importance of organizations' rapid responsiveness to change, particularly in an era in which market share growth is being considerably 'disrupted' by digital technologies. She observes that the focus on value, convenience, ethical consumption and authentic encounters is being driven by millennial tastes and demand and, in her view, there are significant implications for HRM including what kind of employees are required and how they can best be trained, engaged and retained. She argues that competition from digital platforms may finally drive the industry to change its cost-based approach. Recent research shows, however, that digital disruption may just reproduce current precarious employment models. For example, Sigala (2018) draws intriguing conclusions from her study of Airbnb operations in Australia, in which she notes the transition of collaborative economy entrepreneurs into the mainstream commercial world, thus losing many of the social dimensions of networked hospitality.

While there are undoubtedly positive aspects, many of the employment arrangements in peripheral businesses that support larger-scale commercial applications of Airbnb appear to provide 'gig economy' insecure work. Capital is also required for individuals to take advantage of opportunities to rent accommodation 'for hire', hardly a positive antidote to the precarious employment arrangements of globalized hospitality and tourism businesses.

Peripheral tourism studies

In considering how we may better understand the array of complex factors at the macro- and meso-organizational levels, and how they may affect the individual in a specific national context, it is necessary to study local and regional economic factors. In this context, studies that fall outside the mainstream 'hospitality or tourism management' literature add helpful details, in two ways. First, economic geographers such as McDowell et al. (2007, 2009) have looked at how wider labour market and economic forces are replicated in miniature by hotel HR managers. Second, researchers have taken a specific issue, such as labour demand and supply or migrant employment (for example, Riley & Szivas 2009), to examine the effects on local hospitality pay rates. Such studies are not easily classifiable and, equally, are likely to appear in the geographical, social science or business journals. In addition, another rich vein of information to be mined is industrial relations research; for example, Williamson (2017) meticulously examines how changing relationships between hotel owners, trade unionists and state legislators has profoundly influenced conditions for hospitality workers in New Zealand over a long period of time. When the 'benign collusion' between the three ceased, protection for workers reduced dramatically, resulting in a measurable decline in wage rates and working conditions during the period.

Labour geography

In an overview of labour geography's contribution to tourism work and employment research, Ioannides and Zampoukos (2018, p. 1) criticize the approach as 'piecemeal and case based, demonstrating unawareness of broader theoretical discussions and debates within the sub-field of labour geography'. In particular, they decry the attitude of mainly Western researchers who focus on the bad jobs in tourism, but discount the myriad of advantages provided by employment in tourism and hospitality in middle-latitude countries. They suggest that the binary 'good' versus 'bad' job debate skates over the deeper complexities, including geographical issues surrounding hospitality and tourism employment. In their view, discussions in human geography concerning tourism work and workers centre excessively on migration and worker mobility.

Duncan et al.'s (2013) research into labour mobility in New Zealand would, however, be an exception to this rule as it clearly identifies local factors including seasonality and employment conditions, thereby linking macro factors to individual outcomes. Nevertheless, such case-based studies have seriously limited the development of theory, and Ioannides and Zampoukos (2018, pp. 2–3) believe that labour geographers have not really investigated the labour dimensions of tourism and associated services such as hospitality. In their view, Herod's (1994, 1997) innovative conceptualization of 'labour geography' offers 'an alternative viewpoint of work and worker's agency within economic geography [and] recognises that workers are in themselves important agents in producing, shaping and reshaping their everyday geographies'. Similarly, Mooney et al. (2017b), in their study on the intersections of age, gender and ethnicity in hotel work, suggest that workers, even those in the lowest positions of the organizational hierarchy, assert their own agency by choosing to work in supportive environments that respond in different ways to the same meso and macro factors as their competitors.

In a somewhat depressing conclusion, Ioannides and Zampoukos (2018) ultimately attribute the contentious 'low status' of hospitality employment to the growing casualization perspectives. For instance, critical hospitality researcher Guerrier (2008) observes that the fact that so many migrants are employed in very poor-quality jobs in hospitality lessens the appeal of such jobs for local workers. Nonetheless, Ioannides and Zampoukos consider that the notion of mobility is important and should include inter-sectoral and intra-sectoral mobilities, not just the geographical dimensions of migration. Tourism work has always concerned mobility and, in particular, class and gendered aspects of mobility are especially significant. While the international hotel managers are the elite, the invisible workers toiling at the lowest levels of hospitality work are, to paraphrase Bauman (2007), the 'vagabonds and gypsies'.

Diversity management research in tourism and hospitality

As the hospitality and tourism sector in many locations is multi-cultural and otherwise diverse, one would expect hospitality diversity studies to investigate systems and practices that allow employees from different backgrounds, genders and ethnic origins to reach their full potential and, thus, positively influence organizational performance. However, while many studies highlight the critical importance of supporting all front-line employees to deliver high customer satisfaction in service organizations (for example, Michel et al. 2013; Shani et al. 2014), critiques of hospitality diversity research paint a disturbing picture. For example, a systematic literature review by Manoharan and Singal (2017) concludes that most studies are descriptive, United States-centric and do not reproduce the sophisticated theoretical framings common in the general management literature. They also found that the majority of diversity studies are related to gender, a classification which, they observe, appears to relate solely to women in hospitality research – although in wider organizational and diversity studies, 'gender' encompasses men and women, masculinity and feminist studies. A further critical review of diversity management research in hospitality and tourism by Kalargyrou and Costen (2017, p.108) presents similar bleak conclusions, soberly concluding that many studies lack theoretical grounding or the incorporation of a contemporary interpretative paradigm as is typically found in the general management literature. They believe that research on employees with disabilities and on LGBTQ employees is seriously lacking, and that new paradigms are required to study the increasing age diversity in the workforce.

When considering the first area, that is, employees with disabilities, perspectives based on a medical definition of disability have largely been replaced by a social model. The social model of persons with disabilities suggests that the effects of disability are compounded by negative societal attitudes and barriers which prevent, or limit, the full participation of people with disabilities in society. The Convention on the Rights of Persons with Disabilities (United Nations 2016) enshrines the rights of people with disabilities, and its website sets forth the enshrined vision of the United Nations, which has been adopted by 160 countries. The convention takes to a new height the movement from viewing persons with disabilities as 'objects' of charity, medical treatment and social protection towards viewing them as 'subjects' with rights, who are capable of claiming those rights and making decisions for their lives based on their free and informed consent as well as being active members of society (United Nations 2016, para. 2).

When investigating how tourism enterprises integrate people with disabilities into the workforce, McIntosh and Harris' (2018) study analysed societal and workplace attitudes displayed in a BBC television series, which followed a group of young people with various disabilities – including visual impairment and Down's Syndrome – gaining work experience in different types of hospitality establishments. They found that, although in theory the sector can offer many employment possibilities, in reality, this does not occur.

In another study addressing managerial attitudes to hiring people with disabilities, Paez and Arendt (2014, p. 187) establish that most managers do not have 'strong favourable attitudes' towards working with people with disabilities. They suggest a twofold focus would pay dividends; first, managers should be educated and trained so that they have realistic expectations of their employees' capabilities and, second, they should be made aware of their importance as role models and should be educated in projecting affirming attitudes towards employees with disabilities. Supporting this stance, a study on the disability initiatives in ten hospitality companies identified in *DiversityInc.* magazine's 2012 top 10 ranked employers for persons with disabilities (Kalargyrou & Volis 2014) found that employing people with disabilities enhanced creativity, but included a range of caveats. The success of such initiatives 'requires strong commitment from top leadership; an inclusive corporate culture; the creation of alliances with states and vocational rehabilitation agencies; proper accommodation and training of people with disabilities; holding all workers to the same standards; and establishing performance appraisal metrics and incentives to meet disability inclusion goals' (Kalargyrou & Volis 2014, p. 450).

The second area identified by Kalargyrou and Costen (2017), 'generational research', remains fragmented, although talent management has been a topic of considerable interest to the tourism sector. Many reports, such as Deery and Jago (2015), conclude that there is a widespread shortage of skilled labour in the hospitality and tourism sector. It could be said that it has ever been thus, and that the response of the sector has been to bring in migrant workers at the lower levels. However, this does not solve the problem of the talent shortfall at managerial levels. A plethora of studies (for example, Kim et al. 2016; Lugosi & Jameson 2017; Richardson & Butler 2012) explain that a high percentage of hospitality and tourism graduates do not intend to make a career in the sector. More specifically, Weaver's (2009) research shows that while tourism graduates were satisfied by careers in the sector, hospitality graduates were less so, the reasons given for their wish to seek alternative careers being the unsocial hours and the low rates of pay (Richardson & Butler 2012).

Interestingly, Goh and Lee (2018) indicate that members of Generation Z (people born between the mid-1990s and the early 2000s) have more positive than negative attitudes about working in the sector. In comparison to previous studies, such as Richardson (2009), which suggested that low rates of pay were a negative factor, low pay was not in fact proffered as a disincentive; rather Generation Z respondents were more motivated by job satisfaction and career prospects. Goh and Lee (2018) recommend that recruiters emphasize travel opportunities and career paths, and also suggest the need to prepare students for the difficulties of dealing with customers, a major source of anxiety for this generation. In other words, while stating that low pay is not a major disincentive, they recommend that hospitality organizations should be clearer about pay scales and career paths. More generally, retention studies have over time gradually moved from a focus on turnover to a focus on managing talent. Two definitive studies are those by Deery and Jago (2009, 2015), whose meta analyses of talent management, work–life balance and retention strategies in the sector conclude that more humanistic practices, such as flexible work practices, will increase retention and employee satisfaction. However, it must be stated that, in some respects, such studies now appear redundant in a sector increasingly characterized by casualized work arrangements and obscure or non-existent career paths.

Indigenous tourism destinations and community workforces

It would appear logical that any discussion on sustainable tourism development should consider the inclusion and development of local employees, especially where regional culture is a major attraction for tourists. As part of this dialogue, Higgins-Desbiolles and Powys Whyte (2014, p. 94) argue that a primary function of tourism research should be to serve the local community rather than 'being sub-servient to narrow academic interests'. They suggest that one way to achieve this is by adhering to human and special rights codes, whilst areas of critical theorization, such as feminist or indigenous, can further such aims. Therefore, we will now consider what useful future directions can be of interest in this context. Amoamo (2017) suggests that owing to the frantic pace of tourism studies, increased under-standings about indigenous tourism have finally come to the fore and descriptions of cultural tourism experiences have become more complex and fractured. Hence, initiatives that have been developed in response to factors specific to particular locations can offer useful insights. For example, we have much to learn from Mâori perspectives on sustainable tourism development. Mâori are the indigenous people of New Zealand and their cultural knowledge is underpinned by a holistic world-view 'with a relational epistemology that link[s] the natural and cultural worlds, through past, present and future' (Amoamo 2017, p. 165). Therefore, Mâori visions of how a tourism or hospitality enterprise should run are grounded in a sustainable development philosophy, what Amoamo terms a strong iwi (tribal) identity with intrinsic connection to the natural landscape and inter-generational wellbeing. In her study on a tourism destination in the South Island of New Zealand (Amoamo, 2017), she stresses that local communities need greater involvement in the market-ing of their culture and, by definition, the incorporation of Mâori values into how organizations are run.

In a similar vein, when discussing how sustainable objectives are embedded in community tourism enterprises, Wikitera and Bremner (2017) explain that Mâori business models do not necessarily follow a model that focuses on profit maxi-mization. Rather, a Mâori tourism business follows a model that allows them 'to share their culture, while at the same time promoting economic social and cultural sustainability' (Wikitera & Bremner 2017, p. 204). They go on to suggest that there can be challenges in adhering to the sustainable development model identified by Spiller and Erakovic (2005) with its four goals – economic, environmental, social and cultural wealth creation. According to this model, tribal members are able to give input from different aspects and generations. However, in Wikitera and Bremner's example of a thermal village, there is limited capacity for career development due to government control of the guide qualification system, which causes 'tribal experts' to leave the region. Thus, they observe with dismay that this reinforces the New Zealand perception that tourism jobs are not 'real jobs', a point communicated by other studies on the hospitality and tourism workforce (Harris et al. 2011; Williamson 2017).

Summary of contemporary hospitality and tourism workforce management challenges

In this section, we seek to draw together the disparate strands in the rich tapestry of hospitality and tourism workplace research discussed in the above sections. As a starting point, Burke's (2018) analysis of current and future issues in HRM in the tourism and hospitality industries usefully identifies the following challenges:

(1) being selective in staffing and hiring;
(2) offering competitive and fair pay;
(3) providing more supportive, friendly and humane supervision;
(4) using job characteristics and job design to offer more variety and job enlargement;
(5) empowering staff by increasing job engagement and involvement;
(6) reducing levels of some job stressors;
(7) creating a customer service culture;
(8) developing stronger and visionary leadership at senior and executive levels.

Our preceding, admittedly limited, review of authoritative research on the current state of tourism and hospitality workplaces delivers the following key conclusions, which indicate the ideals of a sustainable approach to tourism employment:

(1) In Western society, critical hospitality studies reveal there has been a measurable and marked decline in the working conditions and remuneration of hospitality and tourism workers.
(2) In developing tourism destinations, tourist demand has led to the sexual exploitation of women and, in some locations, men, and the trafficking of children for sex.
(3) Indigenous peoples, ethnic minorities and local communities have been excluded from discussions about the sharing of their environmental resources in tourism destinations and from full participation in the associated financial rewards. Tourism demand has displaced local residents and local workers.
(4) Research into HRM practices has been ineffective in highlighting the necessity of strategic HRM practices, as it has neglected to design effective studies that focus on measurable tangible outcomes of high-involvement work programmes.
(5) Hospitality and tourism strategic HRM research has failed to take human capital, social capital and human behaviour into account.

(6) Hospitality and tourism workforce research has ignored the effect of macro and societal factors that influence HRM practices in different tourism contexts.

(7) Hospitality and tourism diversity research has ignored theoretical models usual in the management literature and failed to test the empirical effect of specific diversity policies and initiatives.

(8) Hospitality diversity research has failed to recognize inter-group differences when looking at the effect of diversity practices and failed to investigate the influence of age, disability and sexual orientation in hospitality and tourism management.

(9) The pace of digital disruption in the hospitality and tourism sector indicates that elements of the sharing economy have replicated intensive precarious labour practices across different types in the sector.

A vision for the future

Building on the evident gaps within existing research across the range of our identified themes, we now address the development of a forward-looking research agenda that operates at two levels, that is, defining a macro, policy-informing plan of action as well as incorporating the meso- or organizational-level considerations that research could usefully address.

Research agenda at the macro level

At a macro level, tourism and hospitality research that focuses on workforce themes should have an ethical focus that includes concerns such as job quality, precarious employment, inclusivity, indigenous tourism, exploitative tourism and the inculcation of a sustainable HRM approach. Policy at a local, national and transnational level should give consideration to these areas in formulating policy for tourism as a considered counter-weight to a predominant focus in tourism development on marketing, increased visitation, infrastructure and services (Baum 2018). Research increasingly shows that diversity targets are only achieved through affirmative actions and quotas (Kalargyrou & Costen 2017). Research should be policy informing in this regard and provide the tools for governments to require organizations to report the gender, sexuality and ethnicity of employees, as well as how many have disabilities, including those on casualized work arrangements. It is only through measures such as this that real change can be effected.

Research agenda at the meso level

There seems to be little appetite among governments to call into account those industry sectors, such as hospitality and tourism, that widely exploit migrant labour, even though recent reports in many locations have detailed practices tantamount to modern slavery, whilst similar evidence has been reported in Australia with respect to foreign backpackers (Berg & Farbenblum 2017). When we look at the practices of successful organizations, there are lessons to be learned. However, it is unrealistic to imagine that organizations will move from the cost-cutting models that have appeared to serve them well over the last 30 years. Research outcomes should promote organizations with ambitious, measurable targets for employee equality and inclusion, as well as robust policies on sexual harassment that protect employees who work for them. They should foster and support consumer organizations that rate and reward businesses that use sustainable labour practices. Much research (for example, Maxwell et al. 2010) details the importance of positive socialization models for new employees in ridding the sector of its temporary work approach. Engaging with industry to see how this can happen could become a priority for researchers.

Sustainable HRM is a model that can provide real and tangible benefits to communities and also enshrine tangible benefits for tourists, hosts and local communities. Zaugg, Blum and Thom (2001, p.1), for example, define sustainable HRM as 'long term socially and economically efficient recruitment, development, retainment and disemployment of employees'. Similarly, Ehnert et al. (2016, p.90) see sustainable HRM as 'the adoption of HRM strategies and practices that enable the achievement of financial, social and ecological goals, with an impact inside and outside of the organization and over a long-term time horizon while controlling for unintended side effects and negative feedback'. Consideration of employment in sustainability terms has emerged as part of a movement to redress what Parkin Hughes et al. (2017) call 'the sustainability skew', by which the primary focus of debate in this area was dominated by considerations of environmental rather than social sustainability. This application of sustainability principles to employment is an emergent field that has only recently seen adoption within tourism (Baum 2018; Baum et al. 2016a) with the somewhat depressing conclusion that 'in general, hospitality and tourism HRM operates contrary to the principles of sustainable HRM' (Baum et al. 2016a, p.15).

Such an approach can ensure that the benefits of tourism are shared within the community, rather than accruing to external organizations. A sustainable approach to HRM can also ensure that different generations can contribute – and have their contribution valued – to the creation of wealth that tourism can bring to rural regions and developing countries. It can also provide some of the multi-generational dialogues that are missing in tourism employment discourses (Manoharan & Singal 2017). As with many other cases of minority group exploitation, there is an intersectional dimension to reports of abuse. It appears that refugees and migrants are more vulnerable to the imposition of conditions of slavery by fellow migrant business owners in environments where residency visas are eagerly sought. Recent high-profile cases before the courts in New Zealand detail modern-day slavery conditions (Dalley 2017; NZHerald 2018). Again, researchers can play a stronger role by working more closely with culturally affiliated organizations to ensure that new arrivals are educated about their rights and entitlements. In similar fashion, there are intersections of ethnicity and gender visible in the disproportionally large number of ethnic minority and indigenous women working at the lowest levels of insecure work in hospitality. Holvino (2010) suggests that we cannot disentangle race from gender and class when looking at workers marginalized in low-quality jobs. This observation of context and nuance must be embedded in future hospitality studies if we sincerely wish to support a realistic and viable debate on sustainable tourism.

References

Amoamo, M. (2017), 'The economic value of identity', in M. Whitford, L. Ruhanen and A. Carr (eds) *Indigenous Tourism: Cases from Australia and New Zealand*, Oxford: Goodfellow Publishers. Accessed 12 February 2018 at https://espace.library.uq.edu.au/view/UQ:690581

Armstrong, R. (2016), 'Modern slavery: Risks for the UK hospitality industry', in H. Goodwin and X. Font (eds) *Progress in Responsible Tourism V*, Oxford: Goodfellow Publishers, pp. 67–78.

Baum, T. (2007), 'Human resources in tourism: Still waiting for change', *Tourism Management*, **28**(6), 1383–99.

Baum, T. (2013), 'International perspectives on women and work in hotels, catering and tourism', Working Paper No. 1/2013, *International Labour Organisation*, 1–77. Accessed 24 February 2018 at http://digitalcommons.ilr.cornell.edu/intl/260

Baum, T. (2015), 'Human resources in tourism: Still waiting for change? A 2015 reprise', *Tourism Management*, **50**, 204–12.

Baum, T. (2018), 'Sustainable human resource management as a driver in tourism policy and planning: A serious sin of omission?', *Journal of Sustainable Tourism*, **26**(6), 873–89.

Baum, T., Cheung, C., Kong, H., Kralj, A., Mooney, S., Ramachandran, S., Dropulić Ružić, M. and Siow, M.L. (2016a), 'Sustainability and the tourism and hospitality workforce: A thematic analysis', *Sustainability*, **8**(8), 1–21. Accessed 14 February 2019 at https://doi.org/10.3390/su8080809

Baum, T., Kralj, A., Robinson, R. and Solnet, D. (2016b), 'Tourism workforce research: A review, taxonomy and agenda', *Annals of Tourism Research*, **60**, 1–22.

Bauman, Z. (2007), *Liquid Times: Living in an Age of Uncertainty*, Cambridge: Polity Press.

Berg, L. and Farbenblum, B. (2017), *Wage Theft in Australia: Findings of the National Temporary Migrant Work Survey*, Sydney, Australia: Migrant Worker Justice Initiative. Accessed 10 February 2018 at http://apo.org.au/node/120406

Bernhardt, A., Dresser, L. and Hatton, E. (2003), 'The coffee pot wars: Unions and firm restructuring in the hotel industry', in E. Appelbaum, A. Bernhardt and R. Murnane (eds) *Low Wage-America: How Employers Are Reshaping Opportunity in the Workplace*, New York: Russell Sage Foundation, pp. 33–76.

Burke, R. (2018), 'Human resource management in the hospitality and tourism sector', in R. Burke and J. Christensen Hughes (eds) *Handbook of Human Resource Management in the Tourism and Hospitality Industries*, Cheltenham, UK and Northampton, MA, USA: Edward Elgar Publishing, pp. 3–39.

Christensen Hughes, J. (2018), 'The changing tourism and hospitality context', in R. Burke and J. Christensen Hughes (eds) *Handbook of Human Resource Management in the Tourism and Hospitality Industries*, Cheltenham, UK and Northampton, MA, USA: Edward Elgar Publishing, pp. 40–63.

Dalley, S. (2017), 'Recent changes to immigration laws: Implications for hospitality employers', *Hospitality Insights*, **1**(1), 1–2.

Davidson, M. and Wang, Y. (2011), 'Sustainable labor practices? Hotel human resource managers' views on turnover and skill shortages', *Journal of Human Resources in Hospitality and Tourism*, **10**(3), 235–53.

Davidson, M., Guilding, C. and Timo, N. (2006), 'Employment, flexibility and labour market practices of domestic and MNC chain luxury hotels in Australia: Where has accountability gone?', *Hospitality Management*, **25**(2), 193–210.

Dedeoğlu, B.B. and Demirer, H. (2015), 'Differences in service quality perceptions of stakeholders in the hotel industry', *International Journal of Contemporary Hospitality Management*, **27**(1), 130–46.

Deery, M. and Jago, L. (2009), 'A framework for work–life balance practices: Addressing the needs of the tourism industry', *Tourism and Hospitality Research*, **9**(2), 97–108.

Deery, M. and Jago, L. (2015), 'Revisiting talent management, work–life balance and retention strategies', *International Journal of Contemporary Hospitality Management*, **27**(3), 453–72.

Dredge, D. and Gyimóthy, S. (2015), 'The collaborative economy and tourism: Critical perspectives, questionable claims and silenced voices', *Tourism Recreation Research*, **40**(3), 286–302.

Duncan, T., Scott, D.G. and Baum, T. (2013), 'The mobilities of hospitality work: An exploration of issues and debates', *Annals of Tourism Research*, **41**(1), 1–19.

Ehnert, I., Parsa, S., Roper, I., Wagner, M. and Muller-Camen, M. (2016), 'Reporting on sustainability and HRM: A comparative study of sustainability reporting practices by the world's largest companies', *International Journal of Human Resource Management*, **27**(1), 88–108.

Figueroa-Domecq, C., Pritchard, A., Segovia-Pérez, M., Morgan, N. and Villacé-Molinero, T. (2015), 'Tourism gender research: A critical accounting', *Annals of Tourism Research*, **52**, 87–103.

Gannon, J., Roper, A. and Doherty, L. (2010), 'The impact of hotel management contracting on IHRM practices: Understanding the bricks and brains split', *International Journal of Contemporary Hospitality Management*, **22**(5), 638–58.

García-Lillo, F., Claver-Cortes, E., Ubeda-Garcia, M., Marco-Lajara, B. and Zaragoza-Saez, P. (2018), 'Mapping the "intellectual structure" of research on human resources in the "tourism and hospitality" management scientific domain: Reviewing the field', *International Journal of Contemporary Hospitality Management*, **30**(3), 1741–68.

Goh, E. and Lee, C. (2018), 'A workforce to be reckoned with: The emerging pivotal Generation Z hospitality workforce', *International Journal of Hospitality Management*, **73**, 20–8.

Guerrier, Y. (2008), 'Organisational studies and hospitality management', in B. Brotherton and R. Wood (eds) *The SAGE Handbook of Hospitality Management*, London: SAGE, pp. 257–73.

Harris, C., Tregidga, H. and Williamson, D. (2011), 'Cinderella in Babylon: The representation of housekeeping and housekeepers in the UK television series *Hotel Babylon*', *Hospitality and Society*, **1**(1), 47–66.

Hawke, A. and Raphael, A. (2016), *ECPAT Report: The Global Study on Sexual Exploitation of Children in Travel and Tourism*, Bangkok, Thailand: ECPAT International and Defence for Children, Netherlands. Accessed 30 January 2018 at www.europol.europa.eu/newsroom/news/ecpat-report-global-study-sexual-exploitation-of-children-in-travel-and-tourism

Herod, A. (1994), 'On workers' theoretical (in)visibility in the writing of critical urban geography: A comradely critique', *Urban Geography*, **15**(7), 681–93.

Herod, A. (1997), 'From a geography of labor to a labor geography: Labor's spatial fix and the geography of capitalism', *Antipode*, **29**(1), 1–31.

Higgins-Desbiolles, F. and Powys Whyte, K. (2014), 'Critical perspectives on tourism', in A. Lew, M. Hall and A. Williams (eds) *The Wiley Blackwell Companion to Tourism*, Chichester: John Wiley & Sons, pp. 88–98.

Holvino, E. (2010), 'Intersections: The simultaneity of race, gender and class in organization studies', *Gender, Work and Organization*, **17**(3), 248–77.

Ioannides, D. and Zampoukos, K. (2018), 'Tourism's labour geographies: Bringing tourism into work and work into tourism', *Tourism Geographies*, **20**(1), 1–10.

Kalargyrou, V. and Costen, W. (2017), 'Diversity management research in hospitality and tourism: Past, present and future', *International Journal of Contemporary Hospitality Management*, **29**(1), 68–114.

Kalargyrou, V. and Volis, A. (2014), 'Disability inclusion initiatives in the hospitality industry: An exploratory study of industry leaders', *Journal of Human Resources in Hospitality and Tourism*, **13**(4), 430–54.

Kim, S., Jung, J. and Wang, K.-C. (2016), 'Hospitality and tourism management students' study and career preferences: Comparison of three Asian regional groups', *Journal of Hospitality, Leisure, Sport and Tourism Education*, **19**, 66–84.

Kusluvan, S., Kusluvan, Z., Ilhan, I. and Buyruk, L. (2010), 'The human dimension: A review of human resources management issues in the tourism and hospitality industry', *Cornell Hospitality Quarterly*, **51**(2), 171–214.

Laws, E. and Scott, N. (2015), 'Tourism research: Building from other disciplines', *Tourism Recreation Research*, **40**(1), 48–58.

Legrand, W., Sloan, P. and Chen, J.S. (2016), *Sustainability in the Hospitality Industry: Principles of Sustainable Operations*, Abingdon: Routledge.

Lugosi, P. and Jameson, S. (2017), 'Challenges in hospitality management education: Perspectives from the United Kingdom', *Journal of Hospitality and Tourism Management*, **31**, 163–72.

Lynch, P. (2017), 'Mundane welcome: Hospitality as life politics', *Annals of Tourism Research*, **64**, 174–84.

Madera, J., Dawson, M., Guchait, P. and Belarmino, A. (2017), 'Strategic human resources management research in hospitality and tourism: A review of current literature and suggestions for the future', *International Journal of Contemporary Hospitality Management*, **29**(1), 48–67.

Manoharan, A. and Singal, M. (2017), 'A systematic literature review of research on diversity and diversity management in the hospitality literature', *International Journal of Hospitality Management*, **66**, 77–91.

Maxwell, G.A., Ogden, S. and Broadbridge, A. (2010), 'Generation Y's career expectations and aspirations: Engagement in the hospitality industry', *Journal of Hospitality and Tourism Management*, **17**(1), 1–9.

McDowell, L., Batnitzky, A. and Dyer, S. (2007), 'Division, segmentation and interpellation: The embodied labors of migrant workers in a greater London hotel', *Economic Geography*, **83**(1), 1–25.

McDowell, L. Batnitzky, A. and Dyer, S. (2009), 'Precarious work and economic migration: Emerging immigrant divisions of labour in greater London's service sector', *International Journal of Urban and Regional Research*, **33**(1), 3–25.

McIntosh, A. and Harris, C. (2012), 'Critical hospitality and work: (In)hospitable employment in the hospitality industry', *Hospitality and Society*, **2**(2), 129–35.

McIntosh, A. and Harris, C. (2018), 'Representations of hospitality at the Special Needs Hotel', *International Journal of Hospitality Management*, **75**, 153–9.

Michel, J., Kavanagh, M. and Tracey, J. (2013), 'Got support? The impact of supportive work practices on the perceptions, motivation, and behavior of customer-contact employees', *Cornell Hospitality Quarterly*, **54**(2), 161–73.

Mooney, S. (2016), 'Wasted youth in the hospitality industry: Older workers' perceptions and misperceptions about younger workers', *Hospitality and Society*, **6**(1), 9–30.

Mooney, S., Schänzel, H. and Poulston, J. (2017a), 'Illuminating the blind spots', *Hospitality and Society*, **7**(2), 105–13.

Mooney, S., Ryan, I. and Harris, C. (2017b), 'The intersections of gender with age and ethnicity in hotel careers: Still the same old privileges?', *Gender, Work and Organization*, **24**(4), 360–75.

Moragra, C. (2017), 'Nature and determinants of informal employment among Grab and Uber drivers in metro Manila', unpublished thesis, Manila: University of the Philippines Diliman.

Morrison, A. and O'Gorman, K. (2008), 'Hospitality studies and hospitality management: A symbiotic relationship', *International Journal of Hospitality Management*, **27**(2), 214–21.

NZHerald (2018), 'Immigration minister on modern day slavery in NZ'. Accessed 7 March 2018 at www. nzherald.co.nz/business-video/news/video.cfm?c_id=1503079&gal_cid=1503079&gallery_id=189794

Paez, P. and Arendt, S. (2014), 'Managers' attitudes towards people with disabilities in the hospitality industry', *International Journal of Hospitality and Tourism Administration*, **15**(2), 172–90.

Paludi, M., Helms-Mills, J. and Mills, A. (2014), 'Disturbing thoughts and gendered practices', in S. Kumra, R. Simpson and R.J. Burke (eds) *The Oxford Handbook of Gender in Organizations*, Oxford: Oxford University Press, pp. 53–75.

Parkin Hughes, C., Semeijn, J. and Caniels, M. (2017), 'The sustainability skew', *Current Opinion in Environmental Sustainability*, **28**, 58–63.

Pritchard, A., Morgan, N. and Ateljevic, I. (2011), 'Hopeful tourism: A new transformative perspective', *Annals of Tourism Research*, **38**(3), 941–63.

Ram, Y., Tribe, J. and Biran, A. (2016), 'Sexual harassment: Overlooked and under-researched', *International Journal of Contemporary Hospitality Management*, **28**(10), 2110–31.

Richardson, S. (2009), 'Undergraduates' perceptions of tourism and hospitality as a career choice', *International Journal of Hospitality Management*, **28**(3), 382–8.

Richardson, S. and Butler, G. (2012), 'Attitudes of Malaysian tourism and hospitality students' towards a career in the industry', *Asia Pacific Journal of Tourism Research*, **17**(3), 262–76.

Riley, M. and Szivas, E. (2009), 'Tourism employment and poverty: Revisiting the supply curve', *Tourism Economics*, **15**(2), 297–305.

Robinson, R. (2013), 'Darker still: Present-day slavery in hospitality and tourism services', *Hospitality and Society*, **3**(2), 93–110.

Shani, A., Uriely, N., Reichel, A. and Ginsburg, L. (2014), 'Emotional labor in the hospitality industry: The influence of contextual factors', *International Journal of Hospitality Management*, **37**, 150–8.

Sigala, M. (2018), 'Market formation in the sharing economy: Findings and implications from the sub-economies of Airbnb', in S. Barile, M. Pellicano and F. Polese (eds), *Social Dynamics in a Systems Perspective*, Cham: Springer International Publishing, pp. 159–74.

Solnet, D., Kralj, A. and Baum, T. (2015), '360 degrees of pressure: The changing role of the HR professional in the hospitality industry', *Journal of Hospitality and Tourism Research*, **39**(2), 271–92.

Spiller, C. and Erakovic, L. (2005), 'Flourishing on the edge: Case study of Whale Watch Kaikoura, an indigenous sustainable business', in *Case in Point: Best Cases from the 2005 International Case Study Teaching and Learning*, Auckland, New Zealand: GSE Publications, pp. 219–40.

Stringer, C. (2016), 'Worker exploitation in New Zealand: A troubling landscape', Report for the Human Trafficking Research Coalition, University of Auckland. Accessed 12 November 2017 at https://researchspace.auckland.ac.nz/handle/2292/33065

Tribe, J. (2010), 'Tribes, territories and networks in the tourism academy', *Annals of Tourism Research*, **37**(1), 7–33.

United Nations Division for Social Policy and Development (2016), *Convention on the Rights of Persons with Disabilities (CRPD)*. Accessed 8 March 2018 at www.un.org/development/desa/disabilities/convention-on-the-rights-of-persons-with-disabilities.html

Veijola, S., Molz, J., Pyyhtinen, O, Höckert, E. and Grit, A. (2014), *Disruptive Tourism and Its Untidy Guests: Alternative Ontologies for Future Hospitalities*, Basingstoke: Springer.

Weaver, A. (2009), 'Perceptions of job quality in the tourism industry: The views of recent graduates of a university's tourism management programme', *International Journal of Contemporary Hospitality Management*, **21**(5), 579–93.

Wikitera, K.-A. and Bremner, H. (2017), 'Mana versus money: An indigenous perspective on the tribal tourism destination of Whakarewarewa', in M. Whitford, L. Ruhanen and A. Carr (eds) *Indigenous Tourism: Cases from Australia and New Zealand*, Oxford: Goodfellow Publishers, pp. 205–224.

Williamson, D. (2017), 'In search of consensus: A history of employment relations in the New Zealand hotel sector – 1955 to 2000', PhD thesis, Auckland University of Technology, Auckland, New Zealand. Accessed 10 February 2018 at http://aut.researchgateway.ac.nz/handle/10292/10412

Zaugg, R.J., Blum, A., & Thom, N. (2001), 'Sustainability in human resource management', *Evaluation Report: Survey in European Companies and Institutions*, Arbeitsbericht Des Instituts für Organisation und Personal Der Universität Bern und Des Eidgenössischen Personalamtes. Accessed 14 February 2019 at www.empiricon.ch/assets/Publikationen/Personalmanagement/03.5-EN-sustainability-in-hrm-200106.pdf

11 Tourism and (re)development in developed nations

David J. Telfer

Introduction

With Canada celebrating its 150th anniversary in 2017, the Salvation Army developed a marketing campaign placing tourists on a bus, showing them not only Toronto's hot spots, but also neighbouring poverty. Commentary on the tour near the Toronto Eaton Shopping Centre highlighted the 50 million people who shop there each year, contrasted with those who find themselves among the one in ten Canadians who struggle to pay for the basic necessities of life, such as food and clothing. A line of restaurants along a street is contrasted with the line of people who go to a nearby food bank and are among 860,000 Canadians who use food banks each month (Lloyd 2017). The media campaign highlighted affluence as demonstrated by tourism coexisting with nearby hidden poverty, a common condition in many developed nations. While the United Nations (UN) is targeting to eradicate extreme poverty, measured as those living on less than $1.25 per day, by 2030, poverty can also be defined as being relative, 'not having enough to meet the expected norms of living standards in the country one lives', and therefore, poverty can also be understood within the context of all countries of the world (Holden 2013, p. ix). With tourism residing next to poverty in major developed cities such as Toronto, what then is the role of tourism in the development and redevelopment process in these nations? This question forms the central focus of this chapter, as areas for future research are presented.

Tourism advocates champion the economic contribution of tourism for its potential to generate foreign exchange, income and employment while diversifying the economy and reducing poverty (Telfer & Sharpley 2016). With established economies, infrastructure and advanced and diversified levels of tourism supply, it would follow that developed nations are in a position to benefit from domestic and international tourism. In 2016, the advanced economies of the world received 55 per cent of all international arrivals (1,235 million) and 64.5 per cent of receipts (US$1,200 billion) (UNWTO 2017). Developed nations are more industrialized and associated with higher standards of living as measured through indicators such as per capita income, gross domestic product (GDP) and even broader-based indicators like the Human Development Index (HDI). Nevertheless, while developed nations rank higher on these indices, national development indicators can mask areas of high unemployment and poverty, even in major tourism destinations. The tourism magnet of Las Vegas, for example, had the highest growth rate in sub-urban poverty from 2000 to 2014 in the United States, at 123 per cent (southern Nevada), compared to the national growth rate of 65 per cent (KNPR 2016; see also Allard 2017). National tourism statistics in Canada reveal tourism supports over 1.8 million jobs, 200,000 businesses and is the largest employer of youth – yet these statistics can also disguise issues of quality of employment (Government of Canada 2018). As Cukier (2002, p. 166) suggests, it is 'not difficult to find testimony from "developed countries" concerning the seasonality, servile nature and low remu-neration of tourism employment'.

In reflecting on the role of tourism in the development process, it is important to consider the economic transformations that developed countries have faced in recent years. From the global economic crisis to the Eurozone crisis and to what de la Dehesa (2006) refers to as the *Winners and Losers in Globalization*, there is a growing awareness of the problems of inequality in developed nations (Molander 2014; Stiglitz 2015, 2018). Indeed, Barr and Malik (2016) argue that the combina-tion of debt, globalization, joblessness, demographics and increases in the price of housing is depressing incomes as well as resulting in prospects for unprecedented inequality among millions of young people across the developed world. Similarly, Moyo (2011, p. 196) notes that 'changing trade patterns, financial destabilization of the world's most advanced economies, and the transition of economic opportuni-ties to the emerging world are defining our world today'.

There are a number of factors that inhibit tourism from contributing more to devel-opment in developed nations, including global and local economic trends, the opera-tion of the industry, the degree of interconnectedness of the sectors of the economy and the level of commitment of respective governments to tourism. Moreover, where tourism (as is often the case) accounts for a small percentage of GDP in large economies, the promotion of tourism barely moves national development indica-tors (Sharma 2013). Nevertheless, it is important to consider geographic scale. For example, regions such as Orlando and Las Vegas, the two largest metropolitan areas in the United States whose principal industry is tourism, are largely supporting state budgets (Danielsen & Lang 2014). At the same time, regions in developed countries that have suffered economic decline are opting to pursue a variety of tourism-related strategies as tools for redevelopment. With manufacturing on the decline, Niagara Falls, Canada, for example, has embraced casinos and wine tourism to further diversify the tourism sector beyond just the famous waterfall.

The purpose of this chapter, then, is to raise questions about future research in tourism and (re)development in developed nations. It begins by considering the nature of development and developed nations. It then examines the relative impor-tance of tourism in developed countries through an analysis of tourism statistics and investigates the promise of the tourism-led economic growth hypothesis. A variety of strategies using tourism as a redevelopment tool are then explored. The central focus of the final section of the chapter is a series of emerging challenges in developed nations related to tourism that are hindering its contribution to development. If developed nations are to effectively utilize tourism to promote development, these emerging trends need to be acknowledged and further researched.

The nature of development and developed countries

Since the end of the Second World War, the nature and scope of development and how it has been defined and measured have become increasingly complex. Broadly, from an initial focus on economic indicators it has broadened to include social and environmental dimensions, whilst the eight UN Millennium Development Goals (2000–15) have transitioned into the 17 UN Sustainable Development Goals (SDGs) adopted in 2015 as part of the 2030 Agenda for Sustainable Development. An interesting dimension to this transition is that tourism is now specifically mentioned within three of the SDGs (8: Employment, 12: Consumption/Production and 14: Sustainable Use of Marine Resources) with two of these focusing on employment (UN 2018a). Specifically, Target 8.9 reads: 'By 2030, devise and implement policies to promote sustainable tourism that creates jobs and promotes local culture'; similarly, Target 12.B states: 'Develop and implement tools to monitor sustainable development impacts for sustainable tourism that create jobs and promote local culture and products'. Given the focus of these two goals on employment, the nature of tourism employment will be returned to later in this chapter. Finally, tourism is also mentioned under Target 14.7, in relation to the sustainable use of marine resources through the 'sustainable management of fisheries, aquaculture and tourism'. Although Target 14.7 is presented in the context of developing countries, many locations in developed nations, such as the Great Barrier Reef in Australia, rely heavily on the marine resources for tourism and are now under threat not only from tourism (Williamson et al. 2017) but also climate change (Goldberg et al. 2018). The importance of sustainable tourism was also highlighted in 2017 when the UN World Tourism Organization (UNWTO) declared it the International Year of Sustainable Tourism for Development. Thus, with the broadening of the scope of development, it is important to investigate how tourism can contribute towards achieving these more complex goals in developed nations.

How development is measured is often guided by the dominant overriding development paradigm of the time. Telfer (1996, 2002, 2009, 2015a) has continued to trace the evolution of development theory and its linkages to tourism (for a detailed examination of development theory paradigms, approaches and strategies, see Telfer 2015a). Table 11.1 presents major development paradigms and the dates when they first gained prominence since the end of the Second World War; notably, new development paradigms do not replace previous paradigms but, rather, offer alternative approaches. A critical point is that development theory can be examined from the perspective of development ideology (the ends) and development strategy (the means) (Hettne 1995). Table 11.1 also includes examples of future research questions for tourism and (re)development in developed countries that reflect the corresponding overriding development paradigms which, in turn, influ-

Table 11.1   Evolution of development theory and examples of research questions for tourism and (re)development in developed nations

Time guide	Development paradigms	Examples of future research questions for tourism and (re) development in developed nations
1950s and 1960s	Modernization	How can tourism stimulate development? How can the benefits of tourism best be circulated through developed economies? How can tourism promote regional development?
1950s and 1960s	Dependency	What are the implications of regions in developed destinations being too dependent on tourism? How can multinational tourism companies such as airlines, hotels and cruise lines influence tourism in developed nations?
Mid-1970s and 1980s	Economic neoliberalism	How have globalization, deregulation and new world financial systems facilitated tourism development? What are the negative aspects of globalization on tourism-based communities in developed nations?
1970s and early 1980s	Alternative development	Is the tourism industry implementing sustainability in developed nations? How can tourism empower women? Is there equal pay for equal work in tourism in developed nations?
Late 1980s and early 1990s	Impasse and post-development	If development theory is at an impasse, how should tourism planning and development proceed in developed nations? How can local knowledge systems best influence tourism development?
1990s and 2000s	Human development	How can tourism contribute to the Human Development Index? How can tourism alleviate poverty in developed nations?
2000s and 2010s and beyond	Global development	How can tourism contribute to the SDGs? How does climate change impact tourism regions/communities in developed nations?

Source: After Telfer 2015a.

ence the strategies used to address the role of tourism in the development and (re) development process. Various development paradigms place emphasis on different strategies. For example, economic neoliberalism favours free and open markets, while human development has a greater focus on poverty reduction. The purpose of Table 11.1 is to allow a consideration of overarching development paradigms while the remainder of the chapter poses future research questions more focused on the empirical examples and challenges presented that are facing developed nations.

Developed nations are often defined in terms of economic performance criteria such as GDP or GDP per capita. The World Bank classifies economies by gross national income ($US GNI) per capita into four income groups: low (less than or equal to $1,005), lower middle ($1,006 to $3,955), upper middle ($3,956 to $12, 235)

Table 11.2   Developed economies

Region/Group	Countries
North America	Canada, United States
European Union	
EU 15	Austria, Belgium, Denmark, Finland, France, Germany, Greece, Ireland, Italy, Luxembourg, Netherlands, Portugal, Spain, Sweden, United Kingdom
EU 13	Bulgaria, Croatia, Cyprus, Czech Republic, Estonia, Hungary, Latvia, Lithuania, Malta, Poland, Romania, Slovakia, Slovenia
Other Europe	Iceland, Norway, Switzerland
Developed Asia Pacific	Australia, Japan, New Zealand
Major developed economies (G7)	Canada, France, Germany, Italy, Japan, United Kingdom, United States

Source: UN 2018b.

and high (over $12,235) (World Bank 2018a). Alternatively, the *World Economic Situation and Prospects Report* (UN 2018b) classifies countries as developed economies, economies in transition and developing economies. Table 11.2 includes the list of developed economies including subgroups based on geographic region and membership in the Group of Seven.

The countries listed in Table 11.2 are similar to those comprising the Organisation for Economic Co-operation and Development (OECD), with the exception of Israel, South Korea, Mexico, Chile and Turkey. Dogan et al. (2017, p. 1703) characterize OECD countries as having 'a large number of tourist arrivals, and a large volume of international trade, industrial production, gas emissions and energy consumption'. The OECD (2018, p. 3) observes that tourism plays a key role in export revenue, job creation and domestic value added contributing 'on average 4.2% of GDP, 6.9% of employment and 21.7% of service exports in OECD countries'. There are, however, significant differences as tourism's contribution to service exports ranges from 11.9 per cent in the United Kingdom (UK) to 40.1 per cent in Italy (OECD 2018).

With development now being measured by more than simply economic indicators, the HDI, published by the UN Development Programme (UNDP), is based on life expectancy at birth, education (expected years of education and mean years of schooling) and standard of living (GNI per capita). In 2016, the Inequality-adjusted Human Development Index (IHDI) was introduced to reflect that achievements in health, education and income are not equally distributed. The UNDP also publishes the Gender Development Index and the Gender Inequality Index, and has added a sustainable development dashboard to its website incorporating measurements of environmental, economic and social sustainability. Table 11.3 includes a list of the top 10 countries based on HDI as well as the remaining countries in the G7. Of particular note, Iceland, ranked ninth in terms of HDI, has recently experienced

Table 11.3   Top 10 countries and G7 for HDI, IHDI and GINI Index

HDI rank	Country	HDI (2015)	IHDI (2015)	Overall loss (%)	Difference from HDI rank	GINI Index and year
1	Norway	0.949	0.898	5.4	0	26.8 (2014)
2	Australia	0.939	0.861	8.2	−1	. . .
3	Switzerland	0.939	0.859	8.6	−4	32.5 (2012)
4	Germany	0.926	0.859	7.2	−1	31.4 (2013)
5	Denmark	0.925	0.858	7.2	−2	28.5 (2013)
6	Singapore	0.925	. . .	. . .	. . .	. . .
7	Netherlands	0.924	0.861	6.9	2	28.6 (2013)
8	Ireland	0.923	0.850	7.9	−2	31.9 (2014)
9	Iceland	0.921	0.868	5.8	6	25.6 (2014)
10	Canada	0.920	0.839	8.9	−2	34.0 (2013)
10	United States	0.920	0.796	13.5	−10	41.0 (2013)
16	United Kingdom	0.909	0.836	8	−1	34.1 (2014)
17	Japan	0.903	0.791	12.4	−8	. . .
21	France	0.897	0.813	9.4	−1	32.3 (2014)
26	Italy	0.887	0.784	11.5	−3	34.7 (2014)
	HD groups					
	Very high HD	0.892	0.793	11.1		
	High HD	0.746	0.597	20.0		
	Medium HD	0.631	0.469	25.7		
	Low HD	0.497	0.337	32.3		
	Developing countries	0.668	0.499	25.2		

Source: UNDP 2016; GINI Index from World Bank 2018b.

tremendous growth in tourism with arrivals growing from 459,000 in 2010 to 2.1 million in 2016. With a population of only 334,000, there are understandable concerns about both excessive numbers of tourists and the inequitable distribution of benefits with most tourists visiting the south of the country (Morris 2018; Sigmundsdóttir 2017). Moreover, inequality more generally is growing in Iceland. In 2014, the country had the lowest inequality rate in the OECD but, particularly since the 2008 financial crisis, it has continued to move away from that position (Ástvaldsson 2018). The child poverty rate in Iceland has also been rising at an alarming rate whilst seniors are also encountering financial difficulties (Ástvaldsson 2018), pointing to a distinction between the 'success' of tourism and development.

Table 11.3 also includes values for the IHDI and, when inequality is factored in, there is a corresponding drop in the HDI values. At the bottom of Table 11.3, countries are grouped into broad categories of HDI for comparison with the IHDI. The 'Very High HDI' countries witnessed an average drop of 11.1 per cent while the 'High HDI' countries saw a 20 per cent drop when examining IHDI. Recognition of this level of inequality is important when considering the role of tourism in developed countries.

Another measure of inequality identified in Table 11.3 is the Gini Coefficient which measures the extent to which income is evenly distributed; the lower the value, the more equitable the distribution of income. Of the nations in Table 11.3, Norway boasts the lowest value, while the United States has the highest. In the context of the OECD countries, Molander (2014) suggests that while the richer countries in the OECD are similar in many respects, there are prevailing differences with regards to income distribution, many of which relate to national economic policies as income distribution can be influenced by transfer and tax systems. Nevertheless, most OECD countries have experienced a trend towards increasing income disparity since the 1970s (Molander 2014), although Moyo (2011) argues that, in the context of developed nations, it is increasingly difficult to distinguish who is financially rich and poor. 'Nearly everyone can go on fancy holidays, buy a new car and live in an enviable home; but the mountains of debt they need to do these things show the true state of their finances' (Moyo 2011, p. 49).

The reduction of inequality within and among countries is Goal 10 in the SDG, reflecting recognition that extreme inequalities tend to 'hamper economic growth, and undermine both political equality, and social stability' (Stiglitz 2015, p. 287). Government policies can be instrumental in addressing inequality. Finland, for example, ranks 23rd in the HDI from 2015 (UNDP 2016) but as Table 11.4 illustrates, ranks very high on a number of other social-economic development indicators. The number of international travellers visiting Finland has doubled since 2000 and while it relies heavily on the Russian tourist market (which has been declining), in 2016 the Chinese market was the top performer with an increase in 29 per cent in overnight stays (OECD 2018). Finnair is promoting Helsinki Airport as a major hub and stopover destination connecting Asia and Europe, offering nearly 40 direct flights a week from seven major Chinese cities (City of Helsinki 2018; Hannonen n.d.). However, this raises the question about the role of corporations such as Finnair having control over tourism flows and how residents will respond to increasing numbers of tourists and the potential for so-called overtourism.

Returning to the discussion of inequality, an important step in addressing inequality was made in January 2018, with Iceland becoming the first country in the world to legalize pay equity regardless of gender, nationality, sexuality or nationality. Inequality can also be explored in the historic treatment of indigenous populations; according to the 2016 Canadian census, for example, four out of five Aboriginal reserves have median incomes that are below the poverty line (Press 2017). Consequently, countries such as Canada and Australia have been expanding indigenous tourism. In its 2017 budget, Canada set out CAD $8.6 million over four years to Indigenous and Northern Affairs to develop Canada's 'unique and authentic indigenous tourism industry' (OECD 2018, p. 139), yet research is required to explore if and how such investments in indigenous tourism alleviate poverty amongst these communities in developed countries, and who controls emerging indigenous tourism.

Table 11.4   Selected social-economic measures of development for Finland

Safety and society	● The most stable country in the world
	● The freest country in the world
	● The safest country in the world
	● The best governance in the world
	● The least organized crime in the world
	● The most independent judiciary in the world
	● The freest and most reliable elections in the world
	● The third least corruption in the world
	● The soundest banks in the world
	● The third best press freedom in the world
Wellbeing and equitability	● The second best country in social progress in the world
	● The second most socially just country in the European Union
	● The best in a comparison of human wellbeing in the world
	● The best in protecting fundamental human rights in the world
Satisfaction and trust	● The people with second highest satisfaction with their life in Europe
	● The people with the second highest trust in others in Europe
Equality	● The second most gender-equal country in the world
	● The second lowest inequality among children in the world
	● The second best country to be a girl in the world
Education	● The most human capital in the world
	● The best primary education in the world
	● The top in education in the OECD
	● The most literate country in the world

Notes: Selected indicators 2016–17; see Kullerg 2017 for further details on original indicators.

Importance of tourism and the tourism-led economic growth hypothesis

At a global level, international tourism represents 7 per cent of the world's goods and services, 10 per cent of the world's GDP and comprises one in ten jobs. Projected international tourist arrivals are 1.8 billion by 2030 (UNWTO 2017). In OECD countries in 2016, international arrivals accounted for 55 per cent of the global total and 60.4 per cent of global travel receipts (OECD 2018). However, the annual growth rate of arrivals in OECD countries dropped from 6.4 per cent in 2014 to 3.9 per cent in 2016, indicating a longer-term slowdown in arrivals and a resulting loss of market share (OECD 2018). Table 11.5 presents tourism statistics on arrivals, receipts, percentage contribution to GDP and total employment for countries of the G7 nations. While these countries have very significant absolute levels of international arrivals and receipts, tourism nevertheless makes a relatively limited contribution to GDP and employment reflecting the diversified nature of advanced economies. At the national level, tourism is often one of many industries that a developed country can rely on to generate income and promote

Table 11.5   Tourism statistics for G7 countries 2016, 2017

Country	2016 international arrivals (1,000)	2016 international receipts (US$ million)	2016 direct contribution % of GDP	2017 % of total employment contribution*
France	82,600	42,481	3.63	9.9
United States	75,608	205,940	2.71	9.4
Italy	52,372	40,246	4.62	12.6
United Kingdom	35,814	39,615	3.42	11.9
Germany	35,579	37,433	3.96	14.0
Japan	24,039	30,687	2.38	6.9
Canada	19,971	18,231	1.82	7.6

Notes: In order of international arrivals; * direct + indirect + induced employment.

Sources: UNWTO 2017; WTTC 2018.

development whilst developed countries often have, to some degree, social safety nets with various programmes to address issues of unemployment and poverty. Ivanov and Webster (2013) examined tourism's contribution to economic growth for 174 countries from 2000 to 2010, and found the contribution is higher where tourism accounts for a higher share of GDP.

It is also important to understand the level of financial support the tourism industry receives from various levels of government, and what policies they have put in place to attract tourism. The 2018 OECD report on tourism trends and policies reveals that although there is downward pressure on public finances, national tourism budgets have largely been maintained or increased; Canada has just released a New Vision for Tourism, whilst Japan's Revitalisation Strategy 2016 has tourism as one of ten key national pillars (OECD 2018). In New Zealand, the Tourism Infrastructure Fund, established in 2017, provides up to NZ$25 million per year for co-funding tourism-related infrastructure, especially in areas where the local population is too small to fund the projects themselves (OECD 2018). The World Economic Forum publishes the Travel and Tourism Competitiveness Index (Table 11.6) on how attractive a country is for establishing businesses in tourism, and Table 11.7 illustrates these rankings for the G7 nations along with government spending on travel and tourism services. Scores are presented on scale of 1–7, the higher the score, the easier it is to do business in tourism in that country. All G7 nations are within the top 10 nations in the Travel and Tourism Competitiveness Index, illustrating the advantages of an advanced economy for tourism businesses. While France has the highest rank in Table 11.7, the United States enjoys by far the largest government expenditure on tourism. Countries in the European Union can also take advantage of the European Commission's (2016) *Guide on EU Funding for the Tourism Sector*

Table 11.6   Travel and Tourism Competitiveness Index

Enabling environment	Travel and tourism policy and enabling conditions	Infrastructure	Natural and cultural resources
Business environment Safety and security Health and hygiene Human resources and labour market ICT readiness	Prioritization of travel and tourism International openness Price competitiveness Environmental sustainability	Air transport infrastructure Ground and port infrastructure Tourist service infrastructure	Natural resources Cultural resources and business travel

Sources: World Economic Forum 2017; World Bank 2018c.

Table 11.7   Travel and Tourism Competitiveness Index 2017 and government spending on travel and tourism 2016 for the G7 countries

Country	Rank	Index score (1 to 7)	Government spending on travel and tourism services (US$ billions) 2016
France	2	5.32	2.27
Germany	3	5.28	1.73
Japan	4	5.26	4.78
United Kingdom	5	5.20	2.12
United States	6	5.12	17.44
Italy	8	4.99	1.58
Canada	9	4.97	1.82

Notes: Travel and Tourism Competitiveness Index in order of world ranking; Government spending figures as of time of writing.

Sources: World Economic Forum 2017; World Bank 2018c.

2014–2020, which offers international sources of funding for various tourism initiatives. An examination of the level of support given by a government in developed nations and the impact that has in the role of tourism in the development and redevelopment process will be an important research topic in the future.

With developed nations enjoying high levels of arrivals and tourism receipts, does this then lead to development? A number of studies, which have become increasingly more sophisticated in terms of analysis, have considered the tourism-led economic growth hypothesis. This is centred on the view that tourism revenues 'can increase income, employment and investment in the tourism sector' (Terzi 2015, p. 165). Thus, not only is tourism income considered a key determinant of economic growth that can stimulate overall economic performance, but also tourism then has the potential to speed up economic growth both in the short and longer term (Terzi 2015). However, a review of the literature (Tang & Jang 2009) found that even though many governments are engaged in tourism development to promote economic growth, inconsistent or contradictory results in terms of the tourism-led economic growth hypothesis emerge from empirical studies. The reasons for these mixed results may be linked to the nature of the studies being conducted, based as they are on different countries with different tourism-economy relationships, or may reflect the fact that tourism businesses are often treated as a homogeneous industry. Hence, Tang and Jang (2009) examined the relationships between the performance of airlines, casinos, hotels and restaurants and GDP in the United States, finding that there was no co-integration between economic growth and tourism industry performance. As a result, they suggest that mechanisms to increase tourism revenue may be successful even in the context of sustained economic stagnation. Tang and Jang note that in the United States, tourism plays a small role relative to the size of the economy, but their results did show a temporal causal hierarchy among the industry subsectors investigated. Specifically, they found that the airlines and hotels were critical in terms of stimulating tourism growth.

In Europe, Cortes-Jimenez and Pulina (2010) similarly examined inbound tourism expansion and economic growth in Spain and Italy in the context of the tourism-led growth hypothesis. In Spain, a bi-directional influence was found where an expansion in tourism assists long-term economic growth and vice versa; conversely, in Italy, a uni-directional influence was found, with international tourism expansion enhancing long-term economic growth. In another study, Tugcu (2013) examined the relationship between economic growth and tourism in countries that surround the Mediterranean in three divisions: European countries, Asian countries and African countries. He found that European countries were better able to generate economic growth from tourism compared to the other countries. While the direction of causality between tourism and economic growth is country- and indicator-specific, some considerations for tourism to generate economic growth include the interconnectedness between sectors of the economy, the level of established tourism attraction and how economic growth is redistributed. In Pablo-Romero and Molina's (2013) later review, it was found that 55 out of 87 studies (developed and developing countries) did support the tourism-led growth hypothesis, with a connection between economic growth and the degree that a country has a specialization in tourism being identified. The authors called for more advanced studies, including into the ability of tourism to generate interregional economic convergence. More generally, as studies on the tourism-led economic growth hypothesis grow in sophistication, additional research is needed not only at the developed country level but also at the regional level.

Finally, there has been increased recognition of the role of domestic tourism in generating growth. In OECD countries such as Australia, Canada, Germany, Italy, Japan, the Netherlands, Norway, the UK and the United States, domestic tourism expenditure represents over 70 per cent of total expenditure in comparison to inbound tourism expenditure (OECD 2018). In New Zealand, Tourism Industry Aotearoa (2014) notes that domestic tourism contributes NZ$14 billion annually, making up 59 per cent of total tourism earnings, hence suggesting that domestic tourism can support the industry in terms of seasonality, regional dispersal and increased domestic spending. Similarly, Tsui (2017) found a low-cost air carrier in New Zealand significantly increased and boosted domestic tourism demand, bringing benefits to regional economies. The issue of low-cost carriers will be returned to later in the chapter but one emerging area for future research is how domestic tourism can stimulate development, especially in areas that may not initially attract international tourists. The chapter now turns to explore the use of tourism as a regional redevelopment tool.

Tourism as a redevelopment tool

While tourism may not contribute significantly to national development indicators in advanced economies, it can be vital at the regional level where it is depended upon to generate employment and income. Generally, then, it will be important to further investigate the role of tourism in regional development, particularly as emerging regions not only generate more investment opportunities but also present additional sources of competition. Tourism has long been used as a redevelopment tool on a variety of scales where economies have seen a loss in manufacturing, where urban cores have gone into decline and where rural economies need additional sources of income (Telfer 2015b). Within the European Union, the European Regional Development Fund provides funding for local and regional tourism development projects, whilst national tourism plans in OECD member countries are increasingly placing an emphasis on regional and local destinations (OECD 2018). For example, in Portugal, the *Valorizar* programme has an annual budget of €30 million for the regeneration and rehabilitation of public spaces for tourism, whilst the Discover England Fund provides up to £40 million to stimulate international visits in destinations throughout England (OECD 2018).

More specifically, following the public-private partnership model of Baltimore Harbour, which transformed abandoned port buildings into a thriving tourism destination, many urban historic waterfronts have been redeveloped, the success in Baltimore being replicated in cities such as Norfolk, Long Beach and Honolulu in the United States, as well as in Sydney, Barcelona, Rotterdam, Osaka and Belfast (Global Harbours Documentary 2008). Equally, the transformative effect of special events and/or iconic destinations have been noted in Spain in the context of the Olympics in Barcelona, Expo 92 in Seville and the opening of the Guggenheim Museum in Bilbao (Blanco & Subirats 2008). Many regional tourism development projects rely on regional branding, strategic alliances and partnerships, not only between businesses but also with various levels of government. However, local governments can enter into bidding wars, offering tax breaks to attract tourism investors, whilst regional development strategies can be expensive, do not always work and, as will be illustrated later, run the risk of gentrification. Rural regions are also turning to agritourism (or agrotourism), including culinary and wine trails, to generate regional development. While this may lead to economic diversification, Phelan and Sharpley (2011) found that in the case of northwest England, many farmers lack the fundamental business competencies to be successful.

Romão and Neuts studied tourism and sustainable regional development in Europe through an examination of natural and cultural resources, and innovative abilities or smart specialization. Their findings, however, suggested that where 'tourism assumes larger socio-economic importance, the contributions of tourism to the achievement of the Millennium Development Goals related to sustainable development was relatively poor' (Romão & Neuts 2017, p. 70). They go on to state that in terms of the utilization of environmental assets, along with the mobilization of resources and knowledge for innovative activities with high value added, specialization in tourism does not reduce the development gap that exists between European regions.

The process of redevelopment has also extended into rural areas or destinations that have become heritage shopping districts. Mitchell (2013) outlines the processes of creative destruction and creative enhancement. On the one hand, in terms of creative destruction, as an area moves towards becoming a rural heritage district, entrepreneurs move into the area driving innovation and seeking profits. In doing so, earlier economic regimes are destroyed and previous economic activities and businesses are displaced, hence changing the character of the destination. Creative enhancement, on the other hand, introduces an additional innovative function but does not cause the displacement of the previously existing economic function, so both co-exist. In the context of development, creative destruction and creative enhancement can generate economic growth, but who benefits and who is displaced are areas that need further investigation. Both options generate change in a community that may or may not be welcomed by locals. Further comparative research is needed to explore why some regional tourism development projects are successful and others are not.

Emerging challenges and research areas for tourism and its contribution to development

Despite the many advantages enjoyed by developed nations, there are several emerging and interconnected challenges facing tourism which have implications for its potential to contribute to development. A number of these challenges, considered below, build on the work by Oritz (2017), and include gentrification, overtourism and the emerging sharing economy; tourism growth, carbon emissions and low-cost carriers; issues of just work and the changing nature of tourism employment; and poverty reduction and inclusive growth. Most of these issues represent a double-edged sword, with tourism bringing benefits to some and difficulties for others. In contrast to the broader development theory-based future research questions raised in Table 11.1, more empirical examples are considered here to further chart a future research agenda for tourism and (re)development in developed nations.

Gentrification, overtourism and the emerging sharing economy

Through the process of gentrification, residences are being renovated – and in some cases rented to tourists – with the overall effect of rising property values and squeezing out local residents. Oritz (2017) argues that 'speculation, gentrification and touristification are creating a new geographical distribution of wealth and poverty' in many of the most visited cities in the world, suggesting that mass tourism to major cities such as Amsterdam, Venice, Barcelona, Madrid and London is driving inequality. Cities are struggling to manage large numbers of tourists, or 'overtourism', and the impact it inflicts on locals. Thus, an important future research question will be how to deal with rising numbers of tourists and overcrowding and the resulting impacts on not only local people but also the property market as the sharing economy continues to grow. For example, Amsterdam is considering raising taxes on tourists by €10 a night, as the city of 850,000 was visited by 17 million people in 2016, up from 12 million just five years earlier (Boffey 2017). Residents there have been protesting about rising house prices and how growing numbers of tourists are forcing them out. Twenty-five per cent of visitors stay in budget hotels which brings in limited income to the city, and the city centre is becoming dominated by tourist accommodation. In response to criticism from residents, the city has negotiated with the property-sharing website Airbnb that apartments rented for up to 60 days would subsequently be removed from the website for the remainder of the year (Boffey 2017).

However, the development of the sharing economy has presented significant challenges for governments in terms of the legality of the operation through existing laws and regulations (Fang et al. 2015), with issues surrounding licences, taxes and short-term rentals among the areas of dispute (Guttentag 2015). Tourists using Airbnb in Japan faced reservation cancellations in June 2018 when operators removed their properties from Airbnb's list after the Japanese government enforced the requirement for all guest home accommodations to have a licence. In the summer of 2017, there were anti-tourism protests in several cities across Europe, including in Barcelona, Palma (Majorca), San Sebastian and Venice, again in part against the rising numbers of unlicensed tourist accommodation units (Coldwell 2017). In Venice there have also been protests over the arrival of large cruise ships, whilst in Barcelona there are approximately 16,000 holiday rentals of which close to 7,000 are unlicensed. This led the city to fine Airbnb €600,000 for continuing to advertise these unlicensed holiday properties (Burgen 2017).

In Iceland, which, as noted earlier, has experienced remarkable growth in tourism in recent years, the number of accommodation units had not kept pace with demand. Again, the solution was Airbnb: in Reykjavik, with a population of approximately 120,000, there were 3,100 properties listed on the Airbnb website in July 2016, representing 1 in 23 apartments being for tourist rental (Sigmundsdóttir 2017). Consequently, it is becoming increasingly difficult for locals to find a place to live as property values and rental rates rise; indeed, local people have been evicted from rental units to make way for higher-paying tourists, whilst some landlords rent properties to locals for only nine months so they are able rent to tourists in the summer months. The average annual rise in property values between 2002 and 2017 was 9 per cent; however, between 2016 and 2017 it was 18.9 per cent (Ástvaldsson 2018). Iceland's population also increased between 2010 to 2015, though this was primarily owing to foreigners immigrating with many taking up positions in tourism. Conversely, Statistics Iceland predicts that, on average, 850 Icelanders will emigrate each year, with one of the main reasons being the lack of housing (Sigmundsdóttir 2017). With complaints also coming from hotels and guesthouses that had gone through official channels to register their businesses, the government took steps in 2017 to regulate Airbnb. Homeowners are now allowed to rent out all or part of their dwelling for up to 90 days a year without a licence as long as it is registered with local police and they pay a nominal fee. It is hoped that this will combat tax evasion, provide the authorities with an understanding of the Airbnb market and derail property speculators who had been purchasing flats to transform into tourist apartments (Sigmundsdóttir 2017). As Sigmundsdóttir (2017, p. 7) summarizes, the Icelandic people have struggled 'to come to grips with this massive influx [of tourists] over so short a period and the resulting changes to their lives'.

In response, Airbnb (2018) posts economic impact studies on their websites, and selected findings are presented here illustrating some of the benefits of the sharing economy. For example, in San Francisco in 2012, Airbnb generated approximately US$56 million in local spending, supporting 430 jobs. The average Airbnb visitor stayed 5.5 days and spent US$1,054, while an average hotel guest stayed 3.5 days and spent US$840. Seventy-two per cent of the Airbnb properties in San Francisco were located outside of the central hotel district. In 2014 in the UK, Airbnb generated US$824 million in economic activity and supported 11,600 jobs. Approximately 80 per cent of UK Airbnb hosts rent the property they live in, earning US$4,600 per year by renting for 33 nights. Sixty-three per cent said the income helped pay bills they would regularly struggle to pay (Airbnb 2018). However, Fang et al. (2015) raised several important questions regarding Airbnb, including whether it was taking over the role of low-end motels or whether the entire tourism industry would benefit owing to the increased demand. They studied Airbnb data for the state of Idaho in the United States to evaluate the effect of the sharing economy on local tourism employment, identifying both positive and negative impacts. On the one hand, the sharing economy did benefit the entire tourism industry, generating more jobs as more tourists were attracted to the lower-cost accommodation. On the other hand, low-end hotels are under threat and being replaced by Airbnb, so employees at low-end hotels could lose their jobs. Fang et al. (2015) conclude that the marginal effect of Airbnb decreases as low-end hotels are substituted and, hence, they argue that governments should regulate the industry so that employment is generated and the drawbacks do not negatively impact society.

The sharing economy can also be examined in the case of Uber, the online ride-sharing platform that allows customers to use their cell phones to contact and pay drivers for a ride to their destination. Unsurprisingly, perhaps, Uber has come into conflict with existing taxi companies in various destinations. Bennhold (2017), for example, documents the conflicts between London's 'black cabs' that can trace their lineage to 1634 and Uber, which began operations in 2012, just before the London Olympics. Uber's 40,000 drivers outnumber the 21,000 traditional cab drivers and their fares are 30 per cent lower than those of traditional cabs. Hence, as Bennhold suggests, the new business model is not only disrupting the traditional cab industry but also has broader social and economic implications that are disrupting Britain. Bennhold (2017) links this to the vote on Brexit, suggesting that results of the vote to leave the European Union exposed a rift between those who have profited from globalization and those who feel threatened by immigration and automation. Thus, the tourism industry in the UK as a whole will have to deal not only with the emerging sharing economy, but also with its transition out of the European Union.

In a study of social exclusion in five large Spanish cities, Blanco and Subirats (2008) found that as urban areas went through the process of redevelopment and increasingly catered to tourists, the property market rose and attracted investors from outside the local area, including those from other European countries. Overall, therefore, while the sharing economy offers the opportunity for many more people to participate in the benefits of tourism, additional research is needed on the impacts it is having on the economies and communities where dramatic transformations of the industry are occurring.

Tourism growth, carbon emissions and the rise of low-cost carriers

With increasing numbers of tourists based, in part, on a growing middle class in countries such as India and China, concern has turned to growth in carbon emissions and tourism's contribution to climate change. A quick check of the skies over any large airport in a major city in the developed world on a website such as www.flightradar24 reveals hundreds of circling airplanes. On 29 June 2018, the website tracked 202,157 flights taking off and landing, the busiest day recorded since its inception in 2006 (Newton 2018). Dogan et al. (2017) investigated energy consumption, real GDP and tourism and trade in carbon dioxide emissions in OECD countries. Unsurprisingly, not only are tourism arrivals growing, but also energy consumption and carbon dioxide emissions are on the rise. In OECD countries there is a positive effect of tourism on carbon dioxide emissions through the use of energy and transport for the promotion of tourist facilities. The authors recommend policy makers impose policies in terms of environmental protection and cleaner technologies.

Similarly, in the United States, Raza et al. (2017) found a positive and significant relationship between tourism development and carbon dioxide emissions. As tourism development increases, so too do carbon dioxide emissions: 'Energy consumption in tourism is dominated by transportation activities, which is associated with combusting fossil fuels and a consequential effect of greenhouse gas emissions' (Raza et al. 2017, p. 1786). With the advancement of aviation liberalization, competition has been encouraged which, in turn, is creating new routes and new business models (OECD 2018). Low-cost air carriers in particular have been using secondary airports charging lower landing fees, thereby opening up other regions to tourism development that previously may have attracted limited air traffic. Ryanair, for example, claims to fly 350,000 passengers every day between 200 destinations (Ryanair 2018; see also Oritz 2017); hence, an important area for future research is the relationship between the rise of low-cost carriers and overtourism as discussed above. More generally, how busy will the skies be in the future and can, and should, future airport expansion keep pace? The decision in 2018 to approve a third runway at London Heathrow took nearly 20 years, and likely will not open until 2026 (BBC 2018). Not only is the nature of the airline industry changing, but the communities receiving large numbers of tourists are struggling with how to deal with recent increases in visitors.

Yokomi et al. (2017) examined 26 UK airports to investigate the impact of low-cost carriers on non-aeronautical revenues (e.g. retail, food and beverages, car hire, advertising, car parks and so on). They found that additional low-cost carriers, at the expense of non-low-cost carriers, would have a negative impact on the non-aeronautical revenues of the airports. While they suggest the reasons for the lower revenues are open to discussion, one possible reason is the lower budget constraints faced by those travelling with low-cost carriers. This then has broader implications in terms of development in destinations hoping to attract budget travellers on low-cost carriers. Certainly, the development of low-cost carriers has continued the process of the democratization of travel and bringing visitors to new locations; nonetheless, destinations need to consider the volume of tourists they want to attract as well as the markets they want to pursue. Raising the issue of the contribution of low-cost carriers to climate change in the United States, Raza et al. (2017, p. 1787) suggest that low-cost air travel 'creates hypermobile travel patterns, while spreading the idea that travel is possible at virtually no financial cost'. While there is increased focus on implementing sustainable tourism across the industry, this raises the question as to whether the overall growth in tourism, facilitated in part by low-cost airlines, will outpace efforts to make the industry more environmentally friendly. Additional research is needed on both the positive and negative impacts of low-cost carriers, and whether they can contribute to development in developed nations.

Issues of just work and the changing nature of tourism employment

As Lacher and Oh (2012) indicate, tourism has been a popular development strategy based on its potential for positive economic impacts and job opportunities; however, little research has been undertaken into the quality of the jobs created by tourism. Future research is needed on levels of pay, job security and future employment prospects in the industry (see also Chapter 10 in this volume). In comparison to developing countries where employment in the tourism industry (both formal and informal) has the potential for remuneration that may be in line with other higher-paying positions in the economy, the situation is not the same for developed countries. Investigating three coastal regions in the United States, Lacher and Oh (2012) found that the jobs generated by tourism expenditures had a lower income distribution; that is, they found that tourism provided a greater number of jobs that have low pay than the overall economy of the regions studied. This finding is similar to that of Marcouiller et al. (2004), who argue that there is an unequal distribution of benefits and a tendency for tourism to create a hollowing out of income distribution. In addition to the need for further investigations on the specific concerns over tourism income, it is also important to consider whether tourism is an attractive field for future employment. In Iceland, for example, the growth of tourism has generated new opportunities and stimulated entrepreneurship. At the end of 2016, there were 1,347 licensed travel agencies or tour operators of which 978 had received accreditation since 2010 (Sigmundsdóttir 2017). However, Sigmundsdóttir argues that many of the new jobs are ones the Icelanders do not care to fill, in part because they are overqualified, having university degrees but no opportunities in their respective fields.

Within the processes of globalization and economic neoliberalism, corporations favour deregulation and inevitably seek out ways to lower their costs, including outsourcing (Oritz 2017). In the context of hotels, outsourcing occurs in a variety of areas, including food and beverages, room cleaning, leisure activities and technology and information services (Espino-Rodriguez & Ramírez-Fierro 2017). In terms of development, further research is thus needed on the impacts of outsourcing for businesses and employees. For example, in 2012, reforms in the labour market by Spain's conservative government allowed the Spanish tourism industry to outsource cleaning services. As a consequence, those who work as hotel room cleaners have seen their employment become increasingly precarious and receive poor levels of pay (Badcock 2017; Oritz 2017). Until 2012, full-time contracts paid €1,200 a month but now hotels are outsourcing to contract firms only paying €800. In some areas of Spain, chambermaids have seen their wages halved and are required to clean up to 30 rooms a day which can mean as little as €1.25 per room (Badcock 2017).

The rationale for outsourcing is often based on costs, yet Espino-Rodriguez and Ramírez-Fierro (2017) found a negative relationship between the degree of outsourcing and the level of competitive advantage. The demand for cheaper holidays and the desire to make a profit along with government legislation is driving down wages and living standards. There is also a growth in informal employment. For instance, in Los Angeles, undocumented workers make up 65 per cent of the city's labour force. Moreover, migrants in Western Europe lack many of the basic civil rights (UN 2016). Hjalager (2007) discusses the use of illegal immigrants in the restaurant sector in Denmark; some are recruited through illegal employment agencies in other countries and some from amongst those seeking asylum. Similarly, in the United States, approximately 1.3 million hospitality workers are employed without legal authorization, including 20 per cent of the country's chefs and 28 per cent of dishwashers (Elejalde-Ruiz 2017). Future investigation on the precarious nature of working as an undocumented employee in the tourism industry will be crucial.

Niagara Falls, Ontario, is one of the major tourist destinations in Canada. However, it is also home to one of the highest rates of unemployment. In June 2017, the unemployment rate in Niagara was 7.2 per cent, compared to the national rate of 6 per cent and the Province of Ontario rate of 6.1 per cent (Benner 2017). In the same year, the tourism industry had a strong year in Niagara, yet many tourism jobs went unfilled. Consequently, tourism companies in the Niagara region were considering bringing in foreign workers to fill these positions, as has been necessary in the agricultural sector. With a higher unemployment rate than the national average and many tourism positions going unfilled, numerous questions are raised about the rate of pay and whether these tourism positions are full time or part time. At the end of 2017, Niagara's youth unemployment rate (between the ages of 15 and 24) was at 9.5 per cent (Hosmar 2018). Braley-Rattai (cited in Hosmar 2018) argues that there are a number of social and economic impacts of high youth unemployment which can be quite severe. These include younger people leaving the region and seeking employment elsewhere; the generation of social divisions and political unrest; and individuals postponing life steps such as developing relationships or having children. The employment participation rate, which includes the numbers of people with jobs or those actively searching for work, fell from 63.3 per cent to 60.7 per cent between 2016 and 2017 in Niagara (Hosmar 2018).

Seasonality is another concern, as some tourism employees in Niagara are laid off in the winter and then rely on government programmes, such as unemployment insurance, for income. On 1 January 2018, the Province of Ontario raised the minimum wage from CDN$11.60 to $14.00 (which will increase to $15 in 2019) along with a number of other benefits related to vacation time and emergency and medical leave (Westoll 2017). Consequently, concerns have been expressed by the food service and hospitality sectors as many of their employees earn the minimum wage (Kostuch 2017). In early January 2018, two responses of businesses to compensate for the increase in minimum wage were receiving media attention; the first included raising prices to customers, while the second involved cutting paid breaks as well as forcing workers to cover their own health and dental benefits (Canadian Press 2018). Raising the minimum wage assists workers and potentially contributes to development, yet it also creates challenges for employers. More research is therefore needed on the quality of work in tourism, as well as on the role of government policies towards tourism employment in developed countries.

A final area in need of further investigation is the continuing expansion and impact of technology, automation and digitalization. The previously mentioned sharing economy is built on new evolving online platforms which visitors can access with mobile devices. As Hsu et al. (2016) suggest, these advancements are leading to a 'disrupted tourism industry', resulting in challenges for those offering traditional products and employment opportunities for those embracing the new technology.

In terms of automation, in Japan, robot hotels have started to open, raising questions as to whether they will replace the need for some tourism employees (Hashimoto & Telfer 2018). Additional research on impacts of technological innovation on tourism employment in developed countries will better help in understanding this issue more thoroughly.

Poverty reduction and inclusive growth

As noted in the introduction to this chapter, one of the main challenges in need of further investigation is how effective the tourism industry is in reducing poverty in developed nations. There is growing recognition that growth itself is not sufficient to reduce poverty (Bakker & Messerli 2017) and, therefore, growth in tourist numbers or receipts does not necessarily lead to poverty reduction. To partly address poverty alleviation in the context of developing countries, the focus in development thought has turned to pro-poor tourism, an approach that involves the adoption of a variety of strategies to ensure the benefits of tourism are extended to those in greatest need (Telfer & Sharpley 2016). The UNWTO, for example, launched the ST-EP programme (Sustainable Tourism – Eliminating Poverty). The increasing evidence of poverty in developed countries raises the question as to whether pro-poor tourism should also be adopted in developed nations. In the city of St. Catharines in the tourism region of Niagara, Canada, for example, a different church is open each day of the week providing dinner and a place to sleep for those in need through the *Out of the Cold Program* (November–March). While the causes of poverty are complex, to what extent can tourism alleviate poverty or reduce the need for these types of programmes in the Niagara region?

Recently, pro-poor strategies have evolved towards inclusive growth (Bakker & Messerli 2017); while pro-poor growth strategies focus on redistributing existing resources towards the poorest of society or those below the poverty line, inclusive growth is about widening the size of the economy and focusing on more macro-level economic policies (Bakker & Messerli 2017). Hence, in the context of Niagara, a better question could be: 'how could tourism policies be integrated to reflect inclusive growth?', not least because the adoption of inclusive growth is receiving more recognition, appearing in two of the UN SDGs (Goal 8: Decent Work and Economic Growth and Goal 10: Reduced Inequalities). Equally, in 2017, the OECD released a policy statement, *Tourism Policies for Sustainable and Inclusive Growth*, recommending a holistic, 'whole of government policy approach'. One of the specific approaches is to 'use tourism as an engine for inclusive growth, to create quality jobs, businesses and regional development opportunities, mitigate the negative impacts on local communities, and spread the benefits to all people and territories' (OECD 2017, p. 3). However, although much of the research on the role of inclusive growth policies linked to tourism to alleviate poverty has been undertaken in developing countries, further research in this area in developed countries is urgently needed.

Conclusion

With advanced economies and interconnected tourism supply and marketing structures, developed nations are often in a better position to benefit from tourism. While national indicators reflect tourism may represent a small proportion of Gross National Product, developed countries still receive significant income from tourism. In Canada in 2017, tourism generated $41.2 billion in GDP (up 6.3 per cent from 2016), representing 2.06 per cent of total GDP (Destination Canada 2018). Specific regions within developed countries are highly dependent on tourism. Nonetheless, as noted in the introduction, poverty resides alongside tourism and rising levels of inequality illustrate the challenges many residents face in developed countries. Indeed, although the focus of developed countries has evolved from solely economic indicators to the broader UN SDGs, it is often the economic dimension that continues to receive the most attention. Yet as Marcouiller et al. (2004, p. 1046) state, 'development policy based solely on aggregate growth is naïve and overlooks important distributional attributes associated with amenities and touristic activity'. It is also important to consider who are the intended recipients of the benefits of tourism, and at what scale. Should it be individuals, private companies or governments or, in spatial terms, should it be communities, regions or nations? Marcouiller et al. (2004, p. 1046) also observe that 'contemporary American public policy fascination with promoting regions for increased tourism rests on a preconception that this industry is automatically beneficial to the economic development of communities it affects; the preconception that it is a developmental panacea rules'.

This chapter has explored a limited set of emerging challenges for tourism and its contribution to development in developed nations, as well as identifying areas of future research. The research questions posed were in relation to broad overriding development paradigms which continue to evolve (see Table 11.1), and were also linked to the empirical examples introduced in this chapter. Overriding development ideology will influence the strategies used when pursuing tourism as a development tool, and so both are inextricably linked. The OECD (2018) has categorized the following four megatrends that may influence the shape of tourism in the future: *People, Planet, Productivity* and *Polity*. The term *People* refers to the evolving visitor demand in tourism, including aging populations and a growing middle class. *Planet* refers to the state of the environment and resources and includes climate change. In terms of tourism, this megatrend is focused on the growth in sustainable tourism. A study by the Economist Intelligence Unit (2017), *The Sustainable Tourism Index*, found France and Germany having the strongest overall commitment to sustainable tourism. *Productivity* refers to growth in technology, innovation and entrepreneurship. This is linked to enabling technologies, allowing people to travel such as the sharing economy, and advancements in automation in tourism. Finally, *Polity* refers to the state of governance, trust and accountability in the public sphere. In tourism, public decisions impact travel mobility through the degree a government supports international transport and facilitates travel. Canada, for example, declared 2018 as the Canada-China Year of Tourism and has opened seven new visa application centres in China. Growth in tourism, however, cannot be expected to solve all developmental problems. These future trends, along with the specific challenges examined in this chapter, collectively illustrate the complexity of the relationship between tourism and developed countries, and present a range of future research opportunities.

Reflecting on the areas covered in this chapter, a number of additional future research questions arise, including: How much tourism growth is too much? If major cities in developed countries are already facing overtourism, what will the future bring? As more people travel by airplane, facilitated by low-cost carriers, what will the impact be on climate change? Can sustainable development initiatives keep pace with the growth of tourism? Why does using tourism as a regional development tool not always work? Should regions heavily reliant on tourism diversify their economies away from tourism? Why do tourism employment opportunities often go unfilled in developed countries? Do we need pro-poor tourism or inclusive growth strategies for tourism to deal with poverty in developed nations? While governments can provide a variety of social, economic and environmental programmes for its citizens through the income generated from tourism, how is this income disbursed?

Poverty and inequality are complex issues. Tourism cannot be focused on in isolation but, rather, needs to be part of a holistic approach to development. While much of the research in terms of tourism and development has been undertaken in the developing world, more research is needed on the nature of tourism and (re) development in the developed world.

References

Airbnb (2018), *Airbnb Economic Impact*. Accessed 21 February 2018 at https://blog.atairbnb.com/economic-impact-airbnb/

Allard, S. (2017), *Places in Need: The Changing Geography of Poverty*, New York: Russell Sage Foundation.

Ástvaldsson, J. (2018), 'Poverty and inequality', *Iceland Review*, **1**, 15–16.

Badcock, J. (2017), 'Spain's hotel chambermaids "Las Kelly" fight for fair pay', *BBC News*, 18 October. Accessed 22 February 2018 at www.bbc.com/news/world-europe-41650252

Bakker, M. and Messerli, H. (2017), 'Inclusive growth versus pro-poor growth: Implications for tourism development', *Tourism and Hospitality Research*, **17**(4), 384–91.

Barr, C. and Malik, S. (2016), 'Revealed: The 30-year economic betrayal dragging down Generation Y's income', *The Guardian*, 7 March. Accessed 19 February 2018 at www.theguardian.com/world/2016/mar/07/revealed-30-year-economic-betrayal-dragging-down-generation-y-income

BBC (2018), 'Heathrow Airport: Cabinet approves runway plan', *BBC News*, 5 June. Accessed 31 July 2018 at www.bbc.com/news/uk-politics-44357580

Benner, A. (2017), 'Jobless rate spikes; tourism jobs unfilled', 10 July. Accessed 30 January 2018 at www.stcatharinesstandard.ca/2017/07/10/unemployment-rate-increases-in-niagara

Bennhold, K. (2017), 'On London's streets, black cabs and Uber fight for a future', *New York Times*, 4 July. Accessed 21 February 2018 at www.nytimes.com/2017/07/04/world/europe/london-uk-brexit-uber-taxi.html

Blanco, I. and Subirats, J. (2008), 'Social exclusion, area effects and metropolitan governance: A comparative analysis of five large Spanish cities', *Urban Research and Practice*, **1**(2), 130–48.

Boffey, D. (2017), 'Amsterdam to increase tourist tax to reclaim city for residents', *The Guardian*, 11 September. Accessed 21 February 2018 at www.theguardian.com/world/2017/sep/11/amsterdam-to-increase-tourist-tax-to-reclaim-city-for-residents

Burgen, S. (2017), 'Barcelona cracks down on Airbnb rentals with illegal apartment squads', *The Guardian*, 2 June. Accessed 21 February 2018 at www.theguardian.com/technology/2017/jun/02/airbnb-faces-crackdown-on-illegal-apartment-rentals-in-barcelona

Canadian Press (2018), 'Ontario minimum wage hike: Companies divided on whether to raise prices or slash benefits', *Huffpost*, 9 January. Accessed 31 January 2018 at www.huffingtonpost.ca/2018/01/09/ontario-minimum-wage-hike-companies-divided-on-whether-to-raise-prices-or-slash-benefits_a_23328466/

City of Helsinki (2018), 'Helsinki reaches out to millions of Chinese travellers with new Helsinki mini program', *City of Helsinki*. Accessed 20 April 2018 at www.hel.fi/uutiset/en/kaupunginkanslia/millions-chinese-travellers

Coldwell, W. (2017), 'First Venice and Barcelona: Now anti-tourism marches spread across Europe', *The Guardian*, 10 August. Accessed 21 February 2018 at www.theguardian.com/travel/2017/aug/10/anti-tourism-marches-spread-across-europe-venice-barcelona

Cortes-Jimenez, I. and Pulina, M. (2010), 'Inbound tourism and long-run economic growth', *Current Issues in Tourism*, **13**(1), 61–7.

Cukier, J. (2002), 'Tourism employment issues in developing countries: Examples from Indonesia', in R. Sharpley and D.J. Telfer (eds) *Tourism and Development: Concepts and Issues*, Clevedon: Channel View Publications, pp. 165–201.

Danielsen, K. and Lang, R. (2014), 'Comparing Orlando and Las Vegas: Understanding industrial diversification in the nation's two largest tourist-led regional economies', Conference Paper, *Association of Collegiate Schools of Planning*, Philadelphia, PA. Accessed 13 March 2018 at www.researchgate.net/publication/271704572_Comparing_Orlando_and_Las_Vegas_Understanding_Industrial_Diversification_in_the_Nation%27s_Two_Largest_Tourist-Led_Regional_Economies

de la Dehesa, G. (2006), *Winners and Losers in Globalization*, Oxford: Blackwell.

Destination Canada (2018), *National Tourism Indicators 2017 Highlights*. Accessed 19 April 2018 at www.destinationcanada.com/sites/default/files/archive/691-national-tourism-indicators-q4-2017/national-tourism-indicators-highlights-2017_final.pdf

Dogan, E., Seker, F. and Bulbul, S. (2017), 'Investigating the impacts of energy consumption, real GDP, tourism and trade on CO_2 emissions by accounting for cross-sectional dependence: A panel study of OECD countries', *Current Issues in Tourism* **20**(16), 1701–10.

Economist Intelligence Unit (2017), *The Sustainable Tourism Index: Enhancing the Global Travel Environment*, Economist Intelligence Unit, London. Accessed 19 April 2018 at www.eiuperspectives.economist.com/sites/default/files/Sustainable_Tourism_Index.pdf

Elejalde-Ruiz, A. (2017), 'Hospitality industry needs more immigrant workers to survive, report says', *Chicago Tribune*, 24 August. Accessed 21 February 2018 at www.chicagotribune.com/business/ct-hospitality-needs-more-immigrants-report-0825-biz-20170824-story.html

Espino-Rodriguez, T. and Ramírez-Fierro, J. (2017), 'Factors determining hotel activity outsourcing: An approach based on competitive advantage', *International Journal of Contemporary Hospitality Management*, **29**(8), 2006–26.

European Commission (2016), *Guide on EU Funding for the Tourism Sector 2014–2020*, Brussels: Europe Union.

Fang, B, Qiang, Y. and Law, R. (2015), 'Effect of sharing economy on tourism employment', *Annals of Tourism Research*, **57**, 264–7.

Global Harbours Documentary (2008), *Global Harbours: A Waterfront Renaissance*, DVD, C. Stein and K. Skeen (producers). Accessed 13 March 2018 at www.globalharbors.org/index.html

Goldberg, J., Birtles, A., Marshal, N., Curnock, M., Case, P., and Beeden, R. (2018), 'The role of Great Barrier Reef tourism operators in addressing climate change through strategic communication and direct action', *Journal of Sustainable Tourism*, **26**(2), 238–56.

Government of Canada (2018), 'New Canadian record for international arrivals set in 2017', news release, 20 February. Accessed 22 February 2018 at www.canada.ca/en/innovation-science-economic-develop ment/news/2018/02/minister_chaggercelebratescanadasbesttourismyearever.html

Guttentag, D. (2015), 'Airbnb: Disruptive innovation and the rise of an informal tourism accommodation sector', *Current Issues in Tourism*, **18**(2), 1192–217.

Hannonen, P. (n.d.), 'Finland targets Asian stopover tourists – but does Helsinki have a chance to become a new Keflavík?', *Euromonitor International*. Accessed 20 April 2018 at https://blog.euromonitor. com/2016/01/finland-targets-asian-stopover-tourists-but-does-helsinki-have-a-chance-to-become-a-new-keflavik.html

Hashimoto, A. and Telfer, D. (2018), 'Evolution of a Dutch cultural theme park to technology entertainment in Japan', in M. Tunkkari-Eskelinen and A. Törn-Laapio (eds) *Proceedings of the International Conference on Tourism Research*, Jyväskylä, Finland, Reading, UK: ACPI, pp. 57–67.

Hettne, B. (1995), *Development Theory and the Three Worlds*, 2nd edn, Harlow: Addison Wesley Longman.

Hjalager, A.-M. (2007), 'The illegal economy in the restaurant sector in Denmark', *Tourism and Hospitality Research*, **8**(3), 239–51.

Holden, A. (2013), *Tourism, Poverty and Development*, Abingdon: Routledge.

Hosmar, S. (2018), 'Brock professor responds to Niagara's high unemployment rate', *Brock Press*, 16 January, p. 5.

Hsu, A., King, B., Wang, D. and Buhalis, D. (2016), 'In-destination tour products and the disrupted tourism industry: Progress and prospects', *Information and Technology and Tourism*, **16**(4), 413–33.

Ivanov, S. and Webster, C. (2013), 'Tourism's contribution to economic growth: A global analysis of the first decade of the millennium', *Tourism Economics*, **19**(3), 477–508.

KNPR (2016), 'Poverty is rising in the Las Vegas suburbs', *Nevada Public Radio*, 2 March. Accessed 23 February 2018 at https://knpr.org/knpr/2016-03/poverty-rising-las-vegas-suburbs

Kostuch (2017), 'Ontario minimum wage increase expected to impact jobs', *Hotelier*, 2 June. Accessed 31 January 2017 at www.hoteliermagazine.com/ontario-minimum-wage-increase-expected-impact-jobs/

Kullerg, M. (ed.) (2017), 'Because we are Finland and you are not', *You Are Here*, Autumn, 28–9.

Lacher, R.G. and Oh, C.-O. (2012), 'Is tourism a low-income industry? Evidence from three coastal regions', *Journal of Travel Research*, **51**(4) 464–72.

Lloyd, J. (2017), 'The Salvation Army's hidden poverty tour', *Strategy*, 4 July. Accessed 12 March 2018 at http://strategyonline.ca/2017/07/04/the-salvation-armys-hidden-poverty-tour/

Marcouiller, D., Kim, K.-K. and Deller, S. (2004), 'Natural amenities, tourism and income distribution', *Annals of Tourism Research*, **31**(4), 1031–50.

Mitchell, C. (2013), 'Creative destruction or creative enhancement? Understanding the transformation of rural spaces', *Journal of Rural Studies*, **32**, 375–87.

Molander, P. (2014), *The Anatomy of Inequality: Its Social and Economic Origins – and Solutions*, London: Melville House.

Morris, H. (2018), 'Has Iceland's tourism bubble finally burst?', *Telegraph*, 8 March. Accessed 14 March 2018 at www.telegraph.co.uk/travel/destinations/europe/iceland/articles/iceland-tourism-growth-slows-bubble-burst/

Moyo, D. (2011), *How the West Was Lost: Fifty Years of Economic Folly and the Stark Choices Ahead*, Toronto: D&M Publishers.

Newton, J. (2018), 'Mesmerising footage shows how more than 200,000 flights took off and landed on one of aviation's busiest days in history', *Daily Mail*, 2 July 2018. Accessed 30 July at www.dailymail.

co.uk/travel/travel_news/article-5909895/Mesmerising-footage-shows-200-000-flights-took-landed-Friday.html

OECD (2017), *Policy Statement: Tourism Policies for Sustainable and Inclusive Growth*, Paris: OECD. Accessed 15 April 2018 at www.oecd.org/cfe/tourism/OECD-Policy-Statement-Tourism-Policies-for-Sustainable-and-Inclusive-Growth.pdf

OECD (2018), *OECD Tourism Trends and Policies 2018*, Paris: OECD. Accessed 14 February 2019 at http://dx.doi.org/10.1787/tour-2018-en

Oritz, E. (2017), 'When mass tourism clashes with the right to the city', *Equal Times*, 27 September. Accessed 20 February 2018 at https://inequality.org/research/mass-tourism-drives-inequality/

Pablo-Romero, M. and Molina, J. (2013), 'Tourism and economic growth: A review of empirical literature', *Tourism Management Perspectives*, 8(1) 28–41.

Phelan, C. and Sharpley, R. (2011), 'Exploring agritourism entrepreneurship in the UK', *Tourism Planning and Development*, 8(2), 121–36.

Press, J. (2017), 'Over 80% of reserves have median income below poverty line, census data shows', *Global News*. Accessed 20 April 2018 at https://globalnews.ca/news/3795083/reserves-poverty-line-census/

Raza, S., Sharif, A., Wong, W. and Karim, M. (2017), 'Tourism development and environmental degradation in the United States: Evidence from wavelet-based analysis', *Current Issues in Tourism*, 20(6), 1768–90.

Romão, J. and Neuts, B. (2017), 'Territorial capital, smart tourism specialization and sustainable regional development: Experiences from Europe', *Habitat International*, 68(1), 64–74.

Ryanair (2018), *Facts and Figures*. Accessed 21 February 2018 at https://corporate.ryanair.com/abo ut-us/fact-and-figures/

Sharma, R. (2013), *Breakout Nations: In Pursuit of the Next Economic Miracles*, London: W.W. Norton & Company.

Sigmundsdóttir, A. (2017), *The Little Book of Tourists in Iceland*, Reykjavik: Little Books Publishing.

Stiglitz, J.E. (2015), *The Great Divide: Unequal Societies and What We Can Do about Them*, London: W.W. Norton & Company.

Stiglitz, J.E. (2018), *Globalization and Its Discontents Revisited: Anti-Globalization in the Era of Trump*, London: W.W. Norton & Company.

Tang, C.-H. and Jang, S. (2009), 'The tourism-economy causality in the United States: A sub industry level examination', *Tourism Management*, 30(4), 533–58.

Telfer, D.J. (1996), *Development through Economic Linkages: Tourism and Agriculture in Indonesia*, PhD thesis, University of Waterloo, Ontario, Canada.

Telfer, D.J. (2002), 'The evolution of tourism and development theory', in R. Sharpley and D.J. Telfer (eds) *Tourism and Development: Concepts and Issues*, Clevedon: Channel View Publications, pp. 35–80.

Telfer, D.J. (2009), 'Development studies and tourism', in T. Jamal and M. Robinson (eds) *The SAGE Handbook of Tourism Studies*, London: SAGE, pp. 146–65.

Telfer, D.J. (2015a), 'The evolution of development theory and tourism', in R. Sharpley and D.J. Telfer (eds), *Tourism and Development: Concepts and Issues*, 2nd edn, Bristol: Channel View Publications, pp. 31–76.

Telfer, D.J. (2015b), 'Tourism and regional development issues', in R. Sharpley and D.J. Telfer (eds) *Tourism and Development: Concepts and Issues*, 2nd edn, Bristol: Channel View Publications, pp. 140–77.

Telfer, D.J. and Sharpley, R. (2016), *Tourism and Development in the Developing World*, 2nd edn, Abingdon: Routledge.

Terzi, H. (2015), 'Is the tourism-led growth hypothesis (TLGH) valid for Turkey?' *Doğuş Üniversitesi Dergisi*, 16(2), 165–78.

Tourism Industry Aotearoa (2014), *Domestic Tourism: The Backbone of the Industry 2014*, Tourism 2025 Growing Value Together Whakatipu Uara Ngatahi. Accessed 27 February 2018 at www.tourism2025.org.nz/tourism-2025-archive/domestic-tourism-the-backbone-of-the-industry/

Tsui, K.W.H. (2017), 'Does a low-cost carrier lead the domestic tourism demand and growth of New Zealand?', *Tourism Management*, 60, 390–403.

Tugcu, C.T. (2013), 'Tourism and economic growth nexus revisited: A panel causality analysis for the case of the Mediterranean region', *Tourism Management*, **42**, 207–12.

UN (2016), *Urbanization and Development: Emerging Futures, World Cities Report 2016, The Widening Urban Divide*, UN Habitat. Accessed 21 February 2018 at https://unhabitat.org/wp-content/uploads/2014/03/WCR_The-Widening-Urban-Divide.pdf

UN (2018a), *Sustainable Development Goals*. Accessed 17 February 2018 at www.un.org/sustainabledevelopment/sustainable-development-goals/

UN (2018b), *World Economic Situation and Prospects Report*, New York: United Nations. Accessed 17 February 2018 at www.un.org/development/desa/dpad/wp-content/uploads/sites/45/publication/WESP2018_Full_Web-1.pdf

UNDP (2016), *Human Development Reports Table 3 Inequality-Adjusted Human Development Index*. Accessed 17 February 2018 at http://hdr.undp.org/en/composite/IHDI

UNWTO (2017), *UNWTO Tourism Highlights 2017 Edition*. Accessed 17 February 2018 at www.e-unwto.org/doi/pdf/10.18111/9789284419029

Westoll, N. (2017), 'Ontario hourly minimum wage jumps on Jan 1, changes to personal leave and vacation coming', *Global News*, 27 December 2017. Accessed 30 January 2018 at https://globalnews.ca/news/3935476/ontario-minimum-wage-increase-2018-personal-leave-vacation-changes/

Williamson, J., Byrnes, E., Clark, J., Connolly, D., Schiller, S., Thompson, J., Tosetto, L., Martinelli, J. and Raoult, V. (2017), 'Ecological impacts and management implications of reef walking on a tropical reef flat community', *Marine Pollution Bulletin*, **114**(2), 742–50.

World Bank (2018a), *How Does the World Bank Classify Countries?* Accessed 16 February 2018 at https://datahelpdesk.worldbank.org/knowledgebase/articles/378834-how-does-the-world-bank-classify-countries

World Bank (2018b), *World Bank Development Indicators GINI Index*, World Bank. Accessed 18 February 2018 at http://databank.worldbank.org/data/reports.aspx?source=2&series=SI.POV.GINI

World Bank (2018c), *Government Spending on Travel and Tourism Service*. Accessed 21 February 2018 at https://tcdata360.worldbank.org/indicators/govt.tat.spend?country=BRA&indicator=24661&viz=line_chart&years=1995,2027

World Economic Forum (2017), *The Travel and Tourism Competitiveness Report 2017: Paving the Way for a More Sustainable and Inclusive Future*, World Economic Forum: Geneva. Accessed 17 February 2018 at www3.weforum.org/docs/WEF_TTCR_2017_web_0401.pdf

WTTC (2018), *WTTC Data Gateway*. Accessed 17 February 2018 at https://tool.wttc.org

Yokomi, M, Wheat, P. and Mitzutani, J. (2017), 'The impact of low cost carriers on non-aeronautical revenues in airport: An empirical study of UK airports', *Journal of Air Transport Management*, **64**, 77–85.

Index

Printed and bound by CPI Group (UK) Ltd, Croydon, CR0 4YY

23/04/2025

14660959-0003